Revised Edition

LANDSCAPING YOUR HOME
WILLIAM R. NELSON, JR.

UNIVERSITY OF ILLINOIS PRESS
Urbana Chicago London

Drawings by K. E. Cessna and Stephen and Paula Wheeler

Contents

Preface

Landscaping Your Home was first published 12 years ago. Although intended primarily for the homeowner, it is now used as a textbook in many colleges and universities. In revising the book for this edition, I have incorporated new subject matter and design techniques that will make it equally useful to the homeowner, the teacher and student, the nursery operator, and the landscape contractor.

The homeowner who has a new house without improvements or one with an established landscape will find here the information necessary to make the property both beautiful and functional. The teacher and student can use the book as an instruction manual and study guide. For the nursery operator and landscape contractor, it will serve as a source of ideas and provide a practical approach for further developing skills in designing and constructing residential landscapes.

Many magazine articles and "how-to-do-it" books describe and illustrate individual landscape units (patio, service area, fence enclosures, flower or shrub borders, etc.) without relating these units to the house, the total site, or a family's particular needs. But landscaping is not merely the craft of growing plants or building structures — it is the art of developing space around your house for convenience, beauty, and pleasure.

Landscaping Your Home deals with the *principles* of landscape design, as well as with the practical application of these principles. Instead of simply telling you "how" to grow plants, construct fences, and pour concrete, it helps you to identify and solve your specific problems. The principles of landscape design are translated into easily understood guidelines that enable you to exploit the full potential of your property through imaginative arrangements of structures and plants. You can then easily determine where plants, paving, and fences should be used and which building or plant materials are most suitable for your situation.

This revised edition (100 pages longer than the original 1963 edition) includes new sections dealing with landscape lighting, the design of townhouses and condominiums, and the unique "backward process" for developing planting compositions and selecting plants; a greatly expanded discussion of landscape structures and construction materials; more comprehensive check lists and charts; nearly 250 new illustrations; and more than 100 additions to the List of Plant Materials.

The assistance of many people is required to produce a book of this scope. I want to express particularly my great appreciation to Richard Moores of the Office of Agricultural Publications for his meticulous review and for his skill and assistance in revising the text to make it clearer and more exact. I also wish to thank Professor John B. Gartner of the Department of Horticulture for reviewing Chapters 12 and 13 and making many helpful suggestions; Professor Michael A. Dirr, also of the Department of Horticulture, for recommending additions to the List of Plant Materials and carefully reviewing the nomenclature of the various plants; and finally, my students through the years, who have taught me at least as much as I have taught them.

This revised edition is dedicated to Ken Cessna (1935-1969) in recognition of the excellent drawings that have contributed so much to the success of *Landscaping Your Home*.

William R. Nelson, Jr.
Urbana, Illinois

1: Establishing Your Landscape Needs

Your home deserves the most attractive setting you can give it. When you bought your home, you provided for your family's comfort and convenience by choosing a house with adequate sleeping areas, living areas, and storage space.

It is important to give equal consideration to the space surrounding your home. If you develop this space properly, you can actually extend your living activities into the landscape.

Many homes are either "overlandscaped" or not landscaped at all. You have seen attractive houses without plants or hidden behind a forest of plantings. Many people surround their lot with a fence, and then plant an unrelated collection of trees and shrubs without considering what their final effect will be. This "shotgun" approach demands as much money and effort as an orderly, well-designed landscape.

Merely planting trees and shrubs is not landscaping. Designing a landscape is an art — the growing of plants is a craft. Landscaping means creating a plan to make the best use of the space available in the most attractive way. It means shaping the land to make the most of the site's natural advantages. It means building such necessary structures as fences, walls, and patios. Finally, it means selecting and growing the plants that best fit the design.

The function of landscape architecture is not only to create and preserve beauty but to make the surroundings useful. The smaller the home grounds, the greater the need for proper planning. Every square foot of space and every dollar must be made to produce maximum results. A professional landscape architect can help you solve problems too involved for you to handle. He is trained in art and design, and has a sound understanding of ground forms and related engineering and site-development principles.

He knows about the use and culture of plant materials. He also has the ability to design needed structures so that they will be in harmony with the other elements of the landscape plan.

A landscape architect does not sell plants or actually execute the plan. His sole responsibility is to design a plan within the terms of agreement with his client. This plan may contain detailed construction and planting designs that will be carried out by the nurseryman or contractor. Either the landscape architect or the client may supervise the job.

There are many landscape architects in the United States, but most of them are located in or near urban centers, where their talents are in demand for large-scale private and public projects. There are, however, some professional landscape architects who design residential properties. The assistance of a landscape architect will pay handsome dividends for the costs involved.

If a landscape architect is not available, contact your nurseryman or garden center. They may be able to offer the services of a landscape designer to help you develop your plans. In most states, landscape architects are licensed; landscape designers are not. You may wish to see examples of the designer's work before making a decision. You can then determine if the designs and use of landscape materials follow the principles outlined in this book.

A nurseryman is also important in home-landscape development. Reputable nurserymen are licensed by the state, and are usually members of their state and national professional organizations. A nurseryman will supply plant materials, and will plant according to the landscape architect's plan. He can advise and assist in the culture and maintenance of your plantings, and will sell you healthy, high-quality stock.

The function of landscape architecture is to make the surroundings both beautiful and useful through the organization of the space around the house into "use" areas. If possible, there should be close communication between living and service areas within the house and living and service areas out-of-doors. Make the best use of available space to create a landscape into which you can extend your living.

Successful landscape planning involves three considerations. First, you should consider your lot or site as a cube of space, very much like a room. The ground is its floor and your property lines are its walls. The ceiling is the canopy created by structures, tree plantings, and the sky. A good landscaping plan is developed in terms of these three dimensions.

Next, study the floor plan, window locations, and primary living areas of your house to establish a relationship between living and service areas in the house and similar areas out of doors. Finally, consider the design from outside the house as viewed by yourself and by others. You can then determine the most effective means of blending your house to its site. Note on your plan those areas that require attention, including views into your property from adjoining areas.

Your final landscape plan will depend upon your lot and its orientation to wind and sun, your house plan, the amount of money, time, and effort you want to spend on maintenance, your family's interests and activities, and even the neighborhood itself.

Try to preserve all of the best natural resources of the site, such as trees, brooks or streams, good soil, rock outcroppings, and turf. Carefully study good as well as bad views. Keep attractive views open and framed for greatest value. Screen out unattractive and objectionable views either by structures or by proper plantings. Develop pleasing lawn and planting areas in relation to the views from the main rooms in the house.

When you are remodeling a landscape, carefully study the walk and drive patterns for convenience, decide which plantings should be saved, and evaluate established activity areas for appropriateness. Do not allow existing developments to prejudice your evaluation. A good approach is to visualize your property as if it had nothing on it. List what you would like to have and what problems must be solved. Then determine what you already have that helps you achieve your goal. Don't keep something simply because it is there. If what you have doesn't work, get rid of it!

Sunshine, rain, snow, wind, heat, and cold will influence your landscape design. Consider plantings that give protection from the summer sun and also allow warmth from the winter sun, wind barriers (fences or plantings) to reduce winds in the outdoor living areas, and grades to carry rain and melted snow away from the house and garden structures.

The main rooms of the house should benefit from both winter sun and summer breezes. When you plan what shade you will need to modify the extremes of the sun, consider possible shade from your neighbors' trees and houses, as well as shade from your own trees and house.

The best orientation for a house is at an angle of approximately 30 to 45 degrees from the east-west line. Since most homes are already sited, however, you must carefully plot future shade patterns from trees to keep sunny areas for gardens and shady areas for the house and patio. To plot these patterns accurately, you need to understand the movement of the sun and its angles at different seasons.

An inventory of your family activities will help you in planning the overall layout and use of your land. Allow space for outdoor living needs, the children's play area, and the service area. If your family does not want to spend much time working in the yard, keep the design simple and the plantings of the type that do not need much care. Base your planning efforts on how much time you can give to your garden and how much money you can spend to develop your property.

It is not necessary for you to complete your total design all at once. Your first job is to put on paper what your development will include when it is completed. Then, as money is available to finish different sections, these sections will fit into the total picture. Completing the entire plan could take five years or more.

Many families have found it helpful to include a set amount each year in their regular budgets for landscaping purposes. Whether this amount is 50 dollars or 500 dollars, it can be made to go a long way when you know exactly what is to be done, how much you can buy, and how much you can do yourself.

You will also need to consider the vegetation already on your property. If you have heavy woods, you are fortunate. But it may take courage to remove unnecessary or undesirable plants. Trees growing in a heavy woods usually become tall, spindly, and poorly shaped because of competition from other trees for light, food, and moisture. Removal of the poorer trees will allow the better ones to develop their natural form and become handsome additions to the total picture. If you have only a few trees on your property, you should protect them against damage during construction.

Geographical location and climate largely determine the plants you can use. For example, people living in the southern areas of the northern states (below the 40th parallel) are able to use many plant materials that will not grow successfully in the northern extremes. Place plants that will grow successfully

Attractive homes are often hidden because of overlandscaping. Planning your landscape design before buying plants will save you money in the initial cost of the plants, and you will not need to remove overgrown material in 10 to 15 years.

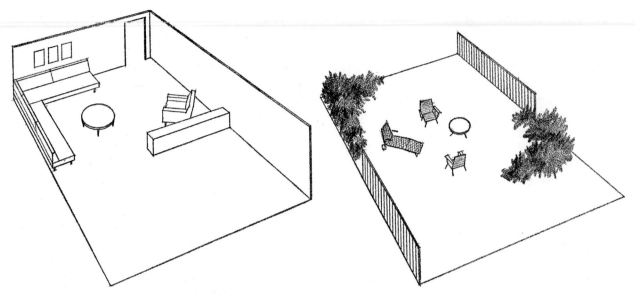

Your landscape can be compared to a room in your house. Each has three dimensions: a floor, walls, and a ceiling. The floor of your landscape is the earth. It may be covered with lawn, ground cover, or hard surfacing materials. The walls of your landscape are structures, shrub borders, etc., and the ceiling is formed by the horizontal plane of an overhead structure and the canopy of tree branches, as well as by the sky itself.

in shade on the north and east sides of your house. Locate shade trees where they will best shade the house, terrace, and outdoor living areas.

Decide how much privacy you will need to make your outdoor living areas useful for family life. Study the total lot area and its relationship to the neighborhood to determine whether you should screen or frame a view. Consider the proximity of your neighbors, the height of the surrounding land, and views of your property from other yards.

Soil type will affect your choice of design and plants. It is easiest to work with those plants best suited to your particular type of soil. You also need to know whether your soil is wet or dry. Poorly drained, wet soil is difficult for any home gardener to work with, and very dry soils limit the kinds of materials that will grow successfully. You must also consider the ability of your soil to support structures. Will subsurface preparations for drainage and footings be extensive?

Your family is probably the most important consideration in planning your landscape garden. An inventory of your family's needs will tell you which basic elements will make a livable, useful, and attractive setting for your home.

For example, if you have small children, you will probably want to locate their play equipment (sandbox, teeter-totter, etc.) so that you can supervise the children from the kitchen. If your family likes lawn games, then you should certainly leave an open area for favorite games.

You might want to develop the total landscape picture to encourage such hobbies as bird watching, collecting butterflies, cooking with special herbs, or growing specimen flowers for arrangements or garden club competitions. If gardening is a family hobby, you might consider a greenhouse for raising plants during the winter or starting seedlings early in the spring.

The frequency with which you entertain is also a consideration. For example, a socially active family might give special attention to parking needs. If your property is large enough, or if you are located in a rural area, you might want to set aside a special area for guest cars so that they will not block traffic in your drive or lane. If you wish to entertain outdoors during the warm months, plan a suitable location.

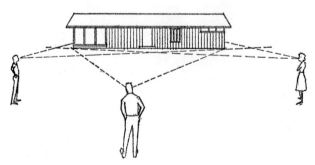

Study the views outside your house from the street and the views from the rear of the house. Note the orientation of the house on the lot, window locations, doors, and architectural materials. In the public area, you should also note setback, the layout of drives and walks, and public and private traffic patterns. In the outdoor living area, check on the need for privacy and shade and the character of off-property views.

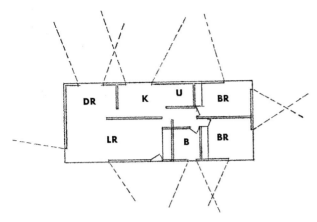

A drawing of the floor plan of your house will help you decide which views from each room should be screened and which should be featured. If you do not have interesting views from the living areas of the house, you will want to create them. A floor plan will also help you establish a correlation between living areas in the house and "use" areas out-of-doors.

If protection from insects at night is important to you, you will want to consider some kind of screening for your terrace or patio. How often does the family want to live outdoors for family cookouts, entertaining, or simple relaxation? If your main interest is entertaining, then the terrace or patio should be large enough to accommodate more than the family itself. A smaller paved area would be enough for your own relaxation and enjoyment.

Do you want to grow vegetables? It is usually best to locate a vegetable garden near the service area. Do you want a garden to grow cut flowers? This special type of garden is difficult to incorporate into a landscape development. Perhaps you should also locate a cutting-flower garden in the service area, where the plants can be put in rows especially for cutting.

Will you need to store equipment? Many new homes are built on a slab with only a small utility room in which to store gardening equipment. If your garage or utility room is not large enough to hold all of your yard equipment, you may want to consider building a garden and storage shelter. You may have a camper, boat, or other recreational vehicle that should be stored away when not in use.

This partial inventory of family interests will help you to organize your thinking. A list of your needs will be helpful in fashioning your final landscaping plan. This list will tell you how to spend your time, money, and effort most wisely, and will be of great assistance in developing a well-integrated living environment, both inside and outside the home.

You should also inventory your liabilities. An unsightly view on neighboring property demands a planting or fence that will screen it out and create an interesting scene on your own property at the same time. You will also need to consider screening for privacy from your neighbors. One consideration is the height of surrounding land and houses. You can screen by fencing and by skillful placement of shrubs and trees.

Another possible liability is the orientation of your lot and house. Do you need to modify the climate and temperature? A house built on a high elevation may catch winds that need to be modified by barrier plantings, windbreaks, or fences. Carefully placed trees will shade and protect outdoor areas, as well as living areas within the house.

Flat or sloping ground can be an asset or a liability. Grade changes are not necessarily a liability. They offer many chances to create an interesting design. A very steep slope is a liability, however, because it tends to erode under heavy rains. It needs a dense ground cover for protection, or terraces and retaining walls to obtain additional level area and to eliminate erosion.

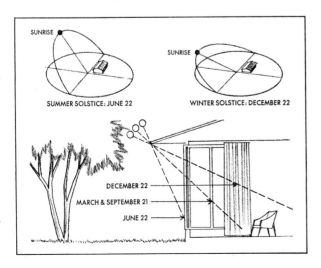

Trees and shrubs can serve dual functions in a landscape. They add beauty and interest in line, form, color, and texture, and they provide screening and enclosure for climate control. Notice the angle of the summer sun as compared with that of the winter sun. The placement of the tree not only gives background to the house but also protects the house from the summer sun, while allowing the winter sun to reach the house for important solar heat.

Completely flat ground can also cause gardening problems because it lacks surface drainage. Flat ground often demands special grading to help move excess water to underground sumps or lower areas on the property.

The relative acidity or alkalinity, texture, humus content, and drainage of the soil need to be investigated. Soils that are extremely acid or alkaline restrict plant growth. A very heavy clay soil will drain poorly and keep needed air from the plant roots. For easy maintenance, it is best to choose plants that will tolerate your particular soil condition.

Trees and other vegetation already growing on the property can be considered assets. Don't be afraid to take out excess trees so that the remaining specimens will develop their most beautiful form. You may want to leave some native vegetation, but be sure that it fits the overall plan. Remember — if you significantly change the general environment of the area, native plants may not continue to thrive, and you may have to use ornamental plantings.

A distant view can create an interesting focal point in the landscape. Special treatment is usually necessary to frame this view. If the view is made up primarily of vertical elements (groves of trees, mountains, buildings, etc.), the framing material should also have dominant vertical lines. A view composed mostly of horizontal elements (low, rolling hills, lakes, cultivated land, etc.) should be framed with low shrub borders that project at right angles from the side planting to repeat the horizontal character of the view. You may want to screen part of a nearby view to focus attention on a distant view.

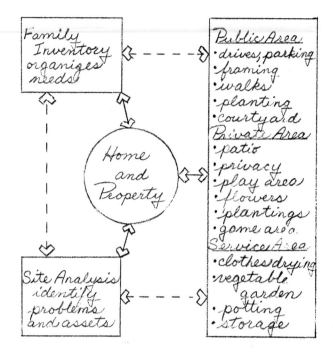

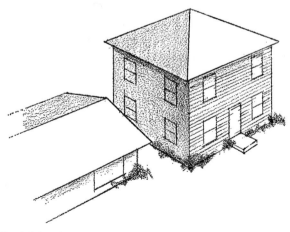

The height of surrounding land and neighbors' houses and views from their property are important considerations in obtaining privacy from above as well as on a level. You should also study the shade patterns cast by nearby structures. These shade areas are important considerations in selecting plants.

Water features such as a stream or brook and rock outcroppings are natural objects that will modify the design of your landscape plan. Feature and accent these objects. Their potential design qualities are most desirable in developing any landscape picture.

Don't overlook the chance to use a pleasant adjoining environment. For example, if your house borders a golf course, a large park area, or any other landscape development, you have an opportunity to use all of this extra lawn area to give a sense of space to your property.

In Chapter 2, you will make a detailed family inventory. Look at this inventory often as you work out your landscaping plan. It will help you to organize your thinking and give you an orderly approach to the greatest enjoyment and use of your indoor-outdoor living area.

Each family's needs are different. Include in your plan only those family interests that will make the living space, both inside and out, most livable and useful for your family. This plan will tell you what you have to work with. You can then determine the space needed for lawn, patio or terrace, game or play area, and planting area.

Your final plan will take the guesswork out of landscaping. It will tell you which landscape elements should be added to those already established by the family inventory. Although you may have to complete the plan in stages, you will be working toward a final, well-organized design.

2: Starting Your Plan

Any good landscaping design is planned on the basis of three major areas: the public area, the living area, and the service area.

Working out the design on paper is very helpful. It is amazing how ideas will develop and mistakes show up on a plan. The more accurate you are, the more effectively your plan will serve its basic function: to control the physical forms (structures, slopes, grades, plants, etc.) and the actual arrangements of these forms on the ground according to basic design principles.

Careful measurement of all physical objects on the property (house, trees, etc.) insures that, when you execute the design later, specific areas will be in scale and in proper proportion to the actual space on the ground. You will need to use a tape. Be sure that the tape is held tight without a sag.

For outdoor measurements, draw a rough sketch of the property and of the shape of the house on an ordinary sheet of paper. Allow enough space to jot down the measurements as you make them. Some of the features that should be measured include the setback distance of the house, the side property lines, the walk and drive locations, and the locations of such other permanent features as sewer lines, septic tank, trees, and other plantings. In measuring from the building, always measure straight out at a right angle from the corner of the building. You can sight down the side of the house to make sure that you are measuring at right angles.

These outdoor measurements should be transferred to graph paper. You can buy graph paper with various scales at most stationery or book stores. A scale of ⅛-, ¼-, or ⅟₁₆-inch equals 1 foot will enable you to use a standard ruler. The preferred scale is ⅛-inch. This scale allows most properties to be drawn on a sheet of paper of reasonable size, and will help you to develop a sense of proportion and to visualize the relative size of the landscape elements.

First, draw the overall lot on your graph paper. Indicate your legal property lines as well as the public property to the curb line, including the walk and planting strip (if any). Now draw your house on the property. The location of the house is determined by your setback measurements and the distance from the house to the side property lines.

Indicate the locations of bedrooms, living room, kitchen, and other rooms. Mark all windows and outside doors to scale. Add the outdoor measurements of the walks, drive, and plantings. This information helps you to visualize the relationship between the house and the lot. You will want to locate certain service activities near the kitchen and utility areas. You will also want a pleasing picture from the family room and the living areas. Fasten with masking tape a sheet of tracing paper over your basic house and lot plan. This "overlay" will allow you to try out various arrangements.

Be sure to indicate any easements on your plan. Typical residential easements may be for underground utilities, surface drainage, or access to overhead utilities. If you do not know the width of the easement or the limitations on developing it, check with the city or the agency involved. You should also investigate legal restrictions on the development of your property. These restrictions include community ordinances such as zoning laws, subdivision regulations, and building codes.

Another set of restrictions may apply only to your particular subdivision. These restrictions, generally referred to as "subdivision covenants," may restrict the placement of structures to specific areas of land within the legal boundaries of your property. A typical example is a subdivision adjacent to a golf course, where no structure, tree, or shrub over 4 feet high can be planted beyond the building space. This covenant prevents one owner from obstructing another owner's view.

Municipal ordinances, which apply to the entire community, may designate the fence and wall heights for various locations on the property, control the number and placement of secondary buildings, and limit the extent to which architectural units can be extended from the house. Find out whether building permits are required for any of your planned construction. Checking the laws and regulations carefully before you undertake any construction may save you considerable money and trouble.

The *public area* lies between the road and the house. It is exposed to the full view of the public. The first impression of your house is the street-side design. Each house on your block adds to or detracts from the appearance of the street. There are four elements that make up the public area or front yard: (1) walks to the front door, the drive, and possible parking areas; (2) tree plantings; (3) shrub plantings; and (4) lawn areas.

The most important consideration in the public area is the front door. This is the focal point of the design for the area, and the spot you will want to

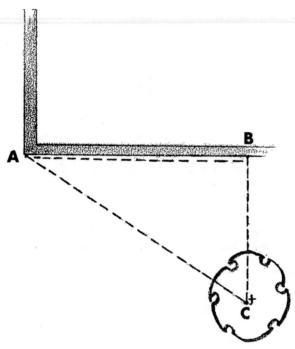

To locate objects between the corners of the house, measure from point (A) along the house to point (B), where a right-angle line intersects the object (C). Then measure the distance from (B) to (C). To check your accuracy, measure from (C) to the corner of the house (A).

feature and make attractive. The walk and drive that lead your guests to the front door comprise the first important design element. Their location, scale, and form deserve serious study.

Walk location greatly affects the appearance of the public area. For example, an uninterrupted front lawn creates an illusion of depth in the foreground between the street and the house. A walk leading from the road to the front entrance cuts the lawn in two, and gives a strong, harsh line that divides the front-lawn area into sections or panels. This division is often repeated by the driveway. A broad, expansive lawn area undivided by these elements gives a more spacious and pleasing setting for your home. The best walk location is parallel to the front of the house, and connecting the front porch or entrance with the driveway.

With this walk location, the driveway should be wide enough to serve as the walk from the street, and should always run into the street at right angles so that the driver can see traffic clearly in both directions before he enters the street. Plantings at the intersection of the drive and the street are not necessary to call attention to the entrance, and often obstruct the driver's view of the street.

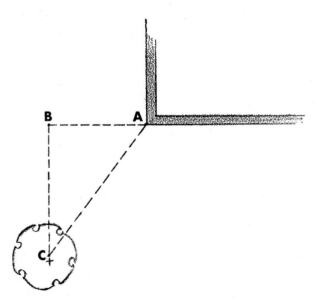

Locate physical features accurately for plotting to scale on your plan. For objects beyond the corners of the house, take a measurement from the corner of the house (A) to a point (B), which is at right angles to the object. Take another right-angle measurement from (B) to locate the object (C). To check your accuracy, take a third measurement from (C) to (A).

THE LANDSCAPE ARCHITECT'S SIGN LANGUAGE

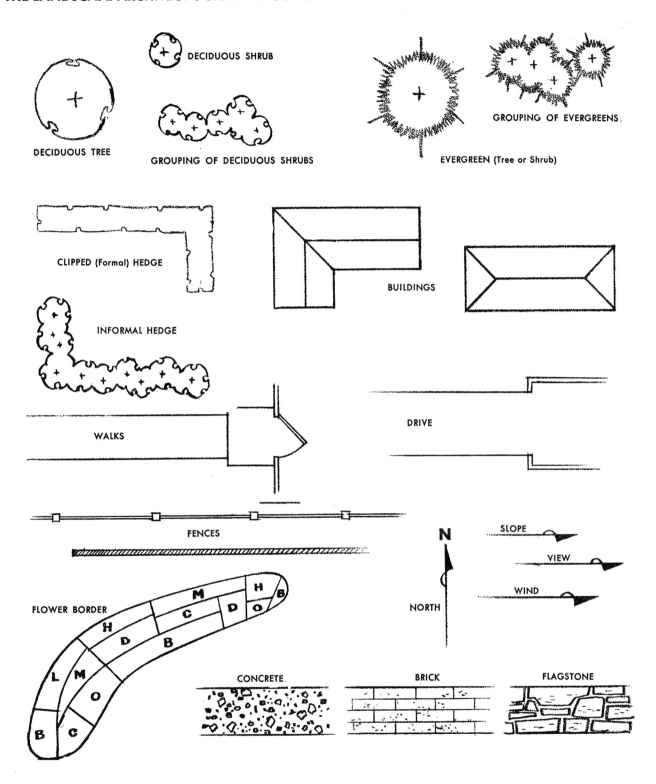

Each symbol represents a physical feature, and is used as a graphic representation of this feature on the base plan. These symbols (especially plants, structures, walks, and drives) should be drawn to scale on the plan. Show the mature size for plants. For example, the symbol for a deciduous tree should represent its mature spread. Letters such as those for the "flower border" are often used as a key for a flower-planting plan.

If you want to outline the drive when snow has drifted across it, drive lengths of scrap pipe into the ground 15 to 20 feet apart flush with the turf. Then fit metal rods or wooden dowels into these ground pipes. Paint the tips of the rods or dowels with black, red, or fluorescent paint. Take them out in summer. Since you want the driveway to be as inconspicuous as possible in the total design, *do not* outline it with painted rocks, plantings, hedges, or flowers.

Driveway width will vary according to your needs and the total area available. Usually 10 feet is wide enough when the drive is surfaced with a permanent material. If you want a circular drive, you will need a width of 14 to 18 feet in the curved section so that all of the car remains on the driving surface. If you wish to park cars on the curve so that moving cars can pass, allow 22 feet of width.

If a double-width drive to a two-car garage would be too massive in the public area, hold the drive to a minimum width of 9 to 10 feet and then flare to the width of the door openings for a distance of 18 feet. This arrangement allows you to drive the car com-

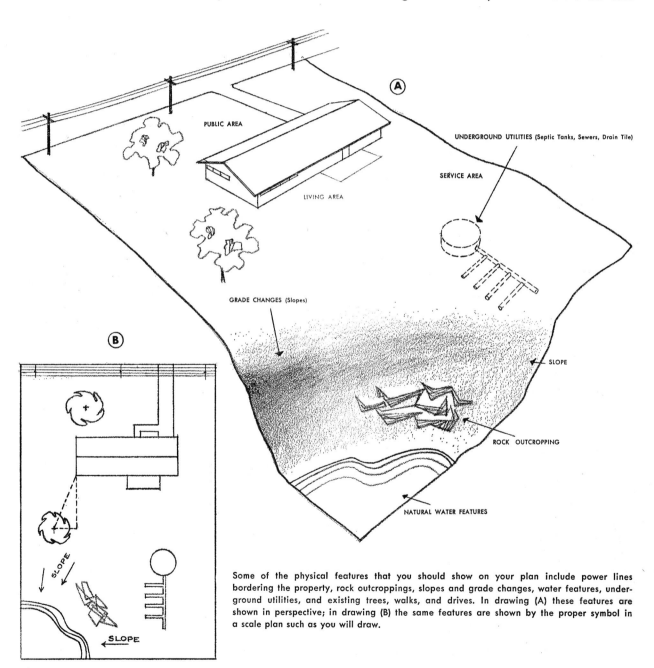

Ⓐ

PUBLIC AREA

LIVING AREA

UNDERGROUND UTILITIES (Septic Tanks, Sewers, Drain Tile)

SERVICE AREA

GRADE CHANGES (Slopes)

Ⓑ

SLOPE

ROCK OUTCROPPING

NATURAL WATER FEATURES

SLOPE

SLOPE

Some of the physical features that you should show on your plan include power lines bordering the property, rock outcroppings, slopes and grade changes, water features, underground utilities, and existing trees, walks, and drives. In drawing (A) these features are shown in perspective; in drawing (B) the same features are shown by the proper symbol in a scale plan such as you will draw.

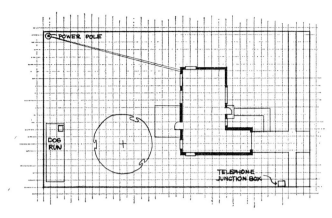

When you have completed the outdoor measurements, plot these measurements to scale on your base plan. Plotting them on graph paper makes it easy to keep the lines parallel and at right angles. Use graph paper with a grid pattern that allows you to work at a ⅛-inch scale.

pletely out of the garage before maneuvering it onto the narrower portion of the driveway.

Tree plantings make up the second design element in the composition of the public area. Trees in the front yard serve to frame the front view of the house, provide shade, and mask undesirable architectural details. You can establish harmonious relations with architectural forms by repeating these forms in your tree selections.

Always use a large lawn shade tree to frame a two-story house — a small flowering tree makes the house look taller. Select only those trees that branch high enough so that you can still see the house from the street below the canopy of foliage. Houses facing the south or west may need more than one large shade tree for adequate protection from the afternoon sun. It may be necessary to use several large, high-headed trees at the front.

The most effective placement of trees to obtain the framing effect is determined by the view of your house at a 30- to 45-degree angle from the street. This is the angle at which passersby will see your house. No one views your house at a hard right angle except those living directly across the street from it.

Shrub plantings comprise the third design element. These plantings are intended to complement the house design and to tie the house to the site or ground. They have been traditionally referred to as "foundation plantings." This term is misleading because it implies that the only location for shrubs is adjacent to the house. In many situations, plantings away from the building result in a better design. Since the house is the most important part of the public-area design, the shrub plantings should not compete with it.

The fourth design element of the public area is the lawn. The lawn serves as the connecting link between all the other elements. It ties these elements into a single composition, and gives a broad, expan-

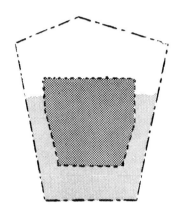

In most communities, local ordinances specify the minimum setback of the house and sideyard widths for every lot (medium-gray area in drawing at left). Certain subdivisions have covenants of additional restrictions that limit even further the placement of the house and landscape elements (dark-gray area).

sive setting to the house. A lawn unbroken by planting, walks, or special features will accomplish this result best. Island flower beds, gazing balls, bird baths, painted tractor tires with petunias, flamingos, and other novelties have no place in the front lawn. The next time you drive past a house with any of these novelties in front, notice that the novelty, not the house and its complementary planting, catches your eye. The novelty breaks the cardinal rule that the house is the most important part of the design.

The *outdoor living area* usually includes all of the property to the rear of the house except that portion set aside for the service area. It may also include side-yard spaces if they are wide enough for use. By using all available space, you gain additional living area, as well as an extension of the house into the landscape. This is especially important when indoor spaces are limited. Once you know what your outdoor activities will be, you can begin to develop a "floor plan" of use areas similar to the one you followed in planning the layout of your home.

The outdoor area usually includes a patio or terrace. This unit must be easy to get to if it is to be used. For this reason, its location must be considered in relation to the door that leads from the house.

However, the shape of the property may not allow enough space at the door location, or another side of the house may be better suited climatically for this outdoor living activity.

If possible, locate the outdoor living area where you can see it from the living room, family room, or dining room. Since the living area will be the most highly developed landscape picture in the yard, it should be located so that it can be enjoyed as fully from inside as from outside.

Many design elements go into the development of the living area. Not all of them can be included in any one landscape. You will want to select those that best meet your family's needs and interests. Some of these design elements are as follows:

1. Enclosures (fences, walls, or screen plantings)
2. Plantings (shrubs, hedges, flower borders, ground cover, trees)
3. Surfaced areas (patio, terrace, walk, paths, sitting areas, steps)
4. Garden embellishments (barbecue pits, seats, water features, garden furniture, portable planters, sculpture, lighting, objects of art, rocks, raised beds).

Enclosure forms the sides of your outside room. It provides privacy and screens the view from the property. It controls the movement of people and pets both within and without, and serves as a partial climate control and noise baffle. The enclosure is extremely flexible. It can be high and solid to screen out neighbors or unsightly views, or it can be low and solid, or high and of open design when you want the garden to be seen. In addition to these obvious functions, enclosure units have a more special and subtle function. They *define space* in the three-dimensional outside rooms, and help to distinguish one space from another. Enclosure gives a sense of form, scale, proportion, and intimacy to the landscape.

Plantings are important, although they are not the only unit of design in the landscape. All plants — annuals, perennials, woody shrubs, and trees — are important elements used to create interest as individual plants or as a mass of material. They provide a pleasing, refreshing, and soul-satisfying setting around a home. The number of plants you use depends upon whether you are interested in gardening or whether you want a garden that needs as little maintenance as possible.

Surfaced areas have become prominent design units in an outdoor living area. If you consider the ground surface as the floor of an outdoor room, you will want material that prevents weeds, dust, heat re-

flection, mud, and dirt. The material must also be suitable for the type of activity planned for the area.

The basic surfacing types are (1) paving for heavy traffic; (2) lawn for medium traffic; (3) sawdust, tanbark, sand, and gravel materials for little-used areas; (4) ground covers where no one will walk; and (5) flower- and shrub-bed areas. Patterns formed by each of these surfacing elements add greatly to the total composition. To avoid too busy a picture, consider surfaces along with detailing and design of the enclosure and shelter elements. Simple forms and patterns are best. They should be strong and bold, but they must never dominate the scene at the expense of the vertical (walls) and overhead units. They also must not reduce the three-dimensional spaciousness of the design.

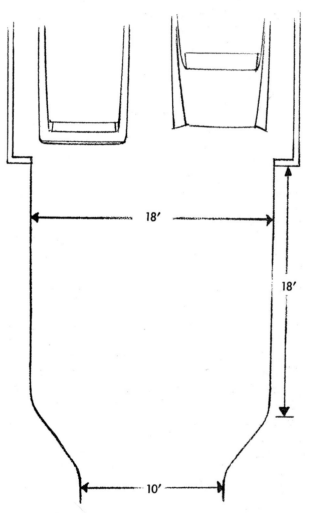

If a double-width drive to a two-car garage would be too massive in the public area, the drive can be held to an 8- to 10-foot width and flared to the width of the door openings close to the garage. Holding a paved drive to the width of the door openings allows for garage corner plantings.

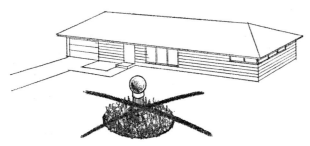

A broad expanse of lawn uninterrupted by bird baths, island flower beds, flamingos, and other novelties is the best possible setting for your house. Banish all novelties from your public area. They detract from the object you want to emphasize most — your house.

Garden embellishments are comparable to home furnishings and accessories. For example, pictures, lamps, and decorator items are used to complement, accent, and contrast with the basic furnishings of the home. Rather than adding superfluous beauty to an already well-designed area, you will want to design each item to be a part of the total landscape.

Select only those items important to the activities in which your family will take part. You may use the outdoor living area for reading, sitting, sunbathing, entertaining (dancing, cookouts), or for lawn sports such as badminton and croquet. You may want to locate the children's sandbox, swings, and teeter-totter in this area; or you may want to use part of it for hobby gardening.

The final landscape area is the *service or utility area*. All of the service functions that can be screened by a fence should be assigned to this area. It may not be practicable to group everything together, since each function presents a separate problem.

Garbage cans should be located close to the house for convenience but far enough away to avoid odors and to allow for adequate structural screening.

Most homes need clotheslines, even with a dryer. Lines that are not used often can be placed some distance from the house. Many types of lines allow the center post standard to be removed. The surface beneath the lines should be of material that will not soil the clothes if they should fall.

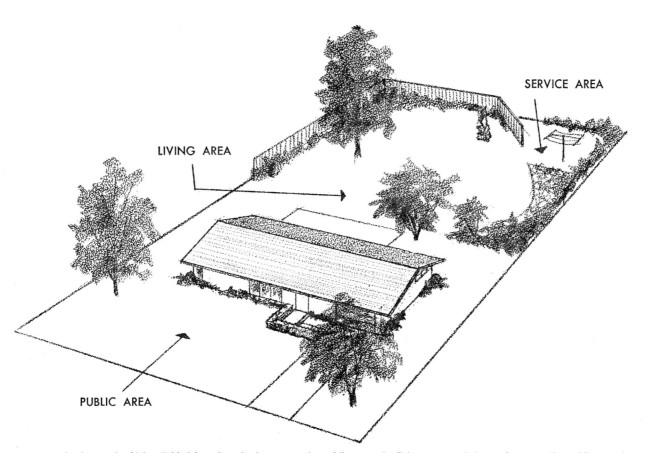

Your home landscape should be divided into three basic areas — the public area, the living area, and the service area. The public area is located from the street to the house. The living area is located at the rear of the property. It should provide privacy and enclosure, and may include a patio, plantings, and sculpture. The service area can be located to the side or rear of the property, depending upon the elements to be included and the frequency with which this area will be used.

The clothes-drying area can be combined with a vegetable or cut-flower garden. You can work storage space into the area for the odds and ends needed for garden work. Compost piles, garden work benches, cold frames, and greenhouses can also be provided.

The amount of available space will determine to a great extent the screening for the service area. A fence is superior to plants as a visual barrier when space is limited. The lines of the fence depend upon the design of the rest of the area. The fence can be in straight lines, angled, serpentine, or curved. Overall landscape layout best determines the actual lines of the fence. The fence is a basic part of the landscape, and its placement, function, and design serve to emphasize a line, create space, or define an area.

At this point, it may be well to consider more specifically the landscaping elements or garden em-bellishments that will go into the public, outdoor living, and service areas. Many of these items will be discussed in detail in later chapters, but the "Family Inventory Check List" below and on pages 15 through 18 will help to clarify your thinking about your interests and needs. As you develop your landscaping plan, you may discover that you will want to move certain items from one area to another. For example, you may plan to locate the children's play equipment in the living area, and later decide to move this equipment to the service area so that the children can be supervised from the kitchen. It is a good idea to refer to this check list frequently while working out your landscape design. After you have read this book, you may wish to modify your inventory in the light of what you have learned.

Notes

Family Inventory Check List

Family Members

Name	Age	Sex	Hobbies
_____	_____	_____	_____
_____	_____	_____	_____
_____	_____	_____	_____
_____	_____	_____	_____
_____	_____	_____	_____
_____	_____	_____	_____

PUBLIC AREA

Driveway _____   **Number of cars in family** _____

Off-street parking needed? _____   **For guests?** _____

Privacy from street _____   **Entry walk** _____

Entry garden or court _____

Utility lighting _____   **Landscape lighting** _____

Structures (fences, walls, decks, etc.) _____

Notes

Family Inventory Check List (continued)

OUTDOOR LIVING AREA

General gardening:

Minimum maintenance _____   Moderate maintenance _____

High maintenance _____

Family allergy considerations _____

Special interests:

Hobby garden (specify) _____

Flower borders: Annuals _____   Roses _____

Perennials _____   Begonias _____

Mixed _____   Other _____

Herb garden _____   Size _____

Container plantings _____   Type _____

Planter boxes _____   Type _____

Dwarf fruit trees _____   Type _____

Small fruits (bush) _____   Type _____

Vine fruits _____   Type _____

Favorite plants _____

_____

_____

_____

Entertaining: Large groups _____   Small groups _____

Formal _____   Informal _____

Paved terrace or patio:

Number of people _____   Material _____

Number of chairs _____   Style (captain's, director's, lounge, etc.) _____

Notes

Family Inventory Check List (continued)

Number of tables _____   Style (dining, cocktail tables, etc.) _____

_____

Permanent seating: Benches _____   Seat-height walls or planters _____

Shade required? _____   Where? _____

Table umbrella _____   Overhead structure _____

Trellis _____   Tree _____   Fabric canopy _____

Lawn games: _____   Area lighted? _____

Badminton (24' x 54') _____   Basketball (40' x 40') _____

Croquet (30' x 60') _____   Horseshoes (20' x 40') _____

Putting green (30' diameter) _____   Shuffleboard (6' x 45') _____

Tetherball (20' diameter circle) _____

Outdoor cooking: _____

Permanent grill _____   Size _____   Gas _____   Charcoal _____

Portable grill _____   Size _____

Barbeque pit _____

Sink _____   Water _____   Electrical outlets _____   Storage _____

Swimming: _____

Investigated legal requirements? _____   Considered liability insurance? _____

Portable pool _____   Size _____

    Wading _____   Swimming _____   Round _____

    Rectangular _____

Permanent pool _____   Size (16' x 34' minimum) _____

    Diving area _____   Shape _____

    Paved decks _____   Size _____   Material _____

Enclosure for pool _____: Plants _____   Wire fence _____

    Architectural wall or fence _____

Lighting _____   Dressing facility _____   Equipment storage _____

Notes

Family Inventory Check List (continued)

SERVICE AREA

Vegetable garden _____   Size _____

Flower-cutting garden _____   Size _____

Compost bin _____   **Cold frames** _____

Greenhouse _____   Size _____

Dog run _____   Size _____   **Doghouse** _____

Other pet requirements _____

Clotheslines: Frequent use _____   Occasional use _____

Permanent _____   Portable _____

Recreational vehicle storage: Camper _____   Size _____

Boat _____   Size _____

Trailer _____   Size _____

Lawn and garden storage: _____

Equipment: Mower _____   Hose _____   Sweeper _____

Sprinkler _____   Spreader _____   Sprayer _____

Tools (itemize) _____

Supplies: Fertilizer _____   Peat moss _____   Sprays _____

Patio furniture (itemize) _____

Trash containers: Number _____   Preferred location _____

CHILDREN'S PLAY AREA

Blackboard _____   **Climbing ropes** _____   **"Junk" playground** _____

Sandbox _____   **Slider** _____   **Swings** _____

Playhouse _____   **Tricycle "freeway"** _____

Wading pool _____   **On paved surface?** _____

Shade required? _____

Trees _____   Overhead structure _____

Notes

Family Inventory Check List (continued)

Fence _____   Height _____   Type _____

Surfacing material: Sand _____   Grass _____

Wood chips _____   Small gravel _____

Storage (toys, equipment, etc.) _____   Size _____

GENERAL GARDEN ACCESSORIES AND FEATURES

Sculpture _____   **Landscape lighting** _____

Water features _____: Fountain or spray _____   Reflecting pool _____

Fish _____   Plants _____

Bird interests: Bird feeder _____   Bird-attracting plants _____

Birdbath _____   Birdhouses _____

3: Analyzing The Site

The character of your land — its slopes and flat areas, soil, existing vegetation, climate, and views — will influence and to a certain extent determine your basic landscape design. To get a "feel" for the many different elements that make up your property, you must make a visual and physical analysis of the site, including the legal boundaries of your property and the visual boundaries beyond it. Repeat this process several times. Each time that you repeat it, you will discover influences you overlooked before.

The most common site conditions with which you should be concerned include topography, drainage, soil, existing vegetation, natural features, climate (macroclimate and microclimate), structures, walks and drives, and the extensional landscape. Read the sections dealing with these site conditions before you complete the checklist in this chapter.

Do not start your landscape design without first considering the original shape of the surface on which it will be worked out. Before moving into the details of the three major landscaping areas and proposed plantings, you will need to study the natural ground forms. Look for their inherent beauty, and decide how you can adapt existing grades so that they will be beautiful as well as usable for family living.

Consider the ground forms on your property as a part of similar ground formations in your locality. One of the first requirements in site development is to keep enough of the present elevations, forms, and shapes of the land so that your overall design stays in harmony with other nearby land forms. Think of your land as one unit of the area, not as an "island" unrelated to the surrounding areas.

Try to preserve the natural features of the land. But don't try to condense on your small area all the patterns that nature has exhibited around you. Instead, try to make the best use of the topography that exists on your property.

Grading can change or emphasize these natural features. Your family inventory will tell you whether you want a patio, a children's play area, areas for lawn games or passive recreation, or areas for special garden hobbies. In some cases, you may want to change the ground form in order to have certain activities. In other cases, you may want to locate an activity on a part of the site already adapted for maximum usefulness and beauty.

Drainage is almost always changed or modified during the course of house construction. To be sure that the basement won't flood, that activity areas will be usable, and that plants will thrive and grow, you should investigate water drainage above and below the surface. You need to know how water flows over the ground. Look for areas where water will collect and stand for long periods. Make certain that water does not flow toward walls and house foundations, where it could build up and undermine the structure or cause seepage into the house.

The volume of water handled on a piece of property increases significantly when structures and hard surfaces are placed on the property. For example, a house with a roof area of 1,200 square feet will discharge 750 gallons of water on the surrounding ground during a 1-inch rainfall.

You must also consider drainage beneath the surface. Water below the surface moves horizontally as well as vertically. The two extremes of subsurface drainage are sand, with fast water movement, and clay, with very slow water movement. It is popularly believed that filling a hole with water will indicate how effectively the soil will absorb the water. But this method is quite inaccurate because of variables in soil-water saturation, hole size, volume of water, evaporation, etc. Check with the neighbors about the drainage on their property. If it appears that you may have drainage problems, you should obtain professional assistance.

Soil is important because it is not only the growing medium for plants but also the foundation for all of our activities and structures. Its ability to promote plant growth and to support activities depends upon its chemical and physical properties.

The chemical properties are best determined through soil tests. Your county extension office can advise you where these testing services are available. To find out whether your soil is suitable for supporting structures and various activities, contact the soil specialists at your state land-grant university or the U.S. Soil Conservation Service. This information is particularly important if you are planning changes in natural grades. Grading disturbs the relations between topsoil, subsoil, and lower portions of the soil profile that could affect later development.

To determine the suitability of your soil for plant growth, ask yourself the following questions:

1. Does my soil need chemical fertilizers?
2. What fertilizer analysis is recommended?
3. What are the rates of application?
4. Should the soil be amended to provide more organic matter?
5. What organic materials should be used?
6. How should these materials be applied and incorporated?
7. Is there a drainage problem?
8. Can this problem be solved with proper grading?
9. Should drainage tile be installed to carry away excess moisture?

Existing vegetation may be native plants found on a new site or ornamental plantings that are a part of an established landscape you wish to remodel. Native plants grow in a delicate ecological balance with neighboring plants, the soil, and the climate. During the course of your home building and landscape development, be sure that you do not disturb this balance to such an extent that the plants can no longer thrive.

Some designers believe that it is inappropriate to use any material that is not indigenous to the area; others claim that native materials are "common" and have no place in the home landscape. But both native and ornamental plants can be used to advantage in a landscape design. You should evaluate both types of plantings on the basis of quality, quantity, kind of material (shrub or tree), and genus and species.

Quality refers to a plant's soundness of form and structure, as well as to its general appearance and beauty. If the plant is one-sided, poorly shaped, or generally a poor specimen of the species, you should consider removing it. The age of the plant is also important. If the plant appears mature, try to estimate how many more years it will survive before declining in vigor and landscape value.

Quantity refers to the number of plants. A heavy population of plants may prevent your using your property for various family activities. By selectively removing certain plants, you may gain the necessary space for these activities. If you have only a few or isolated plants, ask yourself these questions: Will their location interfere with the effective development of my property? Can they be integrated into the overall planting composition?

The *kind of material* — trees or shrubs — must also be considered. Trees are usually valuable assets, and you should protect them carefully during grading and construction. Shrubs require closer study and evaluation. Consider the form, size, and general vigor of each shrub. If the shrub requires heavy pruning, it may be better to replace it. Your final decision should be based on how well the shrub can be incorporated with other plantings in your landscape design.

The *genus and species* of a plant must be known for positive identification. For example, the genus flowering crabapple (Malus) indicates a common group within which there are many species (Almey, Japanese, etc.). Do not assume that the genus will tell you everything that you need to know about a plant. Once you identify a plant by both genus and species, you can check the plant list at the back of this book or other references to determine the desirability of preserving the plant.

Natural features include earth, rock, and water. These unprocessed materials have an importance often overlooked in the landscape design. The merging of natural features with the more refined structural elements of design adds a great deal to the functional and visual pleasure of the landscape. In your analysis, determine how these features can be handled so as to preserve their inherent character and qualities. You must also maintain as close a relationship as possible between the natural feature and the existing materials and land forms around it.

If changes or modifications of natural features are necessary, try to interrelate the materials and the spaces they create to the function of the area. Avoid changes that destroy the natural character of the element. Most natural features need to be presented in a natural context, even though they are part of a more highly organized and refined overall development.

The *macroclimate* is the general expression of temperature, precipitation, humidity, and wind for large regions or areas. The macroclimate gives us a general knowledge of climatic factors that affect both man and plants, including temperature, precipitation, humidity, and the prevailing wind.

Temperature is an important consideration for both human comfort and the growing of plants. Check the average mean temperature and high and low temperatures for both summer and winter in your area. Low winter temperatures establish a limit on the types of plants that can be grown. High summer temperatures determine to a great extent the design required to make outdoor space comfortable for man. Note also the frost dates in the spring and fall. These dates determine the growing season of plants, particularly tender materials such as annuals.

Precipitation is another limiting climatic factor. Find out the number of inches of rain per year in your area and the seasons when rain generally occurs. This information will help you in selecting suitable plant materials, and indicate whether irrigation and supplemental watering will be required. You may even decide to install an underground irrigation system.

Humidity, which is closely associated with precipitation, has a great deal to do with human comfort. Areas with high humidity often have a high incidence of plant diseases. Being aware of potential disease problems will help you to select more resistant types of plants.

The *prevailing wind* in the area should also be considered in the development of your design. Summer winds help us to determine where to provide shelter and protection or where to capitalize on cool breezes. Winter winds must be considered for their effect on the heating efficiency of the home. These winds can also injure tender plants. Low areas collect fog and cold air, and frost occurs because of reduced air circulation. Higher elevations are more exposed to extremes in air movement, and can be an asset or a liability, depending upon the circumstances.

The *microclimate* is a specific expression of the wind, temperature, and precipitation patterns on your property. This microclimate consists of variations of the elements that make up the macroclimate. For example, the influences of buildings, trees, and landscape structures considerably modify wind and rain patterns. High and low spots, areas of extreme light reflection, large paved surfaces, building overhangs, the configuration of the land, and the arrangement of vertical elements may also create microclimates. Study your property carefully to determine the extent of these influences.

Your site does not end with the property boundaries. Consider the areas beyond your property boundaries as the extensional site and landscape. As you

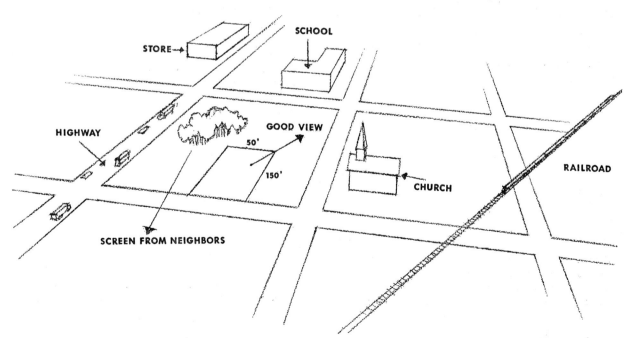

A sound approach to landscape planning is to consider the extensional landscape — those areas beyond your property boundaries. Don't rely on your memory. Make careful observations at the site itself of all features — good and bad — of the total extensional landscape.

study the natural ground forms on the site, draw on your plan the main elements of the surrounding area, as well as the features on your own site. These observations and notes will help you to understand the relationships of your land to neighboring property and to decide which elements to preserve and which elements to remove, screen, or in some way de-emphasize.

If your property is on a corner, check on noise, headlight patterns on the windows, and likely areas for developing private spaces.

The following check list will help you to analyze your site. Go through the list and check "yes" or "no" for each question. A "no" indicates that nothing needs to be done about that item. A "yes" means that the condition needs improving or that it will be an important consideration in designing your plan. Then write down on a separate sheet of paper what needs to be done for each "yes" answer. For example, if you answered "yes" to the second question under "Structures" and the first two questions under "Walks and Drives," your notes might read:

Shrubs are too close to rear door. Move them to a different place or discard them.

Straighten driveway, so that it will come into the street at a right angle.

Make sidewalk wider so that two people can walk side by side.

The check list includes most of the things you will need to consider about your site. You will probably want to add others.

DRAINAGE

Is drainage poor from the house or from other structures and areas? Yes_____ No_____

Is there a natural slope that can be used for septic-tank drainage? Yes_____ No_____

Is there drainage from a neighbor's property? Yes_____ No_____

Is there drainage onto a neighbor's property? Yes_____ No_____

Are there low spots? Yes_____ No_____

Do areas of your property show signs of erosion? Yes_____ No_____

Does water stand on the surface in any area? Yes_____ No_____

Is your property below the surrounding properties? Yes_____ No_____

SOIL

Does topsoil need to be added? Yes_____ No_____

Is your soil too acid or alkaline? (See your county extension office about a soil test.) Yes_____ No_____

Does the structure of the soil present a problem (either too much clay or too much sand)? Yes_____ No_____

Does drainage need improvement? Yes_____ No_____

Should humus be added? Yes_____ No_____

Does your soil need fertilizers? (See your county extension office about a soil test.) Yes_____ No_____

MACROCLIMATE

Does the pattern of the sun indicate a need for more shaded areas? Yes_____ No_____

Does the prevailing wind (write down the direction of it) mean that you will need protection in certain areas? Yes_____ No_____

Will the temperature extremes in your area (write down the usual maximum and minimum) affect your choice of plantings? Yes_____ No_____

Is it necessary to water your plantings artificially? Yes_____ No_____

Is the humidity high in your area? Yes_____ No_____

MICROCLIMATES AROUND BUILDINGS

Since these are situations that cannot ordinarily be changed, you cannot answer the following questions with a simple yes or no. Your notes should describe the location and extent of these microclimates so that you can take them into consideration when selecting plantings.

What areas are in the shade of buildings?

Where are the sunny areas near buildings?

Where are the wet areas and the dry areas?

What wind patterns caused by the buildings do you need to consider?

Where are the frost areas?

EXISTING VEGETATION

Do some trees need to be removed or changed? Yes_____ No_____

Do some shrubs need to be removed or changed? Yes_____ No_____

Is there a need for ground cover? Yes_____ No_____

Does the lawn need to be improved? Yes_____ No_____

Can shrubs be successfully combined with additional plantings? Yes_____ No_____

Are the genus and species of existing plants desirable? Yes_____ No_____

Is the general quality of each plant high enough to justify saving it? Yes_____ No_____

Are there more plants than you need? Yes_____ No_____

Are any of the plants native material? Yes_____ No_____

Has there been any significant alteration of the native plant's original growing environment? Yes_____ No_____

Will the native plants combine well with ornamental plants if a combination of the two should be necessary? Yes_____ No_____

NATURAL FEATURES

Are there bodies of water on your land that you may want to feature? Yes_____ No_____

Are there rock outcroppings on your land that you may want to feature? Yes_____ No_____

Are there sunken areas that you may need to grade and fill? Yes_____ No_____

Are there eroded areas that need attention? Yes_____ No_____

Do you have steep slopes that require retaining walls or special plantings? Yes_____ No_____

Do you have a slope that prevents using the yard for lawn games? Yes_____ No_____

Does your neighbor's ground elevation affect your landscaping? Yes_____ No_____

STRUCTURES (shelter, patio, terrace, fences, or walls)

(On a separate sheet of paper, evaluate the condition and suitability of all existing structures on your property.)

Can the locations be improved? Yes_____ No_____

Can access to the structures be improved? Yes_____ No_____

Do the locations of the structures affect plantings? Yes_____ No_____

Is more protection needed against sun and wind? Yes_____ No_____

Are any of the structures too large or too small in relation to the lot? Yes_____ No_____

Can the construction materials be made to blend with the surroundings? Yes_____ No_____

Are dry walls or retaining walls necessary to obtain sufficient level area? Yes_____ No_____

Do utility meters or air conditioner units require screening? Yes_____ No_____

Do you want permanent seating in any areas of the yard? Yes_____ No_____

Does the children's play area require paved surfacing? Yes_____ No_____

Does the service yard require paved areas? Yes_____ No_____

Are steps needed to provide access between different levels? Yes_____ No_____

Would a ramp be desirable between different levels? Yes_____ No_____

Is a storage structure needed in the service area? Yes_____ No_____

Is a storage structure needed in the children's play area? Yes_____ No_____

WALKS AND DRIVES

Does the walk or drive need to be relocated for greater convenience or attractiveness? Yes_____ No_____

Does either need to be made wider? Yes_____ No_____

Does water drain onto them? Yes_____ No_____

Can the walk be arranged in staggered pattern for greater interest? Yes_____ No_____

Would expanding (modifying) the walk at the entry allow for a courtyard treatment? Yes_____ No_____

Should the walk be colored charcoal gray to reduce glare? Yes_____ No_____

Do you need off-street parking? Yes_____ No_____

Is there adequate lighting along the walks and drives? Yes_____ No_____

Do you *really* need a secondary walk around the house? Yes_____ No_____

Can stepping-stones be used to carry the traffic? Yes_____ No_____

Are walks needed from the rear entry to the service area or to other activity spaces in the outdoor living area? Yes_____ No_____

EXTENSIONAL LANDSCAPE

Do you want to change your neighbor's view of your property? Yes_____ No_____

Do you need to frame a good view or to screen a bad one? Yes_____ No_____

Are noises from a nearby boundary road a problem? Yes_____ No_____

Are there pleasant adjoining areas (golf course, park, grove of trees, etc.) that you can take advantage of in your plan? Yes_____ No_____

Do you need more protection and privacy in the public area? Yes_____ No_____

Do you need more protection and privacy in the living area? Yes_____ No_____

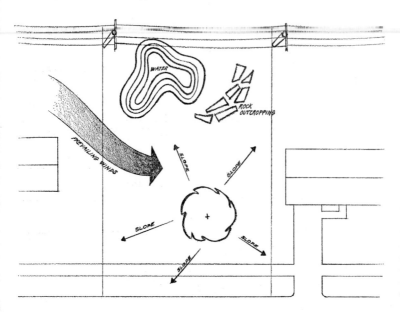

You can best study the site with a scale plan. A plan will help you understand the character of the site and the possibilities for development. Show all natural features (rock outcroppings, water, slope, vegetation, etc.) and man-made features (buildings, walks, drives, etc.) on your plan. If your property has extensive changes in grade, rock outcroppings, etc., a more detailed record of these features, as shown in a topographic survey, may be necessary.

Use this check list along with your base plan when you study the site. Attach a sheet of tracing paper firmly over the base plan with masking tape. Put down information on this overlay that relates to your design. Include any changes or modifications that might be made by grading. Sketch in diagrams and measurements of areas that you want to keep "as is."

Additional information to put on your overlay might include trees to be removed or retained, low spots that need drainage, off-property nuisances, high and low points, such natural features as shrubs, depth of topsoil, eroded areas, water or drainage problems, and any other information that might be important in your proposed project. Use this check list and your tracing-paper notations for adapting, modifying, or eliminating some of the conditions as the design goes along.

In addition to your on-site observations, you will need certain supplemental information. First, you should check local zoning and subdivision ordinances to become familiar with location and height restrictions for fences, walls, plantings, and structures in different areas of your property. Second, if your subdivision has restrictive covenants, there are additional limitations on what you can and cannot do on your property. Covenants cannot contradict local ordinances, but they are often more restrictive. Finally, you should determine if there are easements on your property, and where they are located. An easement is a right-of-way for public or quasi-public use. These could be for telephone, power, or drainage. You should find out what restrictions are involved in developing those areas covered by the easement.

Your site analysis gave you basic information about the negative and positive qualities of your property. To determine how to minimize the negative qualities and maximize the positive ones, it is necessary to put together the base plan, family inventory, and site-analysis information.

The next step is "goose-egg" planning. Place a second overlay sheet over the site-analysis sheet and the base plan. At this point, you are not interested in the specific shape each activity area will take. Simply rough in the approximate locations of the various activity areas (patio, children's play area, service area, etc.) with loose "goose-egg" shapes. This approach will help you to determine the space required for each activity area and the influences of site conditions on these areas.

Goose-egg planning also allows you to study the interrelationships between neighboring activities. For example, you would not want the children's play area adjacent to the patio. You should make several goose-egg studies to explore all alternative activity locations.

As you make your comparison studies, evaluate each activity location for its compatibility with the activity next to it and to the house (floor plan, points of access, and visual prominence). Once you have a logical placement relative to the house, compare the activity location with what already exists on the site, as shown on your site-analysis overlay. You should also doublecheck each activity area against each major category listed in the site-analysis check list.

Study the influence of both the macroclimate and microclimate. If the influences are favorable, you

Do several goose-egg studies. The four studies above show alternative locations for specific activities or elements that need to be included in the design. Notice that the goose-egg shapes are at different locations in each study. At this point, you must decide whether the various activities or elements are compatible with one another, and whether the arrangement best fits the conditions of your site.

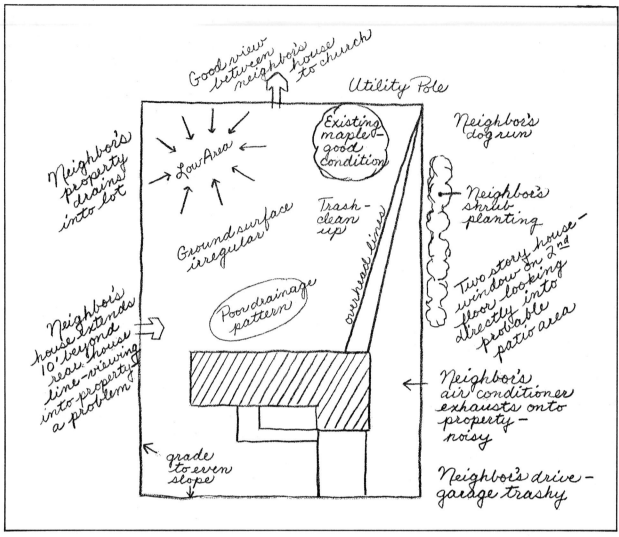

Example of a site analysis sheet with appropriate notations.

have no problem. If the influences are unfavorable, however, you will need to determine if they can be modified satisfactorily through the use of structures or plantings. Similarly, evaluate the impact of the soil, existing vegetation, natural features, structures (both on and off your property), and the extensional landscape. If the impact is neutral or favorable, you have no serious problem. If the impact is negative, you must determine if the problem can be resolved through design or if another location for the activity needs to be found.

The *existing ground forms (topography)* and drainage are of especial importance at this time. You need to determine whether the proposed activity area or structure will work with the natural physical form of the area. Try to locate the activity areas where existing slopes and grades conform as closely as possible to the requirements of the proposed activity. If major

modifications are required, you should investigate other possible locations. If no other locations are available, it will be necessary to alter and modify the land form by grading.

Grading moves earth and remolds, reforms, and resculptures the land. Nearly all landscape construction requires some grading and surface reshaping of existing ground forms to make the areas more useful. But extensive grading results in important technical and practical problems.

It is costly to move soil, and major grading changes have significant impact upon other phases of the design process. If it is necessary to grade your site, strip and stockpile the topsoil. It is a valuable natural resource. Extensive grading disturbs the natural drainage patterns and the relations between the topsoil, subsoil, and bedrock. This disturbance increases problems of settling and of constructing footings and foundations for paved areas and structures. If there are existing trees in the areas that will be graded, the amount of soil that can be added or removed around a tree must be carefully studied. This amount will vary according to the genus, species, and size of tree.

For proper drainage, you must have adequate runoff on "near level" sites and not too fast a runoff on slopes. The steeper the slope, the less water intake by the soil, and the greater the surface erosion problems.

If land has less than 5 feet of vertical fall in each 100 feet measured along the ground, it is considered flat land. Although flat land needs least alteration for outdoor use, moving surface water across it may be difficult, and drainage will be poor if there is tight soil beneath it.

A grade of 1 percent (1 foot in 100 feet) should be maintained for adequate drainage in turf and planted areas. If your soil is especially heavy (clay), or if you get excessive amounts of rain during storms, the grade should be increased to 2 percent. Areas around buildings should have a minimum slope of 2 percent and a maximum slope of 4 percent.

To add variety and interest to the landscape design, you may want to change the levels and grades of flat ground. These may be changed through the use of raised planting beds, or by grading the earth into sculptural mounds.

Because people are perpendicular to the land, they require level or nearly level land to move around easily. Those activity areas with a high level of use should be on land areas that are basically flat (0 to 5 percent). People can still move around with relative ease on rolling or sloping ground that ranges from a fall of 5 to 10 feet in 100 feet. Since this ground is not actually horizontal, only those activities involving

occasional use should be placed on it. Rolling ground offers more opportunity for interesting development than flat ground, but controlling erosion of sloping ground often requires extra construction and grading.

Steep slopes fall more than 10 feet in 100, and are difficult to stand or move around on. Although their soil is likely to be thin and poor, these slopes offer opportunities for dramatic arrangements. The cost of developing steep slopes is considerably higher than the cost of developing rolling or flat ground.

You can measure the percent of slope by means of a 2 x 4 board and a level. The board should be 5 feet long. Place one end of the board at the upper end of the slope. Place the level on the board, and adjust until the board is horizontal. Drop a straight line down from the extended end, and measure from the bottom of the board to the ground slope. Record this measurement in feet and tenths of feet, and multiply by 20 for the percent of slope.

Grading should shape the ground surface so that water will flow away from structures, walks, and surfaced areas. If you have very flat land and tight subsurface soil, you may have to grade so that water will flow into diversion ditches and on into a sump or natural outlet off your property. On the other hand, slopes may move water so fast that is has to be controlled to stop erosion. You can cover steep slopes with vegetation or terrace them with retaining walls.

Grading should fit the various elements of the plan to the site according to the slope and the anticipated intensity of use. For example, you might have to grade enough level space for the house and for an outdoor living area such as a patio or terrace. You might also have to grade steep slopes to obtain more gentle slopes for walks or driveways.

Grading should create a pleasing site appearance. Land sculpture tries to take advantage of existing grade changes and build them into prominent features of the total design. Long, monotonous, straight lines or level ground can be relieved by grading. Grading terraces can make steep slopes more pleasing and useful.

Review your check list carefully to see what changes you are going to make in your landscape that will affect your grading. You will probably need to consider which existing trees, shrubs, and plants should be saved or relocated; where roads and walks should be located for most efficient movement; what grades will be necessary to provide drainage away from new structures but blend in with the general shape of the land; and what utilities and subsurface structures will be needed. For example, a sewer line

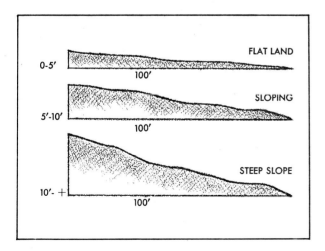

FLAT LAND
0-5'
100'

SLOPING
5'-10'
100'

STEEP SLOPE
10'-+
100'

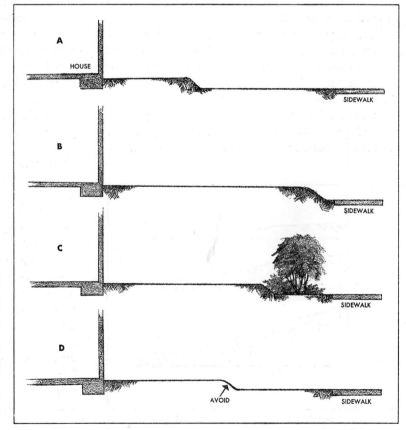

One of the functions of grading is to provide a setting for the house. In the top drawing, it is obvious that a ranch-style house could not be constructed on the original grade indicated by the broken line. By terracing the slope, adequate space is provided for the house. The large two-story house in the middle drawing would not look appropriate on the original grade because the grade is just large enough for the house. Cutting soil away at the rear and filling at the front provides an adequate flat area with a better scale relationship to the house. The bottom drawing shows a house designed to fit the topography so that a minimum of grading is required.

Grading to the front of the house should allow for drainage away from the house and conform to certain standards of design and use. (A) Two level areas have been obtained — the 16-foot terrace area around the house, and the slope to the lower level extending to the sidewalk. If there is not enough space to make the slope gradual, a retaining wall may be required. (B) When the change in grade is made close to the sidewalk, leave a small, level area between the walk and the slope. (C) A 3- to 6-foot level area allows for a planting to screen and soften the abrupt change. (D) Do not divide a space into equal parts with the slope in the middle.

must slope from the house to the septic tank and then to a drain field, or from the house to the city sewer. Catch basins must carry water from the house to city storm sewers or to a sump for disposal.

When you "remold" your property, try to keep its elevations and forms in harmony with surrounding properties. Surface drainage should be carefully controlled, especially in relation to neighboring property. You don't want your neighbor's surface water running over your lawn, and your grading must not dump all of your water onto your neighbor's property.

If your building site is very hilly and has many trees and other natural features, you may want a licensed surveyor to survey it for you. You may have to tell him what kind of survey you want. A property survey gives you the property lines, but a topo-

graphic survey also gives contour lines, indicating the relative heights of the land above a known elevation. You will probably not need a topographic survey if your land is level or nearly level.

If the topography of your site is extremely irregular and the problem of grading is too complex, you should retain a landscape architect to develop a grading plan and design any grading structures that may be needed. As a part of this work, he will have a topographic map prepared that eliminates all guesswork about existing grades.

A landscape architect, civil engineer, or contractor may use a few technical terms that you should understand. For instance, *rough grading* is done before construction work starts, *subgrade* is the top of the material on which surface construction (pavements,

A steep slope may require the development of several levels with retaining walls. A series of low walls is more desirable than one large wall. The most pleasing picture and the best use of these level areas result when changes in grade are made below the house level rather than above it.

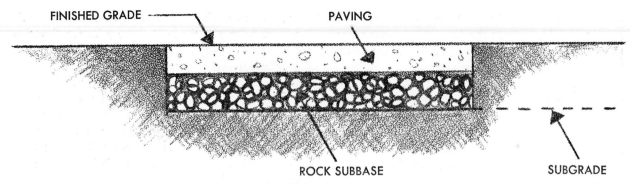

In addition to grading for level areas, you must grade for installation of paving structures. The area between the finished grade and the subgrade must be excavated to the subgrade line.

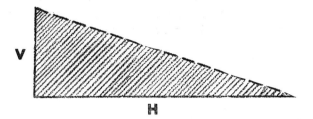

The degree of slope is expressed as a ratio between the horizontal units (H) and the vertical units (V). This ratio is often shown as H:V or H to V.

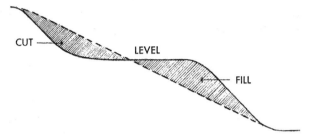

When grading to create level areas, try to balance the cut and fill.

topsoil) rests, and *finished grade* is the final surface after all construction is completed. Excavated material and the resulting space is known as *cut,* and the process is known as *cutting.* When it is necessary to build up existing elevations, the material used and the result are known as *fill.*

Slope ratio is the rate at which a side slope slants from the vertical. In a 20 to 1 (20:1 or 20 in 1) slope ratio, the side slope slants at the rate of 20 units of length horizontally to each unit of height. The expression "the slope had such and such a grade" means the rate of slope between two points expressed as a percentage. A *contour line* is drawn at a constant elevation. Contour lines indicate the shape of the ground surface on a plan. A change in ground form requires changing the contour lines on your plan. Moving a contour line ½ inch on a plan may actually mean moving a ton of earth 50 feet on the site. Know what *contour interval* — the vertical distance between contour lines — was used on your plan. It makes a difference whether these lines are at intervals of 1 foot or 50 feet.

Material taken from a cut is ordinarily used to make a fill nearby. Balancing a cut and fill avoids excess hauling. But if the excavated material is of poor quality or more than you need for fill, have it hauled away.

Before any cuts or fills are made, remove all trees that are not to be left permanently on the site. Work carefully around trees so as not to disturb the existing grade. Leave access for water and air if you are filling around trees. Retaining walls can be built either to hold a grade around a tree or to keep a fill away.

When you have decided on the grade design, strip topsoil into a stockpile to be used later for planting and seeding. Grading over good topsoil covers valuable earth that you will need later for effective planting.

Fills are built up in compacted layers to form a stable section. Finish the surface as indicated on the grading plan. Compacting a fill by tamping is especially important if you plan to put a structure in that location later. Changing a natural grade by filling makes it difficult to provide solid footings for structures. If the fill is not properly compacted, you may need to go down to undisturbed earth to find earth that is solid enough for footings.

Grading requires certain minimum slopes to insure proper surface drainage and practical relations between elements in the site-development plan. Nearly

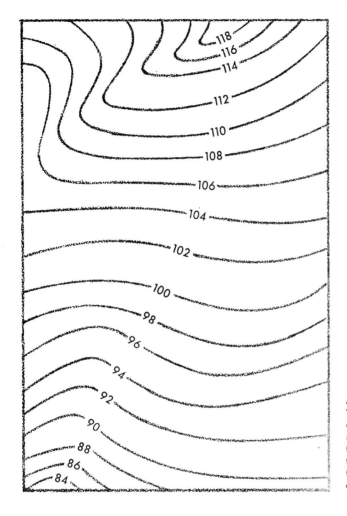

A topographic survey map consists of lines called "contour lines." These numbered lines indicate the elevation in feet measured from an established base point. The contour lines in the center of the map are evenly spaced, indicating an even slope. Contour lines that curve downhill (top of the map) form a ridge. Contour lines that curve uphill (lower part of the map) form a valley. The closer the contour lines, the steeper the slope or valley. Widely spaced contours indicate a gradual slope or level land.

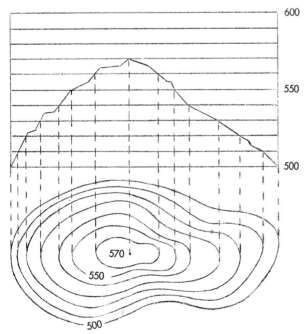

An elevation and plan of contour lines indicating a hilltop.

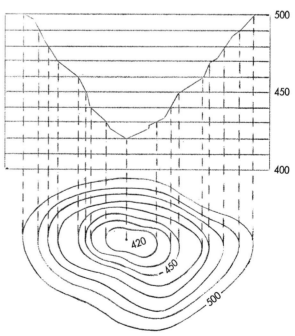

An elevation and plan of contour lines indicating a valley.

	Acceptable H:V (percent slope)		Desirable H:V (percent slope)	
	Maximum	Minimum	Maximum	Minimum
Entrance walks	25:1 (4%)	100:1 (1%)	25:1 (4%)	100:1 (1%)
Ramps................	6.7:1 (15%)	—	6.7:1 (15%)	10:1 (10%)
Grassed banks	3:1 (33%)	—	3:1 (33%)	6:1 (17%)
Planted banks	2:1 (50%)	—	3:1 (33%)	5:1 (20%)
Driveways	6.7:1 (15%)	200:1 (.5%)	8.3:1 (12%)	100:1 (1%)
Steps................	1.5:1 (67%)	—	2:1 (50%)	3:1 (33%)
Patio-terrace	50:1 (2%)	200:1 (.5%)	50:1 (2%)	100:1 (1%)
Drainage swales	10:1 (10%)	100:1 (1%)	10:1 (10%)	50:1 (2%)

level surfaces (lawn, seeded areas) should not have less than a 100 to 1 (100:1) slope. A more desirable slope is 50:1. Although certain landscape areas appear to be level, they must have some slope for drainage. The preferable slope for all flat surfaces is 2 percent, with a minimum of 1 percent. A slope of ½ percent is permissible only if there is no alternative.

The table above shows the grading and drainage slopes for typical units in the home landscape. The two columns on the left indicate the **acceptable** maximum and minimum limits for various slopes; the two columns on the right indicate the **desirable** maximum and minimum limits for these slopes. The maximum limits of acceptable slopes are based on use, and the minimum limits are based on drainage requirements. The desirable slopes listed in the table provide the greatest convenience and safety, are easier to maintain, and have the best visual appearance. In certain cases (entrance walk, ramps, grassed banks, planted banks), the maximum acceptable limits and the maximum desirable limits are the same.

The slopes are expressed as ratios and as percent of grade. The ratio is the relationship between the horizontal (H) measurement and the vertical (V) measurement. For example, the acceptable maximum ratio (H:V) for entrance walks is 25:1 (25 horizontal units to 1 vertical unit). In other words, the slope for the entrance walks should not drop more than 1 foot for each 25 feet of walk. Dividing H into V gives us the percent of grade — in this case, 4 percent.

Before undertaking detailed design of the use areas, be sure that you have proper drainage. Proper drainage is the most important consideration in developing the total landscape design. Without adequate surface and subsurface drainage, neither your activity areas nor plantings will succeed.

Rainwater on the earth's surface evaporates, enters into the soil, or flows across the site. This excess water is called "runoff," and you must make provision for it in your plans. In the design of a drainage system, you need to know the maximum amounts of water that will have to be handled. Find out from the U.S. Weather Bureau the number of inches of rainfall per hour that can be expected in your locality. This information is based on a 2- or 5-year period.

Surface drainage is the easiest problem to solve, but it requires a suitable outlet. You cannot divert surface water onto your neighbor's yard, and you must grade so that surface water is carried off gently to avoid erosion.

Drain surface water into a storm sewer or onto areas where it will not be troublesome. Rain gutters and downspouts discharging roof water directly on the ground create surface drainage problems. One solution is to collect water from each downspout in a catch basin at each corner of the house. Or you can run the water into drain tile laid around the house and discharge it into a large dry well, storm sewer, or roadside ditch.

You should also keep subsurface drainage in mind when you grade. Subsurface water, as well as surface water, will drain downhill toward the house and eventually seep into the basement unless it is diverted. One way to handle this problem is to lay drain tile around the foundation footings, and run the water into a large dry well, storm sewer, or street. You can also connect a downspout discharge line with this system. If you do, be sure to have a drain tile large enough to carry both surface and subsurface drainage and a dry well big enough to handle all the water from a heavy rain.

Sometimes you can take care of subsurface drainage by grading a surface swale. If the ground slopes toward the house, you can start grading up toward the house from a spot about 16 feet away. Runoff water will then collect in this depression and will be diverted around the house.

If you have a high water table on your property, the only solution is to lay extensive drain tile for subsurface drainage. But it is wise not to build on a high water table if you can avoid it.

You can use a drain tile line to carry away downspout or surface water that stands on the property. Lay the line deep enough for water to flow to the sump or ditch. Lay drain tile in rows 8 feet apart. Two to 3 inches of drop in 10 feet is enough slope, but the tile must be laid in straight lines without any bends or twists, either up or down or sideways.

Drain tile lines work best if laid on 4 inches of gravel. Cover the joints with tar paper or roofing paper to prevent soil from seeping in, and then cover with gravel. If there is no natural place off the property where the tile can empty water, you may

have to provide a sump at a low point on your property. A sump is merely an excavation filled with rocks so that water emptied into it can filter into the soil at a slow rate.

Before doing any grading on your site, find out about grading ordinances from your local city hall or courthouse. Check through the requirements and limitations of these ordinances. They may set maximum cut and fill slopes and tell you what drainage controls are required.

You might also have a landscape architect prepare a complete grading plan. A grading plan may save you a great deal of trouble and pay off handsomely in the long run. Many problems and serious consequences can result from moving large amounts of earth without having studied the effect of these changes on your property, as well as on the property around you. The importance of a grading design cannot be stressed too highly. Once the landscaping is in, you won't want to change any grades.

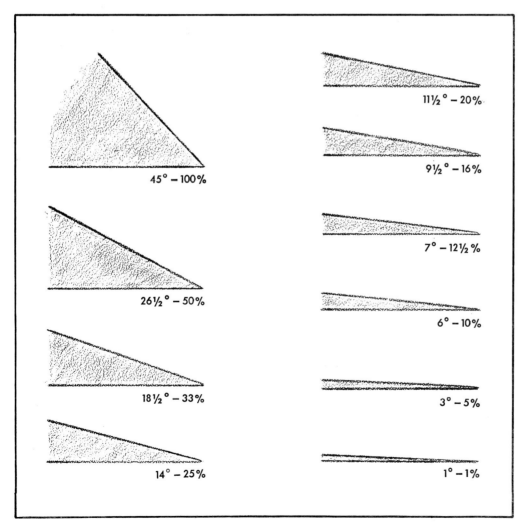

45° – 100%

26½° – 50%

18½° – 33%

14° – 25%

11½° – 20%

9½° – 16%

7° – 12½%

6° – 10%

3° – 5%

1° – 1%

These drawings will help you to visualize the various slopes involved in landscape design. The degree of angle and percent of grade are shown for each slope.

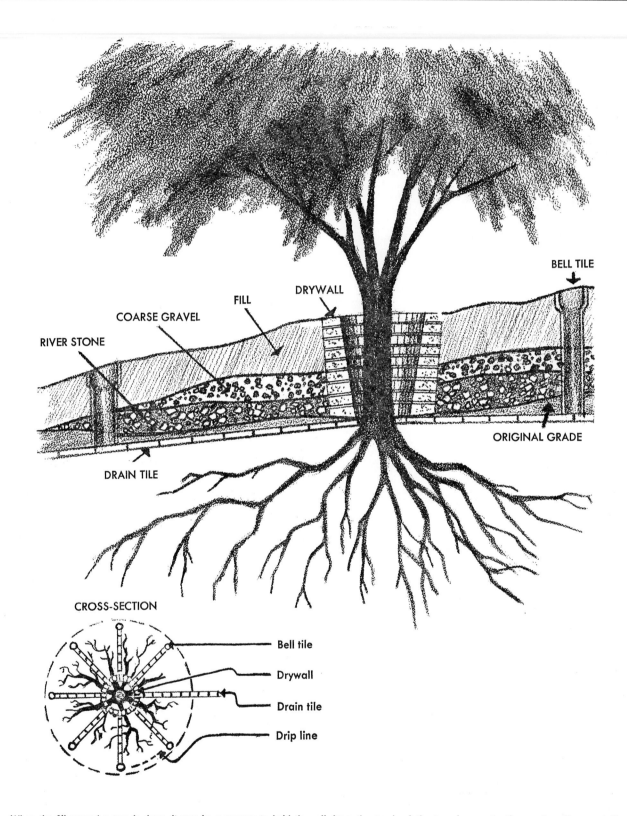

CROSS-SECTION

- Bell tile
- Drywall
- Drain tile
- Drip line

When the fill around a tree is deep, it may be necessary to hold the soil from the trunk of the tree by constructing a drywall around the trunk area to expose the original grade. At the drip line of the branches, place 6-inch bell tile in a circular pattern around the tree. This procedure allows water and fertilizer to be placed as close as possible to the root zone. Lay 4-inch drain tile leading away from the tree to carry water from the trunk. Add 8 to 10 inches of river stone over the tile and original grade. Place a 4-inch layer of coarse gravel over the river stone before adding the fill material.

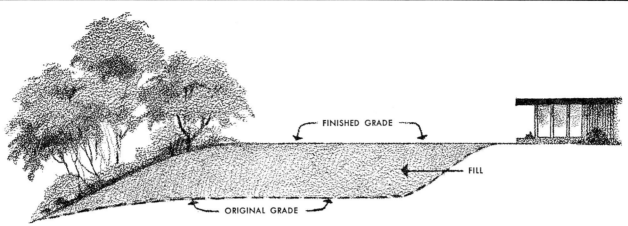

The broken line indicates the original grade — a short level area next to the house sloping rather steeply to a second level area. This grade was extended by filling. As a result, the house has a better setting, and the more gradual slope eliminates the need for a structural retaining wall.

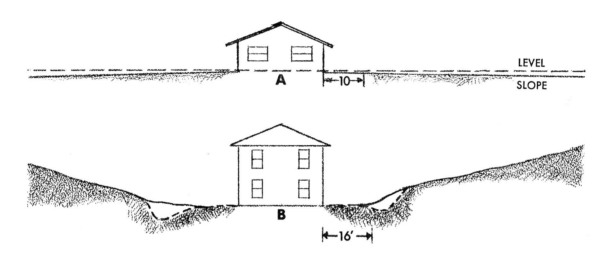

Always grade around structures so that water flows away from them. To assure good drainage, allow at least a 1-percent fall. If your surrounding ground slopes toward the house, you will need to grade a surface moat (indicated by broken line) at a distance of 16 feet from the house. This 16-foot area should be graded to near level with a 2-percent fall.

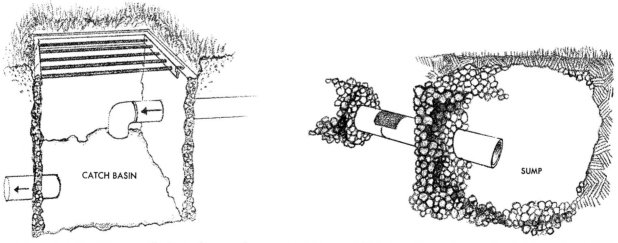

Water collected by underground tile from rain-gutter downspouts can be carried by a catch basin or sump. Notice that the drain tile joints (right above) are covered with tar paper or roofing paper before the tile is covered with gravel.

4: Choosing Construction Materials

The range of materials available for use in the home landscape is greater than many people realize. These materials include natural, unrefined, nonstructural units (earth, rock, landforms, water) and processed, refined, and structural units (metal, plastic, concrete). For every situation, there are several materials that can do the job equally well. You should evaluate each material not only on how effectively it will function in the landscape but on how well it relates in line, form, color, and texture with the other materials around it.

No element in the landscape can be judged in isolation because its effectiveness depends upon its relations with all of the other elements. These relations produce a specific quality of space that becomes important to people as users of space. Whenever you place materials and objects on the land, you are creating space. By emphasizing the character of each type of material (natural or processed) in your design, you strengthen the space articulation of that material and enhance your pleasure and experience in that space.

Your selections should be based upon how well the material combines with other materials, the quality of the space it produces, and the durability, costs, and long-term maintenance requirements. This chapter discusses the physical properties and aesthetic functions of a large number of landscape materials. It is designed to give you a better understanding of the qualities and capabilities of these materials so that you can make the best use of them in your home landscape design.

Earth

Earth is usually thought of only as the foundation for our garden and the growing medium for our plants. You should not, however, overlook its potential as a landscape material with definite three-dimensional qualities.

Since the earth is an accumulation of small particles, it can be graded into mounds or small hills, thus assuming a third dimension in opposition to gravity. The amount (degree) of slope that the earth will hold in this third dimension depends upon the nature of the particles that compose it. If these are primarily sand, the earth will be able to maintain only a very slight angle. Gravel, on the other hand, can maintain a rather steep angle before its sides slough off. Most soils fall somewhere in between these two extremes. This quality is called the "angle of repose" — the amount of slope that the earth can hold without structural retention.

By making use of the earth's three-dimensional qualities within the limitations of its angle of repose, you can manipulate it in a sculptural manner to provide contrast with surrounding landforms. For example, creating earth berms offers topographical relief to monotonously flat land. Earth mounds are also effective in reducing noise and suggesting privacy and enclosure.

To determine the ability of your earth to form sculptural elements, take a shovelful of your soil and allow it to dry. Then pyramid the soil to determine the angle of slope you will have when the earth is graded on a larger scale in the yard. You must also consider possible erosion. How will the surface be covered to prevent future erosion? If you decide to use turf, be sure that the angle of the slope is not so great that mowing will be a problem.

Carefully consider the suitability of earth sculpture to the remainder of the design. The earth must be modeled in such a way that it seems logical and

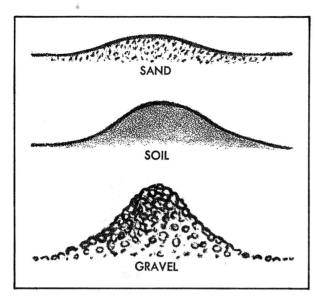

The angle of repose varies according to the nature of the material. Sand has the lowest angle of repose, soil an intermediate one, and gravel the steepest.

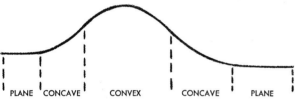

PLANE | CONCAVE | CONVEX | CONCAVE | PLANE

The sculpturing of soil into pleasing berms or mounds requires the use of plane, concave, and convex lines.

compatible with what we know to be natural for the material and the ground forms in general. Forcing a sculptural earth unit (berm) into a small-scaled area emphasizes its artificiality. The resulting mound looks contrived and awkward. There must be sufficient space to provide pleasing transitions, utilizing the basic earth forms — convex, concave, and the plane. If you ignore these forms, the end result may be bumps of earth that resemble molehills or loaves of bread. Finally, be certain that your earth berm is an integral part of your overall design, not something imposed on the design because it is unique.

Rock

Rock is used here as a general term to describe several types of the material, such as boulders, cobbles, setts, stone, and gravel. The earth we live on was produced from rock. It is a material related to the pull of the earth's gravity. For this reason, its appearance in a design must be based on a clear understanding of its character when used as a native, unprocessed resource and as a processed or tooled element.

In its native state, rock can be used as sculptural boulders, flagstone for paving, fieldstone for dry walls, pebbles for ground cover, and gravel for surfacing. Tooled or processed rock might be used in the landscape as cut stone, sawed stone, and polished stone (granite or marble), and for paving or mortared walls. But rock always remains an individualized material. Its appropriateness in any design depends upon how well you use it in relation to the site and to other landscape materials.

In some areas of the United States, rock is a dominant landscape feature, and it should be carefully studied to determine how to emphasize its sculptural and structural qualities. A well-conceived design featuring the native rock can be improved and strengthened by the integration of different types of rock from outside the region. These might offer a contrast or a complement to the form, color, and texture of the existing rock. Do not overdo the use of imported rock. Imported rock must be woven into the overall design to reinforce the natural beauty of the native rock in the landscape.

When rock is not a part of the natural landscape, rock of any scale (boulders to pebbles) can be used as a landscape enrichment. Since the rock in this situation is controlled through design, you should not attempt to reproduce a natural rock area. Similarly, do not use rock in a patently artificial arrangement — like the old Victorian rock garden rising abruptly like a circular dome or tiered cake out of an otherwise flat area. Placing rocks on their narrow edges or in crazy-quilt patterns is also obviously unnatural.

A good rule is that all rock should be placed as nearly as possible in the position that it occupied in nature. For example, rocks laid down in sheets (flagstone, slate, etc.) should always be used horizontally. Odd-shaped rocks should be placed on their largest surface, with emphasis on their horizontal dimensions — longer than wide. In general, place rocks so that they look appropriate and give a sense of stability. Because of a rock's mass, it is subject to gravity's pull. If a rock appears to be defying this natural force, it has been incorrectly placed.

Boulders are large-scaled, individual rocks. Their interest as landscape features is related to their sculptural form and visual interest. For this reason, you should select and display boulders on the basis of form, size, color, and texture.

Remember — boulders are units of considerable mass that must be placed on the land in the same way that they would be found in nature. They may be placed separately or in groups of two or three. You should develop a composition that has dominance, contrast, and tension.

37

Group boulders so that tension results from the differences in size and arrangement between each boulder in a "point-counterpoint" theme.

In placing three boulders, you can achieve dominance by allowing one boulder to have greater importance than the other two — for example, by using the largest boulder with a natural vertical axis. Contrast is introduced by the other two boulders being smaller than the first, but each being of unequal size and having a different axis. For example, the second largest boulder might have a modified vertical axis but a bulkier mass than the largest boulder. The third boulder could be the smallest of the three with a definite horizontal axis. Tension results from the different sizes and the grouping of boulders in a "point-counterpoint" theme.

Natural rock outcropping is a rock mass that emerges naturally from the earth's surface. Because of its large size, it establishes a scale and texture around which you must work. Analyze its form and the line and direction of its mass, as well as its texture and color. Do not treat it as an isolated picture, such as ringing it with flowers or other small-scale materials.

Cobbles are rocks that measure more than 3 to 4 inches in opposing directions. Although several of the surfaces may be relatively flat, a cobble is a basically rounded mass. Cobbles may be found in fields and along riverbeds. When grouped together, cobbles are characterized by their coarse texture. This texture can offer considerable variety to the design. There are wide variations in color, depending upon the area where they are found. Cobbles cannot be obtained in some areas of the United States.

You must give special consideration to the size of the cobbles as compared with the other landscape elements in the immediate area. The relations between different kinds of materials is most apparent in this case. The coarseness must not be poorly proportioned and gross in contrast with the space and other materials. Cobbles obviously have limited use, if any, in small, highly refined areas. When a strong ground pattern or texture contrast is desired, however, cobbles offer a dramatic contrast, as well as a complementary relationship between nearby surfacing materials, plants, and enclosing elements.

Cobbles contained within a strong pattern provide textural variety and contrast when used in combination with hard surfacing materials (concrete, brick, etc.) and plants.

Stone has been used as a building material for thousands of years. It has the qualities of beauty, warmth, human scale, durability, and strength. Builders classify stone as flagstone, fieldstone, and rubble.

Flagstone is any stone with horizontal layering that can be split into large, flat slabs. It is most suitable for paving.

Fieldstone is composed of irregular blocks of uncut stone of varying sizes found both on and under the surface of the earth. It occurs over wide areas of the country. Fieldstone is most commonly used in its natural form in drywalls and stone masonry walls. The individual stone shapes merge into the larger, dominant form of the wall.

Both fieldstone and flagstone can be processed (cut and dressed) with a saw or chisel. This processing produces a modular, dimensioned, smooth-sided unit with a more architectural (regular) appearance than the natural, irregular form.

Rubble is coarse, broken, and ungraded rock debris. Its shape may vary from spheroid to angular. It is often used as fill material and in masonry construction.

Stones most commonly used in the landscape are limestone, sandstone, slate, granite, and marble.

Limestone is formed by consolidated material laid down by water and wind. It is a porous rock, but it has sufficient strength to serve as an important landscape material. Limestone is quarried, and it is usually sawed into dimensioned units for paving and wall construction. Its typical color is gray to grayish white.

Sandstone is also a compacted stone. It is composed principally of sand particles held together by natural cement, and it has about the same structural strength as limestone. Its resistance to weathering depends upon its binding cement. If this binding cement is iron oxide (red to brown in color) or silica (very light colored), the stone will be far more resistant to weathering than those forms with calcium (white, buff, or gray). Sandstone can be used as a structural material and in dry climates for paving. Much of what is called flagstone and blue stone (because of its blue-gray color) is a form of sandstone split into thin plates.

Slate is formed from thin, layered shales. Its most marked characteristic is its distinct cleavage, permitting it to be split into flat sheets. It has a fine texture, and the usual colors are red, green, black, gray, and purple. Slate is a popular landscape paving material.

Granite is rock that is very hard, strong, and durable. It varies in texture from fine to coarse, and it may be gray, yellow, pink, or deep red. It does not weather appreciably. The durability of granite makes it a highly desirable construction stone.

Marble is a crystalline stone of fine texture and compact surface. It takes a high polish, and is available in a wide range of colors. These color variations result from the presence of various oxides. Not all marbles are suitable for landscape use. Some are subject to severe deterioration from weathering. Consult your local dealer in stone and gravel for available exterior marbles. Because of its fine texture, marble has an exceedingly smooth surface. This surface is hazardous to walk on with leather heels and soles or when it is wet.

As a landscape material, stone is used primarily for paving and stone masonry. Limestone, sandstone, and slate are the most commonly used stones for paving because of the ease with which they split into flat pieces as a result of stratification.

Stone is more costly than any other paving material, but it gives a solid pavement with a durable appearance and interesting texture. If properly built, stone pavements will last many years. In the selection of specific stone, be sure that the surface will not slough off or layers peel off because of weathering.

The colors of stone combine well with other elements in the garden.

Paving stones may be used as irregular shapes or as a dressed stone sawed to a modular, dimensioned unit. The natural, irregular forms must be combined carefully to avoid an indiscriminate patchwork of colors or a confusing and busy pattern.

The thickness of paving stones ranges from 1 to 2 inches. You will need the 2-inch thickness if you place the stone on a sand bed. The 1-inch thickness is used when the stone is placed on concrete and set with mortar.

Granite pavers are quarried stone with a color range from gray to white. They are often referred to as "granite setts." These units are usually $3\frac{1}{2}$- to $4\frac{1}{2}$-inch cubes that are fairly square. Granite pavers are set on 1 inch of moist mortar consisting of 3 parts of clean, sharp mortar sand and 1 part of non-staining portland cement. Once set, granite pavers should be swept with a dry joint and filler mixture of 3 parts sand and 1 part cement. The average coverage for pavers is 7 pieces per square foot, or 50 square feet per ton of granite cubes.

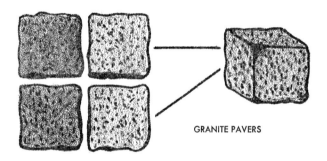

GRANITE PAVERS

Stone masonry may be divided into *rubble work* and *ashlar*. Rubble work does not involve the use of cut stone, although the stone may be split to give a flat face for the wall. It can be used in either a dry-wall or a wall with mortar. A drywall may be a low retaining wall or a freestanding wall. Its construction depends upon the force of gravity and the friction and interlocking of the stones.

Ashlar is a wall with the outside facing constructed of cut stone. The joints are carefully dressed, and the stones are usually of the same height laid in a continuous course. This "regular course" is the opposite of random ashlar, where the stones are of various sizes and the effect of a course is not preserved.

Stones are selected on the basis of appearance, cost, durability, and maintenance. Appearance is judged on the suitability of the stone in color, texture, and aging qualities, and the general characteristics of the landscape to be designed. For example, some stones are more appropriate for a neat, tailored appearance, while others lend themselves to the rustic or picturesque effect.

In color and texture, there is a wide range of choice from marble to sandstone. The aging qualities vary from those types of stone that mellow in tone and outline to the very hard types like granite that retain their hard edges and contours indefinitely.

Costs vary according to the availability of the stone and the ease of processing and installing it. The close proximity of a stone quarry reduces hauling costs, and stone that can be easily quarried and dressed is less expensive. Installation costs depend upon the labor involved in placing the stone.

Durability refers to the lasting qualities of the stone. Frost is the most destructive element. In areas where frost does not occur, almost any stone may be used; but in areas where frost and wet weather occur, porous stone can be seriously affected. Limestone, sandstone, and marble differ greatly in their softness and porousness. Be sure that the stones you select are suitable for your geographic area.

If the stone is to be used as a surfacing material in areas with heavy traffic, the hardness of the stone is an important consideration. This hardness provides an abrasive resistance that helps prevent uneven surfaces after several years of wear. Maintenance must also be considered, particularly for surfacing stone. Find out how easily the stone can be swept, washed, and cleaned, and whether the surface will stain.

Pebbles are small stones worn and rounded by the action of water. They are available in a wide range of sizes and colors. Pebbles are used mostly for paving, where the pebble is pressed into the concrete base. This type of paving provides a texture quite different from that of the exposed aggregate finish to concrete.

The number of design and pattern possibilities with pebbles is practically limitless. You can easily execute a detailed and intricate pattern or use pebbles as a simple textured surface. Since pebbles are placed by hand, you may wish to limit the paving to small areas for accent and design emphasis.

Pebbles are generally available from local building supply firms, and their cost is not excessive. Their general appearance is pleasing because of their natural colors, interesting texture effects, and good scale. There is no glare problem from pebble paving, although sweeping and cleaning may be difficult because of the rough surface. Hosing is the most efficient method for cleaning pebbles. Pebbles are durable rocks. Their durability as a paving depends upon how well they are bonded with the concrete or mortar in which they are placed. The pebble surface is resistant to staining.

Gravel results from the disintegration of rocks by natural forces or blasting. It is distinguished from sand by its size, which is usually over ¼ inch and not over 3 inches. Larger fragments are cobbles and boulders. The cost of gravel is low except for special types and colors that must be shipped into your area.

Gravel is pleasing in general appearance. Its color can vary from black through cinnamon to white. It should be used as a contrast and accent. Do not overuse gravel. Plan gravel areas for interesting shapes and patterns that interrelate with the surrounding ground patterns of the design. Gravel is basically a plastic element, and it can be arranged in curved or straight-lined patterns. It may be used for walks and drives or as a ground cover.

You should buy gravel that has been washed to remove clay and organic materials and then graded into various sizes. It is sold by the ton or cubic yard. A ton of gravel weighs about 3,000 pounds. Pit-run gravel is not graded by screen.

Gravel is difficult to confine and uncomfortable to walk on. Although weeds will grow through it, these can be controlled by laying a double sheet of heavyweight polyethylene plastic beneath the aggregate. You can punch holes in the plastic at intervals to allow water to drain into the soil. Gravel is available in four sizes, ranging from the smallest pea gravel to large rocks. Pea gravel is too small for walks. It sticks to shoes and is easily tracked into the house. The best gravel size is about ½ to 1 inch in diameter.

Gravel may present a glare problem, particularly if it is a light gray or white, and maintenance can be burdensome because of collected litter on the rough, textured surface. Since gravel cannot be broom-swept or raked, hosing is the most common alternative. A gravel "vacuum" can be rented to refurbish gravel surfaces that have accumulated years of fine seeds, dirt, and other debris.

Loose aggregates have not been commonly used as surfacing materials. Aggregates are usually gravel and small rocks that provide a rough and temporary surface. If you apply them directly to the soil in heavy traffic areas, they will sink into the earth over the years with heavy traffic. Small rocks will also kick onto the lawn or planting areas and cause problems. Aggregates can be used to supplement hard-surfaced areas or in low-traffic situations. For example, large rock aggregates may be used around the base of trees for contrast in texture, or as patterned areas in combination with hard surfaces and ground cover.

Mixed rock sizes are not good buys. Smaller rocks work to the bottom, leaving the larger rocks on the surface. Lay rocks 1½ to 2 inches thick, and rake and roll to make firm. One cubic yard of rocks will cover about 200 square feet to a thickness of 1 inch.

In addition to gravel, loose aggregates may include wood chips, bark, tanbark, and pine needles. These are pleasantly soft surfacing materials whose natural color blends harmoniously with the landscape. Tanbark is made of oak-bark chips used in leather tanning. You can get tanbark from a tannery. The availability of the other materials depends upon whether commercial lumbering and paper-making industries are located in your area. Tanbark scatters easily, but you can confine it by defining the area with 2 x 4 headers. One ton of wood chips covers 175 square feet. Put the chips on top of 2 or 3 inches of gravel or a 3-inch pad of crushed limestone for drainage.

Crushed limestone and granite are durable surfacing materials when properly applied. For best results, lay them in three 1-inch layers. Water and roll each layer thoroughly.

Manufactured Masonry Units

Manufactured masonry units include brick, tile, concrete block, and precast concrete paving units. They are manufactured in standardized sizes, rectangular shapes, and relatively uniform colors. Since they are subject to the same gravity influence of the earth as stone, they play a similar role in the home landscape. These units can be used effectively in both vertical structures and horizontal surfacing. Their use in free-formed and abstract curved patterns is limited because of their strong rectangular shape.

Brick is the oldest of man-made building materials. The most common construction brick is made of hard-burned clay. There are two other types — cement brick and adobe brick. Cement brick hardens by chemical action, and adobe brick hardens by drying in the sun.

When clay brick is fired at high temperatures, it is harder and much less porous than brick burned at low temperatures. Well-burned brick has a dark red color, and under-burned brick is salmon colored. One test of hardness is to strike the brick with a hammer. Well-burned brick will give a metallic sound, while under-burned brick gives a dull thud.

Facing brick and common brick are graded on the basis of their weather-resistance capabilities. Use grade SW for exposures to heavy rainfall and severe freezing conditions and grade MW for exposures with average moisture and minor freezing conditions.

Bricks were formerly made in a wide variety of sizes, but now a standard size has been adopted for common brick. The dimensions are 2¼ inches thick, 3¾ inches wide, and 8 inches long. There are special bricks such as Roman brick, which measures 1⅝ inches thick, 3¾ inches wide, and 12 inches long. Special paving bricks are also available. These have the same dimensions as common brick except that they are one-half as thick.

Brick is one of the most handsome paving materials. Bricks can be used in a great variety of patterns to achieve various textures. Their warm color provides a pleasant contrast with plant materials, ground covers, and soil.

Bricks also produce a solid and durable paving surface. When laid on sand, bricks give a slightly irregular or uneven surface. Frost action often results in heaving, but the bricks can easily be reset for the summer. A brick surface reduces glare. Since bricks are quite porous, it is difficult to keep them clean. To prevent weeds and grass from growing beneath the bricks, use polyethylene plastic under the sand bed prepared for the bricks.

Smooth-face brick or rough common brick is ordinarily used for garden surfaces. Face brick is used less often than common brick because it requires matching mortar joints in a professional manner, and it is more expensive.

Wire-cut is a common brick. It is cut square, but it has a rough texture and a pitted surface, and it is smoother laid on edge. Sand-mold brick is smooth and easier to clean than wire-cut brick, and it is slightly larger. A third common type is clinker brick, which is oven-burned and has black spots and irregularities on the surface.

Your local building-materials dealer has bricks in a wide variety of textures, sizes, and colors (red, orange, yellow, brown, gray, and blue-black). Be sure that he has enough bricks of the type you need to finish your project so that you can avoid variations in color.

Brick can give pleasing color effects, provide interest in texture, perform special functions, and satisfy particular site requirements. Bricks are also used for vertical constructions such as walls. Soft bricks have a warm color and agreeable texture, but they are subject to staining and discoloration from airborne area grime. The harder, smoother brick is not subject to staining and grime because rains will wash its surface, but it is cold in appearance and rather forbidding in color. The type of brick you select is a matter of personal preference.

Used brick is popular for both garden paving and walls. Its weathered look, worn surfaces, and traces of old mortar create an attractive and informal appearance. The increased demand for used brick and its limited availability add considerably to its cost.

In choosing your paving patterns, carefully consider the balance of the landscape. Avoid too busy a pattern that will dominate the design. There are several standard designs from which to choose — running bond, basket weave, or herringbone.

Cement brick is a combination of portland cement and a suitable aggregate. It has limited landscape use, and should never be used where a watertight condition is required below grade.

Adobe brick is best used in arid and semiarid climates. It must be protected from moisture penetration and set on a waterproof foundation with adobe mortar. Adobe sizes range from 3 to 5 inches high, 10 to 12 inches wide, and 14 to 20 inches long.

Clay tile is a thin, solid slab of burned clay that is either square or rectangular. The degree to which it absorbs water ("vitrification of fusion") is an important consideration. Clay tile pavers are usually waterproof and weatherproof. Pavers are unglazed. They are available in sizes ranging from 3 x 3 inches to 6 x 6 inches, and are laid individually in mortar on a concrete pad.

Clay tile pavers have a smooth surface, no glare, and are semiresistant to stains. Their common color ranges through tans and reds. This type of surfacing is easily swept and cleaned. It is an expensive surface, but its durability, richness, warmth, and appeal make the investment worthwhile.

Concrete blocks are structural masonry units composed of portland cement, aggregate, and water. The blocks have a rough surface, and they are usually the color of gray concrete. They are available as solid units, and as units with multiple hollow cores. The most common size is 8 x 8 x 16 inches, although other sizes are available. Because of their large individual size, they are difficult to use for warped or curved surfaces.

Concrete blocks were first developed as a cheap, practical, and easily handled unit for wall construction. Although strong and durable, they lack the richness and warmth associated with brick. In recent years, however, designers have discovered that concrete blocks have considerable potential for imaginative uses. This trend has been aided by the development of many colors, sizes, and styles, with a wide selection of textured surfaces. The textured concrete block has a three-dimensional bas-relief design on one surface. The design patterns are quite varied. These textured blocks can be used in conjunction with common concrete block, as well as by themselves.

Another relatively new type of concrete block is the *screen block*. Screen blocks have a variety of open patterns. They are popular because they allow air movement through wall areas while preserving privacy. The light, airy effect of this block combines well with standard solid block for interesting patterns and details, Since screen blocks are not load-bearing, it is not possible to construct a high wall entirely of screen block. There are many sizes available. The most common size is 4 x 12 x 12 inches.

Since the concrete mix is a plastic element, it can be cast into a variety of sizes and shapes (round, square, rectangular, hexagonal). In addition, a variety of colors and textures can be achieved by varying the cement, sand, and rock used in the mix.

Patio block is the most common precast concrete unit. It is available in a wide range of sizes. Solid blocks are 2 inches thick, and hollow core blocks are 4 inches thick. Shapes include round, square, rectangular, and hexagonal. Various patterns can be developed, using one size of block or several different sizes.

Concrete patio blocks can be set on sand or in mortar on a concrete pad. Their surface is resistant to stains, and can be textured or smooth. The amount of glare associated with this material depends upon the color and surface finish. In most cases, patio blocks can be easily cleaned. They are durable and inexpensive. Precast stepping stones are similar in all respects to the patio blocks.

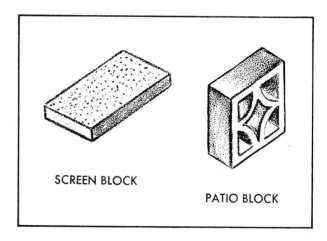

SCREEN BLOCK

PATIO BLOCK

Cast stone is another precast concrete unit that has gained in popularity. It was first developed as an imitation of standstone, limestone, and granite, but it is now being produced for its own distinct character in color and texture. The aggregate used gives a variety of different characters to the stone.

The surface of cast stone can be treated to give specific effects by hand-tooling, hammering, or grinding. The finished product can also be polished if the aggregates cover almost all of the surface.

Cast stone is an enduring and economical material for use in freestanding and retaining walls. Precast curbs can be used as tire stops in parking areas and as continuous curbing, or they can be stacked to provide an inexpensive retaining wall.

Precast curbs are 8 inches wide, 6 inches deep, and 6 feet long. There are 1-inch holes approximately 6 inches from each end and in the middle of the unit. To hold the curbs in place, insert a 1-inch reinforcing rod or galvanized pipe in each hole. These rods should be at least 4 feet long.

PRECAST CURB

Wood

Wood is equaled in importance as a landscape material only by earth, rock, plants, and water. It is familiar and charming, and its color, texture, and grain patterns add a natural richness to the landscape. The abundance and relatively low cost of wood also add to its popularity.

Wood is easy to work with, and has strength and durability as long as it is properly used and treated. To gain the most from this versatile material, it is important to know its characteristics, grading, varieties, and methods of use.

Wood is classified as **softwoods** and **hardwoods**. The softwoods are conifers or conebearing trees, and hardwoods are deciduous (lose their leaves) or broadleaf evergreen trees. Hardwoods are seldom used in landscape construction because of their high cost.

Wood decays as a result of attacks by fungi and small insects that feed on the wood cells and break down their structures. Air, moisture, and a favorable temperature are necessary for this decay process. If one of these requirements is lacking, the fungi and insects cannot function.

Paint prevents decay by keeping out dampness, but the most common preventive method is to poison the fungi and insects by impregnating their food (the wood cells). Commercial preservatives with a coal tar creosote base or a zinc chloride base are used for this purpose. Coal tar creosote is the most effective, but it has an objectionable color and odor. The best preservative with a zinc chloride base is pentachorophenol dissolved in petroleum oil. The oil later evaporates, leaving the chemical in the wood.

The best way to apply a preservative is to pump it into the wood under pressure. The least effective method is brushing. If you use this method, be certain to work the preservative into pores and cracks. It should be applied at least twice. Lumber in direct contact with the soil should be heartwood of redwood, bald cypress, or red cedar. If these are not available, use pressure-treated wood.

Lumber that has not been seasoned is described as "green." Seasoning reduces the moisture content of lumber from an average of 30 to 35 percent down to 12 to 20 percent. Kiln drying is another seasoning process that reduces the moisture content to 3 to 8 percent. Kiln-dried lumber is used when shrinkage is very objectionable. Before the wood is dried, it will shrink, check, and crack. For this reason, it is important to buy seasoned lumber.

Lumber is classified into "grades" on the basis of its appearance and strength. This grading is necessary because wood varies according to species, density, and imperfections that lower its strength and durability.

Softwood — the principal lumber used in landscape construction — is divided into three main classes: yard, structural, and shop lumber.

Yard lumber is used for general purposes. It is the lumber usually sold at lumberyards. There are two groups of yard lumber — finish lumber and common lumber. Finish lumber is graded A, B, C, and D. Grades A and B (often referred to as "B and better") are suitable for natural finishes. Grade A is clear, while Grade B has minor imperfections. Grades C and D are usually painted.

Common lumber is graded according to imperfections that detract from its appearance and construction. No. 1 Common, No. 2 Common, and No. 3 Common are the terms used. No. 1 Common is watertight, and has sound, tight knots. No. 2 Common allows large, coarse knots and imperfections that are considered graintight. Some pitch pockets and decay are permitted. No. 3 Common allows larger, coarser knots, some knotholes, and increased amounts of shake (cracks) and decay. For most landscape work, No. 1 Common lumber should be used.

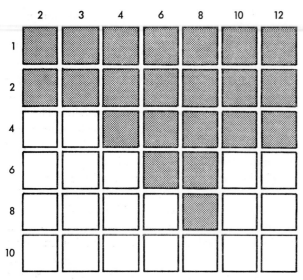

Standard Lumber Sizes. The shaded areas in the above chart indicate the most common sizes of lumber available from local lumberyards.

Structural lumber is graded on the basis of strength, and is used where stresses are required.

Shop lumber is graded largely on appearance. It is used in millwork, trim, etc.

Lumber is cut in even lengths of 6, 8, 10, 12, 14, and 16 feet. The exception is the "2 x 4" (or "stud"), which is also available in 9-feet lengths. After lumber has been dressed or surfaced, it is smaller than the size by which it is identified. Common lumber is ⅜ inch less in thickness and ⅜ inch to ½ inch less in width than the nominal size. For example, a 2 x 4 is actually 1⅝ inches x 3⅝ inches. The actual size of structural lumber is approximately ½ inch less each way than its nominal size.

Lumber is sold by board feet. To calculate board feet, multiply the width and thickness in inches by the length of the board in feet and divide by 12. For example, a 2 x 4 that is 10 feet long $= \dfrac{2 \times 4 \times 10}{12}$ $= 6⅔$ board feet.

The chart on page 45 describes the most common softwoods. Find out which of these species are available in your local lumberyard. Inquire about the dressed dimensions of the lumber, and be certain that it is either air-dried or kiln-dried. Then check the various species available against the chart to determine their suitability for your landscape construction. As noted in the chart, the weathering of wood causes changes in color, roughening and checking of the surface, and cupping. The graded scale for cupping ranges from slight, to distinct, to pronounced, to very pronounced.

The wood finishes for landscape structures can be either painted or stained. Staining is preferable to painting because it enhances and protects the wood, and the color ranges available in stain are more compatible with other landscape materials, particularly plants. Once a surface is painted, you have committed yourself to a high-maintenance program. A painted surface that is unsightly because of fading, peeling, or blistering needs immediate attention. If restaining is delayed a year, however, the landscape scene does not have a neglected appearance.

If you decide to paint, be sure to use a finish lumber. The softwoods are grouped into four categories on the basis of finishing requirements. Those that can be painted with a wide range of types and qualities of paints include the cedars, bald cypress, and redwood. Those for which a suitable priming paint (pure white lead or zincless house paint primer) is necessary include eastern white pine, sugar pine, and western white pine. Those that require careful selection of priming paints and a high-quality finish paint include the firs, hemlock, ponderosa pine, and the spruces. Finally, those that require a most careful selection of priming paints and finish paints include Douglas-fir, tamarack, and southern yellow pine.

Plywood is another construction material available for landscape use. It consists of one or more layers of wood bonded together, with the grain of each layer placed at a 90-degree angle to the adjacent layers. The purpose of this bonding is to decrease the tendency of the wood to warp and split, to reduce shrinkage, and to give nearly equal strength in all directions.

For landscape construction, use either exterior or marine grade plywood. These are bonded with a hot press, using waterproof adhesive. As an added protection, the edges of the plywood board should be covered and protected from exposure to moisture.

Plywood is available in 4- x 8-foot panels with thicknesses of ³⁄₁₆ to 1¼ inches. These panels are made with various surface patterns as well as plain surfaces.

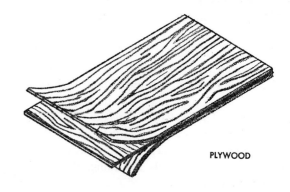

PLYWOOD

TYPE OF WOOD	HEARTWOOD: COLOR, DECAY RESISTANCE	CHARACTERISTICS
Cedar, western red	Reddish brown; highly resistant	Lightweight, moderately soft, low in strength, very small shrinkage. Weathering causes inconspicuous checks and slight cupping. Weathers to dark gray with little or no sheen.
Cedar, eastern red	Brick red to deep reddish brown; highly resistant	Moderately heavy, hard, low in strength, low in stiffness, very small shrinkage. Weathering causes inconspicuous checks and slight cupping. Weathers to dark gray with little or no sheen.
Cypress, bald	Light yellowish brown to reddish brown; highly resistant	Moderately heavy, strong, hard, small shrinkage; one of the most decay-resistant woods. Weathers to light gray with silvery sheen. Weathering causes inconspicuous checks and slight cupping.
Fir, Douglas-	Orange red to red, sometimes yellow; moderately resistant	Unusual strength and density. Softer, less pitchy, and lighter in weight than southern pine. Weathers to dark gray with little or no sheen. Weathering causes conspicuous checks and distinct cupping.
Hemlock, western	Light reddish brown to brown; low resistance	Moderately lightweight, low in strength, hardness, large shrinkage. Weathers to light gray with moderate sheen. Weathering causes conspicuous checks, distinct cupping.
Larch, western	Russet to reddish brown; susceptible to decay	Stiff, moderately strong, heavy, large shrinkage. Weathers to dark gray with little or no sheen. Weathering causes conspicuous checks and distinct cupping.
Pine, eastern white	Cream to light reddish brown; moderately resistant	Lightweight, small shrinkage, moderately soft, low in strength. Weathers to light gray with moderate sheen. Weathering causes conspicuous checks and distinct cupping.
Pine, western white	Cream to reddish brown; moderately resistant	Moderately lightweight, low in strength, soft, stiff, large shrinkage. Weathers to light gray with moderate sheen. Weathering causes conspicuous checks and distinct cupping.
Pine, ponderosa	Orange to reddish brown	Moderately soft, stiff, lightweight, low in strength, little tendency to warp and twist. Weathering causes conspicuous checks and distinct cupping. Weathers to light gray with moderate sheen.
Pine, southern yellow	Orange to reddish brown; resistant to decay	*Longleaf variety:* heavy, strong, stiff, moderately large shrinkage. *Shortleaf variety:* lighter in weight. Weathering causes conspicuous checks and distinct cupping. Weathers to dark gray with little or no sheen.
Redwood	Cherry to deep reddish brown; highly resistant	Moderately strong, lightweight, stiff and hard, small shrinkage. Weathers to dark gray with little or no sheen. Weathering produces inconspicuous checks and slight cupping.
Spruce varieties: Eastern Englemann Sitka	Eastern and Englemann: nearly white; Sitka: light reddish brown; all have low resistance	All three varieties light in weight, low in shrinkage. Eastern is soft, Englemann and Sitka are hard. Weathers to light gray with moderate sheen. Weathering causes conspicuous checks and distinct cupping.
Tamarack	Russet-brown	Intermediate weight and mechanical properties. Weathers to dark gray with little or no sheen. Weathering causes conspicuous checks and distinct cupping.

Adapted from *Materials for Architecture* by Hornbostel © 1961 by Litton Educational Publishing, Inc. Reprinted by permission of Van Nostrand Reinhold Company.

Metals

Metals are not usually listed in an inventory of landscape materials, but the widely held view that the landscape is exclusively earth and plants needs to be modified. In the final refinement of your design, you should use any material that meets the specific conditions of the problem. Some of the metals that can be used in landscape design are discussed below.

Bronze is an alloy of copper and tin. Sometimes additional metals are added to obtain special qualities. Bronze is very strong and resistant to wear. It is primarily a casting metal that is used for a great variety of ornamental purposes. Bronze has excellent resistance to corrosion, and its natural color undergoes changes after exposure to weather. The extent of these changes depends upon the proportion of copper to the other constituents. To avoid galvanic action, do not use bronze in direct contact with iron, steel, stainless steel, aluminum, or zinc. Bronze can be used for grilles, screens, hardware, and sculpture.

Brass is an alloy of copper and zinc. It can be cast or rolled into sheets. Brass is very resistant to corrosion, but galvanic action can be expected when it is in contact with other metals. Avoid using brass in direct contact with iron, steel, stainless steel, and aluminum. Brass can be soldered, brazed, welded, and polished. It is used primarily for ornamental metalwork such as railings, grilles, and hardware.

Aluminum is a silvery white metal characterized by its lightness of weight. It combines quickly with oxygen, and is made corrosion-resistant by the fine oxide film that is formed. Aluminum should be insulated from direct contact with other metals to avoid galvanic action.

Aluminum alloys are classified as casting and wrought. Common wrought aluminum alloys are used as structural members, hardware, gratings, lampposts, and flag poles.

Corrugated aluminum is composed of rigidized sheets with curved or ribbed corrugations. Its brightness limits its usefulness in the landscape, although it can be used as a cheap screening material in areas that are not prominent parts of the landscape.

Aluminum should be shielded from direct contact with lead base paints, dissimilar metals, green wood, certain wood preservatives, and lime mortar, concrete, and other masonry materials. Use aluminum nails. Standard corrugated aluminum is 26 inches wide, and from 6 to 14½ feet in length in 1-foot increments. The depths of the corrugations are ¼ inch, 9⁄16 inch, and ½ inch.

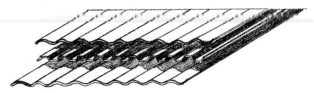

Types of corrugation available in aluminum, plastic, and asbestos.

Aluminum mesh and wire cloth are strong, lightweight, corrosion-resistant materials used for insect screening and fencing. Decorative mesh and wire cloth for guards, grilles, and screening may be obtained in a wide variety of patterns.

Insect screens are available in 50-foot rolls with a maximum width of 6 feet. Chain link fencing is made in woven diamond mesh in two weights — aluminum gauge No. 6 and No. 9. Fencing other than chain link is made from stock aluminum or another compatible metal.

Ornamental aluminum is manufactured from appropriate aluminum alloys. These alloys are used primarily in the landscape as screens, railings, and fences. There are many types and designs. Check with local dealers for information on available shapes and finishes.

Steel is employed in various forms in landscape design and construction. Steel has few impurities. After processing, it has a fine, dense structure with great strength in compression and tension. Steel is used for reinforcing rods and reinforcing mesh for concrete, structural beams, tubular columns, and sheets. The sheets include all types of fencing, mesh partitions, insect screens, and guards.

Wrought iron is almost pure iron that is tough, easily welded, malleable, and resistant to corrosion. It is used for plain ornamental ironwork such as grilles, gratings, decorative columns, railings, fences, screen enclosures, furniture, and small decorative objects. If ornamental ironwork is to be used for structural support, you should check its strength. Prefabricated columnar units are usually either 8 feet or 7 feet 4 inches in height. These can be cut to a minimum of 7 feet 3 inches and 6 feet 6 inches, respectively.

Concrete

Concrete is a mixture of sand, gravel, crushed rock, or other aggregate held together by a hardened paste of cement and water. When first mixed, this material is a plastic mass, and it can be poured into any shape. The variety of shapes is limited only by the materials used for forming.

Forms are the molds in which concrete is poured. They are made of wood and steel. Depending on the kind of work being done, they may require tying, bracing, and extra support to hold the weight of the concrete.

Forms support and hold the concrete until it sets sufficiently to retain the shape or pattern designed. The concrete surface "mirrors" the inner surface texture of its forms. This "mirror" quality can be used to create interesting patterns and textures in walls and other structures. When a smooth surface is desired, the inner face of the forms must be smooth.

Both plain and reinforced concrete may be used in landscape construction. The characteristics of concrete vary widely, depending upon the properties of the ingredients and the proportion of the mix. The techniques used for placing, finishing, and curing can also affect the quality of concrete. If not properly handled, concrete will crack, buckle, craze (hairline cracks), or dust off (powdered surface).

The speed and care with which concrete must be handled limit the size of jobs that the amateur can do successfully. In most cases, it pays to have an experienced concrete man do the job. He has the tools and equipment to finish the concrete pavement in a smooth or rough texture.

A smooth surface, although easy to clean, has a hard commercial appearance that many people find objectionable. The glare from a smooth surface can also be a problem. A smooth surface is necessary, however, if the area is to be used for games or dancing. For vertical surfaces, the finishing process involves filling pockets, removing rough edges and projections, and smoothing out joint marks and blemishes. The designed finish involves using the "mirror" effect or placing small pieces in the forms to create a pattern.

Color can be successfully added to the concrete mix if it is thoroughly mixed with the other ingredients. But red, green, and brown colors seem artificial when compared with the natural colors of other landscape material. They also tend to fade badly. An alternative is to color the concrete a charcoal gray. Six to 8 pounds of pigment (Carbojet, for example) per sack of cement gives a mix that appears black but lightens to a warm charcoal gray when it cures. Lesser amounts of pigment result in lighter shades of gray. Gray is a neutral color that does not dominate the scene, and it blends well with other materials. There is very little fading if it is properly mixed and proportioned. The major hazard when using powdered additives is that the swirls of white and dark in a poorly mixed batch resemble a marble cake.

Concrete is a popular surfacing material because it can be used to cover large areas at moderate cost. Using bricks or wood dividers to form 4- or 5-foot squares will relieve the monotony of a large concrete area. Coloring, tapping in pebbles, brooming, and exposing the aggregates are only a few of the techniques that can be used to obtain a bold design reflecting the color and texture of garden plant materials.

Asphalt

Asphalt as a landscape surfacing material was once confined to drives and parking areas. Since asphalt has been improved, however, it is now used for more refined units such as patios and terraces, walks, and service areas. It is particularly effective when the total surface is broken up into a pattern by combining brick or concrete with asphalt paving.

Wood dividers may also be used to give further definition to the pattern. Asphalt paving must always be installed against a firm edge. Without this edge, the sides of the asphalt will crumble and break away. Bricks, heavy wood header boards, concrete, or steel edging can be used.

Part of the appeal of asphalt lies in its low cost. Since asphalt pavement demands less material than other surfacing materials, larger areas of surfacing can be obtained for less money. Although you can lay asphalt paving yourself, it is far more satisfactory to have it placed by a contractor. You can then be assured of a stable base and proper rolling.

The black color of asphalt causes the pavement to become uncomfortably hot during the summer months. Although this heat is not reflected, it is held well into the evening. Asphalt can be quickly cooled by hosing down with water.

Asphalt is a natural constituent of most petroleums. It has special value because it is a strong cement — readily adhesive, highly waterproof, and durable. Since asphalt is a solid material at ordinary temperatures, it can be readily liquified by the application of heat (asphalt concrete), by dissolving it in solvents of varying volatility (cold-laid asphalt), or by emulsification (asphalt macadam).

Asphalt concrete consists of asphalt cement and graded aggregates of crushed stone or gravel mixed in an asphalt plant at controlled temperatures. The asphalt is then transported to the site, spread over a firm foundation, and rolled while it is hot.

Cold-laid asphalt is made by either of the two types of liquid asphalt that are spread and compacted at normal atmospheric temperatures. These two types are cutback asphalt and emulsified asphalt.

Cutback asphalt has been liquified by blending it with petroleum solvents. Upon exposure to atmospheric conditions, the solvents evaporate, leaving the asphalt cement to harden and hold together the aggregates from which it has been mixed.

Emulsified asphalt is the suspension of asphalt cement in water by means of an emulsifying agent. When the asphalt is combined with aggregates and laid as pavement, the water and emulsion agent evaporate.

Asphalt macadam is laid by the penetration of either hot asphalt cement or asphalt emulsion to a coarse or crushed stone or gravel base. After the base is compacted and smoothed, the asphalt is sprayed on in controlled quantities (1 gallon per square yard for emulsified and 1 pound per square yard for hot mix).

Any of these asphalt pavings can be used in the home landscape. All landscape areas where this pavement might be used, including drives, are considered light-duty. Nevertheless, there must be proper grading, adequate drainage, and sufficient base course for a long-lasting, satisfactory paving.

The thickness of the base course and wearing surface varies according to the type of soil and subsoil. The top course may vary from 1 inch for walks to 2 or 3 inches for drives. The base course should usually be three times the thickness of the surface course. To avoid shifting, cracking, and softening in hot weather, the base course must be rolled by a heavy roller and hand-tamped in areas that are inaccessible to the roller. Your local asphalt company can recommend the thicknesses for your area.

Asphalt pavings create conditions that favor germination of weed seeds in the soil. Weeds and plants can be prevented from growing through the surface by sterilizing the soil before applying the base and finishing courses. Use only recommended soil sterilants. Do not use oil of any kind because oils prevent the asphalt from curing.

If you object to the black surface of asphalt, you can add color by painting or by applying a smooth, colored asphalt mix. Since the colors are often bright and garish, however, it is difficult to blend them with the natural colors of other landscape materials.

Asphalt paving blocks and tiles give a distinctive paving surface that is long-wearing and essentially maintenance-free. They are made by premixing asphalt with graded aggregates and molding the mixture into block or tile form under pressure. Asphalt paving blocks and tiles are available in a wide variety of sizes and thicknesses ranging from 1¼ to 3 inches thick, 4 to 8 inches wide, and 8 to 16 inches long.

The blocks may be rectangular or square, and the tiles are hexagonal. The variety of shapes allows you to develop interesting line and patterned surfaces that you may prefer to the smooth blacktop surface. These asphalt units should be installed over a concrete slab, asphalt binder course, or crushed stone base on a ½- to ¾-inch bituminous setting bed.

Asphalt and cement combined provide a good paving that is durable and easy to handle. The mixture of 6 parts sand, 9 parts crushed rock, 2½ parts asphalt emulsion, and 1 part cement pours like concrete, but it is not as heavy to handle. It dries hard to a compact asphalt surface. The surface is finished by troweling shortly after pouring. The mixture is thinned by adding water until it has a consistency that will pour. If the mixture is too soupy, the asphalt will sink to the bottom. Apply over 4 to 6 inches of crushed rock. A smooth surface is obtained by adding sand to fill in the spaces between the rock.

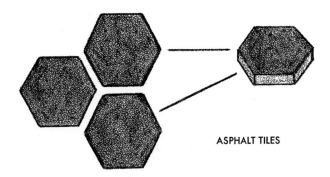

ASPHALT TILES

Processed and Manufactured Products

Processed and manufactured products should also be included in the list of landscape materials. These are products fabricated from raw materials that result in completely new forms of material. The products do not usually display their parent raw material so that it is visually obvious. In this group we include glass, plastics, and asbestos.

Glass is used primarily as a vertical element in landscape design to stop the wind in exposed areas without blocking the view. This view may be a panoramic scene off your property or areas of high interest created on your property.

The glass may be stock commercial units used in architecture, or glass sheets installed into custom-designed frameworks to complement the rest of the design. For example, standard 6-feet-wide two- or three-track sliding doors can be used effectively. Since each door slides independently, you have considerable flexibility in varying the degree of air movement in the area. Various styles of window sash may be used in certain situations. Window sashes can be installed on pivots to direct the breezes, or installed so that they can easily be removed when they are not needed.

Glass is characterized by its transparency, brittleness, and hardness. It has no structural strength, of course, but it is important to know its thermal expansion because of the internal stresses developed and the actual expansion of the glass. Tempered glass is most commonly used in the landscape in areas where there is impact shock and thermal shock. It may be obtained in glare-reducing types: transparent with a neutral gray or other color tint that lowers light transmission but has true color vision; or translucent glass, usually of a white color, that gives wide light diffusion and reduces glare.

Patterned glass is also available as tempered glass. It is semitransparent, with distinctive geometric or linear designs on one or both sides. Some of the types of patterned glass are concave stripes, hammered, pebbled, ribbed, and squares.

Tempered glass diffuses transmitted light, and gives varying degrees of privacy. It is available in ¼- to 1-inch thicknesses, 3- to 6-foot widths, and 8- to 10-foot lengths. Its weight varies with size and thickness. If chipped or punctured, tempered glass will shatter. For this reason, it cannot be cut or drilled, and you must use standard sizes in your design.

The installation of glass is known as "glazing," and the materials used to make the weatherproof joints are called glazing materials. These include wood sash putty, metal sash putty, elastic glazing compounds, and compression materials (molded shapes made of rubber, neoprene, vinyl, or other plastics).

Your glass should be installed by a professional glazier. Be sure that the glass meets design conditions and limitations, including the correct thickness and size to withstand wind loads. When glass is installed in temperatures below 40° F., special precautions must be taken to avoid failure of the watertight seal.

Plastic is a commercial classification of a product of synthetic origin. It is a material that can be shaped or formed in a certain stage of its manufacture. It is often used in place of glass in the landscape. For example, plastic sheet can be used as roofing overhead for climate control on patios and terraces, and vertically for wind control, light control, and visual screening. If you use plastic as roofing, be sure to select colors that transmit less than 35 percent of the sun's heat.

Plastic is obtainable in transparent, translucent, and opaque sheets, and in a wide variety of colors.

Avoid colors that will be garish or eerie when sunlight shines through. Plastic sheets are usually made of fiberglass and polyester plastics. They are treated with acrylic for long life and color stability. They may be plain or reinforced with glass fibers to give the sheet high-impact strength.

The sheets may be flat or corrugated. The flat sheets are best used as vertical units. They may be obtained in thicknesses of ⅟₁₆ to ³⁄₃₂ inch, widths of 1 foot 4 inches, 2 feet, 2 feet 8 inches, and 3 feet 4 inches, and lengths of 4, 5, 6, 8, 10, and 12 feet.

The corrugated sheets are available in the same thicknesses but in a greater variety of widths and lengths. Ask your local distributor for detailed information. There are also several dimensions of corrugations from ¼ to 3 inches. These corrugations correlate with other materials such as aluminum and asbestos sheets, and may be used in conjunction with them.

When choosing a plastic, check its rigidity, durability, and color stability, as well as the effects of sunlight, weathering, heat, and cold. Lucite and plexiglass are the common trade names of plastics most frequently used in the landscape.

Another type of plastic material consists of regular window screen sealed in clear plastic. This screen will block off a view without shutting out any sunlight. It diffuses sunlight in a soft radiance that looks cool, and the silhouette of plants behind the screen gives a quite interesting effect.

Asbestos is a mixture of asbestos fiber and portland cement combined under great pressure. Although asbestos has had limited use in the landscape, it has much to recommend it. Asbestos is resistant to heat, moisture, and corrosion; it is easy to maintain; and its muted natural color (cement gray) blends well with other landscape elements. Asbestos can also be painted.

Asbestos is available in both corrugated panels and flat sheets. The corrugations result in interesting shadow patterns that give continually changing effects when used close to the patio. Asbestos combines well with plastics as alternate panels.

Corrugated asbestos sheets are available in standard and lightweight sheets ⅜ inch thick and 42 inches wide. Lengths range from 10 to 12 feet in 6-inch increments. These sheets are ⅛- or ³⁄₁₆-inch thick, 4 feet wide, and 4, 8, 10, and 12 feet long.

The flat sheets of asbestos provide a simple but handsome enclosure. A vertical screen constructed of these sheets is an effective backdrop for plants. The clean, modern lines make asbestos screens especially suitable for highly used areas where materials and details are subject to close scrutiny.

Sheets of asbestos are also available in several standard colors, pastels, and natural cement color. They have a striated surface that gives a textured effect. The sheet sizes are ⁹⁄₁₆ inch x 2 feet 8 inches x 8 feet.

It is necessary to predrill all holes. Neoprene or lead washers or lead-headed bolts must be used to attach the panels to the frame. Since the panels are heavy, they should be attached to steel posts or to very heavy wood that has been well embedded in concrete. Asbestos sheets should not be used where impact shock is likely to occur.

Miscellaneous Materials

Miscellaneous materials that also may be used in the home landscape include fabrics (canvas, burlap) and bamboo.

Canvas is a heavy, closely woven, rather stiff fabric that can be used to provide shade and climate control for the various activity areas. Canvas can solve many shelter problems at a small cost. If it is properly installed, it can withstand strong winds. The support must be very sturdy, and the material must be firmly anchored to it. Canvas today is made of cotton and synthetic fibers, including acrylic, woven fiberglass, and vinyl-coated nylon.

The cotton canvas suitable for any outdoor use is known as "army duck." It is purchased on the basis of weight by yard. Although army duck is now woven in a great variety of widths, it was originally made only in a 28½-inch width. All commercial references to 7-, 8-, 10-, 12-, and 15-ounce weights are based on this original width.

Canvas can be obtained in a variety of colors, and it can be treated to resist mildew and repel water. It can be vat-dyed (the woven fabric is totally immersed) or yarn-dyed (the canvas is woven after the yarn is dyed). Yarn-dyed canvas provides a variety of patterns and color combinations in the weaving process.

"Painted canvas" is a term referring to vat-dyed canvas that is actually painted with acrylic paints that are water- and weather-resistant. Patterns, floral, and textured effects are possible with this technique. Unlike yarn-dyed canvas, the pattern is seen only on the topside unless it is painted on both sides.

The most expensive, durable, and colorfast canvas is vinyl-coated. A thick film of vinyl is permanently fused to the topside of the fabric. It can be easily cleaned. The vinyl surface itself resists staining, and provides a colorfastness that allows a wide choice of colors from pastels to deep shades.

Synthetic fibers are now used to make canvaslike materials. Although these materials are not canvas, they are commonly referred to as canvas. Among the synthetic fibers used are saran fibers composed of poly-vinyl-chlorides. Nylon is also a popular lightweight material. Both saran and nylon should be treated with a flame retardant and water repellent.

Burlap is jute woven into cloth. It is relatively inexpensive. Burlap is not particularly strong, and it lacks elasticity and durability. It can be a good awning material, however, and its open weave allows for some ventilation. Unlike canvas, which completely blocks the light, burlap will filter the sun's rays. Since it is not waterproof, there is no protection from rain.

Use the heaviest grade of burlap available, and hem with double-stitched flat-felled seams. Use grommets to attach the burlap to either a wood or metal frame. Lace it to the frame with awning twine.

Bamboo screening (commonly called "matchstick") is available in rolls that can be used for a filtered light roof over the patio, and as a vertical screen. In either case, a metal or wood frame is needed to support the bamboo, since it does not have any structural capabilities. Split bamboo is wired together, giving a slightly irregular surface appearance that greatly enriches any garden space through handsome texture contrasts between the bamboo and plants and rocks.

Bamboo is lightweight and easily installed to its supporting frame. It is not as permanent or durable as the other materials discussed in this section, but it is inexpensive and effective in both a functional and aesthetic sense.

5: Choosing Landscape Structures

Structures make your landscape design functional. The structures you can use in your design include grading, circulation, surface, enclosure, overhead, and utility structures. Natural ground forms on your property, your property analysis, and your family inventory will help you decide which structures to use.

The amount of construction is largely determined by the size of the area. Both structures and plantings give privacy, organize space, serve as windbreaks, and hold slopes on a large area, but structures require the least amount of ground space to achieve these ends. Only a few structures are necessary on a large property where there is ample room for plantings. You may need only to modify ground forms with grading and use ground covers and lawn for ramplike connections between levels.

Landscape structures serve the same purpose on smaller city lots or farmstead areas as plantings do on large areas. You can use fences, baffles, and screens instead of shrubs and trees for privacy and as windbreaks. Walls can hold steep slopes and banks, and steps can provide easy access between levels.

Your family inventory might show that you want an outdoor eating area, a level space for lawn games, and some way to break the flow of prevailing winds over the patio. You may have 18 feet of level area behind the house. Beyond this area, the ground is rolling. Your site analysis shows that you will need to screen your neighbor's view and cut down on the prevailing breezes from the west.

Your landscape will need some grading to be level enough for lawn sports. This change in earth form will require a retaining wall between the patio level and the lawn area. You will also need steps for easy movement between the two areas and a fence located along the west side to break the prevailing wind and

provide the necessary screening from the neighbors. Several baffles located to the south will help create space for indoor-outdoor living and provide complete wind control.

A family living on a completely level lot may want to create interest and variety in the dominant horizontal line of the ground by building raised planting beds or low seat walls. A fence and baffles can still be used for wind protection and privacy.

Not all of the structures discussed in this chapter can be included on one piece of property. The key to building functional landscape structures is to blend them into a harmonious combination that is practical and contributes to the overall design.

Grading Structures

Grading structures (drywalls and retaining walls) are used to develop areas for human activities in the home landscape. The extent of the grading operation and the grading structures required depend upon the use for which each area of the site is intended, the size and shape of the site, the topographical relation of the site to the surrounding land, and the influence of buildings located on the site.

The greater the use of the area by people, the flatter the ground surface must be. Achieving a level surface often requires grading structures to retain the earth at different levels. This is particularly important when the property is small and the shape is the arbitrary form of straight-lined subdivision lots imposed on the ground forms.

Grading structures must be carefully designed and placed so that the topography of your site blends with the topography of the surrounding land. Your modifications of the site should always be in relation to whatever borders it, and your grading must blend with the original ground forms just inside or at your property line.

Your house is the main feature of the site, and the grading scheme should be governed by the position and design of your house. The groundline should flow outward from the building, providing a terrace of at least 15 feet to give the house an appearance of stability on the site. The elevation of this terrace must be considered in relation to the floor level of the building. It should be 6 inches below the floor elevation, and it should slope away from the house a minimum of 1 foot vertically for 100 feet of horizontal distance. A slope of 2 feet for 100 feet is preferable.

The major consideration in deciding whether to use a grading structure or to grade the land to a slope between two levels is the angle of repose of the soil. (See Chapter 4 for a discussion of angle of repose.) Structural support is necessary when the normal angle of repose covers ground space that may be needed for activity areas. By using grading stuctures for retention of the soil, you do not lose large areas of land to accommodate the horizontal spread of the soil's angle of repose. Instead, every foot of land becomes available for development and use. Grading structures should also be used when unusual moisture and soil problems (soil erosion and the slipping of earth) make natural slopes impractical.

The function of grading structures is to hold the soil in place between levels. Considerable strength is required to hold the weight of soil and to withstand the hydrostatic pressure of water that builds up behind the structures. The materials used in grading structures must be able to tolerate direct contact with soil and moisture. These materials include rocks, stones, brick, concrete blocks, poured, reinforced concrete, and precast concrete curbings. Redwood or wood treated for decay resistance can also be used. Railroad ties are among the most popular wood materials.

Drywalls are built without mortar. They are also called "gravity" walls because they hold their place by reason of their own weight. Drywalls can be used to hold a slope 6 to 10 feet high, but in the home landscape they are used for shallower slopes.

Since there is no mortar in a drywall, the joints are open, allowing water to flow through and reducing the hydrostatic pressure associated with solid walls. The drywall is usually built of large stones or broken concrete with earth pockets between the stones. (You can plant these pockets with small plants and vines.) The sheer weight and the friction of stone on stone

holds the wall in place. Select stones with reasonably flat surfaces and place them on their longest horizontal surface. Stones should be placed so that the one above rests on part of two stones below for what is called a "bond." With this construction method, there are no long vertical seams.

The drywall does not have to go below frost line, although it needs good anchoring with the soil. Large rocks placed in a slanting position against the slope at a depth of 8 to 12 inches below the surface will hold the wall and prevent any slipping forward. The width of the wall at the base must be wider than at the top. The base width should be equal to one-third of the total height of the wall. The face of the drywall is always pitched in toward the hill or bank to help stabilize the wall against the weight and lateral thrust of the earth.

Retaining walls are used to retain the earth at nearly a 90-degree angle. Since this angle far exceeds the earth's normal angle of repose, the wall must hold its position against the tremendous pressure of water and earth. A landscape architect or civil engineer will design your retaining wall so that the wall will not rotate and overturn as a result of pressure from the earth behind. Check your local ordinances for minimum design standards required in the construction of retaining walls, and to see whether you need a building permit for these structures.

Retaining walls are constructed of rock (rubble), dressed stone, manufactured masonry units, concrete,

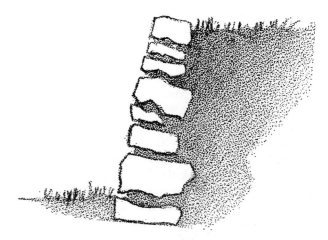

A drywall can serve both as an effective retainer and as a distinctive design element. Notice that the stones are long enough to anchor into the soil, and that they are placed in a backward slant. The front end of the stone slants slightly upward, while the back end is tipped into the ground. The face of the wall should also slant into the slope for greater resistance against the pressures of the earth.

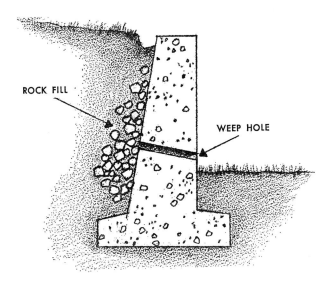

ROCK FILL

WEEP HOLE

A concrete retaining wall should not be less than 12 inches thick at the top. The width of the base should be 48 to 50 percent of the height of the wall. The projecting foot at the front of the wall should be 1/12 of the height. The back of the wall should be sloped from the bottom and waterproofed with asphaltic compound. Weep holes should be set 10 feet apart and slanted to the front so that they will drain about 4 inches aboveground. A rock fill should be tamped in behind the wall, although the top 12 or 18 inches can be filled with soil.

and timber, including railroad ties. A retaining wall should be thought of as an architectural unit that must be designed to blend with other refined landscape elements.

The exposed face of a retaining wall can offer visual interest through texture, light and shadow patterns, and contrasting vertical elements. The degree of visual interest depends in large part upon the material selected. If the retaining wall is 4 feet high or higher and extends over a considerable distance, the broad, unbroken surface becomes monotonous and uninteresting. This surface can be broken by the skillful use of plant material, by a combination of materials carefully blended together, or by variations in the planes of the wall face.

The height of the wall should be well proportioned to the level surface below. The minimum width of the level area should be at least 1½ times the height of the wall. Much wider level areas are, of course, desirable.

If there is considerable difference in vertical elevation, use a series of low walls rather than one high wall. Low walls are more pleasing to the eye, easier to plant, and less likely to lean or topple downhill than high walls. If the series of low walls will be viewed from above, the height of each successive wall should be decreased and the width of the level terrace should be increased.

Since people almost invariably move close to the edge of walls, you may need a railing to provide safety. The height of the railing should be about knee-high or above. Whether the railing is solid or open depends upon the view beyond.

The footings for retaining walls should be below the frost line. The soil water behind the wall can be drained through the use of drain tile and gravel backfill. To relieve hydrostatic pressure, the wall should have weep holes at 10-foot intervals to allow dammed-up water to escape. These weep holes can be formed with 2-inch pipe located just above the base of the wall.

Raised beds are often used for planting compositions. The success of these plantings depends upon having the soil well drained. Since raised beds are above grade, they must be carefully designed to prevent the wall from bulging out of shape, from being lifted up vertically, and from slipping or moving along its base. The soil must be drained so that the plant material will survive.

Both retaining walls and raised beds require reinforcing to avoid surface cracks. Use ⅜-inch bars spaced 2 feet on center and running both horizontally and vertically. These bars should be placed at least 2 inches below the exposed face of the wall.

You can add interest and variety to level ground through the use of raised beds, seat walls, or a combination of the two.

Steps and ramps can be classified as grading structures. Since they function primarily as circulation structures, however, they are discussed on pages 56-58.

Drains and catch basins are underground structures that facilitate the handling of surface and subsurface runoff water. They are a part of a system of surface channels or underground tile used to remove water from activity areas in the landscape. Rainwater should be removed promptly from both paved surfaces and grassed areas. The surface should be graded so that the water is carried to drain inlets placed at frequent intervals. In most residential work, these drain inlets can be relatively small and inconspicuous. Standard drains with 8- x 12-inch grates are available for the collection of water. For easy maintenance, use a drain with a metal basket nested just below the inlet grate for collecting paper, leaves, and other debris. This basket can be easily removed and cleaned. The drain pipe connecting the inlet to the catch basin should be at least 4 inches in diameter.

Catch basins are temporary reservoirs constructed of concrete into which drain inlet water is discharged. The outlet pipe should discharge into a storm sewer, dry well, or low surface area. The pipe should be at least 2 feet above the bottom of the catch basin to allow for the collection of sediment and debris. This debris should be cleaned out occasionally to avoid flooding or clogging of the outlet pipe. Outlet pipes should be at least 6 inches in diameter. If they connect several basins, they should be 8 inches in diameter.

A sump or dry well would be constructed on your own property. It should be at least 6 feet in diameter and 6 to 8 feet deep. The sides of the excavation are walled with stone, and the cavity is filled with coarse gravel. The surface is covered with gravel or concrete slab. The water from the drainage system is discharged into the sump, allowing the water to penetrate into the subsoil at a slow rate. Water discharged on the surface in a low area will dissipate slowly. For this reason, drainage water should not be discharged into a major activity area. If you intend to connect the outlet pipe to a storm sewer, check municipal regulations to find out whether you are permitted to do so.

Clay tiles are used for underground drain lines. These tiles are available in bell, spigot, and plain ends. They are manufactured in two strengths (standard and extra strong) and 2-foot and 4-foot lengths, with inside diameters of 3, 4, 6, and 8 inches. The most suitable tile for your property will depend upon the requirements of your drainage system. The pitch of drain tile should never be less than 2 inches nor more than 6 inches per 100 feet.

Circulation Structures

Circulation structures (drives, curbs, walks, paths, ramps, and steps) provide for the convenient movement of people and vehicles on your property. For the automobile, circulation structures offer access from the public street to the house and garage. For the pedestrian, they provide access from the public street to the front door, as well as to various spaces developed for use in the residential landscape. Since the circulation requirements of vehicles and pedestrians are distinctly different, they will be discussed separately in this chapter.

Drives for urban and suburban residences involve somewhat different design considerations. Since the urban home is usually set back 25 to 30 feet from the street, the driveway should be straight and direct from the street to the garage. The urban driveway is often used as pedestrian access to the house. The rural or suburban drive should be reasonably direct, fitted to the topography, and present a good impression of the house and its surrounding landscape. It should never appear to "collide" with the house. If there is considerable area, the suburban or rural drive may enter the property at the extreme corner and then sweep in a broad curve toward the house. If the area is limited, you may be restricted to a direct, straight-line approach.

The dimensions of the driveway should be carefully worked out to insure ease of movement for the vehicles that will use it. If the driveway is sufficiently wide with an adequate radius on curves, there is least wear on the surface, and less chance of damaging bordering landscape materials. An urban drive should never be less than 9 feet wide. A double drive should be 16 to 18 feet wide. Rural and suburban drives should be a minimum of 12 feet wide. If the drive is 16 feet wide, two cars can pass easily. The drive should be 14 to 18 feet wide on curves to prevent car wheels from overriding the driving surface. (Y turnarounds and parking areas are discussed in Chapter 10.)

A driveway, no matter how well designed, is seldom a thing of beauty. The surfacing material should be attractive, while meeting the requirements of weight support, all-weather use, and durability. You may have to compromise between your desire to have the drive inconspicuous and the practical and economical requirements of driveway construction.

Driveway surfacing materials include cinders, crushed limestone, gravel, concrete, asphalt, and brick. Cinders can be used for an inexpensive driveway surface. Although cinders are not as durable as concrete or asphalt, they will last for many years if properly applied. The cinders should be applied in layers 12 inches deep. Each layer should be rolled a number of times. Topdressing with sand gives a finished surface. This surface will not maintain itself, however, if the road is steep or subject to erosion.

Crushed limestone provides an inexpensive and relatively durable surface. Limestone should be applied, wetted, and rolled in 1- to 2-inch layers to an 8-inch depth. Its white color and brightness when sunlight hits it make it aesthetically objectionable. Since weeds will grow in this surface, maintenance is high. Limestone will erode when surface water flows over it.

Gravel that has passed through a ½- to ¾-inch screen makes a satisfactory driveway surface if applied 8 inches thick. It is difficult to walk over, and the wheels of cars tend to "throw" the gravel into adjacent areas. Its lightness of color and associated glare are major drawbacks.

Concrete drives are the most satisfactory because of their durability, ease of maintenance, and smooth surface for driving and walking. But concrete has a hard commercial appearance, and its light color and high degree of glare make it a harsh material in the landscape. This condition can be overcome by using Carbojet coloring, by exposing the aggregate of the concrete, or by incorporating small gravel or stone chips into the surface for interesting texture and color.

A concrete drive must have a stable, compacted subbase of 6 inches of crushed stone or the concrete slab will crack. The concrete should be a minimum of 4 inches thick. If heavy loads will be carried over the drive, the slab thickness should be increased to 6 inches.

Drives less than 40 feet in length do not require expansion joints. On longer drives, a ½- to 1-inch expansion joint should occur every 20 to 30 feet. Expansion joints are usually an asphaltic matrix. The dark line of the asphalt can be avoided by using latex that drys to a light cream color.

Asphalt drives are a popular and less costly permanent surfacing that concrete. Asphalt is durable and smooth, with only minor maintenance problems. It can be easily patched and repaired, and its dark surface is less objectionable in the landscape than the lighter colored concrete and limestone.

Asphalt drives should be built up in a series of layers: a subbase of 6 to 10 inches of 1½-inch broken stone; a base course of 2½- to 3½-inch crushed stone; and a wearing course of 1¼- to 2½-inch stone and a ¾-inch topdressed layer of broken stone, with a finish layer of gravel or stone screenings. Remember — asphalt must be laid against a firm, stable edge. To prevent weeds from growing through the asphalt, the soil should be sterilized.

A brick drive is probably the most attractive and visually appealing. It is also the most expensive. Vitrified paving brick is used over a 5-inch concrete pad and a 1½-inch sand cushion. The joints may be asphalt or cement grout. Bricks combined with concrete work out very well and reduce the cost. Bricks can be laid on sand against a firm edge, but some relaying is necessary because of surface heaving from freezing and thawing.

With the exception of asphalt, all of the surfacing materials discussed here will stain from engine oil dripped on the surface. Unfortunately, there is little that can be done about this situation.

Walks are major lines of visual approach and physical access to the landscape. In the public area, walks are the major link between the drive and the front entry to the house. If the walk is used frequently, its alignment should be straight (the shortest distance between the two destinations). Curves can be justified only when there is a logical reason (a steep slope, rock outcropping, or heavy planting) for diverting direct movement.

The width of the walk must be based on the dimensions of the human body. Since 2 feet is a minimum space for people walking, the walks should be at least 4 feet wide. A width of 5 feet increases pedestrian comfort and provides better scale relationship with the house.

Walks other than the entry approach are secondary walks. It is a common tendency to include more secondary walks in the landscape than are actually needed. These secondary walks should be located for access to the landscape for pleasure or to utility and service areas (garbage can, clothesline, etc.). In either case, they should be determined carefully after the goose-egg plan has been completed.

Ask yourself whether each secondary walk is really needed. Will the walk be used frequently enough to justify its existence, or can the lawn easily support the traffic? Secondary walks can have smaller dimensions than the entry walk because they need to accommodate only one person at a time. The recommended minimum width for secondary walks is 3 feet, although an absolute minimum of 2½ feet can be used in rare situations.

Both primary and secondary walks should be laid out so that walking is easy. In sloping areas, walks should be extended lengthwise along the face of the slope for ease of movement and minimal grading. This is called "working with the contours." Placing the walk at right angles to the face of a steep slope makes walking more difficult and frequently necessitates unnecessary grading.

All walks should have a cross slope to facilitate the drainage of water over their surface. The surface needs to be "tilted" slightly. A 2-percent cross-slope

(1 inch for a 5-foot width) is recommended; a 1-percent cross slope (½-inch for a 5-foot width) is the absolute minimum. Longitudinal slope is another important consideration. A minimum longitudinal slope is 1 inch in 10 feet. The maximum longitudinal slope depends upon your climate. It can be as great as 8 percent in areas where there is no snow and ice, but 5 percent is the maximum in climates where snow and ice occur.

Since walks are primarily utilitarian structures, they should be as inconspicuous as possible. Avoid using surfacing materials that are glaring, cold, and commercial in appearance. Plain concrete and asphalt are in this category, although the harsh qualities of these materials can be reduced or eliminated through proper detailing and finishing. The surfacing materials should be subdued in color and light absorbing, with a pleasant texture and good scale relationship with the user and the surrounding garden elements. Materials suitable for use as steps include brick, flagstone, concrete, precast concrete units, asphalt, asphalt tile, and granite setts.

Walk construction varies according to the surfacing material used. (For a discussion of surfacing materials and basic construction considerations, see Chapter 4.) Exact specifications for subgrade preparation and finish grade construction vary for different areas of the country. These specifications depend upon soil conditions, drainage requirements, and the extent of freezing and thawing. You should check with a reliable source for the recommended procedures for your area.

Paths are minor circulation units that are usually narrower than a secondary walk and lack the finished appearance of a walk. They are more commonly associated with woodland gardens than with the highly developed man-made landscape on the typical urban and suburban lot. Path widths and surfacing materials vary with topography, frequency of use, and maintenance requirements. A typical path is 2 feet wide. This dimension may vary with the requirements of use and of the site. Try to relate the scale of the path to both human use and the scale of the landscape. The layout of paths on sloping and hilly sites involves the same principles as those for walks. Since the surfacing material is usually not as durable as that used in walks, the possibility of soil erosion and instability of the walking surface should also be considered.

Materials suitable for paths include precast stepping-stones, gravel, crushed granite, wood chips, and pine needles. Precast stepping-stones are a popular means of providing a relatively durable path surface. The precast units are usually 15 inches square. They are set in lawn or a loose aggregate such as gravel or surrounded by wood chips or bark. If you set stepping-stones in the lawn, be careful that they do not become little dots of concrete that are completely out of scale with the remainder of the landscape.

Stepping-stones should be placed on a pad of sand 3 inches thick. The sand helps to reduce the heaving of the stepping-stone that results from freezing and thawing. When heaving occurs, the stepping-stone can easily be reset and leveled. Since the level of the lawn tends to build up over time, you can have a series of little lakes in your path after four or five years. The stepping-stones should then be lifted and sand added to bring the surface of the stone level with the grade of the lawn. Stepping-stones placed in stone aggregate or wood-chip areas also need the sand pad, but resetting for grade changes is not a problem.

The success of a stepping-stone path depends upon the proper spacing of the stones so that the space between stones is comfortable for both men and women. A good spacing that does not require a giant step for women or a half step for men is 24 to 26 inches from center of stone to center of stone. If the area will be used primarily by children, the distance should be reduced according to the children's age and physical size. (For a discussion of the surface materials that may be used for paths, see Chapter 4.)

Ramps and ramped steps are circulation structures that connect two different levels of ground. Ramps are used as a means of access on sloping ground that is too steep to walk up comfortably without horizontal extension and gradation. The ramp is a sloping plane that is particularly useful when you must move wheeled equipment up and down grade changes between levels. The slope of the ramp should not exceed a 15-foot vertical rise over a distance of 100 feet measured horizontally.

Ramped steps are useful where the slope is too steep for a path (over 10 percent) and not steep enough for steps (under 20 percent). However, ramped steps can also be used in place of steps (slopes over 20 percent), particularly when the length of the slope is long and the ramped step can be laid out as nearly parallel with the contours as possible instead of perpendicular to them. The vertical lift of a step is called a "riser," and the risers in a ramp are usually 3 to 6 feet apart, with some slope between each riser. The spacing of the risers on a ramped step should be based on either one or three normal paces (the average adult male-female pace is 24 to 26 inches). The amount of slope between risers should not exceed 1 foot in 6 feet. The height of the risers can vary from 4 to 6 inches.

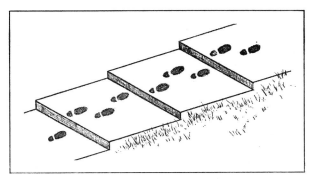

Ramped steps can be used for slopes too steep for a path. The length of the ramp should allow for 1 or 3 paces between risers.

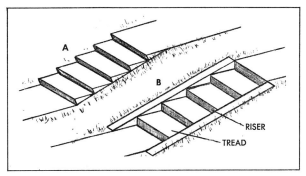

Steps that protrude from the grade (A) become unattractive dominant objects in the landscape because of their sawtoothed appearance. Steps recessed into the grade (B) blend with the slope

The ramp or the ramp portion between steps can be constructed of the same materials as those suggested for walks and paths. Choice of the proper material depends upon the degree of refinement desired and frequency of use. If the ramp is to be used in all seasons, and if you live where ice and snow are common, make your selection on the basis of ease of clearing snow and surface quality that will provide good traction when wet.

The walking surface could be reinforced concrete, asphalt, brick, dressed flagstone, or precast concrete paving units set in mortar or placed on sand. Do not place the paving on sand if the ramp is steep enough to cause erosion of this base course. It is not easy to remove snow from gravel, wood chips, or crushed granite, but these materials are appropriate for ramps if winter use is limited. If it is necessary to retain soil along the side of a ramp or ramped steps, you can use the materials discussed under grading structures.

Steps provide an easy transition between one level and another, particularly when grading structures are used. They are important design elements to relieve the monotony of a wall or slope, to serve as a terminal object for a path or walk, and to facilitate movement through the landscape.

Steps offer a chance to develop interesting landscape arrangements. Unlike indoor steps, garden steps do not need to run in a straight flight. They can have various turns or angles, as long as they are scaled so that they do not look abrupt or pinched.

Even if the vertical rise of a series of steps is extremely steep, they should not be higher than they are wide. Break up a very long flight into smaller groups, and separate these groups with landings. You can also change the direction of a set of steps at a landing.

Keep outdoor steps in scale with the outdoors. Outdoor steps should have a wide tread and a low riser. In other words, you should spread a flight of

steps horizontally as much as possible. For outdoor steps, a 6-inch riser is the absolute maximum, and a 12-inch tread is the absolute minimum. Proper riser-tread relationship is extremely important. Low, broad steps look better and are easier to climb and descend than steep ones. The recommended proportion for outdoor steps is a 5-inch riser to a 15-inch tread, a 4-inch riser to an 18-inch tread, and a 3-inch riser to a 24-inch tread.

Steps should be designed as simply a part of the total composition, not as dominant objects in themselves. They should be fitted to the slope and designed for the user's comfort and convenience when ascending and descending. Steps should never protrude from the bank. They should be recessed into the bank so that the outer edge of the risers is even with or slightly below the surface plane of the bank. This placement avoids the irritating sawtoothed effect of steps placed on top of the slope.

The style of your steps should fit the style of your design. Steps can be rustic and "naturalistic," or they can be a strong architectural form. The strong architectural form should be considered for areas of high use. Each style adds much to the interest of the landscape in controlling directions of traffic movement and views to and from the steps.

One way to make steps is to nail wooden treads to 2 x 10 side pieces called "stringers," leaving the risers open. This type of construction is a poor choice if the steps are intended to be permanent. You can use wooden risers with different kinds of tread materials. For example, you can fill the tread with dirt, gravel, tanbark, wood, or brick. You can use railroad ties for risers, with earth or grass providing a ramplike change in levels. These treads are often long enough for people to take several steps on each tread, depending upon the slope. Another possibility in light-traffic areas is to use redwood or cedar-log risers treated with preservatives, with loose aggregates on the tread.

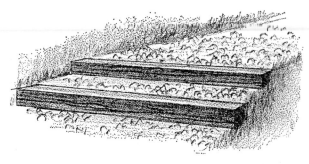

For steps in light traffic areas, railroad ties or redwood or cedar lumber can be used as risers. The treads can be gravel, tanbark, or turf. The same combination of materials can be used to construct a ramped-step connection between levels.

Brick treads and risers set in mortar offer almost unlimited design possibilities. In areas with alternate freezing and thawing, it is important to reinforce the concrete foundation. Brick treads can also be used with wooden risers such as railroad ties or heavy milled lumber. Garden tile treads with brick or concrete risers is another pleasing combination.

Precast concrete slabs are often used, and plain concrete steps with reinforcing steel can be worked into an attractive arrangement. You can also use concrete blocks as risers and treads, or as risers in combination with paving brick, wood, or tile.

Surface Structures

Surface structures are paved units that facilitate the use of the various activity areas. Typical paved units are the patio-terrace, drying yards, service areas, the play area, and game courts.

Since these surface structures are a part of the floor of the landscape, they function in the design as areas for specific uses, as a foreground to whatever exists beyond, as a surface for pattern decoration, and as a setting for objects placed upon them.

Surface structures play a dominant role in the home landscape, and they must be designed and placed with great care so as not to disrupt and overpower the total scheme. In certain cases, however, a paved area (the patio, for example) may become a focal point in the design, depending upon its size (scale), location, and degree of refinement. Those surface structures that primarily serve a utilitarian function — play areas, game courts, service areas, and drying yards — should always fit into and become a part of the landscape without being dominant.

Construction of special-use pavements is similar to that of walks. They must be carefully laid out on well-prepared foundations and graded so that water does not stand on their surface. The materials selected depend upon the use planned for the area. Obviously, play areas and game courts should be constructed of material with a smooth texture and a firm, durable surface. The surface should be easy to sweep or wash off and have a minimum glare. Asphalt or concrete are excellent choices.

In utility areas, you will want a surface that is durable, firm underfoot, and can be easily cleaned or washed off. The texture of the surface (rough or smooth) and its resistance to stains depend upon the type of activity planned for the particular area.

Surfaces for patios and living-activity areas should also be easy to clean, durable, and preferably resistant to food stains. Because of their prominence, surface structures should be a neutral or subdued color and have an interesting pattern that breaks up broad areas and gives a quality of human scale. Most of the paving materials discussed in this chapter are satisfactory for utility areas or the patio.

Brick paving is popular because the individual unit size combines into a restful and harmonious effect. The colors available blend well with other garden colors and absorb light, eliminating glare problems. The surface texture is more pleasant underfoot than smoother pavements. Smooth bricks can be slippery when wet, especially when covered with moss. Bricks, except for the very hard-burned ones, will absorb stains.

Bricks may be laid in various patterns that allow you to control the dominance of the surfaced areas. The most simple and economical pattern is the running bond. The lack of strong pattern makes this a useful layout for walks or utility areas that you do not want to emphasize. Running bond is also suitable for patios.

A more familiar pattern is the basket weave design. This pattern is suitable for almost any situation. A less common pattern that also has a moderate degree of visual attraction is called "jack on jack." In this pattern, each brick course is lined up unit to unit throughout. It can also be used in all types of situations, including walks. The herringbone pattern is the most visually demanding of the four basic patterns. In fact, over large areas it can cause optical illusions that are disturbing.

You can develop other patterns with brick, but avoid complicated patterns that will make the area appear "busy." A simple pattern with repetition of line and form will give an overall harmony to the paved area.

BRICK PAVING PATTERNS

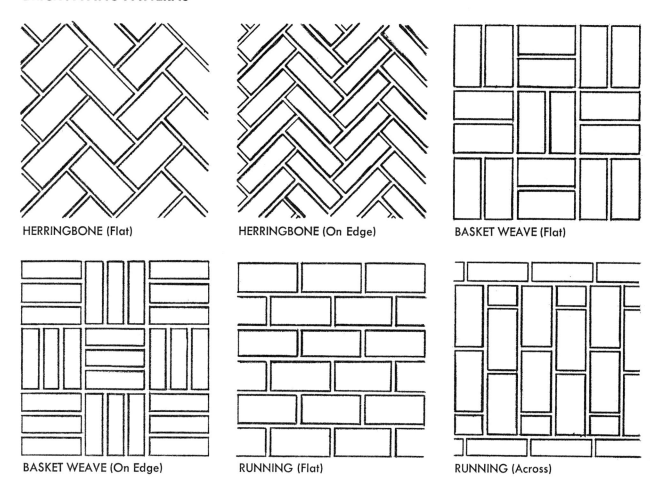

HERRINGBONE (Flat)   HERRINGBONE (On Edge)   BASKET WEAVE (Flat)

BASKET WEAVE (On Edge)   RUNNING (Flat)   RUNNING (Across)

Bricks can be installed on sand or set in mortar over a concrete pad. When installing bricks on sand, it is important to have adequate subsurface preparation. In areas with unstable soil and where winter freezing and thawing are severe, a 4- to 6-inch base of crushed stone or limestone should be laid before adding a 2- to 3-inch sand base. When these conditions do not exist, you can place a 2- or 3-inch layer of sand directly on the soil.

In excavating for your subsurface preparation, be careful not to disturb the subgrade of the soil. If the subgrade is loosened accidentally, stabilize it by moistening and tamping to avoid future settling. Place a 1-inch layer of crushed gravel at a time, then moisten with water and thoroughly tamp or roll. The sand base should also be moistened and thoroughly tamped or rolled before placing the bricks. Mason's sand is superior for this type of paving subbase.

Bricks placed on sand should be kept level without joints. Place the bricks tightly against one another and sweep sand into the cracks. To prevent the bricks from shifting and joints from opening up, lay the

bricks against a firm edge of concrete, steel edging, header boards, or bricks placed vertically (soldier bricks) into the soil or concrete. This method does not prevent the bricks from heaving upward as a result of frost action.

Placing bricks in mortar provides a very stable and durable surface, and eliminates the problem of bricks heaving from freezing and thawing. The subsurface must be excavated to a depth of 8 inches. Do not disturb the subgrade. Place 4 inches of crushed gravel or limestone on the subgrade in 1- or 2-inch layers, moistened and rolled or tamped. Then place a 3-inch foundation of concrete over this base layer. The concrete does not need to be reinforced.

After the concrete has set, add a 1-inch setting bed of mortar in which brick is placed according to the pattern selected. Once the bricks are in place, fill the joints. If the joints are ½ inch apart, use a very wet mixture of mortar to fill the openings. If the joints are ¼ inch apart, use a dry mixture of cement and sand. Sweep this dry mixture into the cracks and moisten with a fine spray until the joints are thoroughly wet.

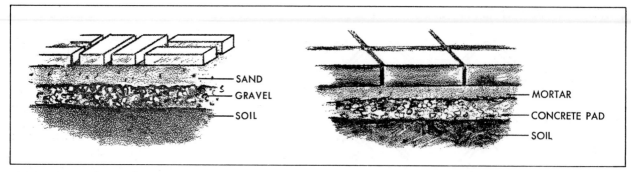

Bricks may be installed on sand (left) or set in mortar over a concrete pad (right).

Bricks installed on sand must be laid against a firm edging. This edging may be concrete, steel, wood, or bricks placed vertically (soldier bricks) as shown above.

Flagstone is sometimes called the "aristocrat" of landscape paving. It appeals to people because of its subdued colors, interesting texture, and durable appearance. Flagstone costs more than any other paving material, but it lasts many years if properly installed. Installation costs are also high, and it is a challenge to work out a pleasing pattern if you are using undressed stone. Your design must be carefully laid out in advance to avoid an indiscriminate patchwork of color or irregularly shaped stones put together in a busy pattern.

Dressed flagstone (square or rectangular) allows you to develop a more orderly and regular paving pattern. Flagstones may be slate, limestone, marble sandstone, and bluestone. Bluestone is a type of sandstone available in blue, gray, red, pink, and various shades of green.

Flagstones are quarried in flat sheets 1 to 2 inches thick. They can be placed on a 2-inch pad of sand with turf joints. This type of installation will not re-

main level where frost occurs, and a subsurface preparation of the kind described for brick on sand paving is necessary. Flagstones can also be set in mortar. The procedure is the same as that for brick paving except that the setting bed of mortar needs to be only ¾ inch thick. Joints should be filled with mortar.

Tile as a paving material has a decidedly formal appearance. It is rich looking, and its unit size (6 x 6, 9 x 9, and 12 x 12), makes it compatible with most other landscape materials. Plan your total surfacing area to fit the tile size you intend to use so that you eliminate the time-consuming job of cutting the tile to fit the space. Since tile has a very hard surface, it does not absorb stains and is easily cleaned.

If the soil is stable, and there are no problems with frost action, tile can be installed on a 1-inch pad of sand placed directly on the soil. When the soil is unstable or frost occurs, installation is the same as that for brick paving except that the pad of sand needs to be only 1 inch thick. If more sand is used, the tile rocks or tilts when merely the edge or corner is stepped on. For a more stable and durable installation, follow the procedure for setting brick in mortar. In this case, the setting bed requires only ¾ inch of mortar.

Precast concrete patio blocks have a paved appearance similar to that of dressed flagstones, but the color and texture are not as warm or pleasant. Nevertheless, they can be used to make attractive walks and paved areas. Since they are cast into modules (standard dimensions), several different sizes can be fitted together to achieve various patterns. But be careful. Because of this flexibility in size, it is easy to end up with a confusing, distracting, or overly elaborate design. Installation of precast concrete blocks is the same as that for flagstone.

Granite setts or pavers give a coarse-textured, uneven surface that is ruggedly handsome in the landscape. Although not suitable for patios or highly used walks, granite setts are pleasant paving for secondary areas. They are frequently used for visual effect more than as a functional paving.

FLAGSTONE PAVING PATTERNS

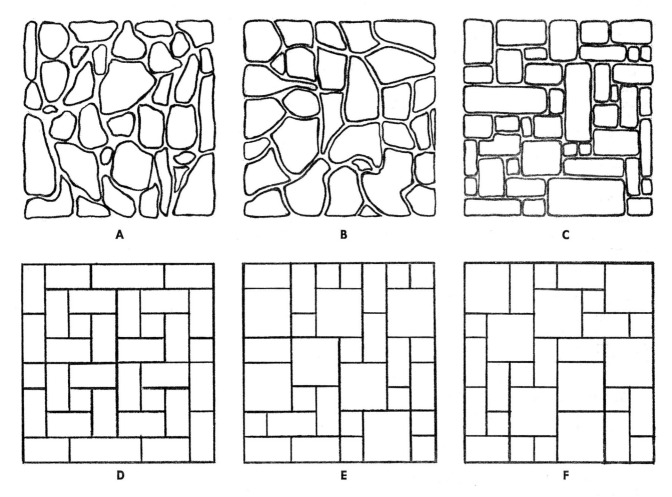

Flagstone may be obtained in its natural quarried form (A, B), in rough-dressed units of various sizes (C), or in dressed units with standard dimensions (D, E, F). The natural quarried form can be placed in an irregular pattern (A) that must be carefully worked out to avoid a confusing patchwork of shapes. The natural form can also be placed in an irregular pattern in which the various stones are fitted as closely as possible (B). Rough-dressed flagstones lend themselves to a random but fitted pattern (C). Because of their uniformity, dressed flagstones are used to develop more regular patterns — basket weave (D), and random patterns using three different stone sizes (E, F).

Granite setts should be installed in 1-inch moist mortar (1 part of non-staining portland cement to 3 parts of clean, sharp mason's sand) placed over a stable subbase of 3 inches of concrete on a compacted gravel base 4 inches thick. The joints should be filled with a dry joint-filler mix of the same proportions as the wet mix.

Asphalt block and tile is another modular paving unit. It is relatively inexpensive and virtually maintenance-free. Many people prefer this unit type of asphalt paving to standard asphalt paving because it has an attractive pattern and texture. It is important to choose the correct thickness. If asphalt block is to be used for driveways or roads, it should be 2½ to 3 inches thick. The hexagonal asphalt tile should be 2 inches thick. For walks, terraces, and patios, both the block and the tile should be 2 inches thick. There

must be a setting bed of portland cement or asphaltic cement at least ½ inch thick laid on a subbase of reinforced concrete 3 inches thick. The joints should be 1/16 inch thick and filled with an asphaltic cement grout.

Asphalt is an inexpensive paving material that can be laid in a wide variety of shapes. Its commercial appearance can be softened by combining it with brick, concrete, dressed stone, or wood dividers. Although asphalt is most commonly used for drives, it is now being used more frequently for walks, living areas, and service areas.

If asphalt is not properly mixed or compacted, it will become soft in warm weather. But if properly laid over a solid bed of rock, asphalt forms a durable, solid surface. Its black surface absorbs the sun's heat, and it will not reflect light as concrete does.

To be successful with asphalt paving, you must plan carefully for adequate subdrainage, using drain tile if necessary to carry off excess moisture. You must also have an adequate base layer composed of 1 to 1½ inches of crushed stone that is compacted and rolled, preferably with a 10-ton roller. Over this compacted layer, spread and roll a ½-inch layer of crushed gravel to fill in the voids of the base layer. To this subbase, apply a 1-inch layer of asphalt for walks, terraces, and service yards, and a 2-inch layer for driveways. If the drive is to carry excessively heavy weight (trucks, for example), the thickness of the asphalt should be increased. The subbase should be three times the thickness of the asphalt topping.

All asphalt paving must be laid against a firm edge to prevent breakup of the sides. The edging can be concrete, heavy wood, steel, etc. Sterilize the soil beneath asphalt to prevent weed and plant growth.

Concrete is probably the most commonly used surfacing material in the landscape. Since concrete assumes any shape into which it is poured, its shape is limited only by the design and construction of the forms. The surface of concrete can be textured by brooming, scoring, exposing the aggregate, or by embedding pebbles. Texturing the surface modifies its harsh, commercial appearance and decreases glare.

There are many types of portland cement designed to meet various construction requirements. Type 1 (normal portland cement) is commonly used for most landscape structures. Under special circumstances, air entraining portland cement is used to produce concrete that is resistant to severe frost action and to the effects of salt applied for snow and ice removal. Concrete made with air entraining cement contains tiny, well distributed, and completely separated air bubbles.

Water and aggregates are added to the cement. The aggregates are graded from fine to coarse and must be clean for the cement to bind them together. The largest aggregates should be approximately one-third the thickness of the slab.

The paving site must be excavated to a depth adequate to accommodate a 4- to 6-inch pad of crushed stone and 4 inches of concrete. In milder climates, the subbase can be reduced in thickness. Next, the forms must be set to the proper grade. They should be braced against the weight of the concrete. After the subbase is in place, you are ready to pour.

In areas where the ground freezes, all concrete should be reinforced with welded wire fabric. This small extra cost will pay dividends by keeping your concrete surface from cracking, buckling, and heaving. Use the 6-inch-square No. 5 gauge fabric for driveways, and No. 8 or No. 10 gauge for reinforcing walks and patios. Be sure to overlap the end of one piece of fabric at least 6 inches with the new end to assure continuous, unbroken reinforcement. The reinforcement mesh should be at least 2 inches below the surface of the concrete.

Once the concrete is placed, the most critical part of the process is finishing the surface. This finishing process should never be started while there is water on the surface because water causes serious problems in scaling, dusting, and crazing.

The finishing process involves the following steps:

(1) Strike off the poured concrete level with the top of the forms.

(2) Fill depressions and level high spots by floating (a process in which a flat board with an attached handle is drawn over the surface).

(3) Use an edging tool to give the concrete a rounded edge that prevents chipping and later damage.

(4) Reduce the slab thickness with a jointer. Grooved joints create a weakened section in the concrete slab that controls cracking from shrinkage or temperature changes. These joints should be spaced at equal intervals. For example, the joints for a walk should be spaced at a distance equal to its width; joints for a drive should not be more than 20 feet apart.

(5) Float the surface again before troweling. Troweling reduces the hard surface.

Curing is an equally important stage. The concrete should be protected so that little or no moisture is lost during early drying stages. Covering the surface and keeping it wet protects the concrete from drying too fast from sun and winds.

This discussion of concrete finishing is necessarily brief. Be sure that you fully understand how to handle concrete before attempting a "do-it-yourself" project. Start small. Concrete has to be handled with speed. If you have a large area to pour, do it in small sections at a time. Be sure to plan for expansion joints at 30-foot intervals. An expansion joint is an asphaltic matrix or latex compounds that allow expansion and contraction of the concrete.

All of the paved surfaces discussed in this chapter must have adequate subsurface and surface drainage. Without proper subsurface preparation, water standing under paved surfaces will cause heaving and cracking from alternate freezing and thawing.

Low-level decks can be constructed at ground level or elevated to whatever height is necessary to provide easy access from the house.

In most cases, the subbase preparation of crushed stone discussed in the section on bricks will provide for adequate water drainage under the paved surface. In some soils such as heavy clay, however, there must be additional drainage protection to collect excess water moving through the subsurface of the soil. This water is collected and removed by installing drain tile under the paved surface and around its edges. Use 4-inch drain tile placed 12 to 18 inches deep. The tile should be laid on a slope that has a 1-foot drop for every 100 feet. The joints of the tile should be left open except for the top of the tile.

Covering the top with tar paper prevents soil and silt from filling the tile. Backfill the drain tile with gravel. The water collected must be carried to a sump or dry well, or allowed to surface in a swale or low area where it can be dissipated at a slow rate that does not interfere with structures or use areas.

Surface drainage must be established at the time you set the grades of the paved surface. Although all paved surfaces should appear flat, their design must include a slight "tilt" to allow surface water to run off. The maximum tilt for a paved surface is a 2-foot drop in 100 feet; the minimum for a smooth surface is a 1-foot drop in 100 feet. The minimum drop on all paved surfaces should be ⅛ inch in 1 foot, although a ¼-inch drop in 1 foot is preferred.

Decks are wood surface structures that can be constructed on or just off the ground or at any elevated height needed for hillside homes. The natural appearance of lumber combines beautifully with other landscape elements, and lumber functions admirably as a surface for outdoor living. Maintenance is low, and wooden decks will last a long time if they are properly designed and constructed.

Low-level decks can be constructed either just above the ground or elevated to floor level to permit direct movement from the house to the deck without a step. Surface decks can also be used to cover old hard-surfaced patios that have cracked because of poor original design and construction. A mini-deck at floor level can give a better transition and connection between the house floor levels and a patio at ground level. The mini-deck functions both as an extension of the house floor into the landscape and as a spacious landing before descending to the lower grade.

Elevated decks are the least expensive means of obtaining outdoor living space for homes located on hillsides or with a considerable drop in grade at the rear of the house. You must consider the deck's structural integrity as well as its appearance. Since elevated decks are highly visible, the number of vertical supports should be kept to a minimum. A landscape architect or engineer should determine the supporting elements needed for elevated decks, maximum span of beams and joists, and the anchoring to the house. Elevated decks must be designed with

railings 36 inches high or combined with benches (16 to 18 inches high) to provide protection to the users.

Deck flooring can have a variety of patterns. The units can be horizontal or vertical to the house, or in a diagonal or grid pattern to prevent monotony. As you develop various patterns in your flooring, check them against the framing spans, bracing along the outer edges, and joist spacing to be sure that they are compatible with the supporting structure.

Since there are many variations in construction practices, lot sizes, and slopes, it is not possible to cover all points in detail. By planning your deck to utilize standard lumber sizes, you will save considerable money in materials and construction costs.

DECK FLOORING PATTERNS

Wood blocks and rounds can be obtained in areas near sawmills. Wooden paving looks more natural in a garden setting than man-made elements. Its color and texture harmonize well with all other parts of the garden. Round disks cut straight through the trunk of a redwood, cedar, or cypress tree, or square blocks cut from railroad ties can be used. The pattern developed from the wood rounds will be a random one, but it should be carefully planned for a pleasant effect. The wood blocks from railroad ties should be laid in a more regular pattern. You may even adapt one of the brick paving patterns.

The wood rounds or blocks can be installed on sand. The thickness of the sand will vary with the surface size and thickness of the unit. Test an area with a 2-inch pad of sand to see if the wood unit is stable. If it rocks, tilts, or gives, you should try a 1-inch thickness.

One disadvantage of wooden paving is that it is not permanent. Plan for eventual renewal or replacement when you put it in. The open grain of the wood soaks up moisture, accelerating decay and deterioration. You can slow decay by applying pentachlorophenol or other toxic wood preservative.

Enclosure Structures

Enclosure structures are vertical elements that organize and define space. The term "enclosure" is used to describe the many types of fences and walls that can be used in a home landscape. Enclosure in this sense does not necessarily mean a high barrier. Enclosure structures separate one use from another and help organize separate activity areas. Two or three spatial relationships may exist within an activity area. For example, in the outdoor living area you may have one cube or volume of space around the patio, another relating to the flower-shrub border, and a third defining the location for lawn sports.

Since more than one spatial relationship may be created on one property, enclosures become important to the development of these areas. The enclosure may be as low as a seat. This "implied" enclosure interrupts movement but does not block vision. It also creates a dominant design pattern and line.

The observer's eye stops at a low enclosure, and his or her imagination continues the vertical effect to separate a particular space from surrounding spaces. This is important because the observer "reads" the landscape and organizes the area into space by enclosure placement. Tall enclosures block both movement and vision and define the space in terms that leave nothing to the imagination. The total view is

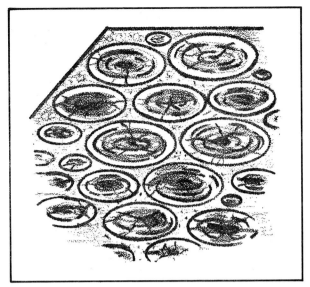

Wood rounds installed on sand.

confined to the enclosed space. Tall enclosures also provide a windbreak, screening, and a sense of protection and privacy.

Privacy is important if you want to make full use of the outdoor living area. People do not feel comfortable in the open with nothing around them, but they can relax completely in the house where walls screen off viewing from the outside. The walls of the house create one large area of space, but the inside walls also define smaller areas of space. Outdoor enclosures should provide both effects.

Enclosures do not have to be continuous elements. For example, a fence does not need to run the full length of the area. Often the baffle effect of offset panels will create interesting spatial relationships, as well as a sense of enclosure and privacy.

Combining a solid enclosure along one side, a low, open enclosure along another, and baffles for a third side often results in a pleasing effect. All the enclosures for one area do not have to be the same, but the materials used should be related. Whatever material is used in a major enclosure should be harmonious in scale, texture, and color with the materials used in all other enclosures.

Landscape construction should extend the house into the outside area. For this reason, it is best to repeat materials used in the house construction — wood, brick, stone, etc. Landscape construction materials should harmonize with house materials in texture, scale, and color.

There are several important design principles for fences and walls that you need to consider. First, the height of the structure should be well above or well

HOUSE

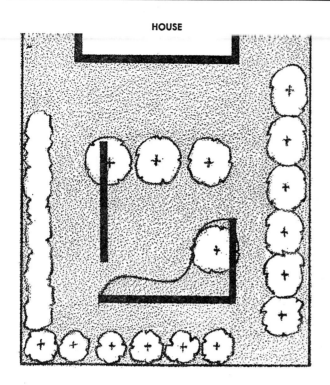

HOUSE

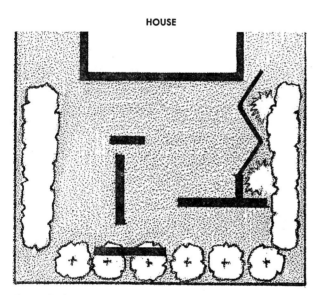

Trees, shrubs, fences, and walls contribute to the creation of space. The drawings above illustrate how these elements create two or three spatial relationships within a landscape.

below eye level. It is irritating to have your vision split with a wall or fence at eye level. The relation between the mass and height of the enclosure element is also important. Implied enclosure is accomplished better by a low wall than by a low fence. A low wall has good proportion because it has sufficient mass in relation to the areas being defined, but a low fence is likely to look flimsy and out of scale with the remainder of the design.

As you design your enclosure element, decide what practical and aesthetic function it is to play in your design. For example, is your enclosure element to be for privacy, partial screening, space definition, or climate control? Should it be inconspicuous and subordinate to the other landscape materials in the composition, a prominent architectural unit, a backdrop for other objects, or a decorative surface? Answers to these questions will greatly influence the design of the structure.

Of all the structures considered in this chapter, enclosure structures are the most important in determining the nature and quality of the space. The design, arrangement, construction materials, and color of enclosure structures can establish a mood (formal, relaxed, etc.), elicit a particular emotional response (serious, gay, etc.), and delineate behavior and activities (games, sitting, eating, etc.).

Fences serve many purposes. They divide outdoor areas, enclose and protect the garden, furnish a background for flowers and shrubs, screen out unsightly views, and shelter the sitting area, patio, or terrace from the wind. They can separate utility space from living space and provide solid enclosure or the lacy openness of a partial screen. They also serve as barriers to keep children and pets within the yard and to prevent people from crossing the yard.

But usually the main reason for a fence is privacy. You can obtain privacy by outlining the area with a fence, but there are other ways. For example, you can build the fence as a series of baffles or sections without respect to the property line. It may swing around an outdoor living area in a curve or angle across at a slant.

The amount of privacy you will get depends upon the type of fence you use. Board fences, horizontal louvers, or close-set grape stakes give maximum screening. Vertical louver, board-on-board, or spaced-slat fences give medium screening. Lattice, pickets, and posts and rail give very little screening.

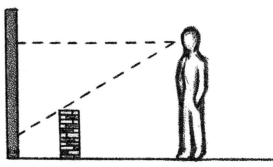

Low enclosing elements block movement but not vision; tall enclosure structures (above eye level) block both movement and vision.

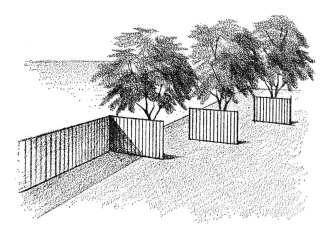

Enclosures do not need to run the full length of the property line. Offset panels provide interesting spatial relationships while retaining a sense of enclosure and privacy.

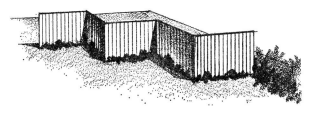

A stepped fence adds dominant pattern and line to a design.

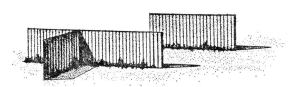

One panel placed at right angles creates a focal point that provides a setting for a piece of sculpture or specimen plant. Another panel is offset for additional enclosure and privacy.

The size of the area to be enclosed will tell you whether to put a fence along your property lines, or whether to use sections and panels within the property. For example, fencing along a property line might be best for a small area, but fences, panels, and baffles built within the garden will do a better job of creating desired enclosure in a large area.

A fence requires only 10 to 12 inches of ground space to function as an enclosure element. A wall may require as much as 3 feet of ground space, and a 6-foot screen with plants requires 6 to 8 feet of ground space. Your decision as to when and where to use fences should depend in part upon the available ground space.

In planning for a fence, select materials adapted to carrying out your landscape design. It is to your advantage to use any easy or inexpensive source of materials.

Avoid design and texture that stand out by themselves. Choose both your design and materials for their simplicity. Some materials are more appropriate in certain localities than in others. For example, rocks are not usually appropriate in highly developed urban areas.

The ways in which materials combine and blend with each other and with the buildings and site are as important as cost and availability. Don't select materials merely because they are pretty. Select them for their appropriateness, their ability to blend together, and their suitability to the materials and architecture of the house.

Wood is the most common material for fence construction, although asbestos cement panels, plastic panels, and various metals such as wrought iron are also available. Glass screens provide some climate protection without interfering with the view.

For fencing, use decay-resistant woods such as redwood, cedar, or cypress for posts and bottom stringers that come close to the ground. If other species are used, be sure that they are treated with preservative to increase resistance to decay and termites. For facing boards or other structural members such as middle and top stringers, you can use lumber that is not decay resistant. Be sure to buy seasoned or kiln-dried wood to avoid shrinkage, twisting, and cupping after the fence is constructed. It is not necessary to buy top grades of lumber, since tight knots are quite acceptable for fences. (Lumber types and grades are discussed in detail in Chapter 4.)

Most fences are constructed with 4 x 4 posts, 2 x 4 stringers, and 1-inch facing boards. If you plan to mortise the stringers into your posts, use a 6 x 6 post. Posts for gates should also be 6 x 6; 4 x 4 posts should be used only for very lightweight gates. Posts should be set at least 3 feet deep and not more than 8 feet apart. They should be carefully aligned and set vertically. Backfill around the post with gravel for several inches to facilitate drainage. The remainder of the hole can be filled with concrete to give good anchorage and support against wind and other stress.

Stringers should be located at the top and bottom of the facing boards. A third stringer halfway from the top and bottom will keep boards from warping and twisting. For heavier structures with more mass and scale, you can use 2 x 6 stringers.

Facing boards can be vertical, horizontal, or diagonal, depending upon the design. For an extremely handsome and refined fence, use either 1 x 1 or 1 x 2 vertical boards. For a lightweight fence, use 1 x 4 boards. Solid board fences are constructed of 1 x 6, 1 x 8, or 1 x 10 boards. Tongue and groove or shiplap can be used for tight fences. The surface texture can be smooth, but resawed wood gives an interesting textured effect. To avoid waste and save money, plan the length of your facing boards to fit standard lengths.

Hardware for assembling the fence should be high-quality, hot-dipped, galvanized aluminum alloy or stainless steel nails or other fastenings. Other types of metal will corrode and stain the wood when exposed to moisture. Use a nail that is three times as long as the thickness of the board you are nailing. Sharp-pointed nails seem to hold better than blunt ones, but they tend to split the lumber. If splitting is a problem, predrill the nail holes.

The design of your fence will be governed by whether you want the fence to be a plain, utilitarian structure or a conspicuous, handsome, and decorative unit. You can choose a fence that is adequate for its function yet not so elaborate as to detract attention from the remainder of the landscape, or you can select one that can function as a major design element in the total scheme. Some of the more common types of fences used in the landscape are described below.

A *picket fence* is one of the few fences that can be used as a boundary in the public area. There are several patterns and widths available. The monotony of these fences can be relieved by varying the width or height of the pickets.

Picket fences are not good barriers, and they need painting often to keep a neat appearance. Since they do not provide much privacy, they are not suitable for the outdoor living area unless shielded by shrubs.

A *lattice fence* can be used to screen out an objectionable view if the lattices are placed closely together. The lattice fence may also serve to create or divide space. Often vines are used on these fences. It is important to blend in a lattice fence as a part of the landscape. For example, do not paint the fence white when everything else is in more natural tones. Lattice fences do not have to be small lath-type structures. Larger posts and wider lumber for the lattice often give better scale relations with the landscape.

A *rail fence* is ideally suited to a country scene, but it can also be designed to work well with an urban landscape. For most homes, a rail fence is a better means of defining the property line and discouraging "pathfinding" than the picket fence. A light rail fence goes best with a ranch-style home, but will look well with many other styles.

A *slat fence* is made of rough-finished wood sawed in 1 x 1 or 1 x 2 strips. The slats may be close together

or far apart. When the slats are close together, leave a little space between them to allow for expansion. The fence can be almost any height you desire. Since slats present a formal appearance, they are usually more appropriate in the city than in the country. Slats have regular edges to give a strong vertical pattern and sense of privacy. Tests have shown that an open slat fence provides more effective wind protection than any other fence.

A *louver fence* is handsome but expensive. Louvers give partial privacy, but also allow as much sunlight or shade as desired for plants on the inside. They can reduce air circulation in the garden and screen off views beyond. Vertical louvers give only partial privacy. For complete privacy, horizontal louvers are needed.

A louver fence should be matched to the house design. It can be painted or stained the house color or a complementary shade. This fence needs careful maintenance.

The split *grape stake fence* is a popular urban and rural fencing. Grape stakes are usually about 2 inches square and 3 to 6 feet high. Redwood grape stakes are decay resistant and need little maintenance, but other types of woods can also be used to make grape stakes. Grape stakes are light, easy to handle, and simple to install. They can be used in many different ways to develop various designs. Grape stakes can be fitted inside a frame to provide a two-sided fence, and they can be attached either vertically or horizontally.

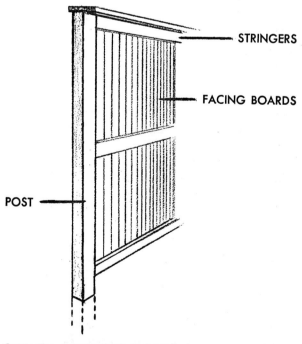

STRINGERS

FACING BOARDS

POST

Construction elements of a fence (rear view).

You can get attractive prefabricated *rustic picket fencing* either in panels or woven together in rows. One of these fences is the stockade type. The typical snow fence seen along highways is another example. Woven pickets are easy to put up, make an effective fencing, have interesting texture, and are built to last.

Although a high **board fence** is easily built, it is expensive because of the amount of lumber used in it. A solid board fence provides absolute privacy, but if it is not carefully designed, it can give a sense of imprisonment and a monotonous view. Applying basic design principles can add interest and pattern to board fences. For a "lighter feeling" and a view of the other side, the boards in a tall fence can be set slightly apart, slanted in a frame to form louvers, or offset by mounting alternating boards on either side of the frame for a board-on-board effect.

Batten siding, tongue-and-groove boards, or alternate panels of vertical and horizontal boards can give pattern or texture to the fence. Using boards horizontally adds the effect of length to the fence and the area surrounding it. Designing the structural supports (vertical post and crossrails) to give strong lines and shadow patterns makes the fence interesting on either side. Or you can solve the problem by fitting the boards within the frame so that they appear the same on both sides.

The popular **basket weave fence** provides complete privacy and interesting shadow patterns. The woven boards give the impression of a texture variation and are attractive on both sides.

Some interesting materials are available today for solid fences. **Plywood** is an old standby that can be attached straight or curved. Use only exterior or marine plywood. Plywood edges need protection from moisture. A cap atop the upper edge will shield it from rain. Wide, solid surfaces put up a tremendous resistance to the wind, and must be installed on substantial framing.

Corrugated asbestos panels have a handsome appearance. Their muted natural color is satisfactory for garden use. They can also be painted. The corrugations result in constantly changing shadow patterns when used close to the patio. This material combines well with plastics used as alternate panels. A fence constructed of corrugated asbestos panels makes an effective backdrop for plants. Since the panels are heavy, they should be attached to steel posts or to very heavy wood that has been well embedded in concrete.

Corrugated aluminum has a bright opaque surface, while **corrugated plastic** sheets give a soft, filtered glow of light to enclosed areas. These plastic sheets are available in various colors and sizes. Use the pastel shades for the best combination of plants and material.

Corrugated aluminum and plastic can be nailed, drilled, or sawed, and are easy to install. If you want a corrugated effect without the reflecting or translucent qualities of aluminum or plastic, you can paint either of these materials to harmonize with garden colors.

Another new type of fence consists of regular window screen sealed in clear plastic. This material can be stretched between posts and stringers to reduce light in the area.

Before you design your fence, check local regulations on fence styles, placement, and heights. Your community building inspector should be able to give you this information.

Walls can be attractive additions to a landscape design. They can enclose an area within the property or be used along a property line. A wall does not have to be of the tall screening type. Low walls are often used to mark boundaries between different parts of the garden and to tie together related elements in the garden plan. A wall can be built for use as a seat, and to create raised planting beds.

Seat walls have become popular. A seat wall 16 to 18 inches high can be a useful and attractive garden addition. Often a low seat wall can also serve as a curb or retainer around planting beds, a temporary table, a potting bench, or a potted-plant display shelf.

Taller walls are often used along property lines, as well as within the property itself. A tall wall can be an attractive structure that makes a good screen. Masonry walls are probably the most effective in reducing noises, but they must be located where they will not trap cold air and create a damp, humid area in the garden.

Whenever a masonry wall is introduced, it offers an opportunity for variety and beauty in design through the rich texture of its building material and its mass and form. In certain situations, neither a hedge nor a fence will function as well as a wall. This is particularly true for the low implied enclosures in the home landscape.

There are four major materials from which walls are constructed — brick, stone, concrete block, and poured concrete. Brick is commonly seen in free-standing garden walls. Brick walls are strong, have an elegant appearance, and weather well over the years. The common running bond pattern is most frequently used. More elaborate bonding patterns include English, Flemish, or Garden Cross.

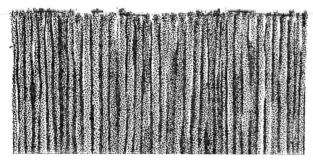

Grape stakes are used to construct a popular rustic-type fence. Redwood stakes weather to a soft gray that complements plants, bricks, and stonework. Nail the stakes to your fence frame. Leave a small space between each stake to allow for expansion. For a two-sided effect, you may want to fit the stakes into a frame.

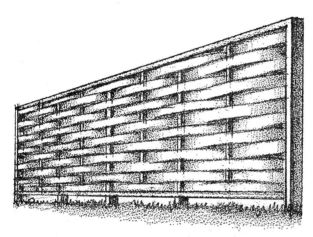

The basket weave fence has the advantage of providing an attractive pattern on both sides. Rough finish lumber is desirable for a softer texture.

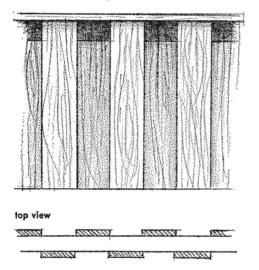

top view

The board-on-board fence reduces strong wind currents while allowing air to circulate between the boards. This fence provides privacy, and the alternating boards form interesting shadow patterns.

The louver fence is a strong design element. For this reason, it should be carefully integrated into the design and not concealed by plantings. The louvers not only allow air to flow through but also form attractive light and shadow patterns. These fences are expensive to build. They require a great deal of lumber and labor to make them structurally sound.

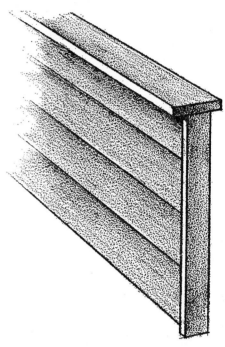

The horizontal louver fence gives complete privacy and a dominant horizontal line to the design. This fence is especially suitable for areas in which you want to give an illusion of greater depth.

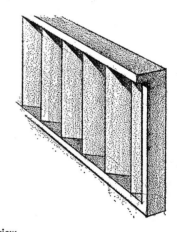

top view

The vertical louver fence gives a partial view of the other side as you move along the fence. Because of its refined construction and airy effect, this fence is a good one to use close to the house.

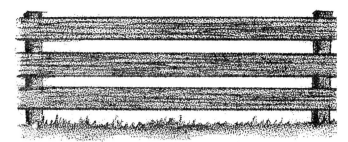

A rail fence is appropriate with low ranch-style houses and in the country. The strong horizontal lines of this fence blend with level or gently rolling land, and the open design allows the viewer to see the landscape beyond the fence. A rail fence provides an efficient barrier, and it is inexpensive and easy to build.

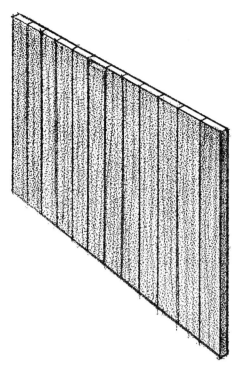

Although a solid board fence allows complete privacy, it is expensive to construct. It serves well as a wind barrier, screen, and background for plants, and extends the walls of the house into the yard.

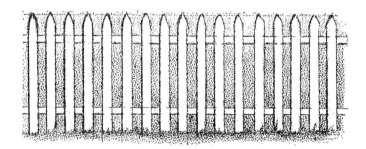

A picket fence is one of the most common types of fences. A wide variety of picket designs can be used. Varying the width of the pickets helps avoid monotony.

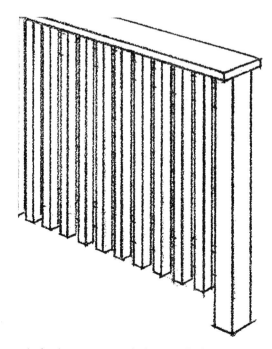

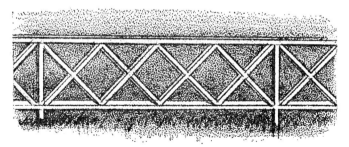

A tightly woven lattice fence gives privacy and serves as a screen. An open-lattice fence provides an open screen that creates space, line, and direction. If plants are grown on these fences, be sure that the fence will support the weight of the plants.

A slat fence, constructed of narrow lumber set vertically, defines an area with clean, crisp lines and provides maximum privacy. The vertical lines offer a pleasing visual effect. The fence shown here is a typical slat fence built of 1" x 1" or 1" x 2" milled lumber set close together.

WALL MASONRY PATTERNS

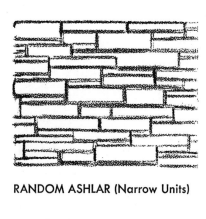

RANDOM ASHLAR (Narrow Units)

RANDOM ASHLAR (Wide Units)

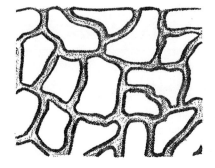

RUBBLE

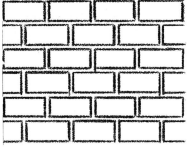

BRICK (Running Bond)

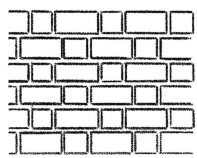

BRICK (Flemish Bond)

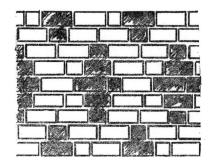

BRICK (Garden Cross Pattern)

These bonding patterns can give a pleasing variation to the surface. For example, bricks make an interesting open grid wall or a seat wall with a redwood cap. It is usually best to avoid mixing brick colors. You should also be cautious about adding texture emphasis by projecting an occasional header beyond or recessing it into the wall face. The results can be visually chaotic and disrupting to the total scene.

The thickness of the wall varies with its height. Low walls may be only 8 inches thick; walls up to 6 feet high should be 12 inches thick. Tall walls should be designed and constructed by professionals. A good foundation below frost line is essential to prevent settling and cracking.

Stone is a natural wall material that is durable and pleasing in color and texture. It is not easy for the amateur to build satisfactory stone walls. The stone may be either dressed and laid in courses called ashlar or uncut stone fitted together in rubble masonry. (See Chapter 4 for a discussion of ashlar and rubble stone.)

In ashlar walls, the face of the stone may be either sawed or naturally rough, depending upon the degree of refinement desired. The rough, uneven surface makes it difficult to achieve a smooth wall face.

In rubble walls, the individual stone units must be in scale with the overall wall mass. Small stones give the wall an unstable appearance. When laying up the wall, do not intermix sizes so that a large stone is next to a small stone. Maintain good proportional relations between one stone and another. The stone should be laid so that the horizontal character of the wall is reinforced by the placement of the stone. Stones should always be placed in the wall in the same way that you find them in nature. Keep the largest stones near the base.

Concrete blocks make a suitable garden wall. Their porous texture and pleasant color can give interesting garden effects, and they can be put together in various combinations and sizes. Regular foundation blocks are better than pumice or cinder blocks because they are more water resistant. If you do not lay concrete building blocks too many rows high, you can hold them together by lining up the holes and filling the holes with pipe reinforcement and cement.

Concrete blocks are the least expensive of all the materials available for wall construction. You can use several different sizes to develop a surface pattern that closely resembles ashlar stonework. Concrete block walls should have a firm concrete footing extending below the frost line. Use steel reinforcing rods in all concrete block walls over 4 feet high.

Poured concrete walls can be formed into a variety of curves and angles. The surface face can be textured or smooth according to the needs of the design. Like retaining walls, freestanding concrete walls should be reinforced for strength and durability.

You can overcome the bleakness of a tall concrete wall by using brick capping, or by curving the wall and adding appropriate plantings. A wooden seat bench constructed along the wall also reduces the sense of height by creating a strong horizontal line.

Overhead Structures

Overhead structures are used to shelter use areas such as the patio, and to help create the third dimension of our cube of space — the ceiling. The ceiling in the landscape is composed of three basic elements — the sky, the spreading branches of large trees, and architectural structures. Overhead structures are important in areas designed for the extension of indoor activities (sitting, reading, relaxing, eating) into outdoor spaces.

The definition and limitation of overhead spaces have strong psychological impact, giving that sense of protection, safety, and comfort that we associate with the complete enclosure (floors, walls, and ceiling) of rooms within the house. By incorporating overhead structures in your design, you can establish a connection between the house and the landscape that is difficult to achieve in any other way.

The overhead structure does not have to be a solid roof to provide a sense of overhead covering and protection. It can be an open grid formed by the crossbeams; it may be partially open with lath spaced between the crossbeams; or it may be a framework with vines providing coverage. Whether overhead protection is partial or complete depends in part upon the amount of control you want over sun, shade, rain, and wind.

The overhead structure may be attached to the house or be freestanding. In either case, it assumes visual importance because it is an architectural structure of definite form, texture, and color. Its design must be compatible with the architectural style and building materials of the house.

Although the overhead structure must be considered an extension of the house into the landscape, this structure is a plane that exists above eye level. For this reason, it should not be the object of fussy or ornate design and detailing. A good rule to follow is that the overhead element should be "sensed," not seen. It is not comfortable to look up — that is one reason why house ceilings have plain designs. This same principle should be applied to the overhead structure.

Check local building codes and ordinances to find out whether you need to obtain a building permit. There may also be restrictions on the total area that the overhead structures can occupy, or limits to

An overhead structure is an extension of the house into the landscape that provides a sense of protection and comfort. Whether the ceiling is open or solid, the overhead structure must be compatible with the architectural style and building materials of the house.

the distance they can project into the yard. These considerations are particularly important if the structure is located in the side yard or front yard of the property. In some cases, no building permit is required if the structure has an open ceiling. If the structure has a solid roof, there may be specific design requirements for footings, the anchoring of supporting members, bracing, and roof construction.

Supports for the overhead may be metal poles or 4 x 4 or 4 x 6 wooden posts. The vertical supports should be large enough to hold heavy crossbeams and any additional roofing material. To avoid the appearance of a forest of timbers, use crossbeams (2 x 6, 2 x 8, or 2 x 10 lumber placed on edge) that are heavy enough to span a considerable distance without sagging. The crossbeams can be used to create an open-grid framework. This structure is sufficient for a person to "sense" space definition and overhead covering.

Since the crossbeams provide the basic framework for the overhead structure, secondary and lighter weight crosspieces can be placed at right angles so that there is a space between each crosspiece, giving a filtered light to the area below. Bamboo screens, woven reed, plastic sheets, canvas, and wood decking can also be used.

Vines are also appropriate for covering the overhead framework. They can be supported by the crossbeams and secondary crosspieces or by wire. Wire is an inexpensive means of supporting vines, but it will sag under the weight of the vines unless it is taut and firmly anchored to the structural frame. The wires should be spaced close together so that the vine grows across the wires instead of along each wire. Turnbuckles will help keep the wires from sagging. Be sure that the wire frame is high enough so that even if the vines sag slightly, they do not interfere with the use of the area below.

Utility Structures

Utility structures for storing furniture and equipment may also be a part of your landscape plan. Plan the location and design of these structures carefully. They should be located for convenience and ease of access without becoming prominent elements in the outdoor living area. The service yard is a logical location for utility structures, since it is screened from the rest of the landscape.

If the utility structure is to be used only for storage, its size will depend upon what you plan to store in it. If the structure is also to be used for other purposes, the size must be adjusted accordingly. For example, one section of the structure could serve as a playhouse for small children and the other section for storage. Then, when the children have outgrown the playhouse, this section can be used for additional storage.

Since a utility structure is an architectural element in the landscape, the building materials selected for it should fit harmoniously with the house and other structures and plantings. Prefabricated commercial units are poor investments unless they can be totally hidden from view. These "outhouse" units have shiny metal siding and roofing that seldom blend well with the architectural materials of the house or with other landscape elements. An excellent way to obtain storage space without introducing a freestanding structure into the design is to incorporate storage units into the design of fences.

In some communities, only one outbuilding is allowed, and its location on the property is restricted to specific areas. In other communities, no outbuildings are allowed. Check local zoning and subdivision ordinances to find out whether secondary outbuildings are permitted on your property. You may need a building permit to build a service structure.

6: Selecting Plants To Fit Your Design

Plants are one of the major building materials in a landscape design. Good design with plants is something more than merely putting shrubs here and there. It requires understanding each plant's individual qualities and environmental needs.

Form, growth habits, texture, and color are important considerations in selecting plants to create a picture with lasting beauty. What is the mass effect of buildings in the area — the forms and lines that your plants must blend with, complement, or screen?

Choose specific plants for a planting composition only after you have considered the total environment in which they will have to live. Study the soil, temperatures, water, light, and wind exposures on your property. What is your soil type? Is the area shady, damp or dry, windy or protected? Each plant has certain conditions that best promote its growth and well-being, and you should choose your plants from those that "like" your conditions.

In this chapter, we will discuss the environmental needs and the design characteristics — color, form, texture — of plants, as well as some of the principles of design that apply to landscape compositions.

Soil is the loose surface material of the earth in which plants grow. It is continually moved about, carried away, and redeposited by wind, water, and ice. Plants add their decaying organic material to change the composition of the soil. But this organic material is almost entirely lacking in some areas. Clay, sand, silt, or gravel resulting from decomposition of rocks alone is not fertile.

Soils are classified into three major types according to the size of their mineral particles. These types are *sand, silt,* and *clay.* An ideal soil mixture contains all three types.

Soils are usually composed of five intermingled materials: (1) minerals; (2) humus, or the organic materials; (3) minute living organisms such as bacteria, protozoa, and fungi; (4) water, which holds dissolved mineral salts in solution; and (5) air.

Humus is the key to good soil. It readily absorbs the sun's rays that warm the soil and promote early plant growth in the spring. Humus helps prevent leaching of certain soluble plant foods, increases bacterial action in the soil, and makes it easier for plant roots to penetrate the soil in their search for food and water.

Humus also increases the water-holding capacity of the soil and modifies the arrangement of the soil particles. Mineral particles in the soil hold water only on their surface, but humus absorbs water like a sponge. Humus improves soil structure so that the soil is easily worked. For example, clay soils will compact and bake hard when dry, and will get lumpy and full of clods if worked when wet. But humus binds soil particles in larger aggregates to give a new texture that will not clod when worked.

Plants cannot grow without water. Even in the best soils artificial watering is often necessary to get water to plants. But too much water drives air from the soil and "drowns" the living plant cells by cutting off the air they need to live. Excess water may also remove nutrients too fast and leave the soil infertile. Too much water limits plant life to the bog types, and too little water limits plant life to desert types.

Plant growth and vigor depend in part upon the amount and circulation of air and water in the soil. Plowing and cultivation have important effects on both water and air content of the soil. Pore spaces filled with air mean too little water, and pore spaces filled with water mean too little air. Balances between air and water determine the natural plant growth in various areas. Cultivation aids proper soil aeration. Working an overwet soil will cause compaction and interfere with air circulation.

The level of the natural water table helps determine the vegetation of a particular area. A high water table usually means a less fertile soil. Drainage is often needed to restore a proper balance between air and water so that desired plants may grow in the area. Air also affects soil temperature. A well-aerated soil is warmer than a wet soil. Good drainage means higher soil heat.

Air circulation over the earth's surface affects plants. Circulating air, breezes, and wind increase evaporation from both plants and the soil. Weak or brittle plants cannot grow in high wind regions because of breakage. General air circulation has a direct effect on plant growth. Cold air flows downhill to collect in low pockets and valleys. Frost occurs earlier in the autumn and persists later in the spring in these low areas, and plants must be able to withstand the still, cold air that collects.

For proper plant growth, the soil should be porous enough to allow air, water, and roots to penetrate it, and yet have enough humus for bacterial activity and to hold water and nutrients. It must also have good subsoil drainage, and the mineral particles (sand, clay, and silt) must be in such proportions as to avoid the dryness of pure sand and the excessive moisture of pure clay.

Too much lime or an alkaline soil allows only alkaline-tolerant plants to grow. Too much acid limits plant life to plants that like an acid soil, such as most of the broad-leafed evergreens. Certain plants will grow under a variety of conditions, but most plants are "choosy" about their living conditions.

Temperature and sunlight also affect plant growth. The energy of the sun's rays combines with other elements to manufacture the food that the plant needs for growth.

Some plants can use more sunlight than others. For example, full summer sunlight will damage shade-loving plants. Other plants grow best in full summer sun. Intense sun can scald the bark of newly planted trees. Sunlight in winter speeds moisture loss from evergreen foliage. Since the evergreen cannot replace this moisture from the frozen ground, its leaves turn brown, resulting in "winter burn."

Plants with colored foliage often need full sun to develop their rich coloring. Nearly all annuals and most perennials must have full sunlight to bring out an abundance of flowers. Since plants vary widely in their habits and needs, it is important to know what environment each plant likes best.

Temperature affects the transpiration (evaporation of water from the leaves and stems) and aspiration (taking in carbon dioxide) of plants. The best temperature for most plant growth is between 50° and 65° F. Both air temperature and soil temperature have a great influence on plants.

Soil temperatures vary with different soils and in the shade of buildings or trees. Differences in soil temperature explain why some plants will grow better in one garden area than in another.

A plant reference book or the list of plants at the back of this book will help you to select plants that are hardy for your area. The planting zones indicated in this list have been determined on the basis of past experience with plants, but they are not entirely foolproof. Some plants will live where they are supposed to die and die where they should live.

Microclimates exist within the limits of your own property, and must be considered when selecting your plants. For example, the corner of a building may have much higher winds than the sides of a building. Narrow spaces between houses and streets or driveways can act as wind tunnels. Wind patterns can be greatly altered by your plantings and fence locations and those of your neighbors. Your own prevailing wind may vary markedly from the prevailing southwest wind.

Plant growth is affected by various artificial conditions imposed by man. You cannot assume that soil in any city or suburb is in its natural condition. Housing developments nearly always change drainage patterns. Moving the soil changes its natural stability. Loosening the soil might permit water and air to circulate too freely; compaction has the opposite effect.

Man also changes conditions aboveground. Structures cast shadows, and their surfaces reflect heat and light to alter natural conditions. Your choice of plants should be influenced by local variations of heat and light in different parts of your garden.

If you ignore a plant's natural preference for certain living conditions, you will have to work harder to keep it healthy. Plants can live with minimum care under favorable conditions, but you will have to watch and care for them constantly if conditions are unfavorable. And even with the best of care, they may not look as you want them to and may even die.

Choose plants that are relatively free from insect and disease problems. You will find that plants grown out of their natural habitat will be more subject to these problems than plants growing in an environment that they like.

Select each plant according to its mature size, growth rate, and life-span. Choosing a plant on the basis of its mature size, not its size at the time you purchase it, assures that you will have sufficient ground space for the plant, and that its ultimate height will be compatible with buildings and surrounding areas. Other important qualities that need to be analyzed include the plant's natural form, structure and silhouette, texture and color of bark, foliage, flowers, and fruit.

Each plant has certain characteristics that hold true under a variety of conditions. The height and spread, texture, growth habits, and shape are usually fairly constant. But too much or not enough sunlight, competition from other plants, or improper soil conditions will affect these design characteristics, as well as the plant's growth rate and size and even its ability to survive.

Many people select plants without considering the mature size, shape, texture, and growth habits of these plants. As a result, plantings often overpower the landscape. If you have ever had to cut out a man-made wilderness around a house, you know how important it is to choose plants on the basis of what they will look like when they are full-grown rather than on their appearance as small plants.

Microclimates are modifications of the general climate. They are a result of the structures and plantings on your property and those on your neighbor's property. Corners of buildings often have winds that are much higher than the winds along the sides of the buildings. Your house, garage, fences, and plantings, as well as those of your neighbors, direct and change wind patterns, create shade conditions, and increase light and heat by reflection. Corners of buildings and the narrow spaces between buildings and along drives can be wind tunnels.

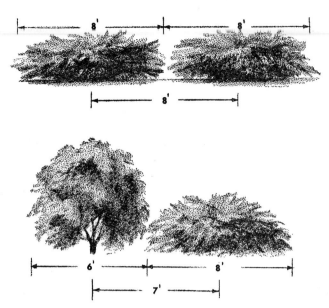

To space plants properly, be sure that the distance from the center of one plant to the center of the next plant is equal to one-half the mature spread of each plant. The spread of a deciduous plant should be two-thirds the height or equal to the height of the plant.

Overplanting is a big mistake. It is difficult to visualize an 18- to 20-inch evergreen spreading 5 to 6 feet across at maturity. Learn the mature spread of plants, and then be sure to space each plant at least one-half the total spread of the two plants. For example, if a plant spreads 4 feet at maturity, set it at least 4 feet away from another plant of the same species. The spread of a deciduous shrub should be approximately two-thirds the height of the shrub or equal to the height of the shrub unless the shrub is columnar in growth habit.

You should also consider the plant's life-span. Many plants grow fast but have short lives. If you choose a fast-growing tree because you are desperate for shade, you may solve the shade problem quickly but be faced with replacement in 15 years. Such rapid-growing trees as Siberian elm (often mistakenly referred to as Chinese elm), poplar, and willow are brittle. High winds, ice storms, and other natural events will damage them severely. Other fast-growing trees, such as hackberry, tulip tree, and sycamore, do not damage as easily, but long-lived plants offer more lasting benefits.

Form

Form is the first design quality of plants that you should consider. If you choose plants that will be natural-looking and graceful when they are full-grown, you won't have much trimming to do. Don't depend on pruning to get the shape you want. It is far more practical to choose a plant that will mature into the desired shape. Each shape has its own place in a landscape design. For example, deciduous shrubs are usually upright, round, or spreading. Deciduous trees are round, weeping, oval, vaselike, erect or columnar, and pyramidal. Evergreens are columnar, narrow pyramidal, broad pyramidal, round, spreading, or creeping.

These basic forms range through all degrees of symmetry and irregularity. The more extreme the form, the more the plant attracts our attention. The intervening forms cannot hold our attention on the basis of shape alone. For this reason, color and texture are important qualities that should be considered along with the form of a plant.

The form is more than the outline of a plant. It also includes the three-dimensional mass of the plant. Form is determined by the line, direction, and arrangement of branches and twigs. The resulting mass influences the scale of the plant and the space in which it is located. For example, weeping and pendulous forms lead the eye back to the ground; ascending and vertical forms lead the eye upward, giving a sense of height and narrowness to the space.

Since the ascending form (evergreens, for example) gives an accent to the design, it should be used sparingly. Horizontal and spreading forms emphasize the lateral extent and breadth of the space. They are "comfortable" forms because their direction corresponds with the normal direction of eye movement. Most plants have rounded forms. These allow for easy eye movement, and provide a pleasant undulation that lends itself to group and mass compositions. The basic plant forms are repeated in herbaceous (non-woody) plants, shrubs, and trees, allowing you to develop harmonious plant compositions by repeating forms at different levels.

Conical-, pyramidal-, and columnar-shaped plants should always have foliage to the ground to look well in their surroundings. To reduce the striking accent of pyramidal plants, combine them with neutral (round or spreading) forms.

There is a definite relationship between the plant form and the topography in nature's landscape compositions. In a mountainous area, for example, the predominant plants are the conical or pyramidal evergreens. Plants are definitely horizontal in the Great Plains. On the rolling prairies, the dominant plants are rounded. Use this relationship in planning your own landscape design. Rounded plant forms should be used most often in your garden.

Using all plants of any one shape will be monotonous, of course. Different shapes provide variety and interest by accenting the major type with other forms.

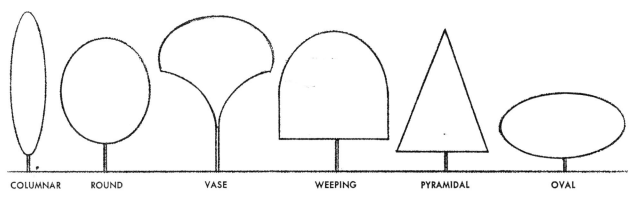

COLUMNAR   ROUND   VASE   WEEPING   PYRAMIDAL   OVAL

The form of a plant is one of its most important design qualities. The basic forms shown above can be found in the three major categories of plants — herbaceous plants, shrubs, and deciduous trees. For this reason, plants from each category can be easily combined into one composition. Study the structure and silhouette of various plants. Do not try to include one plant of each shape. Limit your selection to several plant types that will serve as the dominant forms in the design.

The foliage of conical and pyramidal evergreens should extend to the ground (left) for an attractive appearance. A flowering tree on either side of an evergreen (right) will modify the harshness of the pyramidal form.

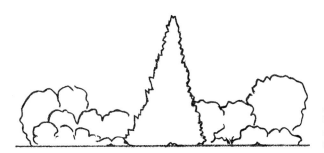

Avoid strong conical or pyramidal forms that dominate the total planting. The pyramidal evergeen shown at left (perhaps a Colorado blue spruce) overwhelms the balance of the shrub border because of its size, unique color, and central placement.

MOUNTAINOUS   PLAINS   ROLLING PRAIRIE

There is a direct relation between plant forms and topography. The basic form of the topography is repeated in the native plant materials. For example, if you live in the Midwest, where rounded forms are predominant (right), be sure that these forms are also predominant in your landscape plantings.

This shrub border is the same as that illustrated on page 79 except that a smaller pyramidal evergreen is used as an accent. This evergreen is in scale with the overall planting, and its placement is off-center — located approximately one-third of the distance from the left end of the shrub border.

With flat or rounded ground forms, for example, you can often create an interesting picture by adding conical or pyramidal evergreens with the dominant round types of plants. But the blend must be so skillful that the conical plants do not dominate the total picture. Scattering them throughout a shrub border will only result in a distracting composition.

Texture

Texture is the second design quality in planting composition. It is a plant feature that is often overlooked or discounted as not being important, but it offers you another chance to add variety and interest to a planting picture. Texture can be defined as the relations between the foliage and twig size and the remainder of the plant. But you must qualify this definition in terms of the distance from which the plant is to be seen. Close up, texture comes from the size, surface, and spacing of leaves and twigs at different seasons. At a distance, texture is the entire mass effect of plants and the quality of light and shadow.

Basically, texture is a plant's qualities of coarseness or fineness, roughness or smoothness, heaviness or lightness, thinness or denseness. Plants that are large when seen close up become smaller with distance, and may blend together or disappear at long range.

The texture of leaves depends upon the quality of the leaf surface, as well as the spacing and size of the leaves. For example, large leaves that are glossy on one side and white on the other have a finer texture than other large leaves because of the effect of light and shadow. Leaves set on long, slender petioles (the stem connecting the leaf surface to the branch) or with a long tapering shape have more motion in breezes. This motion results in a greater play of light and shadow, giving the effect of a finer texture. Small leaves and short petioles have the appearance of strength and coarseness because there is less motion and fewer light and shadow patterns. Density of foliage added to coarseness gives an effect of strength; sparse foliage has a weaker appearance.

The patterns created by light and shade are an important part of texture. These patterns vary from season to season and even from hour to hour. The shadows cast by fine-textured plants are weak because of the spacing and size of the mass and because of light filtering through the foliage. The shadows cast by coarse-textured plants are strong because the foliage is large or dense and light is reflected from the surface. This play of light and shadows emphasizes the fineness or coarseness of the plant's texture.

Texture also varies with the age of the plant. Young plants often have a coarser texture than older plants because they have larger leaves and more lush growth. Since very old plants have smaller foliage, their normal texture is modified to a somewhat finer texture.

When viewed at a distance, the texture of a plant is the light and shadow effect of the entire mass. When viewed at close range, texture is determined by the size, surface, and closeness of leaves and twigs during the various seasons.

Good planting design for a right-angled planting arrangement usually strengthens the extreme ends of the arms with coarser texture and a more solid mass of plants. Use material of medium texture and density for the next group of shrubs in the sequence, and more delicate plants with finer textures in the center or at the intersection of the two arms. By subordinating this natural focal point, you can introduce a high-interest feature such as a specimen plant, flowers, or sculpture.

TEXTURE IS . . .

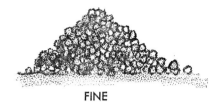

FINE

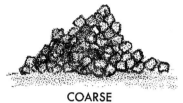

COARSE

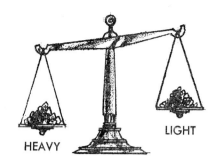

HEAVY   LIGHT

THIN

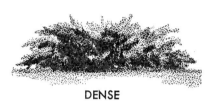

DENSE

LIGHT AND SHADE

TEXTURE RESULTS FROM . . .

LENGTH OF PETIOLE

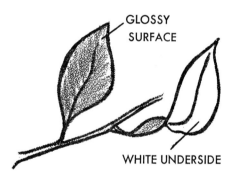

GLOSSY SURFACE

WHITE UNDERSIDE

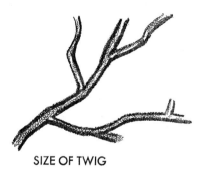

SIZE OF TWIG

SIZE OF LEAF

ENTIRE OR CUT LEAF

SPACING BETWEEN LEAVES

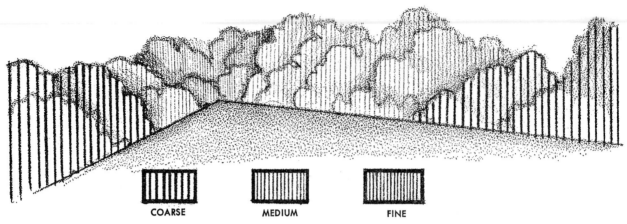

COARSE   MEDIUM   FINE

For an attractive border mass that forms a corner planting, start with the coarsest texture for the end plantings; then grade into medium texture for the next group of shrubs, and use a fine texture at the center of the mass.

Do not use coarse textures in a small area. They decrease the apparent size of the area and appear harsh.

Too much texture uniformity results in monotony. Use variations to get contrast and a play of light and shadow, but avoid extremes. Never put the coarsest plant next to the finest one. Avoid putting coarse textures in small areas — they will apear harsh and cut down on apparent space.

Change textures in a graduated pattern. Move by steps from the plants with the coarsest texture in the composition to those with the finest texture. The leaf size of each plant should be about one-half the leaf size of the plant that precedes it. As you move to plants of finer texture, use proportionately larger numbers. For example, you might move from one extremely coarse plant to 3 plants with one-half the leaf size of the first plant; then to 7 plants with the next finest texture; and finally, to 11 plants with the finest texture. Unless your area is extremely large, keep texture changes simple and gradual, and avoid too great a contrast. Your plantings should allow the viewer's eye to move smoothly from the coarsest to the finest textures.

Another plant characteristic is *habit*. This is similar to texture and may be considered part of it. Habit of growth refers to the looseness, density, or irregularity of the plant's branches. Loose, irregular plants are difficult to combine with plants that have compact surfaces. These two types of plants can be combined, however, to create a strong contrast.

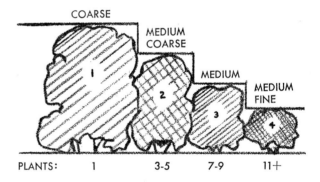

PLANTS: 1   3-5   7-9   11+

You can develop interesting compositions by grading from the coarsest texture to the finest. For a group or linear planting, a stairstep sequence (above) is often effective. This sequence requires decreasing the height and increasing the number of plants used as you move down from the coarsest texture. A possible arrangement of these plants in the ground is shown below.

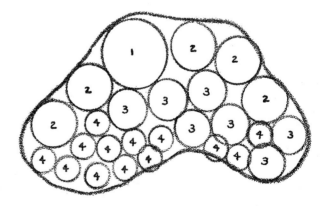

Color

Color is the third design quality of plants. It is the element that has the greatest appeal and evokes the greatest response. This does not mean, however, that a design should be developed exclusively on the basis of color.

The light of the atmosphere is composed of rays of varying lengths. When directed through a prism, these rays separate, and each ray produces a color — red, orange, yellow, green, blue, etc. In landscape design, we are primarily concerned with color that results from light, although the color of pigments (paints and stains, for example) may also be important.

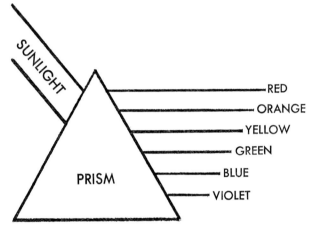

Color results from light. Black is the complete absence of light, and white is a combination of all the light wave lengths. When white light (sunlight) is passed through a prism, the waves of various lengths are sorted, resulting in a rainbow effect. In the drawing above, the colors are shown in the order of their wave lengths.

Each color has three dimensions — hue, value, and intensity. *Hue* is the name of the color, and it also indicates the warmth or coolness of the color. *Value* or brightness refers to the lightness or darkness of a color. In other words, value is the amount of light reflected — a large amount reflected will be a light value, and a small amount reflected will be a dark value. Since yellow has a higher light value than blue or green, it appears as a lighter (brighter) value than the other two colors. *Intensity* is the third dimension of color. It indicates the actual color content — its purity, strength, and saturation as determined by the quantity of the dominant hue. For example, pink or maroon are lower intensities of pure red. These three dimensions are so intricately related that varying one of them has an impact on the other two.

The pure colors of this light spectrum can be arranged in a color wheel by placing each color next to its most similar neighbor. Starting at the top of the wheel and proceeding clockwise, the colors are red, orange, yellow, green, blue, and violet. The mixing of any of these hues produces intermediate colors such as yellow-green, blue-green, red-green, gray-green, and black-green.

This color-wheel arrangement allows us to group colors into *warm* and *cool* colors. The warm colors are yellow, orange, and red; the cool colors are green, blue, and violet. The warm colors are conspicuous, cheerful, and stimulating. They tend to come toward us — advance — while cool colors recede and suggest distance. Cool colors are usually inconspicuous and restful.

Colors on the wheel are grouped according to their relationship to one another. Those directly opposite each other are called *complementary* colors; those adjacent to each other are called *analogous*. Complementary colors are always a combination of a warm color and a cool color. They offer a strong contrast by bringing out the differences between the two hues. Since analogous colors are closely related, there is a greater mixing into intermediate hues, and the resulting combinations are pleasing and balanced.

Color is the result of absorption and reflection. For example, a green leaf absorbs all light rays except green, which is reflected back and perceived by the eye. Yellowish-green leaf is an intermediate color resulting from the "mixing" of light rays reflected by the surface. In this case, one hue is more dominant than the other. All the colors mixed together equally result in white light.

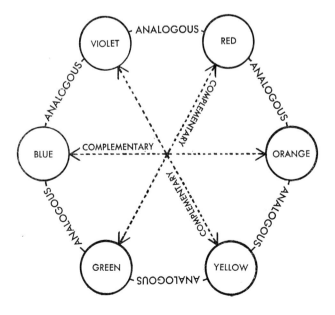

The color we see in the landscape is affected by the reflective values of the surface, by the quality of light, by the color reflections of adjacent objects, and by shadows. Color appears much brighter when the surface is glossy than when it is dull. Small surfaces reflect light differently from large ones. Since a fence is large and flat, its color appears uniform, but color in plants is not uniform because the plant surface is not flat. Some leaf surfaces are in shadow and others in full light, with corresponding modifications of the perceived color and the actual leaf color. The shade color has a darker value and lower intensity because of the lower quality of light. The percentage of color reflection from its surface is lower than that of leaf areas in full sun. In fact, under intense light a color may seem lighter than it actually is.

The color we see is also modified in the context of surrounding colors of structures or other plants. This visual phenomenon is called *simultaneous contrast*. Essentially, it is the visual mixing of two hues seen simultaneously that results in a color change. This change can be good or bad, depending upon whether the combinations are complementary or analogous hues, and the value and intensity of the colors.

A harmonious color design is most easily obtained by providing a dominance of one color. Colors of all parts of the composition must be considered, including plant materials and their changes, as well as structures and pavements. The effects of simultaneous contrast suggest that fences, pavements, and buildings should have a neutral color of low value and intensity that will make them appear smaller and farther away. Then the plants and resulting space become dominant in the composition. You must decide which elements will be dominant and which will be subordinate in each landscape that you develop. If each element has equal importance, the result is visual chaos. Conversely, if every element is subordinate, the result is monotony. It is the planned contrast between the two extremes that gives a "spark" to the design.

The main purpose of plants in a garden is to provide a leafy, green setting that gives the garden an atmosphere of peace and restfulness. This background is more important than a shrub's flowers. Flowers are interesting for only a short time, but the tree and shrub foliage dominate the garden scene for the entire growing season. Green foliage in the garden should outnumber "showy" plants (those that are unusual in form or color) 9 to 1. When you use only a few plants, select them for foliage, not for flowers.

You must also consider *foliage color*. The greatest ornamental value of some deciduous trees and shrubs is the color of their leaves in the fall; others are interesting because of their many shades of green. Some ornamental trees and shrubs also have purple or yellow leaf colors in summer to contrast with the usual green. Foliage color must harmonize with the colors of existing or proposed buildings. The wrong choice can result in color clashes.

Color can either tie together or contrast various kinds of woody plants. For example, if you want to use a variety of forms and sizes of plants, it may be desirable to tie the planting together by selecting plants with similar foliage color. Variations of green can add contrast and interest to a planting. Use golden, purple, and variegated foliages cautiously as a strong accent. Remember — the ratio of brightly colored foliage plants to green foliage is 1 to 9.

Plants have color qualities in addition to foliage color that should be considered. Flowers blooming at the same time should harmonize with one another, as well as with the color of nearby buildings. Clashing colors of flowers disrupt the beauty of the scene. Some plants, like redtwig dogwood or whitebark birch, have color in their bark and twigs. You can often get a harmonious blend of plant and background colors. An example would be an evergreen background for whitebark birch or redtwig dogwood. The foliage contrasts strikingly in the summer, and the colored bark against the deep green evergreen foliage is attractive in the winter.

In developing your landscaping design, be sure that the plants you choose are compatible with the soil, temperatures, light, and wind exposures on your property. You must also consider the form, texture, and color of the plants, and understand how to use the principles of design to achieve a unified landscape.

Principles of Design

You can manipulate form, texture, and color to create a visually pleasing and unified planting composition. To achieve unity in your composition, you must apply the design principles of simplicity, variety, balance, emphasis, sequence, and scale.

$$\text{Unity} = \begin{matrix} \text{simplicity} \\ \text{variety} \\ \text{balance} \\ \text{emphasis} \\ \text{sequence} \\ \text{scale} \end{matrix} \xrightarrow{\text{applied to}} \begin{matrix} \text{form} \\ \text{texture} \\ \text{color} \end{matrix}$$

Unity is the quality of oneness. The purpose of unity is to attract and hold attention, to help the viewer "grasp" the design, and to organize all parts into orderly groups. When a great many objects

A unified composition has a coherent organization that eliminates the need to deal with each plant as a separate detail. *Unity* is gained through the application of the principles of design. Each plant is related to the others through repetition of form, yet with variety in scale (size) and habit growth. *Balance* is achieved by the arrangement of materials (three small, treelike shrubs on the right balance two more open shrubs and the tree on the left). The tree, somewhat separated from the two shrubs, provides *emphasis* by location, scale, form, and texture. From the right side, *sequence* is achieved by linear gradation in the sizes of plants, leading the eye to the point of emphasis (tree). From the left side, there is a more abrupt sequence, including alternation of height and modified linear movement.

In this composition, the pyramidal evergreen form has been added to the predominant rounded form. *Variety* may also be achieved by varying form and color while keeping texture constant, by varying color and texture while keeping form constant, or by varying texture while keeping both form and color constant.

(plants, for example) are presented to our attention, we try to *relate them in patterns* so that we can perceive as many as possible at one time with minimum effort. If we can discover a pattern, we experience pleasure and satisfaction.

A design, no matter how complex, must convey an impression of coherent organization. Each part must relate to the others so closely that we do not need to deal with each part as a separate detail. Unity, then, is pulling together the separate elements that make up a composition into an arrangement that *conveys to the viewer the quality of oneness.*

Simplicity implies the elimination of every detail that does not contribute significantly to the composition. It also implies a degree of repetition rather than constant change, with enough variety to stimulate interest. Repetition suggests the use of only one or few design qualities repeated over and over. Repetition can be irritating if overdone. Simplicity, then, acts as a control over too much variety, but it must not dominate in the form of repetition to the point of boredom.

Variety implies diversity and contrast in the use of the design qualities of form, texture, and color. Variety prevents monotony through avoiding uniformity. By adding contrast (opposite or nearly opposite qualities), you can intensify the visual interest and heighten your satisfaction with the scene or composition. In a good design, variety is inevitable. The only question is "How much is necessary?" The answer depends upon you and the purpose of your design. The degree of variety can range from subtle differences to sharp opposition or conflict. Variety suggests several different lines well used, several different forms well arranged, several different textures well combined, and several different colors well blended.

Balance implies equilibrium on each side of a vertical axis. Formal balance is symmetrical — a mirror image of the other half of the object. Informal or asymmetrical balance has the weight or attractions on each side equated but not identical. Formal balance gives a sense of stability, stateliness, and dignity. Informal balance arouses curiosity, suggests movement, and has a dynamic quality.

Any element of design can be balanced by any other element, provided that both elements are applied in a similarly interesting manner. For example, an area of dark or subdued color can be balanced with a spot of bright color, or a bulky, undifferentiated form with a smaller, more interesting one.

Balance acts as a *control* over variety by keeping the various colors, shapes, sizes, and textures in proportion with one another.

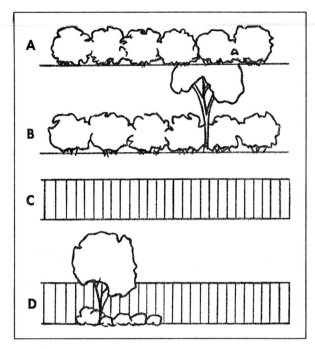

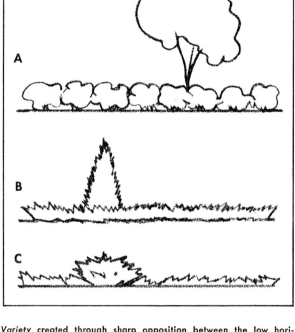

A shrub border composed of the same size, form, or type of plant (A) represents *simplicity* but the result is monotonous. A plant of contrasting size, form, or texture adds *variety* to the composition (B). The monotony of a fence (C) can be relieved by using a small tree to interrupt the horizontal line and small shrubs to contrast with the flat plane of the fence surface (D).

Variety created through sharp opposition between the low horizontal mass and the vertical are illustrated in (A) and (B); (C) shows a more subtle kind of variety through using a larger size of the same plant form.

Formal balance is always built around a central axis or feature and the mass and arrangement on one side are identical with those on the other.

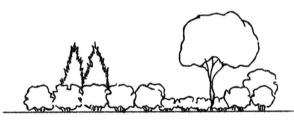

The composition above has *simplicity* through *repetition*, yet with *variety*. The lower rounded plants are used in sufficient numbers to provide a pleasing balance and proportion to the two small evergreens and the small tree.

Informal or asymmetrical balance is achieved when the mass and arrangement on each side are visually balanced. The weight of the mass on the left in the drawing above is balanced by the attraction of the tree and large shrub on the right.

Too much *variety* results when there are too many vertical elements or too many different forms. The composition above is distracting, even though the low-growing shrub is repeated throughout, because there is no focal point that allows the viewer to differentiate the more important elements from the less important ones.

Emphasis is the process of differentiating the more important elements from the less important ones. It implies dominance of certain elements and the subordination of others. The viewer is pleased when he can easily determine what is important in a design. Through the use of emphasis, we can capture the viewer's attention by stressing one element over others. Emphasis can be gained by limiting the number of dominant points in the design; by stressing differences in the size of the elements; by grouping several elements together to give them significance; by introducing the unusual or unexpected; and by the decisive use of bold shapes, intense color, or dramatic texture contrasts.

Sequence is a sequential change in form, color, texture, or size. Not all of these elements should change at once, of course, because then there would not seem to be any sequence at all. Sequence may also be defined as an arrangement of compositional units (plants, architectural materials, etc.) designed to control the viewer's attention and direct it from one unit to another in a linear, alternate, or random pattern.

In its simplest form, sequence is the recurrence of units in linear movement. Sequence can also be obtained by an orderly and logical progression from one element to another, or by a gradation like the stair-step examples of texture or color. Through this gradation, you can bridge extremes in contrast by a series of rhythmic steps.

Sequence can also be achieved by alternation — for example, by alternating large areas of one shape with small areas of another. A sequence of repetition and emphasis establishes a simple rhythm that can be carried to whatever degree of complexity is desired.

Scale is a measurement that indicates the absolute or relative size of objects. *Absolute scale* refers to the size of an object with relation to a designated standard such as a building, a linear foot, or the dimensions of the human body. *Relative scale* is the relative size of objects within a given composition. The object may be compared with an adjacent building or the space or area involved.

Scale is a device to evoke emotion. Monumental scale may overwhelm the viewer, and intimate scale (underscaled or smaller than expected) may increase the viewer's sense of self-importance. Normal scale gives a sense of security — it is what we expect.

Scale helps people to become oriented, to understand the immediate environment, and to comprehend distance because people measure what they see in relation to the dimensions of their own bodies. Scale is also determined by the original area within which the designer starts to work. It is judged by the relative size of one part or object to another and of each part or object to the total area.

Proportion is a part of scale. It is a ratio that expresses the comparative value or size of two quantities (space, length, area, or individual units). Good or bad proportion relates to objects of specific dimensions. Proportion is a device to relate and tie together two identical elements on a ratio basis. These elements may include area, mass, space, height, length, form, color, or texture. Since proportion and scale are both elements of measure, one term may be used for both. "Scale" will be used here to designate the fundamental principle of organization, but you should remember that the term also embraces proportion.

Although the use of the principles of design to obtain unity has been discussed in the context of fitting plants to your landscape, it should be understood that these principles also apply to the use of structural materials. Everything used in the landscape, whether plants or structural materials, has the basic design qualities of form, texture, and color. How you apply the principles of design when manipulating these qualities determines how successful your total landscape composition will be.

You will need a detailed plan showing the location of each planting. Before selecting specific plants, note on your plan the form (oval, horizontal, arching, etc.), height, spread, color, and texture of each planting. Your selection will also be determined by available space, exposure, and the need for structural enclosures.

Plants that repeat the lines and forms of the house and the texture of the house's construction materials give unity and harmony to a landscape design. Another way to achieve harmony is to select materials of contrasting or complementary colors. For example, dark-green Japanese yews offer a striking contrast against a white house. Or the gray-green leaves of Russian olive or white fir complement a gray house with white trim.

Keep landscape arrangements simple and unified. To achieve unity, use one material several times to tie the design together. A landscape has harmony when colors of the various plantings blend with one another and with their surroundings.

The front door is the focal point of the public area around which all landscape elements are balanced. For example, a large tree on one side of the property will balance several small trees on the other side; or a medium-sized tree on one side will balance a group of shrubs on the other side.

Monumental scale (left) is overwhelming, and may result in a sense of insignificance. *Intimate scale* (right), in which objects are underscaled or smaller than expected, gives the viewer a sense of complete control over the environment.

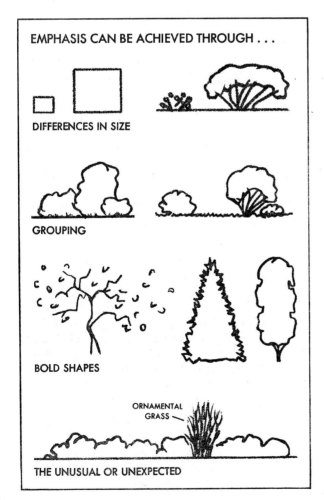

EMPHASIS CAN BE ACHIEVED THROUGH . . .

DIFFERENCES IN SIZE

GROUPING

BOLD SHAPES

ORNAMENTAL GRASS

THE UNUSUAL OR UNEXPECTED

A short section of fence gains emphasis because of its limited use in combination with other materials. When a fence is extended around three sides of an area, however, it loses emphasis.

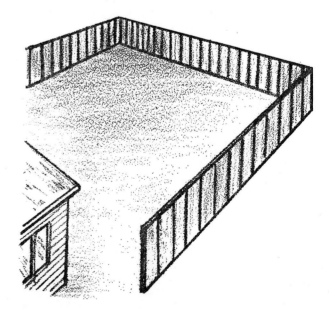

Sequence can be achieved most simply through changes in size (indicated by arrow). It can also be gained through the use of color, texture, and form.

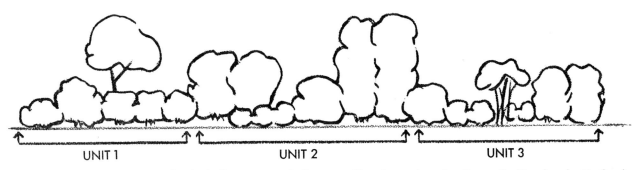

UNIT 1   UNIT 2   UNIT 3

Sequence can be a reoccurrence of units in linear movement. The composition shown above has three units. The viewer's attention is initially drawn to unit 1 because of the tree form. The viewer "reads" this unit as a self-contained element that is satisfying because of its emphasis, balance, simplicity, and variety. The viewer's attention then moves to unit 2, and finally, to unit 3.

Sequence is obtained in the above drawing by alternating a large mass of shrubs with a small mass of trees.

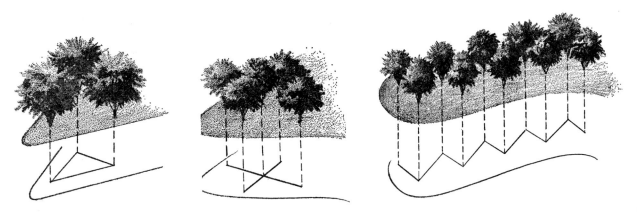

Plants may be set in a triangular staggered line (left), in a checkerboard pattern (middle), or in a staggered flowing line (right).

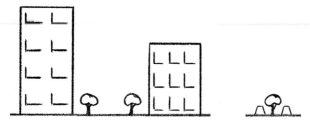

Relative scale results from the comparison between objects, structures, or space in a composition. The small tree is the same size in both of the above drawings. When viewed next to the buildings, the tree appears smaller than when it is bounded by two low hedges.

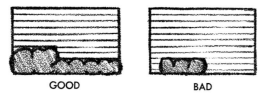

GOOD BAD

Proportion is an expression of the comparative value or size of two quantities, such as mass, area, height, etc. The two drawings above represent proportional relations between masses (plantings against a building or wall). The two drawings below illustrate the importance of proper proportional relations between heights of elements (house and tree).

GOOD BAD

You might consider repeating attractive materials at several places. You can tie your design together by using roof colors, exterior finishes, dominant building lines, and the same plants (or plants with similar qualities) in several locations. But remember — too much repetition results in monotony.

Try to make the best use of the cube of space that surrounds your home. Tall plants give a sense of enclosure and add to the overall beauty of a landscape by serving as a special planting background. They can also be used to frame a house or a view. Low plants give line and pattern to the design, and, in a less obvious way, enclose and define space. Focus attention on plants with interesting branching habits by using them as specimens near walls, on a board fence, or as a foreground element in a shrub border.

Plants used in groups should be planted in cultivated beds to eliminate unnecessary maintenance, such as mowing grass between shrubs, etc. Plants placed in beds give a unified massing effect. The line formed between the lawn and the bed becomes a dominant element in the design that can be reinforced by the arrangement of the plants in the beds. Select the planting arrangement that best emphasizes the lines of your basic design.

Fitting plants to your design is a *backward process.* The steps in this process are as follows: (1) determine the shapes and sizes of the plants needed to carry out your design; (2) decide what textures and colors you want; (3) list the environmental conditions that the plant must be able to tolerate; and (4) select the plants that meet these specifications. The exact procedure for this process is discussed in Chapter 8. After reading that discussion, you will understand why you should not try to mold the design to fit a specific plant.

You can get information about plants from reference materials in your local library or from your state land-grant university or college. Nursery catalogs or your nurseryman can also give you valuable information.

If you know exactly what plants you want, be firm in your demands and order only the plants you need. Do not allow substitutions to be made. If your nurseryman doesn't have what you want in stock, he will be able to order the plants for you. You can also order by mail, but be sure to order plants from a reliable nursery that grows its stock in a climate similar to yours. The plants may be hardy, but they will grow best if they are already acclimated.

7: Fitting Trees To Your Plan

In this chapter, we will discuss fitting trees to your plan. Chapter 8 deals with the selection of shrubs to fit your plan.

The proper selection and use of trees is important because trees are the most permanent of all plant materials. There are many points to be considered when selecting trees for your landscape. For our purposes here, these points can be grouped under cultural, functional, and aesthetic considerations.

First, the tree must be able to grow and thrive in your particular location. You must consider the tree's *hardiness* (tolerance to temperatures and climate) and its resistance to breakage from wind. Hardiness is determined by *planting zones* (geographical areas with common low temperatures that limit the types of woody plants that will survive). You cannot use trees of higher numerical zones than the zone in which you live. You can, however, use trees in lower numerical zones if growth conditions (rainfall, soil, summer heat, etc.) are comparable. (See page 205 for a detailed discussion of plant selection according to zones.)

A tree's resistance to wind and ice damage depends upon the tree's branching habits and the brittleness of the wood. Fast-growing trees usually have weaker branching structure and are subject to greater breakage under stress of wind and ice than the slower growing varieties. Trees that are particularly subject to breakage include silver maple, box elder, Siberian elm (mistakenly called Chinese elm), and willows.

Trees vary widely in their soil requirements. Some trees will tolerate the drouth conditions of sandy soils; others prefer moist to wet conditions; and still others thrive in good loam or even heavy clay soils. Be sure that the trees you select can tolerate your soil conditions.

The production of flowers and fruit is sometimes overlooked. Note the flowering dates and flower colors of trees you are considering. Be sure that the colors are compatible with other plants flowering at the same time, as well as with the colors of nearby structures and buildings. The fruiting habits of trees are an important consideration in deciding where to place trees and the amount of maintenance that will be necessary. Trees with soft fruits should not be placed close to walks, drives, or patios, where fallen fruit can be tracked into the house and possibly stain the surfacing material. Trees with hard fruits, such as nut trees, make good lawn trees, but you must be willing to rake the fruit regularly, especially before mowing.

You must also decide what functions you want your trees to perform. Shade is often the only function we consider when selecting a tree, but trees are a versatile landscape material. In addition to providing shade, properly placed trees can frame a view, mask awkward architectural features, and provide a backdrop for the home or other landscape units at the same time. Trees provide a permanent structure to the design, establish the scale of the landscape, give visual proportion and sculptural and architectural form to open space, and define the overhead limits or "ceiling" of the space.

The largest trees in your design will establish the basic framework of the landscape. The smaller trees should be used as accessories. You need to decide whether you want the trees to be individual elements that develop as perfectly shaped specimens, or arranged so that they will grow together as a mass. The spacing of trees for specimens must allow for the mature spread of each tree used. The group effect of trees is achieved by a much closer spacing. The fact that individual specimens stand alone gives them power and dominance. They serve as focal points. The massing of trees is particularly useful when the

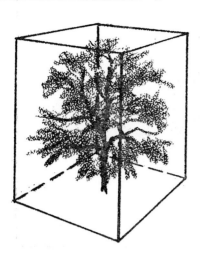
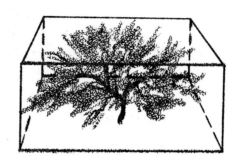
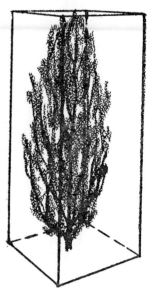

Trees occupy a certain volume of space, and your choice of trees will be limited by the space you have available.

trees are intended to divide space and to provide a background for other landscape elements.

Do not use more than two or three different species of trees to compose each planting group in your design. The trees should be combined according to the six principles of design — simplicity, variety, balance, emphasis, sequence, and scale. Be cautious about combining extremes in form within the same group. When variations in form are used, group similar forms (pyramidal, rounded, etc.) together so that there is a clear distinction between the forms. The trees to be planted together should have certain differences that are easily recognized. Try to have one tree of the group dominant and the others subordinate. For example, one large tree could be combined with several smaller spreading types, or a tree with a very dense texture could be combined with several trees with loose, finer textures. Color can also be varied. Two species of trees that possess equal qualities are seldom visually satisfying.

Tree groups must be related to the entire scene — shrub groupings as well as structures. In addition, study your combination for its effect from the principal place from which it will be seen. Make certain that it is also acceptable from secondary viewing points, particularly when one tree is dominant and the others subordinate.

The individual tree in your design should have sufficient visual strength and character to justify isolating it from other materials. For this reason, the tree's form, color, and texture must be considered carefully. The tree should not, however, be treated as an "art object." It should have harmonious relations with the line, mass, color, and texture of other nearby plantings, or with the house architecture if it is to be viewed against the building.

Locate trees in your planting plan first. Large trees are valuable for their shade. They also frame a big house when placed to the front, and provide a background for both one- and two-story houses when located at the rear of the property.

Plan tree placement with care. Show a tree on the plan as a circle that represents the mature spread of the tree. To help you visualize the differences in trees sizes, draw the circles for large shade trees proportionately greater than those for small trees. Use tracing paper over the basic plan, and plot possible locations with respect to the house and its room arrangements so that you can get shade where you want it. You will want shade on the patio or terrace or the children's playground area, but don't overlook the possibility of using large trees to frame a good view off the rear of your property. A properly placed tree can shade the bedroom areas, provide a frame toward one side of your off-property view, and still serve as a background for the house.

A second large tree might be used to frame the other side of the view, and to shade the outdoor living area, the children's play area, and the daytime living area of the house. The crown of the tree may also serve as a screen for an unwanted off-property view. You will need to keep all of these functions in mind to get the most out of any tree you use.

You must also consider underground utility locations when you place a tree. It is not advisable, for example, to put trees over a septic tank, its drain

TREES CAN BE USED TO . . .

Frame a view on or off your property

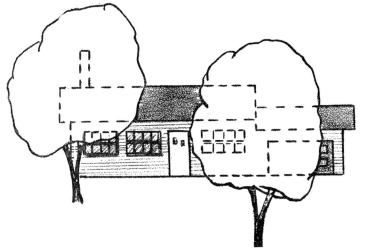

Mask awkward architectural features

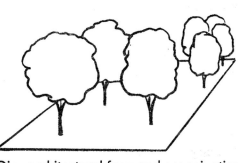

Give architectural form and organization to large spaces

Frame and provide a background for a house

Add variety to a shrub border silhouette

Specimen trees are unique in form, color, or texture. They are placed as individual units separated from surrounding trees, and may be used as focal points or to direct attention to or away from an area.

field, or other underground tiles. Some trees with shallow root systems will interfere with underground utilities. Although tree roots do not "seek" water, they will thrive on any source of underground water. The roots may clog drain tiles, sewers, and other underground tile lines.

Keep trees away from power and telephone lines running to the house and along the sides or rear of your property. Often large trees growing too close to utilities will engulf the wires. When the utility company trims out the trees to clear its lines, you will find ugly holes in the crowns that disfigure your landscape design.

When you use large trees for plantings, consider the scale relationships between buildings and plant materials. A large tree will frame a large house, but it may overpower a small one. The house is the most important part of the landscape development in the public area. Don't put trees where they will compete with your house or blot it out.

Large trees affect the entire planting scheme. For instance, a dense crown provides so much shade that any plants you put near the tree must be able to live under limited light conditions. It is difficult to grow plants or grass under a densely crowned tree. Often the only green mat you can establish is some kind of ground cover.

Trees also compete for soil nutrients and water. This competition can seriously affect the growth of grass, shrubs, flowers, and other nearby plantings.

You will need to consider the rooting habits of trees, as well as the shape and spread of their crowns. The surface roots of a tree affect what can grow beneath the tree. A tree whose roots are primarily near the surface should not be placed where it will overlap a planting area (see the list of trees at the end of this book) because the tree roots will compete with other plantings. A rule of thumb is that the spread of the root system is roughly equal to the spread of the crown.

Since trees establish scale, they should be in proper proportion to the house and its surrounding space. On smaller properties and one-story homes, use small to medium trees to avoid dwarfing the house and overpowering the rest of the design. A very large tree will make a yard seem smaller than it actually is; small trees with a big, two-story house will make it seem even bigger. Use large trees with large homes.

The number of trees you can use depends upon the size of the trees. The larger the trees, the fewer you can put on your property. Often only one large tree can be placed in the rear yard of a small property. When you select a tree, consider soil conditions, tree hardiness, maintenance needs, exposure, and rate of growth. Be sure that the tree will be suitable to your site conditions.

Trees can be planted close together to form a screen (above) or a windbreak if foliage goes all the way to the ground.

When their foliage is high, trees can also be planted close together to create a tracery that divides space and provides a partial screen.

The spreading branches of a single tree create a canopy that forms a part of the ceiling of your outside room.

The shape and branching habits of a tree are important. Upright or columnar trees have vertical ascending branches, downward deflected branches, or horizontal branches. Other trees have oval forms, round forms with horizontal or ascending branches, or irregular branching.

Although trees are larger than shrubs and are often used individually, they can be related to the shrub groups through similarity of form. The same forms that are found in trees can also be found in shrubs and herbaceous plants. For this reason, all three can be combined harmoniously. Do not judge form on the basis of young trees. Many trees change in form as they mature, and, in some cases, once again in old age. Make your selection on the basis of the tree's mature form.

If you plant young shade trees in your lawn, you will probably have to grow sun-loving plants in surrounding areas for the first several years. As the trees mature and their crowns grow more dense, you can shift to more shade-tolerant plants. If you do not want to make this shift, you should select trees that provide a light, filtered shade.

Trees lining a street provide a delicate canopy of foliage overhead, relieve the monotonous lines of houses, and give a sense of character to the street and community. Choose a street tree carefully. An ideal street tree is easy to maintain; does not cause damage to curbs, sidewalks, and sewers; does not drop fruit, foliage, or twigs; will not block street lights or interfere with overhead utilities; and does not have branches so close to the ground that people cannot walk under them.

The trees must be tolerant to smoke, soot, dust, and gases in the atmosphere, and must be free from insect pests and diseases. Because the requirements for street trees are so demanding, the number of recommended trees is quite limited. In some communities, certain types of trees are not permitted along streets. Find out whether there is a shade-tree ordinance or other legislation in your community that affects the plantings of trees along streets.

The following recommendations will prove helpful in selecting a street tree:

1. If parking strips are 4 feet to 8 feet wide, plant the smaller growing trees, such as redbud or European mountain ash.

2. If parking strips are over 8 feet wide, seed to lawn and plant the larger growing trees, such as maples and oaks.

3. If the sidewalk is next to the curb, plant trees on the inside of the sidewalk. Locate the tree a minimum of 5 feet from the edge of the sidewalk.

4. Do not plant trees closer together than one-half of their total spread.

5. Avoid plantings that will interfere with motorists' vision at intersections and with the effectiveness of street lights. A tree should be planted a minimum of 25 feet from the corner of a block.

6. If there are overhead utility lines, *be sure* to select a tree whose ultimate height will be less than the height of the lowest utility line.

7. Restrict the planting of wide-spreading trees to broad streets and boulevards. For most residential streets, use trees whose crowns are somewhat compact.

Small trees are among the most valuable garden plants, and should be used even more than they are now. In addition to giving shade, small trees interrupt the monotonous straight lines of a building or the top of a fence. Because of their height and form, they can screen objectionable views, provide more privacy by adding height to a fence, and give interest and variety to shrub plantings. Often their attractive flowers, foliage, fall coloring, or bark add seasonal beauty.

The "showiness" of small flowering trees makes these trees popular in landscape plantings. The length of this floral display varies from one to two weeks, depending upon the weather at the time of flowering. Since the flowering period is brief, your choice of small trees should not be based exclusively on the tree's flowers. Many small trees produce highly ornamental fruit that often persists for longer periods than the flowers. This fruit greatly enhances the landscape scene, and has the bonus feature of attracting birds.

Avoid combining trees with extremes in form into one group.

Properties with an acre or more of lawn area may require extensive tree plantings. Trees should not be scattered indiscriminately over the area, but should be planted in groups of three or more with only one tree form in a group. This separation of forms by groups makes distinction between forms much more obvious. One form should be dominant through its use in several groups.

Choose trees with a deep-descending root system that will not interfere with underground water, drain, and sewer lines, and that will not break curbs or sidewalls. The mature height of trees is also an important consideration. Be sure that the crowns of the mature trees will not engulf overhead power lines.

Trees may be grouped on the basis of identical form or similarity of form. One of the tree forms must be dominant and the other subordinate. In this drawing, the dense, solid, and rounded tree form in front is allowed to dominate. The other two trees, although rounded in form, are looser, more open, and irregular in the crown, giving them a finer texture.

The density of the crown is important. The shade may be so heavy that grass won't grow beneath the tree. As the tree matures and casts longer shadows, you must consider whether shrub and flower plantings close to the tree will tolerate the shade or partial shade, or whether it will be necessary to change the flower or shrub plantings.

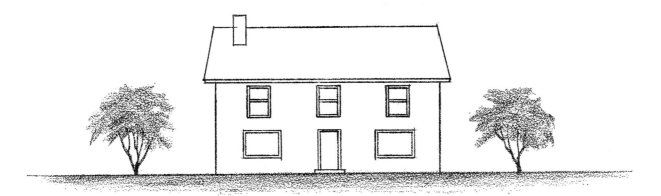

Trees to frame the house must be in scale with the building. A large house framed with small trees (above) appears even larger than it actually is, and a small house framed with large trees (below) appears smaller than it actually is.

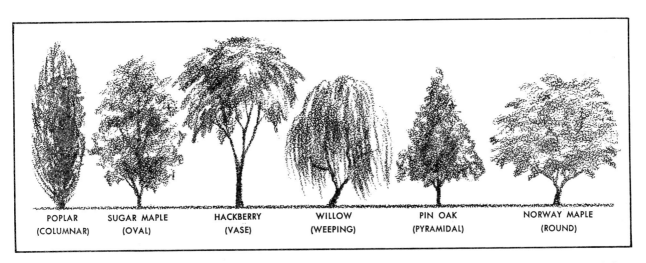

POPLAR	SUGAR MAPLE	HACKBERRY	WILLOW	PIN OAK	NORWAY MAPLE
(COLUMNAR)	(OVAL)	(VASE)	(WEEPING)	(PYRAMIDAL)	(ROUND)

Deciduous tree forms. These are the most common forms that can be used to establish the basic framework of your landscape design. When grouping trees, do not mix different forms within a single group.

Trees can be used to relieve the monotony of a long section of fence (left). Several trees placed in front of or back of the fence (right) provide additional privacy. The crowns of the trees combined with the fence give maximum vertical screening without overwhelming the landscape space.

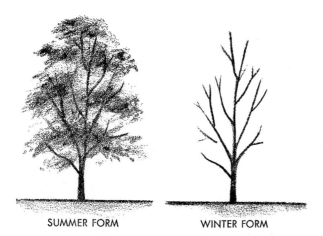

SUMMER FORM   WINTER FORM

Select trees with interesting structure and branching habits so that they are attractive in winter when they are without foliage, as well as in summer when they are in full foliage.

Some flowering trees produce their fruit in full color as early as June; others do not reach complete maturity until late summer and fall. Those varieties that hold their fruit for a long period add welcome color during the fall and winter.

Most properties need both small and large trees. Small trees may be used to frame a house if they are planted close to the point from which the house will be viewed. They are also valuable in providing structural accent and strength to the planting design. You can use small trees as individual specimens in lawns, or include them in your shrub groups or shrub border for additional height, visual strength, or accent to the balance of the composition.

A tree that serves as a specimen must be outstanding in one or more of its design qualities of form, color, and texture. It is often effective to combine three flowering trees of the same type. You can use this mass effect if you have adequate space.

When planting around your house, do not plant directly in front of a door or window, near cesspools or underground pipe lines, close to walks and drives, under overhead wires, or where the mature tree will overhang the house.

The forms of evergreens are related to the mountainous regions where these trees are native. Since their striking appearance tends to dominate the landscape in relatively flat areas such as the Midwest, evergreens should be used sparingly in these areas. Evergreen trees are well suited to provide an accent or an interesting silhouette in a shrub border. Most tall evergreens gradually narrow at the top. This pyramidal form creates a "saw-toothed" effect that does not fit harmoniously with the dominant round forms found in areas with little geographical relief. When tall, narrow evergreens are used, they should be grouped together in clumps of three or four to form a single wide mass.

Remember the following points when choosing your trees:

1. Select trees that are hardy for your area.

2. Do not select trees that have "nuisance" litter, such as messy fruit, seed pods, and broken twigs. This consideration is especially important when trees are near walks or drives.

3. Do not select trees with roots that are heavy surface feeders. These trees will interfere with the growth of lawn and nearby plantings or will cause surrounding pavement to heave.

4. Do not select rapid-growing trees, such as black locust or Siberian elm. Although these trees will give shade quickly, they are shortlived and are prone to breakage from ice, snow, and wind.

5. Select trees that are longlived and resistant to ice and wind, as well as to insects and disease.

6. Select trees that will fit into the available overhead space when they are fully grown.

Because of their strong vertical form, evergreens make striking accent plants in shrub borders. Evergreens do not harmonize easily with the topography and plant forms of the Midwest, and should not be overused in that area.

In the drawing above, an accent is achieved by using evergreen forms, but their dominance is neutralized by the heavy, rounded forms of the background plants.

If you want evergreens without supporting plantings, use at least three evergreens in a group to reduce their vertical effect and to conform to the rule that a planting should be wider than it is high.

The effects of land forms can be modified by plantings. An abrupt change in grade can be given a more pleasing transition by locating plants at the base of the slope (above). The dominance of a higher piece of ground, such as a knoll or hill, can be reduced by planting at the base — not the top — of the rise (below).

When a tree is used in a shrub border, the border should be 1½ times as deep as the tree is tall. This rule applies only to the area where the tree is located.

8: Fitting Shrubs To Your Plan

The word "shrub" usually refers to a woody perennial that flowers during the growing season. Shrubs should be selected with great care. Study their line, form, color, and texture carefully. Since shrubs are lower growing materials than trees, we can see them in much greater detail. Their smaller size is also important in reducing the scale of an area to one that compares favorably with the human body.

Shrubs bloom for only a short time. For this reason, you should select them not only for their flowers but also for their foliage, branching habits, and suitability for a specific location. There is a wide range of shrubs to choose from, and, with a little searching, you can find a plant that will exactly fit your plan. The fact that shrub forms (round, spreading, oval, ascending, and vase) are similar to tree forms is a great advantage in developing shrub compositions that are compatible with the tree forms used in your design.

People too often choose the same standard materials. Using something new to the neighborhood can bring you personal pleasure and still do its job well. You may not be able to find what you want at your local nursery because most nurserymen carry stock that is in greatest demand. But a nurseryman will usually order less common material if that is what you want.

Shrubs can be used as specimens, accent plants, group plantings, shrub borders, hedges, screens, foundation plantings, and planter-box plantings. Vines and ground covers will also be discussed in this chapter.

Specimen Plants

A specimen plant is one that has special qualities that warrant its use as an individual plant in such a way as to display those qualities. A specimen is usually a perfect example of the type it represents, and is outstanding in form, texture, or color, or a combination of these elements.

Because of their unique qualities, specimen plants are usually placed where they can be enjoyed. You can use a plant as a specimen in a border, but it must be superior to any other plant in the border, and it must be planted so that it can be viewed as an individual plant. A single specimen shrub can often take the place of a small tree. You may want to use a specimen shrub as the end feature of an axis (a major line of vision), or as a dominant element at the end of a straight line in a formal design.

If a specimen plant is not the same as the border plants, it must be similar to the group in a least one of the following: size, shape, foliage, texture, or color. Do not use a totally different kind of plant. You can often use specimen plants at special points to frame a building, to accent a corner of special areas or flower beds, or to add interest to an open lawn area. Use these plants sparingly. Too many of them are distracting in a landscape design.

Accent Plants

Accent plants are closely related to specimen plants. A specimen plant usually stands alone; an accent plant is part of the shrub mass but of a different height. It may also differ in form, color, and texture from the shrub mass.

Shrubs can be used for accent plants in both formal and informal gardens. Accent shrubs can be used to vary the height of the shrub border. They break up the silhouette and relieve the monotony of a group of plants of similar height.

REPRESENTATIVE SHRUB FORMS

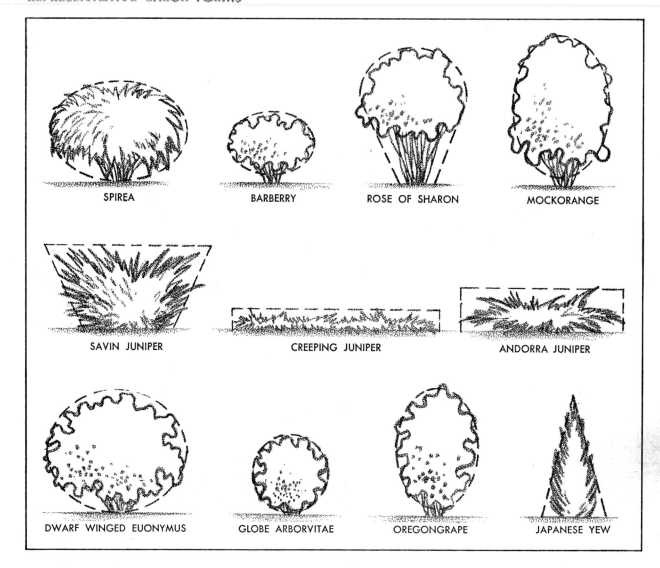

SPIREA · BARBERRY · ROSE OF SHARON · MOCKORANGE

SAVIN JUNIPER · CREEPING JUNIPER · ANDORRA JUNIPER

DWARF WINGED EUONYMUS · GLOBE ARBORVITAE · OREGONGRAPE · JAPANESE YEW

If the composition is made up of broadly rounded masses, accent plants should be taller than they are wide to provide the necessary contrast. If you can't find deciduous shrubs that are suitable, you can use one of the pyramidal or cylindrical forms of evergreens for accent in a deciduous shrub border. Using the same kind of accent plant at several locations in a long border adds similarity and sequence to a garden design. To keep from destroying the unity of your plantings, limit the number of accents in each composition.

You can also use accents where you want to direct attention to a specific area because of some special-interest feature or design element. The accent plant should be sufficiently different from the total composition to arrest the eyes, yet not so extreme that it detracts from or competes with the special-interest element.

Group Plantings

A group planting has less individuality than a specimen plant, since three to five different species are used to form the composition. It should, however, have more interest than the shrub border. The value of a group planting depends upon the relations between height, form, and arrangement of the individual plants that make up the composition.

The primary silhouette of the group can vary. For example, one type of silhouette may have a strong vertical emphasis counterbalanced with several lower plants of different heights. These lower plants may also contrast with the taller plants in form and texture.

A group silhouette can also be low and horizontal in line emphasis. In this case, you can use rounded plants of varying heights but without the extreme height difference in the silhouette with strong vertical emphasis.

The type of group silhouette you choose will depend upon its purpose in the design and its relations to the total composition, including other nearby plantings. Groups with strong vertical emphasis can function as space dividers, provide a focal point of special interest, and relieve the monotony of fence lines. The lower silhouette groups can direct and reinforce pedestrian and vehicular movement, as well as divide areas. Both types can frame a view or provide spot screening of an undesirable element.

Make sure that the group planting is compatible with other plantings and the entire composition by following the principles of design discussed in Chapter 6. To be interesting, a group planting must have a striking outline and arrangement with visual complexity and tension. You can achieve this effect through skillful counterplay of line, form, color, or texture between the plants.

As you plan the placement and design of the group, consider the point from which it will be seen, as well as the intervening distance. The group should be designed so that the strongest interest of the composition is in the direction from which it will normally be viewed. Since the group is freestanding, you cannot ignore its appearance from other views, but these are subordinate to the primary view. Too much variety in your group planting lessens its effectiveness. Follow the procedure outlined under *Shrub Borders* to determine the silhouette of the group through the use of abstract forms.

Shrub Borders

In developing your landscape, remember that you are dealing with a cube of space. This space can be divided into subspaces for various activities through the use of fences, walls, and woody plants. For example, a border mass planting of shrubs can create the outdoor living room. This border may act as a background for flowers and establish the walls of the outdoor living room at the same time. A shrub border may also serve as a screen if you need one for privacy or to block out an objectionable view.

A simple but effective method for designing a planting composition is the *backward process*. Since the last step in this process is naming the plant, you do not "stifle" the design by trying to make it fit a particular plant. The steps in the backward process are discussed on the following three pages.

A specimen plant used as a part of a right-angle planting to emphasize the importance of an area.

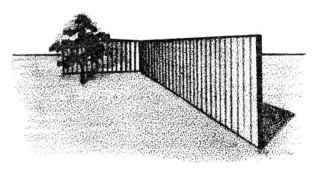

A specimen plant used as the terminus of the main axis of view. The fence shows off the plant's special qualities.

A specimen plant adds interest in a shrub border when surrounded and framed by neutral plants.

TYPES OF SHRUB PLANTINGS

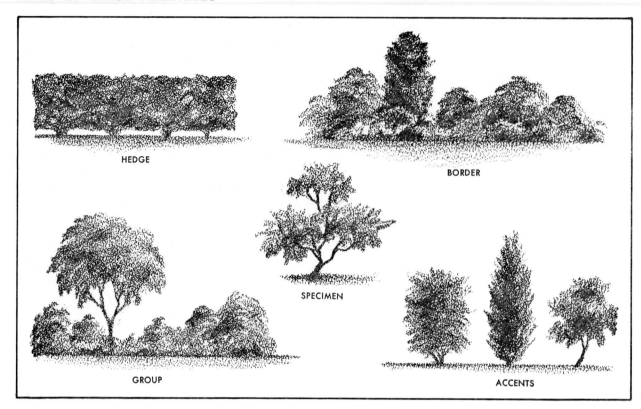

HEDGE

BORDER

SPECIMEN

GROUP

ACCENTS

Step 1. Consider the mass and silhouette of woody plants as a series of abstract blocks or rectangles of various sizes and proportions. Combinations of these abstract forms can be quickly sketched on a sheet of paper. It is helpful to keep their size related to the scale of your base plane (⅛ inch = 1 foot). If you find this scale too difficult, draw a thumbnail sketch that is not to scale. Each abstract form should be in proportion to every other form on a ratio basis that can later be converted to your plan scale.

If you are working to scale, you should first mark off the linear distance that the planting will occupy. (At this stage, you needn't concern yourself with the depth of the planting materials or their arrangement in the bed design.) Now begin to combine the abstract forms into a pleasing silhouette. The tall, rectangular forms may represent a shrub or tree. If the form is intended to be a tree, you do not need to show the full spread of the tree or its canopy effect, since you are now primarily interested in the height variations of the silhouette. The low, horizontal, rectangular forms can represent a series of plants in an informal or formal hedge. Other square or rectangular forms may represent individual shrubs.

After you have a pleasing silhouette drawn to scale, the exact width and height of each abstract block will tell you the size of each plant. You should make at least half-a-dozen abstract studies. Examine these carefully, and evaluate each pattern for its conformity with the six principles of design. (See Chapter 6 for a discussion of these principles.)

Once you have decided which abstract study you prefer, check it against the base plan and your site analysis. Be sure that you have the desired height, screening, openness, etc. where you want them.

Step 2. Place your abstract composition at the top of a sheet of tracing paper so that you have space to develop a second series of studies below. (At this point, your composition must be drawn to scale.) Begin to think of the abstract blocks as tree or shrub forms. These can be either evergreen or deciduous.

You must decide whether the plant form will be rounded, pyramidal, cylindrical, etc. Do a number of studies, using various combinations of forms to explore all the possibilities. Be sure that you keep your plant-form studies exactly equal to the abstract forms they replace. Dropping a dashed line from the center of the abstract box to the plant-form study will help you to keep everything in the same alignment. At this point, you must show the tree form (canopy) or shrub form for the tall rectangular blocks. It will be necessary, however, to check the height of each plant form to be certain that it equals the height of the abstract form.

When you have decided on a particular abstract composition, don't convince yourself that it should never be changed. After replacing the abstract forms with plant forms, you may find some problem that can be solved only by modifying the abstract study. A typical problem is bunching too much medium or medium-tall material around your tallest vertical unit. This problem can frequently be solved by shifting certain units in the abstract study. At this stage, you should be shifting back and forth between the abstract and the form studies — modifying and changing where necessary to achieve the best possible result.

Step 3. To achieve a harmonious sequence and balance in the pattern, you must now consider texture and color. This step is worked out on the abstract study. Place a sheet of tracing paper over the abstract study and indicate by cross-hatching or letters (C = coarse; MC = medium-coarse; M = medium; MF = medium-fine; F = fine) the texture for each mass.

Avoid extremes in texture, such as coarse next to fine. Try to keep texture changes gradual — coarse to medium-coarse to medium. You can, however, combine coarse with medium if you increase the number of medium plants in the composition. The large area of medium texture will be able to hold its own against the one coarse texture.

In studying texture, keep in mind the distance from which the group will be viewed. If the group is close to the observer, the details of the plant will determine the texture. If it is viewed from a distance, the mass and light and shadow will determine the texture.

After you have the texture combinations you want, place a second sheet of tracing paper over the abstract study to analyze foliage color. You can designate your choice with letters or colored pencils. Foliage colors include G (emerald green), BlG (blue-green), YG (yellow-green), RG (red-green), GG (gray-green), and BG (black-green). The value (brightness) and intensity of color now become important. A middle value and high intensity will be visually stronger than a light value and low intensity. Color is modified considerably by the plant's texture. Texture influences the amount of light reflection because of leaf surface, leaf size, petiole length, etc. These, in turn, affect the value and intensity of the foliage color.

When you have a good color composition, combine it with your texture study to compare the relations between the two. Estimate the percentage of the mass that is coarse, medium-coarse, medium, medium-fine, and fine. Make the same evaluation for color according to the color scale. Both the texture and color should be measured against the six principles of design.

Study the balance carefully. The balance should be asymmetrical, with the visual weight on one side of an imaginary vertical line equaling that on the other. The location of this vertical line will depend upon your silhouette arrangement.

Step 4. This final step involves (1) selecting the plants that will be used in the composition; and (2) arranging the plants in plan view. It should not be difficult to select the plants, since you now have a complete set of specifications that each plant must meet. From your abstract pattern, you can determine the mature height and spread of each plant. The color and texture, of course, have already been determined. Check the list of plant materials at the end of this book, as well as other references. Usually, you will find several plants that might be suitable. Make a list of these plants, and then make your selection after looking at them in the nursery.

After you have selected the plants you will use, you are ready to arrange the plants in a bed design. This arrangement is always drawn in plan view. The bed design may be predetermined from your overall pattern development. (Pattern development will be discussed in Chapter 11.) In certain cases, however, you may be designing the bed as you arrange the plants in plan view, especially in group-planting design.

The bed design for a group planting may be composed of straight-line patterns, an arc-and-tangent combination, and possibly curved lines. Curved lines are the most difficult to work with, since considerable space is required to obtain strong, bold curves. Avoid snaky lines and bed designs with many curves that give a wavy effect. The straight line or arc-and-tangent are preferred. The design of this bed must fit with other design patterns established in your overall plan. As you proceed to arrange the plants, be sure to produce the silhouette you have designed in Steps 1 and 2. It is not until this stage that you know how many plants of each group will be required to fill the bed area.

When you have arrived at a suitable plan arrangement, study the design as it will be viewed from directions other than the primary view. Even though these other views are subordinate, the plants must be arranged so that they present a satisfactory appearance from all sides. This principle applies primarily to the group planting, since shrub borders usually have only one viewing direction except possibly at the ends.

The plants should be arranged in the bed so that the form of the plant complements and strengthens the form of the bed. In a freestanding planting such as a group, the taller plants are often located more in the middle of the bed, while in a shrub border the larger plants are at the rear of the bed.

Arrange shrub masses to give an appearance of strength to the border and to create line and direction. The appearance of strength is gained by using larger specimens and perhaps coarser textures at the ends of the border. Repetition of this strength occasionally throughout will help give a cohesive quality to your design, but the internal portion of the mass must not be equal in dominance and emphasis to the ends. Perhaps the easiest way to integrate these materials is to be sure that their arrangement develops a pattern based on the principle of *unity*.

Unity helps the viewer grasp the design through organizing all parts into orderly groups or subgroups. Because your field of vision is limited, you need to develop subgroups within an exceptionally long shrub border. In selecting materials for these subgroups, you can repeat some of the stronger materials. By this means, the viewer is able to organize the many different plants that compose the shrub border into an orderly pattern.

Since the shrub border is made up of a number of different plants, they should be arranged so that the branches of one "meld" into the other. This slight overlap subordinates the individual to the mass. If each plant in your shrub border stands out as an individual separated from its neighbor, you should rearrange the plants so that they touch one another. This is not true for group plantings, where the different plants stand as individuals for contrast and emphasis.

Since you do not want the subgroups of the mass to stand out, they must also be subordinated to the whole; yet there must be satisfactory movement of the eye over the shrub border and between subgroups. This involves the principle of *sequence*. The eye automatically follows the outline of any form or group of forms it views. Check your silhouette to see if visual movement over the total mass is encouraged by a predominance of rounded forms and limited use of extreme accents that tend to stop the eye. Try to correlate the pattern of eye movement over the silhouette with the bed-pattern outline.

The eye movement in the composition may be linear (from one end straight through to the other),

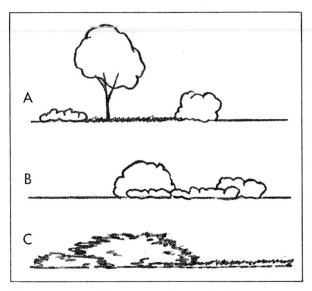

(A) group planting with strong vertical emphasis; (B) lower growing materials arranged as a group without vertical emphasis; (C) group with strong horizontal emphasis in line and movement.

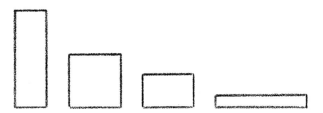

The *backward process* involves the use of a series of abstract blocks or rectangles of various sizes and proportions.

or it may move from either end toward the middle. In the latter case, you must develop a focal point in your design. In certain situations, you may have a linear movement that directs the attention to a focal point outside the planting mass.

Hedges

Hedges can be clipped (formal) or unclipped (informal). Formal hedges demand a great deal of maintenance, and the individual plants impart little of their own character. If the hedge is well above eye level, it forms a wall effect against which other landscape elements are seen. For this reason, the color and texture of a tall hedge must be carefully planned so as not to overpower or compete with whatever is seen against it. Low, formal hedges below eye level have a strong horizontal form that clearly defines an area. They also function as a means of tying together diverse planting units. Since both formal and informal hedges repeat the same material, they form a strong

BACKWARD PROCESS

A

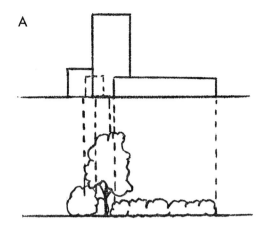

B

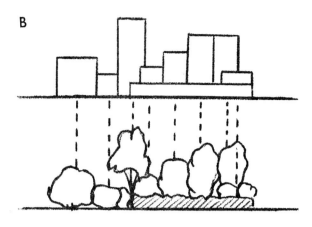

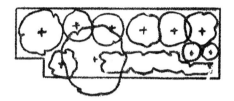

C

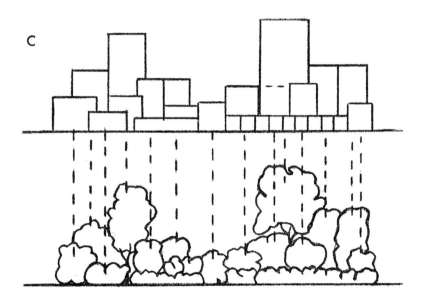

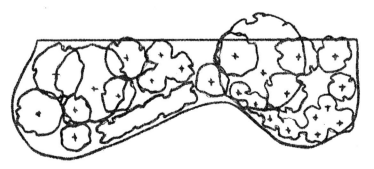

A Group planting

B Limited shrub border
   with a more complex
   combination and ar-
   rangement of materials

C Extensive shrub border
   with the most complex
   combination and ar-
   rangement of materials

structural element in the design. In choosing hedge and screen plants, you will want dense foliage that cannot be seen through and plants that are able to survive close together.

Shrubs for hedges must be able to tolerate a regular shearing. Shearing makes the plant thicker. Small twigs covered with leaves set close together eventually create a solid wall of foliage. Shrubs for hedges should also have a strong branching habit that will hold a load of ice and snow. (See the list of plant materials for suggested shrubs for hedges.)

A formal hedge (above) requires maintenance to keep it well groomed. The plants must tolerate shearing and not break under the weight of snow. Material for a formal hedge should be spaced 24 to 36 inches apart. An informal hedge (below) is not pruned, and the plant material is allowed to grow in its natural form. Spacing varies with the plant selected, and can be as wide as 3 to 3½ feet between plants.

Screens

To use shrubs as a screen, plant a solid mass of one variety to give the effect of a living wall. An ideal shrub for a screen is tall and narrow but with heavy foliage to the ground. If you cannot find this kind of shrub, use tall plants that lack foliage at the base and put lower growing plants ("facer" plants) in front. This combination of plants may closely resemble a hedge. Since the plants aren't sheared, however, the screen doesn't have formal shape and is considered an informal screen. A screen planting can be a background for flowers, lawn, or a mixed shrub border.

The height of a screen or hedge is a compromise between the height needed for screening and the limitation of scale given by the area. For example, in a small area where screening is necessary, a high screen might make the area seem even smaller than it actually is.

Screen plantings are usually composed of neutral materials arranged in harmonious groupings so that the plants do not draw attention. You don't have to block out an unpleasant view completely. A hedge or screen in harmony with the rest of the landscape will hold the viewer's attention to such an extent that he is not conscious of the unpleasant view behind the hedge or screen. You can also subordinate an unattractive outbuilding by placing some striking material in the foreground. Special-interest plantings may even be placed at another angle to divert attention from what is being screened.

Foundation Plantings

Select shrubs for the foundation planting around your house that will make the house look natural and appropriate for its site. Choose shrubs that will not grow large enough to need heavy pruning. Pruning destroys the natural shape of shrubs.

A few plants at the foundation are usually much more satisfactory than many plants. If you decide that your foundation planting calls for at least two different kinds of plants, choose those that look well together. For example, you might use a compact winged euonymus with Waukegan juniper around the base.

Screen plantings are used to obstruct movement, block vision, and reduce noises. A screen planting (above) is a low-cost means of obtaining an enclosure. Since many tall-growing shrubs do not have foliage on their bases, lower growing shrubs can be planted in front of them (below). These "facer" shrubs mask the bare stems of the taller shrubs, and the increased foliage mass serves as a more effective sound and visual barrier.

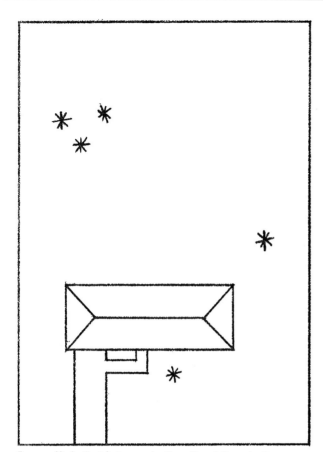 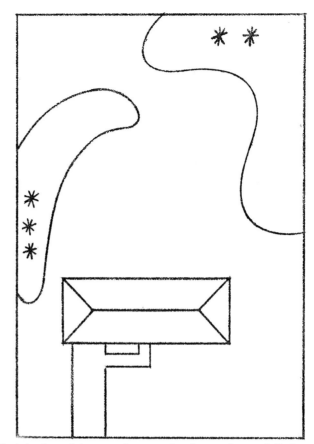

For a unified effect between plantings (foundation plantings, groups, shrub borders, etc.), repeat the same plant in several areas (left). Repeat flowering shrubs at least once in the same general viewing area (right).

Branching habit is another important feature of foundation plants. Those with round or spreading shapes are preferable to those with a stiff, upright appearance. By selecting the correct type of shrub, it is easy to keep the planting proportions in scale with the house. Upright evergreens cannot be used as corner plantings unless they are severely pruned. Select foundation plants that will blend man-made objects into the natural surroundings by providing a transition between the strong vertical lines of the house and the strong horizontal lines of the ground. For example, the plant form should be rounded so that the eye is directed to the ground.

One basic use for shrubs in the foundation planting is around doorways. The doorway is the center for all plantings in the design of the public area. It should provide a pleasing and attractive focal point. Doorway plantings should be interesting, but they should not compete with the doorway for attention. They should be no higher than one-fourth to one-third the distance from the groundline to the eave.

A rule of thumb for corner plantings is that the maximum height of the mature plant should not be more than two-thirds the distance from the ground to the eave. Round-shaped plants tend to direct the eye to the ground and to break up vertical lines better than upright evergreens, giving a desirable transition between man-made objects and the natural surroundings. An upright evergreen at the corner emphasizes rather than softens the vertical line. If upright evergreens are used, there should be adequate room for additional plantings of low-spreading evergreens or rounded deciduous shrubs to give a better transition to the groundline.

Planter Boxes

Planter boxes are often used in contemporary architecture. They may emphasize the horizontal lines of a house, define front-door areas, or, in many cases, simply parallel the front facade. There is considerable doubt about the value of a planter box as a planting area. Often the builder sets a planter box at such a point, scales it to such a height, and makes it of such proportion that it balances a particular area in front of the house. Adding plant material to the height of

SHRUB BORDERS

A shrub border may be located along the property line or within the **property** as "arms" extending from the sides to divide or form areas. It might also serve as a background for flowers, to screen objectionable objects, to frame views, and to modify the effect of changes in ground elevation. If you use too many different types of plants in a shrub border, you will have a plant collection rather than a pleasing composition. Select only a few varieties, and repeat them at various locations in the border. It is not necessary to repeat the variety in the same arrangement or number. To overcome monotony in a shrub border, use shrubs that are of contrasting heights or are outstanding in color, texture, or form.

GROUP PLANTINGS

the box, however, can completely throw the balance or continuity out of kilter.

Planter boxes are often tacked on wherever it suits the designer's or owner's fancy. Certainly some of the planter boxes that you see illustrated in popular magazines appear to be very desirable additions to a home. But to keep a planter box as neat and attractive as those shown in the magazine pictures would be almost a full-time job.

Plants in boxes or other containers above ground are subject to greater temperature and moisture variations than plants in the ground. As a result, they are much more sensitive to light, drouth, wind, and temperature. For example, soil in a masonry planter box will freeze and thaw much faster than the same soil

in the ground. Planter-box materials must have the ability to survive lack of moisture and these extremes of freezing and thawing. Box plantings also demand special soil preparations and drainage.

A good growing medium for planter boxes contains one-third peat, one-third sand or perlite, and one-third soil. If your soil is extremely heavy, the proportions of this mixture may have to be varied. The effects of freezing and thawing can be reduced by lining the container with 1-inch-thick styrofoam sheets. These sheets act as an insulation.

Tubs, movable planter boxes, and other types of portable gardens also need special soil preparation, and the plants in them are subject to the same problems as those in fixed planter boxes.

Vines

Vines are not used in American gardens as much as they should be. Perhaps they are not properly cared for, or owners are not familiar with the basic needs of vines. You can use them in your garden in many effective ways — for green foliage, screening, shade, overhead protection, or simply for their beauty. They are especially valuable in a small garden because they need little space to grow.

Vines are usually classified by their climbing habits. Some vines twist around for support, some have tendrils that reach out and attach to a support, others cling by little rootlets, and still others cling directly to stone or brick. Some sub-shrubs are not actually vines, but have long, flexible branches that can be tied in place to establish patterns.

Landscape designers divide vines into those that grow densely to form a solid covering, and those that grow loosely to provide a tracery effect that you can see through. You can thin out densely growing vines to get a tracery effect, but it is a great deal of work.

It is better to select the vine needed for the specific location. A light vine can be used as a tracery to break up the flat surface of a wall or fence. It can also be used to create an open tracery against the lattice or wire fence that serves as the vine's support.

Vines can be used for overhead protection over patios and other areas where shade trees might not be high enough to give the desired protection. This is an inexpensive way to get summer shade. A vine can help soften harsh construction lines, particularly on a two-story house. A vine across the porch can prevent the viewer's eyes from running up and down the full vertical height of the house. And vines can give a full, rich effect in narrow spaces.

The support for a vine should not be conspicuous unless it is a screen or baffle. A fancy trellis design against a house or fence is out of place and should not be used. A simple support of dowels and wire is far better than a highly designed, intricate support. A vine should blend into the total effect and not be shown off as an individual specimen.

If the vine is in direct sunlight, use insulated wire, slats, or wood dowels for support rather than bare wire. Wire heats up tremendously in the summer sun, and will burn the tips of young shoots.

You can often use two different types of vines for overhead or upright screening — one for dense foliage, and the other for its flowers. Usually the flowering vines are most satisfactory for the home garden.

Vines may be used on a porch for shade or as a screen. They may also be used over the patio and other areas where shade trees may not be high enough to give the desired protection.

Ground Covers

Although ground covers are not shrubs, they combine with shrubs for interesting ground patterns and textures. Since ground-cover plants do not have form in themselves, their form in design is determined by the shape and pattern of their growing area. The ground-cover design can be strong and bold, contrasting with the bed design and plant arrangement, or it can be neutral, serving as a unifying device that ties together the separate elements in the composition.

Ground covers improve the appearance of the ground and, in some cases, hold soil and prevent erosion. Your selection of ground-cover material will depend upon exposure to the sun and the degree of refinement or finish needed. In general, the nearer the observer is to the ground cover, the more refined and dense it should be; the farther away, the more loose and open the ground cover can be.

Ground covers are often used instead of grass. In the past, ground covers were used mostly on banks to hold soil and reduce mowing. But they can also be used in front of shrubbery, in shrub-bed areas, or in a large panel to increase the scale of a small area. Ground covers are sometimes difficult to establish, and it takes some time for them to cover an area.

Keep the soil moist with frequent watering while the cover is spreading, and cultivate carefully so that the roots are not damaged. You will need to hand weed until the bed is established. Once established, a ground cover should crowd out any weeds and be relatively weed-free. Ground cover does not wear well, and should not be used in heavy traffic areas. Traffic areas need lawn or hard surfaces.

9: Fitting Flowers To Your Plan

Flowers are essentially *accessories* in the landscape. Woody plants (trees and shrubs) and structures should be used to form the permanent framework of the design. Flowers die back during the winter. For this reason, they are used most effectively with woody plant material that provides a frame and background for the floral display. Flowers must fit into the total landscape picture, and they should not be so spectacular that they stand out more than any other feature.

Since the house is the most important element in the total design of the public area, all planting and construction should complement the house, not compete with it for attention. Keep island flower beds, for example, out of the front yard.

As a general rule, flowers should be restricted to the rear of the property, to the outdoor living area, or to the service area. It is best if there are no flowers in the public area at all, although sometimes a planter box or an area within the foundation plantings can be planted to flowering annuals satisfactorily. Only one type and color of flower should be planted, and the flowers should be planted in masses. Color in harmony with the house can give a pleasing contrast, but the color should not be so vivid and dominant that it holds the viewer's attention.

You may hear people say that their parents or grandparents had flowers in the front yard. In the past, people spent a great deal of their leisure time on the front porch; and since they wanted to see and enjoy their flowers, they put them in the front lawn. But outdoor living has moved to the rear of the house — flower beds should be there, too, where you can enjoy them.

Flowers add considerable color and interest when seen from the patio or interior of the house. If you enjoy gardening, you can work a flower border into your landscape design that will provide contrast and variety to the overall composition. But if you want an attractive place with a minimum demand on your free time, you can create a pleasing landscape picture around your house through the use of trees, shrubbery, lawn, and ground covers only.

If you use a flower border in the outdoor living area, be sure that it does not dominate the entire garden. Flowers — like screening shrubs, flowering shrub borders, trees, and surfacing materials — should be only one element in the landscape picture. A flower border should capture the complete attention of the observer only when it is used as a surprise feature tucked away behind an arm of shrubs that projects out toward the center of the lawn. Too lavish a display of color destroys the restful atmosphere of the outdoor living area.

The structure, form, and texture of the plants are important in a flower border. But if you intend to use flowers for indoor arrangements or garden club competition, the flower itself is of primary importance. A cut-flower garden in the service area will allow you to grow flowers in rows, as individuals. Then you will be able to give your flowers the necessary care to produce fine specimens.

Landscape design distinguishes between a flower bed and a flower border. A flower bed is designed to stand by itself. It is used in formal gardens as a display, and is not meant to supply cut flowers, since it is a definite design element surrounded by walks, lawns, or possibly a low hedge.

A flower border consists of flowers planted in front of a shrub border. It has informal patterns, and its flowers are set off by the shrubbery. It is much easier

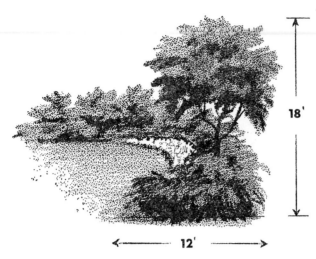

A planting border should be designed so that the incurve is located at the corner of the property. Locate flowers to the front of the incurve and shrubs behind the flowers for background. The shrubs in the outcurve should have a coarser texture than the shrubs behind the flowers. It is often desirable to use a small flowering tree in the outcurve. The tree should be about 1½ times as high as the bed is deep.

to design a flower border than a flower bed. Since a flower border is seen from one side only, you simply plant low flowers in the front, medium-sized flowers in the middle, and tall flowers in the rear. High shrubs provide the background.

To be most effective, flowers must be seen against a background that will show off their colors. Most flowers need a neutral background — the green foliage of shrubs or the brown of a stained fence. Flowers planted against a light background lose much of their effectiveness.

A flower border located in a shrub border may be a part of a long, sweeping curve that is pleasing to the eye because of its informal effect. Shrubs are arranged from coarse at the corners to fine at the center so that they provide a backdrop and focal point for the flower border. In an asymmetrical, straight-line design, flowers must be used in a more controlled and architectural pattern. Annuals are particularly suitable for this type of design. Regardless of the design that you select, limit the depth of your flower border to 5 feet so that you can work easily in the border from the front edge of the planting.

Keep a flower border in reasonable proportion to the rest of the garden, especially to the shrub wall in the rear. For example, a 2-foot-deep border planting of flowers against a 10-foot-deep shrub planting would be only a shoestring of color rather than a garden feature. A 10-foot-deep flower border against a brick wall would also be out of proportion.

Annuals are plants that make all their vegetative growth, flower, and produce seed in one growing season, and then die. Most annuals propagate by means of seeds. Biennials generally use at least part of two growing seasons to complete their life cycle, with a more or less dormant period in the middle. Perennials normally live more than two years.

It is difficult to plan a flower border of perennials and biennials that is spectacular at all times during the growing season. These plants should be used to create a display of peak effectiveness in one season — spring, summer, or fall. The area does not have to be bare the rest of the year. It can have touches of color throughout the growing season, but the enframing and background shrubs should carry the interest at other times. For seasonal effect, most of the flowers used should flower at the same time. Annuals might be an exception, since these plants bloom throughout the season and can be used where a continuous floral show is desired.

To successfully design a flower bed of any scale, you must be familiar with the material that you are working with. Like any other landscape material, flowers should be evaluated and used on the basis of their form (foliage and flower), texture, and color. By carefully controlling and blending these qualities according to the six principles of design, you can easily develop a pleasing composition.

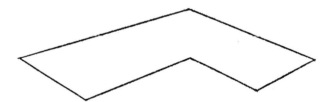

A planting border is a cultivated area in which the soil may either be exposed or covered with a mulch or an underplanting of ground cover. The border area should contrast sharply with the lawn and form a strong, dominant line and pattern in the design. Straight, angular lines (above) are usually considered uninteresting because they are repeated in walks, drives, the house, and property lines. Straight-line borders can be used, however, when the total design is composed of strong patterns that form an overall design. (See Chapter 11 for illustrations of the use of straight-line borders.) A curved bed pattern (below) is restful to the eye and provides an informal effect.

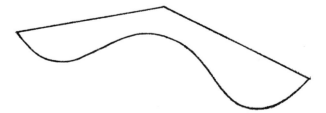

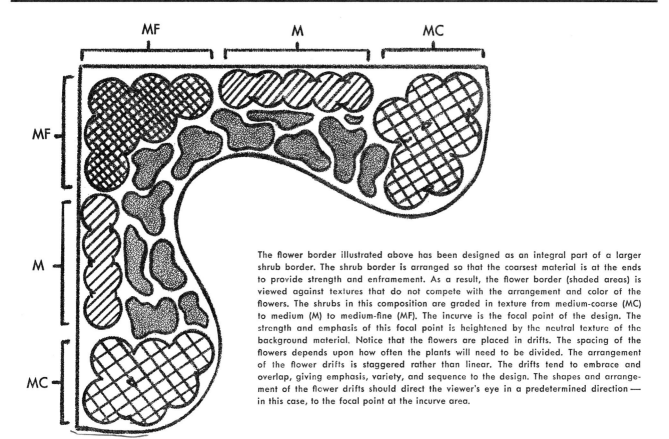

The flower border illustrated above has been designed as an integral part of a larger shrub border. The shrub border is arranged so that the coarsest material is at the ends to provide strength and enframement. As a result, the flower border (shaded areas) is viewed against textures that do not compete with the arrangement and color of the flowers. The shrubs in this composition are graded in texture from medium-coarse (MC) to medium (M) to medium-fine (MF). The incurve is the focal point of the design. The strength and emphasis of this focal point is heightened by the neutral texture of the background material. Notice that the flowers are placed in drifts. The spacing of the flowers depends upon how often the plants will need to be divided. The arrangement of the flower drifts is staggered rather than linear. The drifts tend to embrace and overlap, giving emphasis, variety, and sequence to the design. The shapes and arrangement of the flower drifts should direct the viewer's eye in a predetermined direction — in this case, to the focal point at the incurve area.

Flower forms are a basic design element. The three major classifications are the spike form, the round form (either with individual flowers or flower clusters), and the intermediate forms. Examples of the spike form include delphinium, lupine, and snapdragon. Peonies, oriental poppies, geraniums, and dahlias exemplify the round form. Bearded iris is considered intermediate.

In a flower border, the spike-form flowers are used as an accent comparable to the pyramidal form of evergreen in the general landscape. Used flagrantly, they become a disturbing force that may break up the entire composition. If you do not use the spike form at all, however, you run the risk of monotony and lack of interest.

The plant forms and foliage texture of herbaceous plants are quite similar to those of shrubs and trees. The repetition of these design qualities at all levels of plant materials is most important in achieving a unified composition. Flowers differ from the other kinds of materials, however, in the wide range of colors available for designing.

The same basic color principles apply to flowers as to woody shrubs and other ornamental plantings, and to such color sources as structures, paving, house color, and trim. Color expresses individual tastes, and no one can tell you which colors you should use to dominate your own composition.

Color must please the eye. The color wheel is a good guide for obtaining pleasing color combinations. Red, yellow, and blue are the *primary* colors, and orange, green, and purple are the *secondary* colors. Red, orange, and yellow are *warm* colors. Blue, green, and violet are *cool* colors. A warm color is always opposite a cool color on the color wheel.

Since warm colors are closely related, they can be used together in vivid color combinations. As a general rule, use warm colors in a sequence. For example, a sequence could be a gradation from red to white. But the sequence must be smooth and gradual, such as from red to scarlet, to orange scarlet, to orange, to orange bronze, to orange yellow, to yellow, to pale yellow, to cream, and finally, to pure white. A jump from red to orange to yellow to white is too abrupt without the intermediate colors.

There is no rule of thumb for how much warm or how much cool color to use. But the smaller the area, the fewer warm colors you can use, and the shorter the sequence you can develop. If your proposed flower area is small, you may be able to develop a sequence from orange through light yellow or deep pink through white.

Avoid wide extremes in value (brightness) when using a predominately one-hue combination. This is particularly true of warm hues. For example, violet-red against an orange-red is jarring. These hues are too widely separated in gradation. Intermediate hues are needed for pleasant transition.

Two-color compositions using *complementary* colors (those opposite one another on the color wheel) work well when one complement is allowed to be dominant and the other is used for accent at strategic points. The amount of the accent complement needed depends upon the quantity and intensity of the dominant hue. The purest or strongest of these complementary or contrasting colors create a gay, lively effect — for example, the yellow of snapdragons with blue delphinium. The larger the area and the more brilliant the intensity of the dominant color, the greater the amount of the accent needed.

As a general rule, it is better to use brilliant, high-intensity colors sparingly. They become too dominant and overpowering and, like too many accents, tend to break up the scene. A good policy to follow when using color in a composition is to restrict the number of hues when a variety of values is used. Conversely, when the number of values is held to a limited range, you can increase the number of hues. Most important of all, your color scheme should be *restful* rather than stimulating.

To begin your color scheme, decide what color you want to use; then decide whether a light or a dark value of this color will dominate.

Establish the largest amount of the dark color you will use (this will be determined by the scale of the area). The darker and purer or more intense the color, the more it will show up and dominate the scene. For this reason, you will not want to use too much of the darkest shade. Select your next lightest shade, and increase by one-third the number of plants used. Then go to the third lightest shade, and increase by one-third the number of these plants over the preceding group. Continue this ratio until you reach the lightest shade in your color gradation.

MAJOR FORMS FOR A FLOWER BORDER

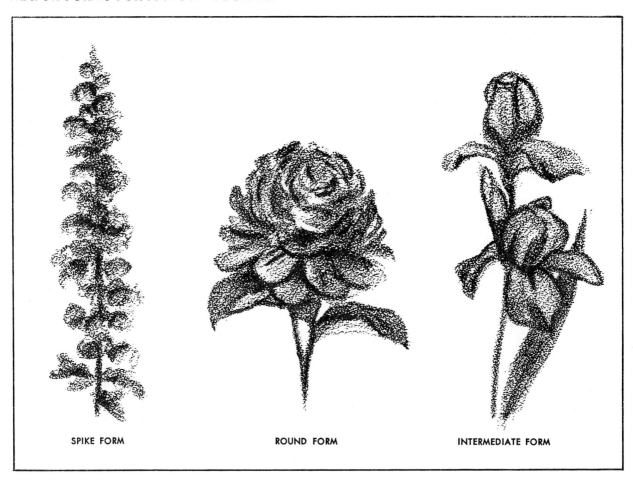

SPIKE FORM   ROUND FORM   INTERMEDIATE FORM

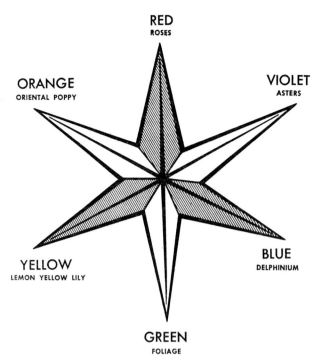

RED
ROSES

ORANGE
ORIENTAL POPPY

VIOLET
ASTERS

YELLOW
LEMON YELLOW LILY

BLUE
DELPHINIUM

GREEN
FOLIAGE

This color wheel lists flowers that are examples of the primary colors (red, yellow, blue) and the secondary colors (orange, green, violet). The warm colors (red, orange, and yellow) are closely related to one another, and are best used in sequence. The cool colors (violet, blue, and green) are used most effectively as contrasts to the warm colors.

Use the darkest shades or the pure, intense flower colors at the point of principal interest, but avoid too much variety where it might add confusion. Although cool colors (blue, green, purple) can be used in a sequence, they can be combined more effectively in a series of contrasts.

You can obtain the most effective color contrasts by using different shades of color opposites. For example, you can get pleasing effects by using a light shade of one color with a dark shade of its color opposite — perhaps light yellow columbine against dark violet lupine. But too many striking contrasts of light and dark shades can become disturbing in the composition, and give a mottled effect. Contrasting bright colors are useful for accent and emphasis, and contrasting muted or neutral colors result in a more restful picture.

Colors can create various illusions. Predominantly cool colors in a garden or at the back of a very short yard give an illusion of depth. Strong, warm colors at the rear of a garden or yard tend to make the garden or yard look shorter than it actually is.

Start your flower-border design with a scale plan on paper. Show each area to be planted to annuals,

biennials, and perennials. Sketch in accent points, and then build a sequence of related sizes and shapes around them, making sure that the round flower form predominates. To develop an interesting silhouette for a flower border, use the "backward process" described in Chapter 8.

The spacing of plants is important in flower border design. Some types spread rapidly and need frequent division, while others do not need to be divided for several years or more. The branches of trees and shrubs have permanent structure, but the stems of flowers die each fall. Since flowers do not have permanent structure, they should be used in groups rather than as individual specimens. Keep some space between groups and between plants within each group to avoid overcrowding and to give form to the border. Consider growth rates as well as the spreading habits of the different plants.

Flowers can be classified into three groups according to their spread and growth habits.

Group 1 plants spread rapidly and need to be divided and replanted every year, or at least every other year. This group includes asters, Michaelmas daisies, sunflowers, buttercups, goldenrod, helenium, wormwood, and rudbeckias.

Group 2 plants spread more slowly than those in Group 1, and need to be replanted every four or five years. Group 2 includes artemisia, perennial spirea, bellflower, Shasta daisy, pink delphinium, comb flower, daylily, coral bells, flax, cinquefoil, painted daisies, violas, and violets.

Group 3 plants spread slowly and should not be disturbed for 8 to 10 years or more. Since the mature spread of these plants is quite wide, they shouldn't be planted close together. Examples in Group 3 include heliotrope, clematis, bleeding heart, gas plant, globe thistle, baby's breath, lavender, lupine, bluebells, peony, and oriental poppy.

Decide the shape of each plant grouping or unit, and then space plants according to how often you will need to move them. Space Group 1 plants 6 to 8 inches apart and divide them every year. Space Group 2 plants 12 to 18 inches apart so that they will not be overcrowded for 4 to 5 years. Space Group 3 plants at least 3 feet apart so that they won't need to be transplanted for many years.

An informal planting bed is usually designed in a series of incurves and outcurves. Each outcurve reaches its greatest width at a certain point and recedes from that point. These curves resemble snowdrifts as they build up against a fence. A snowdrift formed by a low-velocity wind has a very broad out-

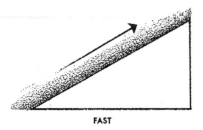
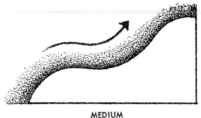
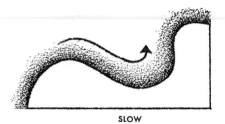

FAST   MEDIUM   SLOW

Snowdrift patterns formed by various wind velocities. The wind velocity parallels the rate at which the eye moves along a straight line, a slightly curved line, and a pronounced curve. These patterns are used in the design of a shrub border to concentrate the viewer's attention on the flower planting. A flower border is usually located in the incurve because any change in direction slows down the movement of the eye.

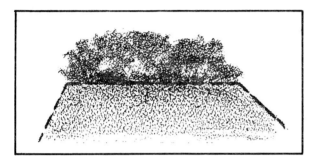

Colors can be used to create an illusion. Cool colors recede, while warm colors advance. If you have a short yard (above), use cool colors to the rear to make the yard appear deeper. If you have an extremely long, narrow yard (below), use strong, warm colors to the rear to make the yard appear shorter.

curve and a deep incurve, while a snowdrift built up by a moderate wind has less incurve. Drift buildup under a high wind is almost a straight line from the ground to the fence. The driftline is the result of wind velocity. The velocity of the wind parallels the rate of eye movement along these driftlines. The shape of the total shrub and flower-planting area should be developed by using these same principles.

In planning a shrub background for a flower border, you might allow the shrub groupings to come out to the edge of the bed at the point of the most extreme outcurve. Shrubs used at this point should have the coarsest foliage. Use deciduous shrubs with finer texture behind the flowers. A deep-bay inset of flowers framed on each side by a bold outcurve of coarse foliage grading into medium-textured foliage, and, finally, into a finer foliage behind the incurve of flowers, makes an attractive planting picture.

Everything flows from the point of the outcurve to the point of the incurve — flower groups flow toward the center of the incurve, which is the focal point of the composition, and shrubs grade from the coarsest to the finest textures. Be sure to use bold curves. A number of wavy lines show direction feebly and can be irritating.

Relate planting height to border width. Usually, the shrub background or fence should be 1½ times as high as the bed is deep. For example, if the bed is 10 feet deep, the tallest planting should be about 15 feet high. But you don't have to conform strictly to this rule. Bold outcurves become planting high points, and these same outcurves, carefully located, can screen undesirable views or objects, or provide some of the privacy that you want for outdoor living.

Don't put an outcurve in the corner of your lot — that's the place for an incurve. Use facer plants in front of shrubs on the outcurve if you want to hide the "leggy" bare stems of the shrubs. You may want to use some small flowering trees for height and accent at the center of an outcurve with ground cover underneath. The full-grown trees should also be about 1½ times as high as the deepest part of the bed.

Remember that herbaceous plants (those having little or no woody tissue), such as perennials and annuals, are *accessories* to the garden structure. The basic structure is made up of the trees and shrubs. Perhaps the most common mistake in designing a flower border is assigning the structural job of trees and shrubs to herbaceous plants.

Most herbaceous plants are attractive for only a short time. They need much more care than trees or shrubs, and are unattractive for long periods unless the area is constantly groomed. For this reason, short-term herbaceous plants should be backed up with good shrub plantings.

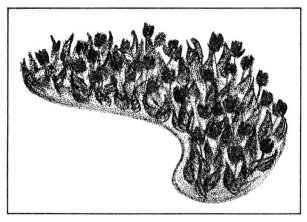

Flowers in the flower border *should not* be planted as individuals. Using flowers as plant groups and masses (above) will give a far more pleasing effect.

Plan the background to supplement the flower border rather than to compete with it. A background should be subtle and subordinate in the total picture. Walls and shrubs make effective backgrounds, but a fence design must be neutral without any detail or it will dominate. Another reason why you should not plant flowers against the house is that the house is architecturally "busy" with windows, doors, and trim. Flowers in the foreground must share interest with the house features.

Keep flower plantings simple. Mass materials in drifts — don't spot them here and there. Group your plants in a staggered or irregular pattern that allows the mass of one plant to embrace, overlap, or drift into the adjoining mass. In this way, you avoid straight-line planting that diminishes the design potential of flowers.

The drift technique eliminates the spottiness typical of many flower borders, where only one plant of each perennial is used. The effectiveness of drifts lies in the use of 3, 5, or more plants of each variety in a drift. If your border area is small, you will be limited in the number of different perennials you can use. By limiting the number of kinds of flowers, you keep the drifts simple but bold, and the border has a strong visual framework that "reads" from a distance. Too many small drifts results in a busy pattern that resembles a patchwork quilt.

Study the arrangement of your drifts on paper before planting. Use the form of your drifts to establish a flowing movement through the border. You may wish to use this movement as a means of leading the viewer's attention to a focal point, a special-interest flowering group, or a specimen plant.

Remember the following points:

1. It is very difficult to keep a border in bloom all summer. If you are limited in space, you can expect only one good show a season. Plan for peak effectiveness either in the spring or fall, and depend upon flowering shrubs to carry the interest at other times.

2. All plants in a grouping should be either sun-loving or shade-loving, and they should require the same conditions of soil, moisture, light, air, and temperature. The environmental needs of trees and shrubs discussed in Chapter 6 also apply to herbaceous plants. If you select a plant that is not suited to the environment, the plant may die or you may have to work very hard to keep it going.

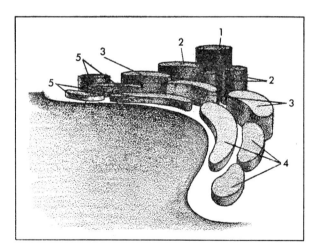

Since the darkest shade and pure intense color dominate a composition, it is wise to use the darker and more intense colors sparingly. You can balance the dominance of the dark color by selecting a lighter shade of harmonious color. To achieve this balance, increase the number of plants of the lighter shade by one-third. In the drawing above, Group 1 represents the darkest mass, Group 2 the mass of the next lightest shade, etc. Notice that the masses increase in size as they become lighter.

10: Designing The Public Area

Every home needs a well-designed landscape to make it more livable, attractive, and valuable. The public area — the space from the front of the house to the street — does not lend itself to family living activities. If it is properly designed, however, it can greatly enhance the appearance and market value of your property. This is particularly true for modest tract houses whose design may be repeated with minor variations throughout the development.

The public area involves design considerations quite different from those associated with the outdoor living area. The most prominent element in the public area is the house. The landscape development is always seen against the house when viewed from the street or public sidewalk. For this reason, your design should be dictated largely by the architecture of the house.

Since the house is the most important element in the public-area landscape, all construction features (walks, drives, fences) and all plantings should complement it and provide a proper setting for it — not compete with it. Fundamental landscape principles for developing the public area are (1) to soften the architectural lines of the building; (2) to frame the building with trees; and (3) to maintain open lawn areas.

Your main purpose in developing the public area should be to blend the structure of the house with the general surroundings so that the house looks natural on its site. You can achieve this combination by softening and blending the vertical house lines with the strong horizontal ground lines. A good transition between these two dominant lines creates a natural and attractive setting for the house.

The center of interest and focal point for all plantings is the doorway. The plantings may be immediately adjacent to the house (often referred to as "foundation plantings") or located in the foreground area away from the building. A third planting arrangement is a combination of these two techniques. Key plantings are adjacent to the building, but supporting materials extend toward the street so that one or several subspaces are created for visual interest from within the house or from the entryway. The advantages of this arrangement are that you can effectively soften and blend architectural lines by planting next to the building, where necessary, but that you avoid the linear, decorative effect of plants paralleling the walls. This third planting arrangement also eliminates the problem of the plantings "floating" in the lawn. (The floating effect results when plants are used as isolated units located in the foreground away from the building.) Regardless of the planting arrangement you choose, remember that the major planting areas to consider are those at the corners, where there are strong vertical lines, and on each side of the doorway.

The design of the public area involves only four landscape units: (1) the necessary structures (walks and drives, fences, walls); (2) trees; (3) shrub plantings; and (4) lawn. These units will be discussed in this chapter, along with special design considerations relating to flowers, flower boxes, lighting, water features, and sculpture.

Before you make any design studies, carefully consider the topography and drainage of the foreground area between the house and the street. Proper grading for drainage will protect your investment in both your house and the landscape. If you have any doubt as to what is to be done and how, consult a professional landscape architect or a nurseryman or contractor experienced in determining proper grades.

(A) The point of balance (fulcrum) is not the doorway, and different elements of different proportions and arrangements are located on either side of the doorway. This is an asymmetrical design. (B) The number, arrangement, and proportion of the elements to the left and right of the doorway are exactly the same, giving a formal design. By making elevation drawings like these, you can study the massing, proportions, and balance of your house.

If your property has much slope, you may need a retaining wall. Decide well in advance where you want grade changes and how these changes will affect your landscaping plans. With retaining walls, you can establish flat areas that help to solve erosion problems and provide enough area for landscape development.

Retaining walls are frequently necessary between the drive and lawn areas. Be sure to choose a construction material (see Chapters 4 and 5) that will blend well with the architecture of the house. Because of the dominance of the house, retaining walls should be refined in appearance and architecturally strong in design. The materials and design should not be so "naturalistic" that the walls present a jarring contrast to the design of the house. Informal walls are inappropriate in an area dominated by precise lines, forms, and masses.

If the slope from the house to the street is too steep for landscape development, you can use a series of low walls to create several terraces, thus eliminating the need for one high wall at the sidewalk or street. Be certain that there is a generous level area (at least 15 feet) immediately surrounding the house. If several walls are used, the width of the intervening terraces should be well proportioned to the height of the wall. Instead of dividing the area into equal amounts of terrace that compete for attention, you might design one terrace so that it is larger and more dominant than the others. This effect is more pleasing to the eye.

If your land slopes gradually, the natural slope often requires no modification. If some change is needed, however, the final grading should be planned to achieve a convex slope from the house to the street. The transition should not be abrupt at the point where the slope "feathers" into level areas or surfaces. If it appears that the convex slope will be abrupt, grade to a concave curve as the transition to the level area.

If your land slopes gradually or is almost flat, you may need only to grade a slope away from the house so that there will not be any standing water around the foundation. A minimum of 1 inch in 100 feet is necessary, and the preferred slope is 2 inches in 100 feet.

Basic construction for the public area usually includes a drive, parking space, walks, screens, and baffles. The color and texture of the material used in the public area must harmonize with the house. For example, a flagstone walk is not appropriate with a brick

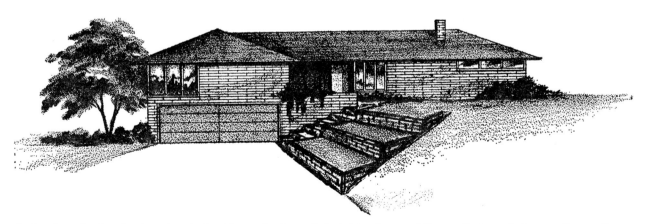

In the above drawing, the steep slope to the driveway has been eliminated by the use of three walls to create terraces. These walls are faced with brick to blend with the house. A drywall of natural stone (limestone, for example) would be inappropriate because the house has a brick facade. If the house had clapboard siding, a limestone drywall with a finished surface would be acceptable.

A small fence baffle may be used to create an interesting planting as viewed from a picture window facing the street, and may also serve to block the view into the house from the street. This fence baffle should be highly refined in detail, and should be constructed of the same material as the house or of a contrasting material that harmonizes in color, texture, and scale with the house.

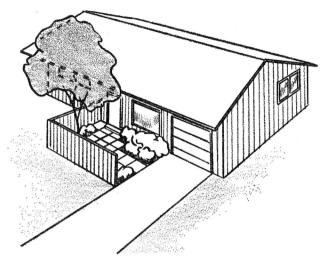

Structures in the public area can be used to create entry spaces, to block viewing into streetside picture windows, or to screen parking areas. These structures should be simple in design, subdued in color, and constructed of material that complements the architecture of the house. Check local regulations to be sure that structures are permitted in the public area in your community.

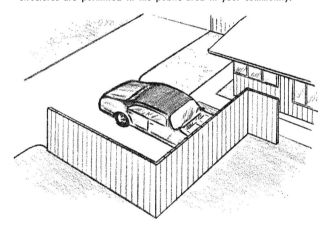

house. It is best to repeat home-building materials in landscape construction. If this is not possible, use materials that will blend and harmonize pleasantly with your house — the focal point of the landscape.

Walls, fences, or baffles in the public area are not generally used as a barrier along the edge of the property. Usually, you cannot justify building a fence along the side yard or across the front of the house. The best setting for a home consists of plantings across the front with an open lawn that is uninterrupted except by trees and necessary walks and drives.

In many communities, local ordinances prohibit the use of vertical structures in public areas. If vertical structures are permitted, their location, height, and possibly design are often controlled by zoning or subdivision ordinances. Be sure that you are familiar with the regulations in your community.

Vertical structures should be used only when they serve a functional role in developing the public space — for example, screening a parking area, creating an entry court, or providing privacy from the street. The design of vertical structures should be aesthetically pleasing but simple enough to avoid competing with the architectural detailing of the house. The color of the structures should be neutral — neither white nor any other color that demands attention.

Large picture windows often open onto the public area and directly to the street. By building a baffle, small wall, or fence that complements the design of the house, you can cut off the view from the street directly into the house and create an intimate garden that can be seen from within the house. Plantings on the street side will soften the harshness of this added structure.

Every landscape development needs walks and a drive. Since these circulation structures are useful rather than beautiful, they should be as inconspicuous as possible. To keep them from attracting attention (and to hold down costs at the same time) restrict their area to a minimum.

In designing a short drive, paths, and walks, remember that curves are usually superfluous design features that do not direct either a pedestrian or an automobile the shortest way to your home. Although an unnecessary curve is not artistically successful, a long drive may curve toward the house to form a dominant line that helps direct the eye to the house. A short driveway or walk should not curve except to go around an obstacle that cannot be removed, or when the planting around the house is so arranged that it seems natural for the walk or driveway to follow it.

Put walks where people naturally tend to go. You cannot justify curves in walks and drives except when the grade is too steep for people to walk in a straight line. In most urban homes, the driveway should handle both foot and car traffic. The walk to the front door from the drive then parallels the house. Keep the walk at least 6 feet from the house so that plants weighted down with rain will not hang over the sidewalk and prevent its use when most needed.

Often the spaces between the walk and the house are under the overhang of the roof, making it difficult to grow plants successfully in this area. An alternative to plants is a textured ground cover of cobbles or contrasting sizes of gravel combined in a pattern.

The width of the walk that leads to the front entrance must be in scale with the size of the house. A narrow ribbon of concrete leading to a large house presents a jarring visual contrast. The walk must be

Doorway plantings for a house with formal balance should carry out this balance. The plant used on one side of the doorway is repeated on the other.

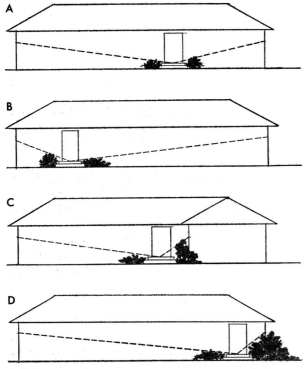

If your house has asymmetrical balance, do not use the same plant on either side of the doorway. To determine the approximate height of the planting for each side of the doorway, make an elevation drawing of your house. From a point at the corner one-half to two-thirds the distance from the ground to the eave, draw a line to the center of the door's threshold. The distance from the ground to this line, as measured 3 to 5 feet from each side of the door or porch, will give you the height that the plant should be to balance the asymmetrical design. (A) Although this house has almost true balance, it is slightly asymmetrical. For this reason, the plant on the right is slightly taller than the one on the left. (B) With this door location, the taller plant should be located to the left of the door and a low-spreading evergreen should be located to the right. (C) When the door is close to a projecting wing, measure the guide line from the corner of the wing closest to the door. (D) When the door is very close to the corner of the house, the doorway planting and corner planting should be combined.

wide enough to allow two people to walk side by side. Since each person needs 2 feet, the minimum width is 4 feet. A 5-foot walk is preferable because it is in better proportion with most houses.

You can add design interest to your entry walk by using an exposed aggregate surface, by introducing wood or contrasting materials as dividers, and by designing an attractive layout pattern. The typical parallel-edged, linear strip of pavement can be transformed into a strong ground pattern by using offset but overlapping units or by staggering the linear line.

Precast or cast-in-place slabs offer a wide variety of colors, textures, and patterns. Avoid a dizzying conglomeration of colors or patterns. Dark material with a textured surface is best from both a functional and aesthetic standpoint. Full sunlight reflects brilliant glaring light from light-colored, smooth surfaces, and a textured surface reduces this reflection.

Precast units may be hexagonal, circular, square, or rectangular. They can be combined in a number of linear walk patterns, including hexagonal, circular units in straight-edged forms, a regular square pattern, squares separated by bricks or concrete, and a random pattern of different sizes of the same shape. The units used for the main walk to the front door should be set in mortar. If the mortar is struck so that the finished level is slightly below the surface of the paving unit, the pattern formed by the units will show to better advantage.

One of the most satisfactory treatments is to have small stones exposed as an aggregate. A textured surface makes a pleasant pavement for pedestrians. Remember — the dominance of the straight lines in the building demands that you adhere to straight-line patterns. Avoid ragged edges. The units should produce a smooth edge regardless of the pattern.

If concrete is used, coloring it charcoal gray will reduce its glare and dominance. Green, red, and brown coloring should be avoided, since they have an artificial appearance, will fade under intense light, and do not blend well with the natural colors of plants and earth. You can obtain a rich charcoal-gray color by adding Carbojet (a liquid that mixes readily with cement and aggregates) to the concrete at the ready-mix plant. If a powdered coloring is used, be sure that it is mixed thoroughly enough to avoid a marble cake appearance. Order 8 pounds of Carbojet per sack of cement (94 pounds) for a very dark finish, 6 pounds for a medium-gray finish, and 4 pounds for a light-gray finish.

Do not pave secondary walks from the main entrance to the opposite side of the yard. Since secondary walks are used mostly by the family, stepping-stones

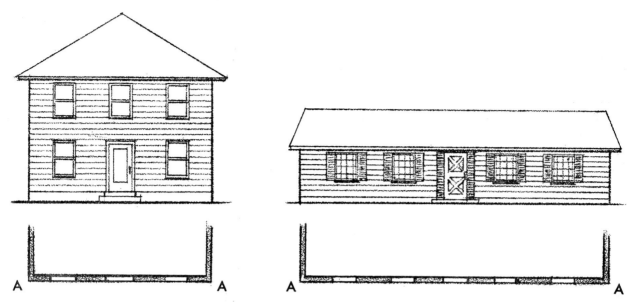

The primary objective in developing a foundation planting is to make the house look appropriate for the site on which it is placed by softening and blending the vertical house lines (A) with the strong, horizontal ground lines.

are generally satisfactory. Place the stones 24 to 28 inches on center for a natural step. If you want them spaced more exactly for your own pace, count your steps for 50 feet and divide 50 by the number of steps taken.

Over a period of four to five years, the grass builds up around the stepping-stones, trapping water and creating a series of "lakes." This problem can be solved by lifting each stone and adding sand to the original 2- to 3-inch pad to bring the stone level with the grass. The advantages of stepping-stones over a hard, solid line of pavement more than justify this occasional maintenance.

The urban home drive usually needs to serve only the family car or cars. The minimum width for one car is 9 feet, and 10 feet is preferable. Double these widths for two cars. If you also use the drive as a walk from the street, add 3 feet to the drive width. Always keep the drive straight and direct when the house setback is relatively short.

Many urban homes have attached garages or carports, but others have separate garages. You may want to provide a Y turnaround between the garage and street so that cars do not have to back into the street. A Y turnaround requires a turning radius of 18 feet between the garage and the turnaround apron. The inside edge of the apron should be 22 feet from the front of the garage. The width of the Y at its narrowest point does not need to be more than 8 feet. The radius of the short side of the Y should also be 18 feet. If properly designed and located, the Y turnaround can also be used for parking one car.

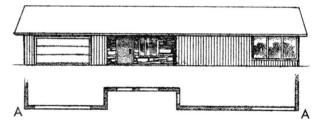

The center of interest and balance point for all plantings focuses on the center of the doorway. For this reason, the two major planting areas are the outside corners (A) and each side of the doorway. Vertical lines formed by projections along the facade should be softened by plantings, although these plantings should not be as tall as those at the outside corners of the house.

A rural drive must be designed so that is accommodates traffic going to the house, and allows continual movement of farm equipment between the road and the farm court. The drive should be at least 10 feet wide. This minimum width does not allow for the widest machinery that will occasionally move over the drive. It is important to leave the sides of the drive clear of all planting and fences or other objects for a minimum width of 15 feet.

Farm court and house traffic need to be separated. Daytime traffic to the house often gets in the way of business traffic. One solution to the problem is a circular drive. A circular drive should measure at least 70 feet across the widest part of the circle. Traffic going to the house then moves along the curve closest to the house, while farm court traffic follows the outer curve. To find out whether you have the necessary width and clearance, drive the largest vehicle that you will use around the area planned for a circular drive.

As an alternative, you might design a hammerhead or head-in area for parking at right angles to the drive. You will need at least 20 feet on the house side of the drive to park a car at right angles. Allow at least 10 feet for each car you wish to park. For example, an area 20 feet by 20 feet would handle two cars.

To solve the problem of getting people to use your front door, locate a hammerhead parking area at the front and to the side of the house. A car pulling into the parking area will then face the door you want people to use. If you have a straight walk from the parking area to the front door, your guests will use that door. If you have two doors at the front of your house,

you may have to put up signs indicating which door you want guests to use. To make this design work, the parking area must be well defined. Do not allow parking space near the rear or side entrance for vehicles other than the family car or cars.

For rural or large suburban properties, a circular or hammerhead drive should be located at the side of the house, not directly in front of the house itself. Your house is the most important part of the public-area design, and the best setting for it is a broad expanse of unbroken lawn. Roads, parking areas, or circular drives cutting up the front lawn divide the lawn into sections or panels of grass similar to the division caused by a front walk from the doorway to the street.

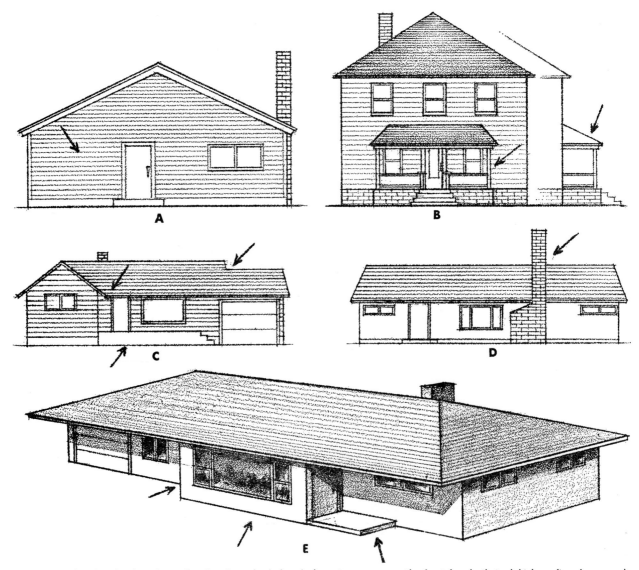

Study your elevation drawings for awkward and poorly designed elements or areas on the front facade that might be softened, screened, or balanced by plantings. (A) Poorly proportioned or large blank wall areas. (B) Large masses and dominant porches. (C) Disturbing angles, jogs, or changes in roof line (note the dominance of the porch across the front). (D) Disturbing contrasts of lines such as the strong vertical line of the fireplace chimney breaking up the dominant horizontal lines of the house. (E) Small jogs or recessed areas that have an "afterthought" or "tacked-on" appearance.

RELATING ARCHITECTURE TO PLANTINGS

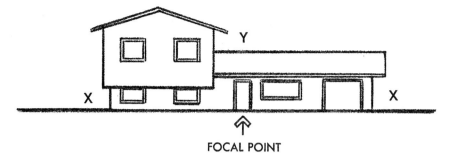

FOCAL POINT

Blending your house with the general surroundings involves creating a pleasing transition between the vertical lines of the house and the horizontal lines of the ground. In this elevation drawing of a house, the major vertical lines are at the outside corners (X). The (Y) corner is secondary and should not be given the same emphasis as the (X) corners. The front door should be the focal point.

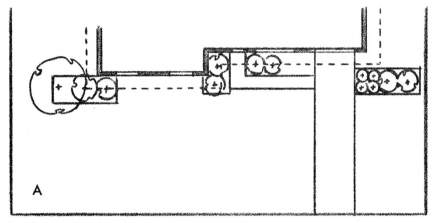

A

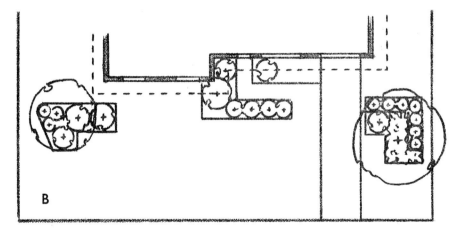

B

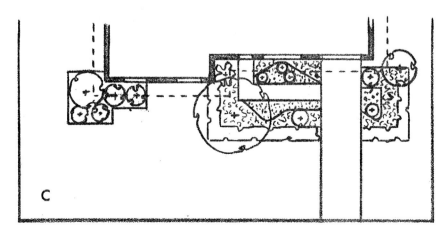

C

Planting designs shown in plan view for the house illustrated above: (A) The traditional "foundation" planting, with the material located directly adjacent to the house. (B) Plantings placed in the foreground eliminate the problem of overhangs, while continuing to lead the eye to the focal point (front door). (C) A combination of (A) and (B). The corner plantings are adjacent to the house, but the planting at the doorway projects from the house toward the street to create a subspace that can be developed as an entry garden or patio court.

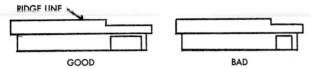

RIDGE LINE

GOOD   BAD

Changes in roof line may be good or bad, depending upon the proportion of the lower ridge line to the length of the house. As a rule, if the lower ridge line is less than one-third of the overall length of the house, you should use the crowns of trees to mask the change.

Lay walks and drives on a 4- to 6-inch gravel base that has been placed on well-compacted or undisturbed soil. You can keep stones out of the grass by placing a metal or wooden strip or some other kind of divider between a gravel drive and the lawn. A border strip also prevents weeds and grass from growing over the drive and helps prevent the edge of an asphalt drive from breaking away.

The various surfacing materials for walks and drives are discussed in Chapter 4. If you use gravel for your drive, select angular rock that will bind together for a firm surface. This binding quality results in minimal "throwing" of the aggregate.

Drainage is very important for a driveway or walk. Build drives and walks with a minimum drop of 1/10 inch every 10 feet. In addition to the longitudinal slope, you should also have a cross-slope. A 2-percent cross-slope (1/4 inch in 1 foot) is preferred, and a 1-percent cross-slope (1/8 inch in 1 foot) is the minimum. These slopes are for removing water that falls on the walk or drive surface. The surrounding ground should be graded so that surface water from adjacent areas does not also flow across the paved surface. This "sheeting" of water makes the surface unusable for pedestrians during heavy rains. In many communities, the sheeting of water across public walks is unlawful.

The organization and layout of the drives and walks must be for *functional convenience* — providing access to your property. For this reason, you should plan your drives and walks before planning the remainder of the public-area design. They should not become dominant elements that overpower the other elements in the public area. Once you have established a satisfactory drive-walk combination, the next step is developing the planting design for trees and shrubs.

Before you can choose specific plants and arrange them in front of your house, you need to analyze the architectural lines and masses of your house. Study window locations, cornice detailing, the doorway and porch arrangement, and any other architectural details or ornamentation. Ask yourself if all of these elements on the front facade are pleasing, tastefully de-

signed, and balanced into an attractive overall design. One element may seem awkward, poorly conceived, and ill-designed. If so, you can arrange plantings to soften, blend, or mask this element so that it doesn't dominate the total picture.

Study the balance of all the facade elements. Is the window arrangement on the left side of the door the same as that on the right side? Is the door exactly in the middle of the front facade? You may have true balance, with an identical repetition of windows and other elements on each side of the door; or you may have an informal or asymmetrically balanced arrangement. If your door is off-center and the other elements of the front are not balanced, you can use a planting composition to restore visual balance.

As a preliminary step to placing trees and shrubs in the public area, make an analysis of the lines, masses, and balance of your house. Draw a rough sketch to scale of the front of your house with windows, doors, and porches properly located. (You may use a black and white photograph if it shows the front facade — not the sidewalls — of the house.)

Indicate with colored pencils the dominant horizontal, vertical, and diagonal lines, shading in major architectural masses and defining main shadow patterns. These building features form the bases for developing your planting design. At this stage, you also need to establish the balance of the building. Draw an axis line or sawhorse at the center of the doorway, and imagine the house as a teeter-totter to balance at this point. From this sketch, you can see where you will need plantings to achieve better balance. If the front door of your house does not face the street because of its location on a projecting wing at right angles to the street, use the center of the front foundation lines as the balancing point on the sawhorse.

Exterior construction materials are also important in helping set the scale of the plant textures and construction materials to be used. Extremes in textures are seldom satisfactory. Do not place fine textures next to coarse textures. For example, heavy siding calls for coarse-textured plant materials. Any other construction in the public area would have to be identical with the siding or in scale and harmony with it.

You should consider views to the outside from rooms that overlook the public area, as well as views into these rooms from the street or houses on the opposite side. The fact that passersby or neighbors across the street can look into your house can make you uncomfortable. Remember this fact when considering window size and location with respect to the elevation of the public walk, street, and the houses

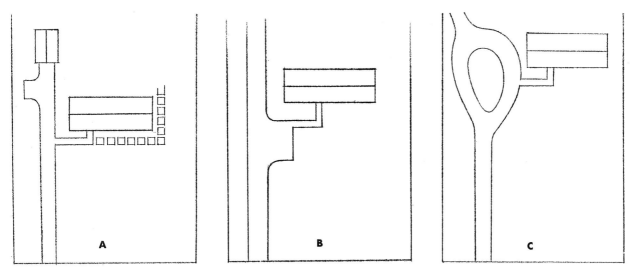

A broad, clear expanse of lawn is the best setting for your public-area design. Walks and drives cut into your lawn, dividing it into small sections. By using the driveway as both a walk and a drive, you eliminate one of these divisions and keep an uninterrupted foreground. Any secondary walks should be stepping-stones to avoid additional hard lines of concrete. (A) The garage is located to the rear of the lot with a Y turnaround. This arrangement eliminates backing a long distance to the street and into traffic. (B) The hammerhead parking areas require a depth of 20 feet beyond the edge of the drive. When located on the house side of the drive, as shown in (B), the parking area should not overlap the front facade more than several feet. (C) The circle drive requires more space than the hammerhead parking area. You can quickly determine if you have adequate space by driving over the area with the largest truck or car that will be driven regularly around the circle. The circle drive should be at the side of the house. Do not locate it across the front of the house.

across the street. In many subdivisions with curved street patterns, the angled positions of the houses located diagonally from your house sometimes establish lines of sight not ordinarily considered. These curved street patterns can also cause lights from passing cars to sweep across the house and into windows.

Note on a pad of paper the views that you see; then decide whether these views are acceptable. Outstanding views should be dramatized, while unsightly views from or into your house need to be screened out. Note on your plan where plantings might frame a good view or screen a bad one, or where construction or plantings might be needed for privacy.

Since trees establish the basic framework of the public-area planting design, you should determine their placement before developing the shrub planting. Remember that trees can perform many functions in addition to providing shade. As you study their location, form, and size, consider how each tree can frame the house, repeat dominant lines or forms in the architecture, and soften, mask, or hide awkward or ill-conceived architectural units.

The house should be framed with trees. Before you place trees, decide from which point or points you want your home to look its best. Since most people view your house at an angle of 30 to 45 degrees as they walk or drive past, your framing should be based on this angle of vision rather than on viewing the

house "head on" from across the street. You should establish this point or these points of viewing either at the edge of your property or some distance beyond the property line.

Since it is difficult to frame the house effectively from all directions, you may need to establish the framing from only one side of your property. In this case, the framing should correspond with the most common approach to your home. Locate the trees for the framing effect upon the side that you and most other people use to reach the site.

To determine the location of the trees that you will use for framing, stand at the primary point of viewing and visualize where trees should be placed so that they will form a graceful frame for your house in later years. The closer the trees are to the viewer or to this primary point of viewing, the smaller they can be in size; but small trees located some distance from the viewer will not frame the house as effectively as larger trees.

Frame your house to concentrate interest *on the house*. As a general rule, the scale of the house should dictate the scale of the trees to be used. For example, a large house needs a large frame. For a small house, it is better to use large shade trees in the outdoor living area to serve as a background from the street. Use small to medium trees in the public area unless a large tree is required to give adequate shade.

Tall two-story houses can be made to look lower and wider by extending the corner plantings beyond the house and angled toward the street. The planting at the corner is one-half to two-thirds the distance from the ground to the second story. The remainder of the material gradually increases in height as it extends from the corner, terminating in a small tree. This arrangement serves to "funnel" the eye toward the front door and reduces the effect of extreme height created by the house. If a drive is located close to the house, the wing planting can be started on the other side. The viewer's eye will carry the line across the drive.

You should not remove trees on your property simply because they do not fit these proportions. If there are no trees on your property, base your selection of new trees upon the scale relations between the trees and the house.

A one-story house requires small trees; a two-story house requires large ones. Placing small trees against a large house emphasizes the size of the house, and results in a poor scale relationship between the trees and the house. You can use a clump of small trees on one side of the house and a large tree on the other side for asymmetrical balance.

Repeat dominant lines in the house as often as possible in planting arrangements and structures. Don't choose a tree simply because you happen to like it. Horizontal lines call for trees with horizontal branching habits. Houses with dominant pyramidal forms in roof line, dormers, etc., require pyramidal tree forms. Study tree lists in reference books and at the end of this book, and note which trees are suitable for both lawn or street trees and which are suitable *only* as lawn or shade trees.

To use trees effectively for masking poorly designed elements or to soften architectural lines, consider again the line and mass analysis described earlier in this chapter. The crown of the tree is most important in this situation. The architectural zones you can modify most effectively with trees are between the roof-eave line and roof-ridge line on a two-story house. Within this zone, the crown of the tree can be used to mask disturbing angles, jogs, or changes in roof line, as well as to soften disturbing contrasts of lines. For example, a strong vertical line or mass in opposition to dominant horizontal lines can be effectively modified.

Sometimes it is difficult to judge if the change in roof-line direction over a projecting wing is good or bad. The same problem occurs when the ridge line is dropped in height over the garage area. A rule of thumb that should help you is based upon the proportion of the changes with respect to the overall mass of the house. Generally, if the change in roof line or drop in ridge line occupies close to one-third of the total linear distance of the front facade, it can be considered in good proportion to the remainder of the house. If the area is less than one-third, you should consider using trees to alleviate the problem.

Compare the proposed tree locations for framing the house to see if the crown of the tree you have chosen will hide poorly designed architectural elements in the upper portion of the building. If the first location is unsatisfactory, shift the tree until you achieve the framing effect at the same time that you mask these architectural elements.

Plantings in the public area are not difficult to design once you understand that they must be designed upon the masses and lines of the building. These two elements — the building and the planting — should result in a single pattern. Remember — the house is the most important element in the public area, and the focal point of your design is the front door. The corners and doorways are the two major areas of concern, regardless of your planting style — traditional "foundation" plants, freestanding compositions in the foreground, or a combination of the two. The extensiveness of these compositions depends upon the lines, masses, shadow patterns, and balance in the house design. The greater the extent to which you can express these architectural features in your planting composition, the greater the harmony of your public-area design.

It is now necessary to return to your architectural analysis for a review of the location and dominance of

When space between the side property line and the house is limited, a modified wing planting can be achieved. Plant the lowest plant on the front facade near the corner, and build up the height of the plants in the direction of the arrows.

vertical, horizontal, and diagonal lines. Draw these principal lines on a sheet of tracing paper placed over the rough sketch of your house. Do not include any other part of the architecture. Next, with a pencil of a different color, lightly shade in the dominant masses. For example, a bilevel home has a long, horizontal mass in its one-floor portion, and a blocky to square mass in its two-floor portion. Your planting design should repeat each of these architectural masses at the end of the house opposite to the end where the mass occurs. This reversal of location gives a pleasing counterplay of mass in building to mass in plants.

If the lines (horizontal, vertical, diagonal) are prominent and the masses are subordinate, these combinations of lines and masses should dictate the silhouette outline of the total planting. The lines should not be repeated as individual plants — they should be reflected in the mass. The shadow patterns are related to line, and are reflected in the planting composition in the same way.

You should now indicate your planting masses with abstract blocks as described in Chapter 8. Do not be concerned at this point with the plant form or what plant will be used. Block out the planting group based upon your study of architectural masses or dominant lines and evaluate these proposed groupings in terms of the balance. Your earlier analysis has given you an indication of which side appears heavy and

which appears light. You must now adjust your abstract blocks of plantings to reestablish balance. This is *visual balance* — in other words, it is how the house appears that is important.

Finally, because the building is the most central and dominant element in the design, you must study its architectural detailing. The most important features are the windows and the front door connecting it to the landscape. Their size, arrangement, and location must be carefully evaluated. If the windows, for example, are of equal size and evenly spaced across the facade, they will have a pleasing, rhythmic appearance that should be reflected in the planting. If the windows are of different sizes and are located at random over the facade, the planting should be strong in line and pattern yet simple in composition to divert attention from them.

Other architectural details such as shutters, wrought-iron railings and roof supports, changes in building materials, two-color combinations, etc. give a "busy" appearance. When these are present, the planting must be simple and neutral in color and form to avoid adding to the visual confusion.

Ordinarily, plants at or near corners should be larger than those on either side of the entrance. Plants at the doorway should not be higher than one-fourth to one-third the distance from the groundline to the eave. If you stay within these proportions, you won't be faced later with a "peek-a-boo" situation in which your house is nearly hidden behind a mass of plantings.

Mature corner plantings should not be higher than two-thirds the distance from the groundline to the eave. The taller plants at or near the corners and the lower plants at the doorway form a concave line that directs the eye to the doorway. These same proportions apply to freestanding plantings in the foreground area of the house.

Instead of the concave line formed by the tops of plants from corner to doorway to corner, you can introduce a taller plant at the doorway. The taller plant will not result in a "roller-coaster" effect if the outside corner plantings are modified in height. This is another way you can satisfy the requirements for blending the house to the site at the corners, and still focus attention to the doorway without disruptive eye movement across the front of the house.

Another technique that strengthens the planting design is based upon the arrangement of the plants in the composition. You work with the principle that the eye follows the outline of any form or mass. By arranging your freestanding group so that the plants grade down in size from the largest material, you provide a definite direction of movement for the viewer's eyes.

This gradation in height should always be in the direction of the front door if the group is located beyond the sides of the house. For example, a house with corner wraparound windows should not be covered, since the corner plantings will be lower than the windows. A small flowering shrub or tree combined with lower shrubs of graded height could be planted toward the property line (away from the corner windows) to give the desired blending effect without blocking the view. The planting is effective because it continues to direct attention to the front door.

Do not use conical or pyramidal evergreens for a public-area planting. The only exceptions are a house with high-peaked gables, narrow windows or dormers, a formal facade arrangement, or natural surroundings that include pointed evergreens and sharp mountain tops. You cannot tie a house to the ground and soften its strong vertical lines with upright, pointed evergreens that emphasize these lines. If you have upright evergreens at the corners, you can soften this vertical effect by placing low-spreading plants around the evergreens, although this kind of planting requires considerable space.

You can make a house look lower and wider by extending the foundation planting to add plant "wings" to the building. This is one example of a combination planting, since it begins with the corner plant and arcs into the foreground. Wing plantings serve to "funnel" the view from the street toward the house and center it on the front door. The wing planting is particularly useful for two-story houses. It can also separate the public from the private living area.

It is not usually a good idea to plant under extremely low windows. If the soil is exposed, however, mud will splatter onto the windows, and you may need to use either plants or gravel ground cover. Of course, if the foundation wall shows 3 feet of unattractive concrete or block, you can conceal it with plantings across the front. Do not place plants so that they will grow up to cover the windows. It is unnecessary to frame a large picture window with an upright evergreen on each side. A picture window already has all the framing it needs for good design. Framing it with plants is comparable to putting two frames around a picture.

In selecting plants, you must consider their mature spread. Usually, the spread of an upright deciduous plant is about two-thirds of the height of the plant or equal to the height. Spreading evergreens are an exception to this rule. Check garden reference books or catalogs and the list of plant materials at the end of this book for the spread of evergreens.

To be sure that plants will fit into the space provided, show their final spread by circles on your plan. Plotting the mature spread of plants prevents overcrowding as the plants grow. The spacing from the center of one plant to the center of another should equal one-half the spread of each plant.

You can drive down nearly any street and see

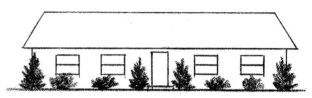

FIFTH YEAR

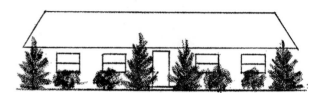

TENTH YEAR

FIFTEENTH YEAR

Know the mature height and spread of the plants you use. The "peek-a-boo" house (fifteenth year) shows the result of lack of information and planning.

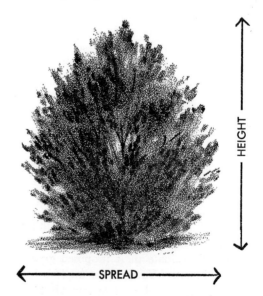

HEIGHT

SPREAD

homes lost in a forest of overplanting. The desire for a completed look immediately after planting is understandable, but you must have the patience to wait two or three years for a balanced and organized appearance that will last for many years. Most modern homes are attractive in themselves, and need only a few plants at the front foundation. This landscaping approach not only lowers landscaping costs but results in a more attractive composition.

You can combine deciduous and low evergreen plants for a highly interesting composition. Deciduous plants usually grow faster than evergreens, and offer interest throughout the year: flowers in spring, full foliage in summer, attractive fruit in late summer and early fall, fall coloring, and finally, after the leaves have fallen, twig patterns and shadows cast on wall areas. The addition of spreading evergreens with their permanent green foliage makes a pleasing combination. You might also consider using all evergreens or all deciduous plants. The deciduous shrubs you select should be the rounded or horizontally branched types.

If your house has a wide overhang, plant the materials at least 1 foot beyond the drip line so that they will get some natural rainfall. Plantings set under the eaves need regular artificial waterings to survive. If there is a walk in front of the planting, allow 6 to 12 inches in addition to one-half the total spread distance so that the plants will not overhang when laden with water or snow.

Shrub plantings should not be placed in the lawn. They should always be in a cultivated bed for ease of maintenance and to reduce damage to the plants from mowing. The bed outline and pattern become important components of the planting design. Bed patterns can be developed from curved, straight, or arc-and-tangent lines.

The *curved line* is the most difficult to deal with because of the prominence of straight lines and right angles that are expressed in the architecture, property lines, streets, and walks. Flowing curves imposed against the house often look incongruous and contrived. To be successful, curves must be bold and strong, with considerable space for reverse curves to provide transition from one direction to another, and from curved forms into straight lines. Never use small, wiggly lines that are constantly changing direction. They are distracting and "busy" in appearance. Although curves are the lines most commonly used in public-area design, they are usually the weakest part of the design.

When the foundation is not exposed, it is not necessary to have a solid planting across the front of the house. A possible planting design (above) is to have an area of ground cover (A) under a large window to tie the corner and entrance plantings together. (B) is a panel of grass or ground cover extending to the house. Breaking up the planting in this way avoids the dwarfing effect of solid planting. Be careful not to have (B) out of scale with the house. It should be approximately one-third the length of the house. Plantings for a house with an exposed foundation should be designed to mask the area (below). Low materials that are equal to the height of the foundation wall can be used effectively with other plants of different heights to provide contrast. The plantings on either side of the door reflect the architectural masses (A) and (B). Notice that changes in plant selection are related to the architectural features of the building facade. For example, the plants under the bedroom windows at right are taller than the plants extending from the doorway to the windows.

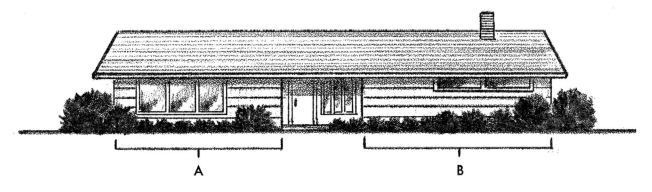

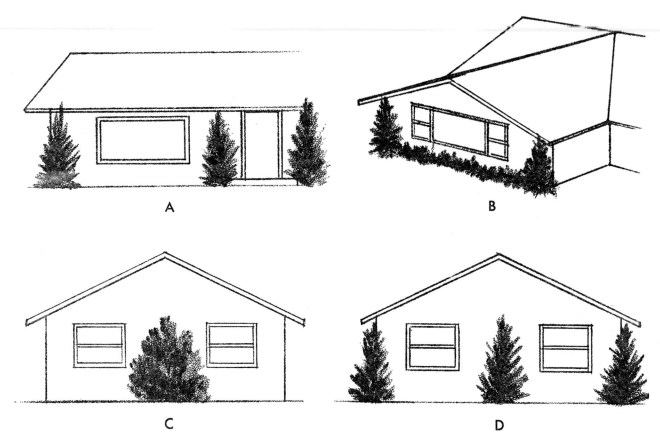

A

B

C

D

(A) *Do not* use conical and pyramidal evergreens at corners and doorways or to frame windows. These areas are already framed architecturally. Conical and pyramidal evergreens emphasize vertical lines and do not provide a transition to the groundline. They also disrupt the scale relationship between the house and other plantings by growing too tall. (B) *Do not* plant the projection of an L- or U-shaped house as a separate facade from the balance of the house. Elevation drawings are helpful in visualizing that the face of any projecting wing must be considered as being in the same plane as the other face areas of the house. (C) *Do not* plant shrubs against every blank wall area, such as between windows at the side of the house. This type of planting tends to dwarf the house, as well as to hide it. (D) *Do not* plant upright evergreens or other plantings that divide an area into smaller parts. These plantings make the house appear tall and narrow.

Straight-line bed patterns are desirable because they repeat the architectural lines of the house. In most cases, these patterns have greater visual interest than curved lines. Additional interest in lines and movement — even curved movement — can be achieved by the manner in which the plants are arranged in the bed.

Arc-and-tangent is an effective combination for planting-bed patterns. It is a pleasant compromise between a design composed of all curves and one composed of completely straight lines. As the name indicates, the curved portion is restrained to the form of an arc that provides for a transition between varying directions of straight lines (tangents). The pattern-development techniques described in Chapter 11 will help you to establish an interesting bed pattern.

You should consider starting or terminating plant-

ing beds at architectural features in the house, especially if the planting is the next-to-the-building "foundation" type. But these guidelines also apply to freestanding groups and combination plantings. All beds should begin or end at architectural features in the house — the edge of a window, a jog in the facade, etc.

Begin or end a bed along a blank wall at a point one-third or two-thirds the distance across the wall. Carefully planning these small details can make the difference between a harmonious and unified design and one that is disjointed, scattered, and haphazard.

Entry gardens and patio-courts can also be used to create delightful entry spaces to your home. As used here, the term "entry garden" means a composition made up entirely of plants, and "courtyard" means a walled open space that may result from the architectural design of the house. Few houses are designed with a totally walled court, but a patio-court can be created through a combination of an entry garden and a court, even though the enclosing element may be no more than a low hedge.

The entry area can be an exciting and highly satisfying landscape feature that is much more elaborate than placing two different plants on either side of the doorway. The patio-court results in space that enhances the view from inside the house and provides a pleasant transition between the street, drive, and the front door of the house.

Even though your house may resemble other houses in a subdivision because of similar facade design, an imaginatively designed entry can add individuality to your home that will distinguish it from the other houses in the neighborhood. The entry garden or court is a worthwhile landscape treatment for any home except some of those with front porches.

The entry garden depends upon permanent plantings for its basic structure, but it may be supplemented with container plantings for seasonal color. A low, raised planting bed for a specimen plant or a small group planting might be used to define the entry space. Make the raised bed no more than 3 bricks high so that the planting is actually in the ground. In this way, you can avoid freezing and thawing damage to plants.

Or you may want to emphasize the ground plane of the entry area. You can develop a strong ground pattern by carefully planning the pavement and planting areas so that they become strong, interlocking design elements. This ground pattern can be further reinforced through surface patterns, textures, and dividers in the pavement, and through plant selection

Trees for framing may also be used to screen, soften, or break disturbing angles, jogs, changes in construction and lines, small projections, etc.

and arrangement and the pattern forms of ground-cover or gravel-cover areas.

The entry garden is not intended to be an over-elaboration of the traditional doorway planting described earlier in which two plants are located parallel to the house and on either side of the door. The distinctive quality of the entry garden is gained by projecting the plantings into the foreground area so that they give a greater definition and form to the entrance area.

The plants you choose must not result in an over-growth that blocks windows or hides the architecture. Select plants on the basis of the available space. Their mature height and spread should be accommodated in the proposed location without requiring excessive pruning to keep them in scale. Be careful not to overplant.

Since you are trying to develop an entry garden with strong visual appeal, the plants used may include small trees or large shrubs with treelike habits of growth counterbalanced with low, rounded (mounding) or spreading forms of shrubs. Lower plants of varying heights may be used where texture and pos-

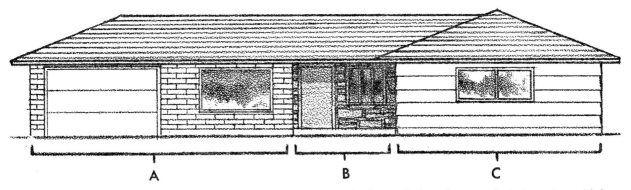

Do *not* combine different materials. The differences in texture, color, and scale often results in unpleasant contrasts. Proportion and balance are lost when one material overpowers another. In the drawing above, (A) is brick, (B) is crab orchard stone, and (C) is board siding. (A) and (B) overpower (C) and dominate the entire facade. If areas (A) and (B) were either all brick or all stone, the result would be the same. If (A) and (C) were siding, and (B) were either stone or brick, there would be proper proportion and balance. Brick and stone should never be used together. They are out of scale with each other and give a poor contrast.

Roof lines forming strong, pointed shapes, such as gables, should be repeated in the plant form whenever possible. For example, the small-leafed linden tree in the drawing above repeats the form and line of the roof. In the drawing below, the gable shapes are repeated through the use of pyramidal evergeens.

sibly color will play a more dominant role. If the available space is small, you should probably not use more than three different kinds of plants. The intervening ground space between the major plantings would then be covered with ground cover or gravel or a combination of the two.

The patio-court design involves developing space by the entryway and next to the house that is shielded either partially or totally from public view. Total shielding may result from the walls of the house; partial shielding can be created by using a low (30- to 42-inch) hedge or wall or structural screens of greater height. Partial shielding will be discussed here.

Like the entry garden, the patio-court projects from the house. Unlike the entry garden, however, the total area to be developed is rigidly outlined by a low shielding element. Within this architecturally defined area, the development of the entry patio-court depends upon the strong use of architectural materials, natural plant forms, and ground patterns. The success of your design depends upon an effective interplay of all three of these elements.

Architectural materials include surfacing structures (patio, walk), enclosure elements (low wall, trimmed hedge), containers and raised beds, and possibly a water feature or sculptural element. Any architectural unit incorporated in this space should have strong, bold design to contrast with the natural character of plant forms, textures, and colors. The hedge is not considered a natural plant form, since it is sheared into an architectural shape.

The same considerations for selecting plants discussed in the entry garden apply here. The major difference is that the plants do not have to be arranged to form the framework of the area, since this framework is achieved by the rigid outline of the patio-court. The ground pattern, which should complement the design, results from the manner in which the architectural and plant materials are combined.

The entry patio-court is a near-view landscape composition. In other words, all elements are viewed at close range — each is seen in detail as to its form, texture, and color. The patio-court is more impressive when all the elements are skillfully combined so that each element strengthens and reinforces the others either through similarity or contrast. No one element (architectural, plant, or ground pattern) should be so dominant that the other two appear as mere frills or ornamentation. All three elements must be integrated so that there is a balanced interplay between them for a high degree of visual interest without any one element "shouting" for attention.

The size of the entry court can vary according to the available space. An entry court can be easily developed if the house is L-shaped or has a recessed entry, but it is also suitable for houses with a straight, uninterrupted facade.

If your community ordinances and subdivision codes permit structures to the front of the house, you may want to use decorative panels or screens as a part of the entry patio-court. They can provide privacy from the street, add interest to a simply designed house, emphasize the entry location, and provide a backdrop for plants that enhances the views from within the house. These screens or panels may be solid or open. They may be constructed of wood, of wood

Plantings that are adjacent to the house should begin or stop at architectural features (windows, jogs, etc.), as shown by the arrows in the above drawing. On wall surfaces without any architectural features (below), the planting should begin or end at a point that is either one-third or two-thirds of the distance across the wall.

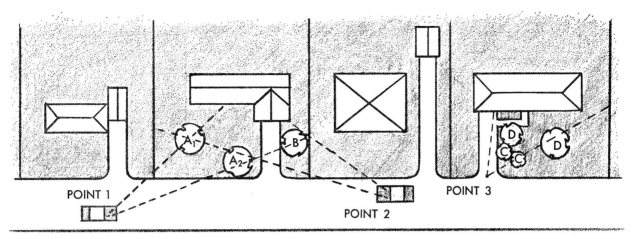

To locate trees for framing, you must first determine the point from which most people will view your house. The house and its immediate foreground are usually all that can be seen when approaching your property along the street. You may establish the primary viewing point from a position well to either side of your property line (points 1 and 2) or at the intersection of your drive and the street (point 3). The tree symbols represent possible locations for framing from the various points. *Point 1*: the major path of approach to the house is from left to right, requiring trees to be located at A_1 and A_2. *Point 2*: the flow of traffic is from right to left, and trees A_1 and B can be used for framing. *Point 3*: the intersection of the drive and the street. The scope of vision from this point is 60 degrees. Trees placed at locations (C) can be small trees because they are close to the viewer. Trees at locations (D) must be larger than the (C) trees because of their greater distance from the viewer. Points 1 and 2 allow greater flexibility in placing the framing trees than point 3.

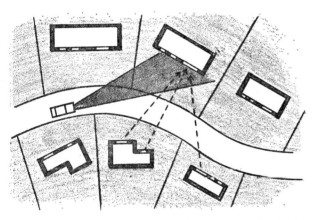

In determining the location and extensiveness of plantings in the public area, consider the views both from and into your house. This is particularly important if the living areas are in the front of the house. You should also study traffic movement for headlight sweeps, especially if your site is on a curved street or if your house is on a corner lot.

combined with smooth sheets of plastic, or of bamboo, expanded metal, plywood, and translucent glass.

If you decide to include an entry garden or patio-court in your public-area design, you must modify the balance of the plantings. You should still consider using corner plantings to soften the architectural lines of the house and to provide a pleasing transition with the groundline, but these plantings must not be competitive with the entry design. Study the mass, line, and balance of the architecture to determine whether the plantings should be next to or away from the

house. You must also decide whether the plantings should be tall, or whether lower groupings would be satisfactory.

Another principle of good public-area design is an open lawn. This principle may be the most unpopular one. Front lawns cluttered with circular and diamond-shaped flower beds, gazing balls, bird baths, petunia patches, unnecessary lattices, pergolas, and specimen shrubs or perennial flowers are a hangover from the Victorian era. If you really want to use these objects, locate them in the living or service areas, not in the public area.

The best setting that you can give your home is a broad expanse of open lawn from street to house, with foundation plantings and framing trees broken only by needed drives and walks. The more compact the drives and walks and the less cut up the lawn, the more pleasing the total picture will be.

Vines may be useful in the public area if your house is too tall for its width. A vine can make a conspicuous horizontal line across part or all of the front of a building to keep the observer's eye from running in an unbroken line to the top of an awkward house. When planting space is limited by the closeness of the sidewalk, vines can also be used to relieve the harshness of the house.

Never use a window box in the public area if the house is attractive without it. Window boxes can be used, however, to disguise badly proportioned architectural features. For example, window boxes can prevent the viewer's eyes from wandering all the way

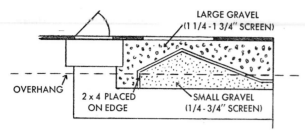

LARGE GRAVEL
(1 1/4 - 1 3/4" SCREEN)

OVERHANG

2 x 4 PLACED
ON EDGE

SMALL GRAVEL
(1/4 - 3/4" SCREEN)

Ground areas under the eaves of the house can be designed so that they are attractive but require little maintenance. Redwood or treated 2 x 4 lumber placed on edge forms a strong ground pattern that "breaks up" a large rectangular area into two pleasing units. In the above drawing, more space is allotted to the smaller gravel because it is not as dominant as the larger, coarser gravel. As a result, a proper proportional balance is achieved between the two areas.

up the vertical lines of a tall building front. They may also improve window proportions by extending beyond the sides of windows that are too tall or too small. Horizontal lines are much more pleasing than vertical lines because the viewer's eyes and head move naturally in a horizontal plane.

Flowers also do not belong in the public area. Many people insist on planting them there because they love flowers. One way to have flowers in the public area and still not have them dominate the house is to put them behind "wing" plantings so that they can be seen from the house but not from the street. Or you can plant flowering bulbs between shrubs in the public area if you place them carefully so as not to create a vivid splash of color. Don't plant bulbs in rows like little soldiers. Throw them on the ground and plant them where they land. Splashes of color in the public area detract from the house.

Special landscape lighting is an important part of the public-area design. In general, lighting in this area is used to illuminate walks, paths, or drives, or to highlight landscape plants for their pictorial effect.

The most common need for lighting is to help people see their way from the street to the house. This lighting often consists of only one light midway between the street and the house. Many people mount this light at eye level. Instead of showing the way, the light temporarily blinds pedestrians and is more hazardous than no light at all. To be effective, the light for walks needs to be either well above or (preferably) well below eye level. If the light is above eye level, it is usually attached to or under the eave line of the house. Be sure that the light source does not create an objectionable glare, and that it is not aimed at the neighbors.

You must also consider the shadows cast by lights. Floodlights placed close to the ground create distorted shadow patterns of people walking. These shadow patterns have caused accidents. Floodlights are best used on drive areas.

Low lighting with the bulbs concealed and the light directed downward is the most effective for walkways and garden paths. Several types of fixtures are available for this use. The most practicable is the mushroom light with a half-dome shade that shields the bulb and directs the light downward.

The spacing of downlighting fixtures should usually be about 14 to 16 feet, although closer spacing is desirable in extremely dark areas. If you are uncertain about the spacing, try several different locations before installing the fixtures permanently.

Avoid the ornate fixtures that resemble owls, frogs, flowers, lanterns, etc. They are usually poorly designed and distract from the landscape. Select fixtures with a simple, straightforward design that will blend handsomely with the rest of your composition. If you use post lights, be sure that they are well above eye level — the minimum height is 6 feet.

The amount and intensity of light needed varies

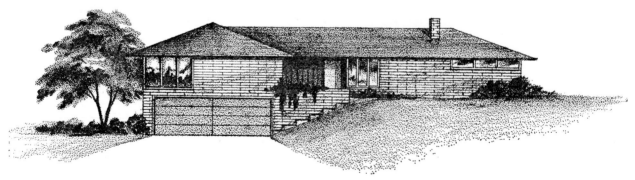

Select corner plantings for a split-level house according to the rule of thumb for height of shrubs at corners. In other words, keep the scale of the plants proportional to the scale of the building. Plants should be taller on the higher corner, with the facer shrubs extending beyond the end of the house. The lower corner would be as shown in preceding drawings.

The window boxes on the side of the house shown above keep the viewer's eye from moving up the full height of the house.

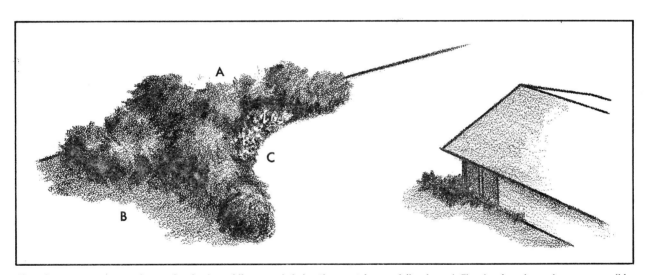

Since flowers attract so much attention in the public area, their location must be carefully planned. The drawing above shows one possible location of a flower border. The planting has been extended along the side property line (A); then curved toward the center of the lot (B) to form a bay for flowers (C). The flowers can be seen from the house, but are screened from the street so that they do not compete with the house for attention.

according to the area to be lighted. For example, steps need more light than walks, and walks need more than drives. Since a dark paved surface absorbs light, it requires more light than light-colored paving. Pre-testing various lighting patterns will help you to determine your requirements.

If you have developed an entry garden or patio court, you have selected high-interest plants that can be effectively underlighted or silhouetted by special lighting techniques. (These techniques are described in detail in Chapter 11.) If you illuminate plants and objects at the entryway, walk lighting may not be necessary because of the "overwash" of light from your pictorial lighting.

Water features and sculpture are optional elements that must be well integrated with the design to provide an appropriate setting and backdrop. For this reason, they are most suitable in the entry patio-court.

ENTRY WALKS

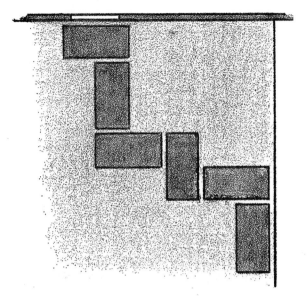

The approach to the front door does not have to be a linear strip of concrete. Large concrete pads placed at right angles provide an attractive approach and create an interesting pattern between the house and the drive that lends itself to an entry planting.

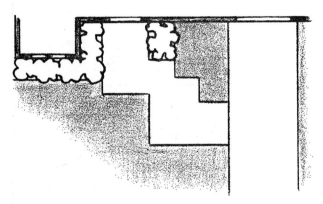

The common straight-lined walk can be transformed into a handsome paving pattern by using offset, staggered, or overlapping units or masses in designing the entry approach.

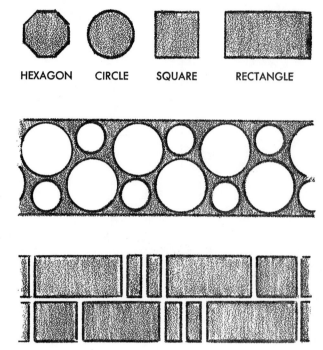

HEXAGON   CIRCLE   SQUARE   RECTANGLE

Precast units are available in a number of different patterns. Individual units of the same pattern may be combined into attractive paved areas. If you prefer a design with greater visual interest, you can combine several different sizes of the same pattern. Avoid making the design too "busy" in appearance.

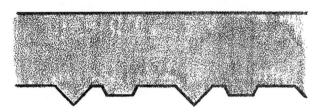

All paving should have smooth, linear edges. Irregular edges are "fussy looking," and it is difficult to keep turf from growing adjacent to the edges.

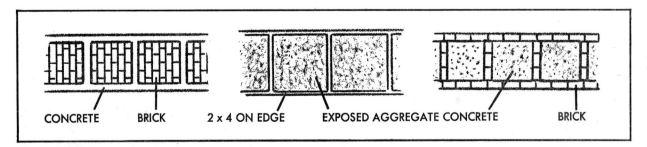

CONCRETE   BRICK   2 x 4 ON EDGE   EXPOSED AGGREGATE CONCRETE   BRICK

Using wood, concrete, or brick to form dividers or modular units (squares) adds interest to the design, introduces human scale by reducing the mass and area, and provides a textured surface that distinguishes the paved area from the area intended for automobiles.

BED PATTERNS

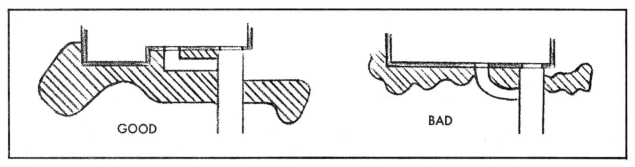

Bed patterns should be simple. Too many curves are distracting or "busy." If you use curves, be sure that they are bold and strong enough to serve as a pleasing contrast to the straight lines of the building.

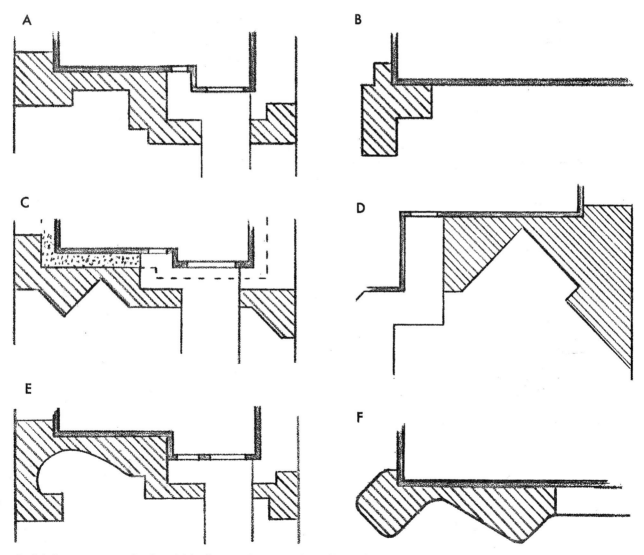

Straight-line patterns are visually satisfying because they repeat the architectural lines of the house. Notice that a strong pattern is achieved by changing direction and varying the size of the areas defined (A) and (B). The lines can be parallel to or at an angle of 45 degrees from the walls of the house (C) and (D). A straight, continuous line would be monotonous. Arc-and-tangent (E) and (F) combines straight and curved lines that are harmonious with the architectural lines of the house. The curved portion (the arc) can be either bold and strong or restrained — serving merely as a transition between straight lines running in different directions.

ELEVATION DRAWINGS TO STUDY HOUSE FEATURES

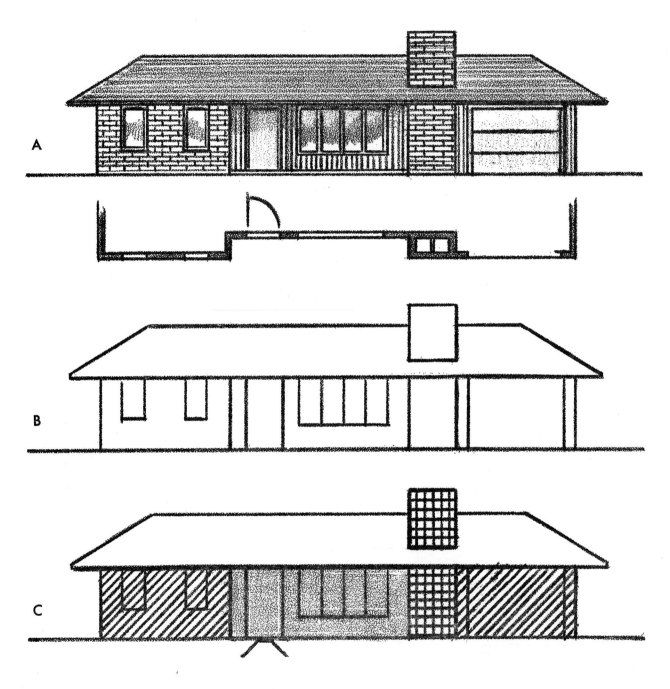

The elevation drawing of the house shown above (A) indicates a recessed area and a projection of the fireplace. The sketch of your house would simply be a line drawing (B), with no attempt to depict construction materials or garage-door detailing. Use colored pencils to show the line, mass, and balance of the house (C). The heavy, dark lines indicate dominant architectural features. The shaded middle area is recessed, with a change of construction material. The checkerboard pattern emphasizes the dominance of the vertical mass of the fireplace. A fulcrum placed at the middle of the door indicates that the balance is heavy on the right side. Since the house facade is broken into four units, the planting design should be a strong, horizontal line. For example, a hedge from the doorway area to the garage would serve to carry the eye across the disruptive units of varying planes and materials. A heavier corner planting mass is needed on the left to balance the heaviness of the house on the right side of the door. A small tree could be placed to break up the prominent line of the fireplace chimney.

ELEVATION DRAWINGS TO DEVELOP PLANTING DESIGN

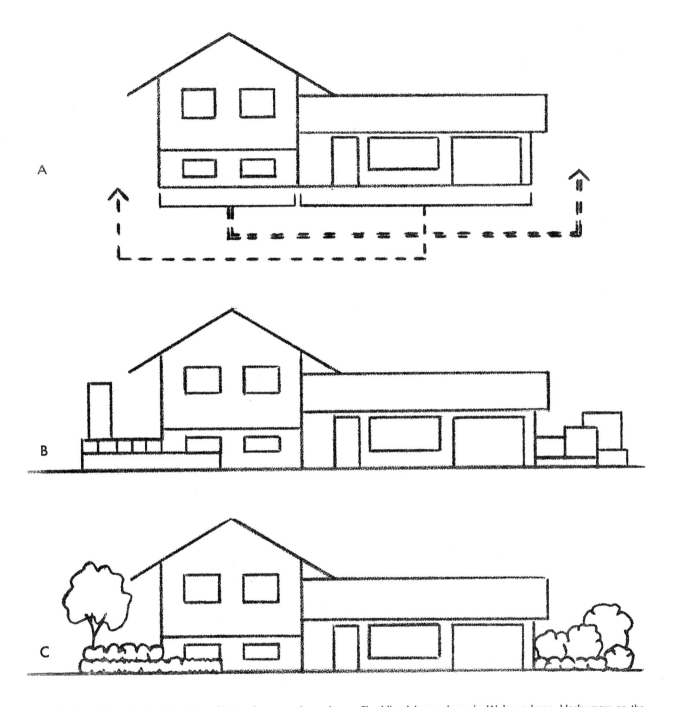

Your planting design should reflect the architectural masses of your house. The bilevel house shown in (A) has a large, blocky mass on the left. This mass should be repeated in the planting mass on the right corner of the house. The horizontal portion on the right should be repeated in the planting composition at the left corner. This is an example of *reversal of location* of the masses. Use the "backward process" in planning your public-area plantings. Notice how the architectural masses are repeated in the plant masses (abstract blocks) in (B) above. The planting arrangement (C) can be adjusted to fit the pattern developed.

CORNER PLANTINGS

  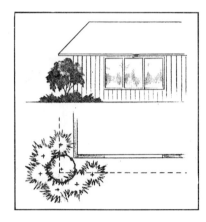

Use tall, medium, or low shrubs at the corners, with lower growing plants at their base to blend the vertical line of the corner into the horizontal line of the ground. Corner plantings should range in height from one-third to two-thirds the distance from the ground to the eaves, depending upon the size of the house. For a small, low house where a tall planting would be too massive (left), the use of shrubs one-third the height from the groundline to the eaves would be desirable. Taller shrubs used with lower growing types and low-spreading evergreens (middle) give a pleasing transition between the dominant vertical and horizontal lines. The distance that the planting extends along the front of the house will depend upon the distance of the window from the corner. The height of the window must also be considered. Begin or stop plantings alongside the house at a logical point — at window edges, jogs in the facade or roof, etc. Tall deciduous shrubs may be combined with spreading evergreens at the base (right). Notice the effectiveness of rounded forms of deciduous shrubs in giving a smooth transition to the groundline.

Corner windows require special treatment so as not to obstruct the view. The planting shown above is composed of a small tree with lower plantings located away from the house. Notice how the lower planting steps down toward the house corner, directing the eye to the front facade. If the space from the side property line to the house is narrow (below), a small flowering tree can serve as a corner planting. Plant away from and to the front of the house. The corner plant can be a small or medium shrub.

SIDE PLANTINGS

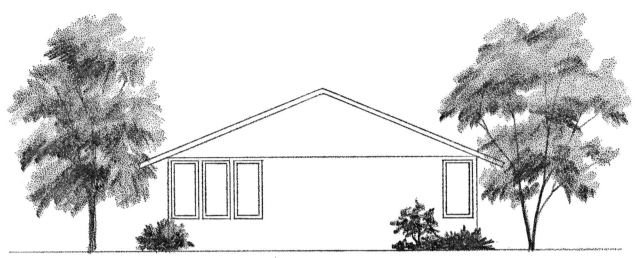

It is not necessary to have a solid planting across the end of the house unless the foundation is high. Plant at both corners. The planting may be extended from either corner with low plants of the same variety running from one-third to two-thirds the width of the house. It is desirable to start or stop plantings at a logical point — at window edges, jogs in the facade or roof, etc. To relieve the monotony of a long blank wall, divide the wall into a small area and a large area (perhaps one-third and two-thirds) as shown above.

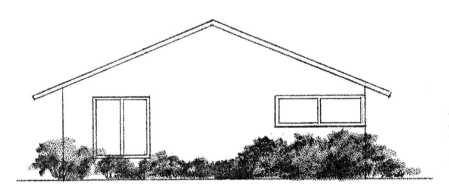

If one kind of small shrub spanning the area would be monotonous, use two kinds of shrubs. One shrub should be slightly taller than the other. Do not divide the plantings in half. Plant two-thirds of the area to a low shrub and one-third to slightly higher plants.

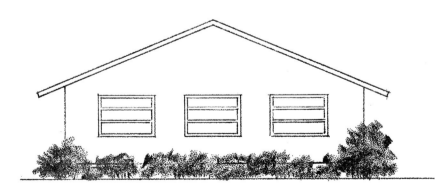

Use a planting across the entire length of a house with a high foundation. At the back corner, select a shrub that is somewhat shorter than the front foundation planting. If the distance between the two corners is not too great, use a low planting of only one kind of shrub.

PORCH PLANTINGS

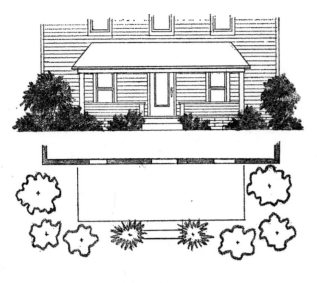

Porch plantings vary according to the height of the foundation, the type of porch railings (open or solid), and the general balance of the facades. If the railing is open, use lower plants; if the railing is solid, use larger growing plants. Wing planting can be continued beyond corners if the house is tall.

When the porch entrance is off to the side, locate the largest shrub at the corner of the house (inside the front walk) and lower shrubs off the street side of the steps. The remainder of the planting is similar to the plantings shown in preceding drawings.

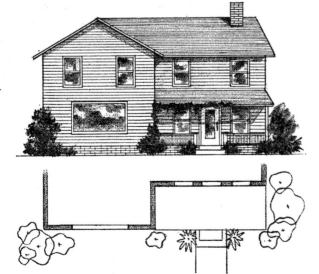

When the porch is to one side of the front facade, low shrubs are used at the entrance, medium shrubs at the porch corners and larger shrubs at the house corners. Vines are used to soften the vertical line in the middle of the facade and to create a dominant horizontal line along the porch eave. This horizontal line keeps the viewer's eyes from moving up the full height of the house.

11: Designing The Living Area

The *living area* should be designed for both utility and beauty. You need to develop this area into subspaces that are comfortable and convenient, as well as visually pleasing when viewed from within the house or from the patio. Exactly how you will develop the private living area depends upon your interest in gardening, outdoor living, and other activities. There are no specific guidelines for the design of the living area like those for the public area. Your family inventory and your own good taste will determine the design.

The public area should be designed on the basis of how it will appear from the street. The view is dominated by the house against which the landscape design is seen. The house gives strong structural form to the area, and the landscape composition must respond to this form. In the private living area, however, the view is from the house into space that is defined only by an imaginary line extended vertically from the property lines along the sides and at the back. You must establish a structural framework that organizes this undefined space into orderly, usable, and beautiful units.

You can use any of the landscape materials (enclosures, plantings, surfaced areas, garden embellishments, overhead structures) to create and organize these units, but don't try to put all of these design elements into one landscape. Choose only those elements that meet your family's needs and interests. Think of the private area as an extension of the house to the outdoors. In effect, you are creating another room for the house with walls, floor, and ceiling. Enclosure structures and plantings, surfaced areas, overhead units, and garden embellishments must be considered for their suitability in developing this area.

Enclosure units are vertical elements that organize and define subspaces, provide walls for your garden rooms, screen out views, and give privacy and protection. Enclosures are especially important in urban areas where lots are small and the houses close together. Screening and privacy are not usually as essential for rural homes, although some enclosure elements should be used to develop subspaces in the landscape.

Garden enclosures are not as rigid or complete as enclosures within the house. You can vary garden enclosures between those that are high and solid for screening, privacy, or protection, and those that are low and open for defining space without blocking the view. This flexibility in combining solid and open enclosures gives your design a strong three-dimensional quality and avoids the problem of a dull, flat landscape. It also allows you to introduce form, scale, and proportion into the design, since there can be variety in height, degree of openness, and general arrangement of the enclosure elements. (Landscape materials and structures are discussed in detail in Chapters 4 and 5.)

A fence is one of the most popular and efficient ways to enclose the private area. A fence located along the property lines provides maximum yard space, while reducing maintenance of land outside the fence. In a large yard, fencing within the property itself can provide a better screening effect than a property-line fence. Clotheslines, storage space, and other items in the service area also need to be screened by vertical enclosures located inside the property line.

A fence gives privacy, protects the garden, provides a background for flowers and shrubs, screens out unsightly views, and shelters the patio or terrace from

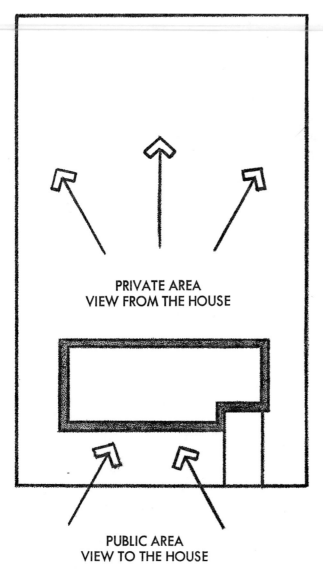

PRIVATE AREA
VIEW FROM THE HOUSE

PUBLIC AREA
VIEW TO THE HOUSE

Unlike the public area, which is viewed against the architecture of the house, the outdoor living area is open and undefined. The design of this area depends upon the creation of three-dimensional space through the use of surfacing, fences, walls, trees, and shrubs.

the wind. It may be used as a barrier to keep children and pets within a yard, or as a strictly ornamental feature. The kind of fence you should build depends upon the purpose it is meant to serve. For example, an open-wire fence will keep out animals. It is also less expensive than a solid wood fence, and you can plant dense shrubs against it as a screen.

The surface of a fence is an important design consideration because a fence intercepts the viewer's line of sight. It is usually best to use a simple, plain fence as background for garden plants. Fancywork on a fence is expensive and often detracts from the garden design. A fence can be made attractive merely by exploiting the design potential of its materials. You

can also add interest by introducing contrasting materials for a single panel or several panels of a long fence. You can use one plastic, asbestos, or brick panel in a wood fence, or one or more panels of a contrasting design achieved by a different use of the same material. You do not need to limit yourself to one type of fencing. For example, you can use a highly refined panel fence around the patio and a less refined board fence in the rest of the garden. Do not change fence style at a corner — it will draw attention to that particular spot. The fence at the rear of the property should be the same height as the fence along the sides. You can use short sections of panels of fencing for interest. By dividing the garden, they make it appear larger and stimulate curiosity. A panel set at a right angle on a diagonal or curve may emphasize a specimen tree or vine, or serve as a place to put a garden feature or piece of sculpture.

Plant materials may be used to create enclosures that are high and solid or low and defining. When used as an enclosing element, plants are usually limited to one type or variety for each section of enclosure. Plants can be arranged in more architectural and linear patterns that are straight, curved, staggered, or in a baffle arrangement, and they have the advantage of relatively low cost and easy upkeep.

For equal height in screening, however, plant materials require more ground space than a fence. A 6-foot fence, for example, requires only 10 inches of ground space; most plants require 6 to 8 feet of ground space. Do not allow your plant enclosures to become a "collector's museum" by using only one of every type of plant you like. Since the more elaborate shrub masses are composed of vertical units, they

Although fences along the property lines provide privacy, they often cannot be built high enough to screen views effectively from surrounding higher elevations. If space is available, tall shrub plantings or trees are often more effective than a fence. Since a fence does not require as much ground space as plants, it is frequently used on small properties.

Fencing within the property lines can give better screening effect and climate control than a property-line fence. Fences close to the living areas need to be more refined (such as panel or solid fences) than those used along property lines.

also function as enclosure elements. (The design of shrub borders is discussed in detail in Chapter 8.)

Masonry, concrete, and rock walls can be used either as tall, solid units or as low, defining masses. Although the costs for materials and construction are high, these walls have the advantage of low maintenance and permanence, and seem to "belong" in the landscape.

Any garden development involves the balancing of open structures against plantings. Both should be used. A landscape made up exclusively of plants or of structural elements can be dull and uninteresting.

The units of the outdoor living area need various types of surfacing, depending upon the function of each unit or the activity that will take place in it. The various surfacing materials — lawn, ground cover, paving, and loose aggregates — give different effects that should be carefully developed into an overall pleasing pattern. The surfacing pattern should reinforce and strengthen the rest of the design, but it should not be allowed to dominate the enclosures, overhead units, or garden furnishings and embellishments. Simplicity and restraint in forms and patterns is the safest approach. (See page 170 for examples of ground patterns.)

Even if you believe that more complex forms and patterns are needed, you must develop a design that is balanced with the remainder of the three-dimensional units of space. For example, several surfacing materials such as hard paving, loose surfacing, ground covers, or lawn can be used together to form a design. The pattern may be a simple combination of paving and lawn or paving with loose surfacing. Three surfacing materials can be made into more complicated arrangements by carefully working out interesting area

shapes and using materials with pleasing texture and color contrasts. You can develop an unlimited choice of patterns for various surfacing materials. A pattern can be formed with straight, curved, or diagonal lines, and one shape may help form another. The edgings that hold the ground cover or paving will emphasize the pattern.

The most popular and most functional surfacing material is a lawn. Lawns have certain advantages that no other surface can match. A lawn is cool and pleasant to sit or lie on in hot weather; it makes a good play surface for small children; and it provides an attractive foreground to set off plants and flowers in the garden. The one disadvantage of a lawn is that it needs almost constant care. Keeping the lawn in good condition is a never-ending job from the moment you start to establish it.

Not all plant surfacing has to be lawn. You can use ground covers for additional green surfacing in areas where there is no traffic, or you can provide usable open space with other kinds of paving materials. Many loose surfacings are both inexpensive and attractive. Many sizes of gravel are available, ranging from very small pebbles for a sitting area to large rocks for an entrance driveway. Bark chips, brick chips, and other materials can be used for surfacing "light-use" areas or where textural contrasts are desired.

Surround lawn and ground covers or loose aggregates in the garden with a flat edging of lumber or metal or a strip of paving. This edging makes trimming easier and separates the lawn from ground covers or aggregates to prevent their intermixing. A wide buffer separating gravel and lawn keeps gravel out of the grass and prevents mower damage.

The terrace, patio, or any other area (walks, steps, special game area, etc.) with a high concentration of use should be designed with a hard surface. Although a hard surface may be expensive, it is by far the most satisfactory surface because of its durability, permanence, and low maintenance. (For more information on the various types of materials available for surfaces and basic construction details, see Chapters 4 and 5.)

The ceiling of the outdoor space has been described as a combination of sky, the canopy of trees, and architectural structures with varying degrees of protection. This ceiling is more flexible in the degree of overhead definition than the ceiling of a room within the house. The sky is a delightful, constantly changing element that is necessarily a prominent part of your overhead design, but it should not be "overused." You should *manipulate* the sky — its areas of dominance or subordination — in much the same way that you would any other landscape element.

FENCE FORMS

STEPPED DIAGONAL

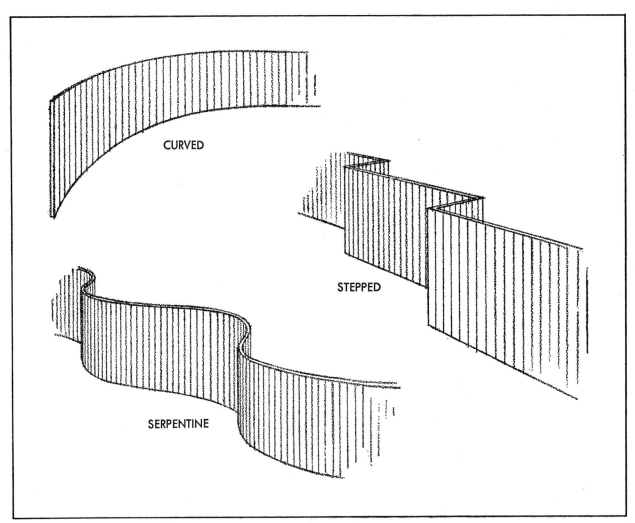

CURVED

STEPPED

SERPENTINE

Decide where you want areas open for weather variations such as sun and rain; then decide where it would be desirable to have partially sheltered areas of shade and reduced light intensity, air temperatures, and heat absorption and radiation. Trees might logically be placed in these areas. Since most small properties cannot accommodate more than two large trees in the living area, the choice and location of these trees deserve careful study. The same trees will also provide a background for the house as it is viewed from the public area, and establish a transition between the architecture of the house and the landscape.

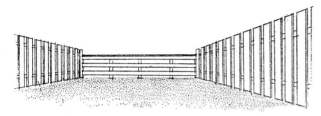

Do not use fencing at the rear of the property that is lower than the fencing along the side property lines.

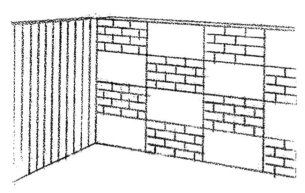

Do not change fence designs at a corner. A change in design emphasizes that particular spot and draws attention to itself.

Do not use fancy, highy embellished gates. They clash with the remainder of the fencing. Gates should be of the same material and basic design as the fence. If contrasting material is used, it must harmonize with the fence in color, texture, and pattern.

Obviously, these trees should be large shade trees that will branch high enough to allow physical movement and unobstructed viewing beneath their lower branches.

You should also decide whether there is a need for structural shelters for total or partial protection in primary outdoor living spaces and areas within the house. These shelters are justified when it is necessary to control sun, rain, wind, heat, glare, dust, and insects, or to allow for more nighttime use or longer seasonal use. Your decision about overhead elements depends upon what you want to control and when you want to control it (day, night, or season); the degree of control (total or partial); and how soon you need it. Can you wait for a tree to grow? Does the overhead element need to be attached to the house, or can it be a freestanding garden structure?

Architectural structures should not be designed with great detail or pattern in the ceiling plane. The ceiling should be "sensed," not seen. You should consult a landscape architect or an architect to be sure that these structures will be compatible with the design of your house.

Whether you add architectural details to the three basic spatial units (walls, floors, and ceiling) depends upon the extent to which you plan to add accessories and embellishments. If you decide that furniture, water displays or pools, sculpture, mosaics, sand castings, boulders, driftwood, container plantings, special planters, unique flowers, or plants are elements that you would like to feature, you should design the three basic spatial units in a simple and straightforward manner so that they will serve as a foil and backdrop.

If you do not wish to emphasize accessories and embellishments, you can use a more elaborate design in the enclosures and, to a lesser degree, in the floor and ceiling. Do not become so interested in accessories and embellishments that you ignore the basic spatial units. You must maintain a balance between these elements in your design. For example, you can use special points of interest to dress up a garden in the same way that accessories are used in a room. These attention-catchers could well be some of the objects banished from the public area (gazing ball, bird bath, etc.), provided that you have a suitable backdrop and integrate them into the total design. Unusual construction or a bright spot of color becomes an immediate point of interest important enough to make the use of other garden ornaments unnecessary. If special garden embellishments are used, create a setting for them and place them as focal points. This setting usually requires a background such as plants or a fence to set off the feature. Be sure that it is well located and in scale with the rest of the design.

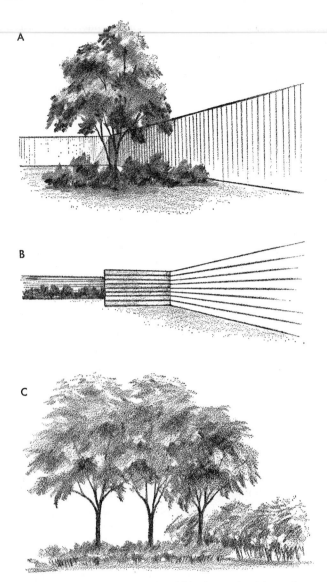

Fence panels or plantings help divide the garden into sections, create space, define areas, and stimulate curiosity. (A) Baffle effect established by low shrubs and a tree. (B) Baffle formed by a panel placed at right angles to the property-line fence. (C) Baffle effect created by trees and ground cover located at right angles to shrub border.

Since the private area extends the indoors to the outdoors, you will need ready access to this area, preferably at floor level. The private area should also be located close to the kitchen so that it is handy for cookouts and outdoor eating. If your door is at the house-floor level, which is above the ground level, you will need to provide steps with low risers and broad treads. An alternative is to design a mini-deck at this location. A mini-deck will give you a large landing before you descend to the grade level of the yard. It is hazardous, particularly when carrying food, dishes, etc., to have to descend steps immediately after step-ping out of the house. The large landing gives you an opportunity to become oriented and prepare yourself for descending the steps.

A patio in a small home-grounds design gives a good vantage point from which you can enjoy the yard. Analyze the terrace or patio in your proposed plan early in the pattern-development process. The rest of the garden should be planned to take advantage of the patio location, since the patio is the first major unit we experience when we enter the landscape from the house. For this reason, the patio pattern more or less establishes the overall pattern design for the balance of the area. The line, direction, and form of the patio should be reflected in other major design units.

Slopes can be handled in several ways. Grading in the private area is the same as that for the front lawn. To obtain a usable flat area, you may need to level a steep slope by filling soil behind a retaining wall. This flat area should slope away from the house and drop at least 2 inches every 100 feet. A slope is less expensive than a retaining wall, but the latter requires less space, is permanent and attractive, and weathers well over the years.

You can work out some interesting effects with retaining walls. Retaining walls may be curved, angled, or straight. On a steep slope, a series of low walls is far more pleasing than a large single wall. If your wall is too tall to serve as a seat wall, consider building a low bench against the wall to make the wall look lower and emphasize its length.

Several low retaining walls make a better design than one high wall. If a high wall cannot be avoided, the effect of height can be reduced by the addition of a seat bench against the wall. A seat bench gives a strong horizontal line to the design.

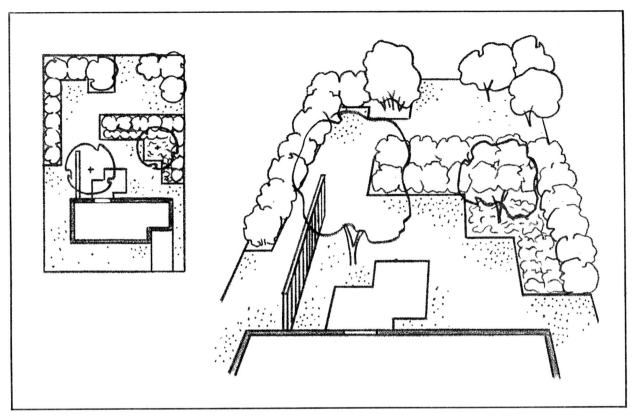

Natural and architectural materials should be used in the outdoor living area to subdivide large, open spaces into smaller units that will accommodate the various functions planned for this area.

Steps may serve both as a retaining wall and as a means for getting from one level to another. Although steps are more expensive to construct than a ramp, they offer more opportunities for interesting design arrangements. If you need to move wheeled equipment up and down a grade change, however, a ramp is preferable to steps.

Garden steps do not have to be in a straight flight. They may be constructed with various turns or angles so long as they do not look abrupt or pinched. The steps should have a wide tread and a low riser. The general recommendation is for a 15-inch tread with a 5-inch riser. The height of a flight of garden steps should not be greater than the width. If the flight is extremely long, break up the steps into smaller groups and separate these groups with landings. You can change direction at a landing.

If you want to set aside a special area for the children, be sure that you have allowed enough space for all play equipment — sandbox, swings, teeter-totters, etc. Don't overlook the possibility of including junk building material (bricks, scrap lumber, boxes, etc.) that children can use to create their own play. Swings, slides, and other standard play equipment usually become boring after a short time, but the creative chal-

lenge of manipulating and building play elements will occupy a child for many hours. Children are constantly seeking new challenges. They want to test themselves and the world about them. Junk play is one way for them to meet these challenges.

You can partially hide the play area with shrubs, although it should be located so that the children can be supervised from the kitchen window. Sand, bark, or wood chips are suitable under play equipment, since you cannot grow grass successfully in this area. Because a child quickly outgrows the need for a restricted play area, this area should be located and arranged so that it can be easily incorporated into the landscape when the child no longer uses it.

Although volleyball and basketball courts do not usually improve the appearance of your property, they can be justified if sports are an important part of your family's leisure activities. If you are interested in lawn games, be sure that you have allowed adequate open space in your plan for these games.

If you have an off-property view that you wish to develop, make your garden a foreground opening up and framing this view. Broad, flowing lines of plants, walls, and paving will lead the eye from the house toward the view. Use planting arms to dramatize

Header or divider boards may be used between two types of surfacing materials to keep one from intruding upon the other. The divider boards should be redwood, cypress, cedar, or a wood that has been treated with wood preservatives. (A) Headers dividing loose gravel and lawn or other surfacing materials. (B) Headers dividing ground cover and lawn. (C) Headers dividing brick and lawn.

Raised planter beds create interest and dramatize a tree or other plantings. The top of the retainer may serve as an excellent potted-plant display shelf.

or emphasize any part of the view. A garden should appear wider than it is deep. If your property is longer than it is wide in the direction of the view, you can create an illusion of width by putting in or emphasizing lines running at right angles from the side property lines. For example, you can make a change in level by building steps across the width of the garden or by extending low shrubs toward the center of the lot. Everything else in the garden should be on a large scale. Anything delicate or small will be dwarfed by the size of the view off the property.

A flat, open space, such as a lawn and paving or gravel, should serve as the foreground. There should be nothing to mark the end of the property — the gar-

den should flow directly into the view. If you can see housetops or other disturbing elements at the bottom of the view, you can block them off with a low hedge or other low planting. Plant only a few varieties and repeat them often. Avoid specimen plants that draw attention from the view.

Now it is time to review your family inventory, site analysis, and goose-egg plans to understand how they will influence the design of the basic landscape units.

The family inventory, which forms the basis for your outdoor living-area design, will tell you the number and types of spaces you need for general and specific activities. In your home, you have rooms for general living (family, dining, living, recreation, etc.); for work (kitchen, utility, shop, sewing, etc.); and for private living (bedrooms, bath, etc.), and you should have similar activity spaces in the landscape. General living spaces include the patio, terrace, outdoor courts, and children's play areas; work spaces include the service yard, vegetable garden, flower garden, and storage; and private living spaces include small, private patios and suntraps off bedrooms and possibly bathrooms. Study your inventory carefully to be sure that you have explored all of the possibilities the landscape can offer your family.

After you have reviewed the family inventory, return to the site analysis and study the assets and liabilities of your lot, your house, and the surrounding neighborhood. This process is necessary if you are to successfully combine your needs as identified in the inventory with the site analysis. Your goal should be a serviceable and orderly arrangement that takes advantage of the assets and requires the least disturbance to the land.

The design process must be carefully correlated with both the family inventory and the site analysis. The combination of these two earlier studies forms the basis for the goose-egg planning described in Chapter 3. After you have reviewed the goose-egg planning process, you should make three or four different studies for your property. Analyze these studies on the basis

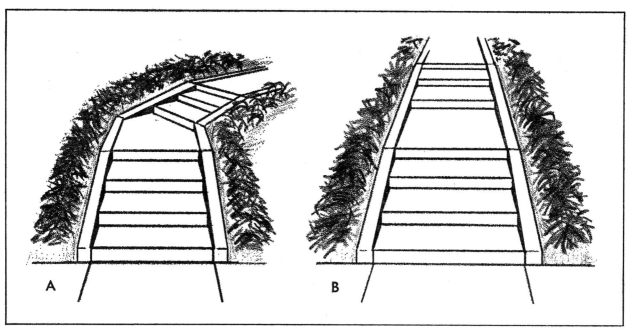

Steps can serve both as a retaining wall and as a means of access from one area to another. Outdoor steps should be of greater scale than indoor steps. Avoid making them so narrow that they look pinched. Garden steps should have a wide tread and low risers. The height of a flight of steps should not be greater than the width. (A) Make any change in the direction of the steps at landings only. (B) If the flight is extremely long, break the steps into smaller groups and separate these groups with landings.

of each activity location and its compatibility to the site, house, and neighboring activities.

You should now consider the typical traffic patterns that will probably develop between the house and the various areas of the landscape. Try to anticipate which of these "trip" lines will have heavy use and which will carry only occasional traffic. Draw lines from primary house doors to the areas involved. The heavier the traffic, the darker and wider the connecting lines should be. This study will help you to decide whether you need to provide walks or paths, and whether you should integrate these circulation units with your patio or terrace design. Turf is probably adequate for light-traffic routes unless the area will be used during the wet months of spring, fall and winter. In that case, it may be necessary to choose a more durable surfacing material.

You are now ready to develop the ground-pattern design for your property. This is the next step toward achieving your spatial framework in the third dimension. Before you begin the actual pattern design, consider the various alternatives in style that can be used. For example, the pattern can have traditional style with symmetrical balance; or, for a more natural setting, it can be informal with strong, bold curves arranged with an asymmetrical balance. Or you may prefer an informal architectural-type garden with definite patterns, lines, and forms contrasting with one another in a geometric design that has asymmetrical balance. An informal, asymmetrical layout tends to have more interest. Symmetrical balance is rigid and formal; asymmetrical balance is more subtle. An informal design has the additional advantage of not needing to be as "spic-and-span" as a formal design.

Most formal gardens are rectangular, even when curves are added for ornamentation. This rectangular shape should have a ratio of 7 to 3 or 7 to 4. One major axis should lead from the terrace or picture window to the rear of the property. Any special feature midway down the line must be low and unobtrusive. A formal garden is symmetrical, with regular and balanced shapes and patterns for each element of lawn, paving, and shrubbery.

Shapes should be *informal* in an informal garden. These shapes don't have to be regular or symmetrical or even pleasing in themselves, but they should fit together in a visually satisfying combination. A broad, simple curve is usually preferable to a series of small curves. Pattern shapes should be well proportioned and not too long, narrow, or irregular. There should be enough difference between lengths and widths to create interest. Plan a design that you believe would be most comfortable for you and your family. As you work out your plan, think first only of patterns and activity locations. Allow yourself plenty of time — ideas sometimes come slowly.

It is best to start your design of the living area by developing the ground pattern. Your goose-egg study

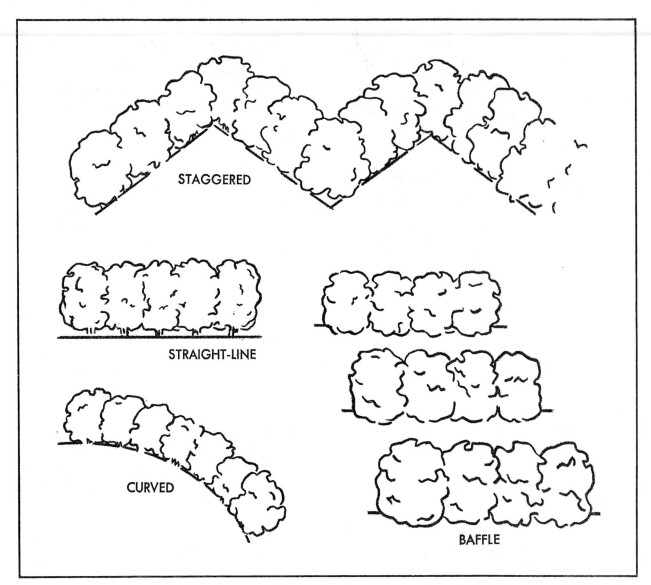

STAGGERED

STRAIGHT-LINE

CURVED

BAFFLE

Plants, as well as walls and fences, can be used for suggested or total enclosure. A plant below eye level organizes space without obstructing the view; a plant above eye level both defines space and limits the view. Plants can be used in straight-line, curved, or staggered patterns, or in a baffle arrangement.

will tell you the best locations for the activity areas on your property, but it does not indicate the specific size, shape, or detail of each area. These should now be determined.

There are three basic patterns — *straight, diagonal,* and *circular* — from which you can develop your design. The straight-line pattern has lines that extend at a 90-degree angle from the house, with cross lines that are parallel to the back line of the house. The diagonal pattern has lines at a 45-degree angle to the back plane of the house, with cross lines also at a 45-degree angle, forming an intersection of 90 degrees. The curved patterns include free-flowing curves, as well as the arc-and-tangent style.

It is better to work out your pattern studies as thumbnail sketches rather than at full-scale on your base plan. Sketch freehand on scratch paper the general shape of your lot. These thumbnail sketches should not be much larger than 3 inches. It is important, however, that the shape of your lot and the areas between the rear of the house and the property lines be approximately the same proportions as those shown on the scale drawing. If you fail to relate your freehand sketch to the base plan, none of the pattern development that follows will have value for you. Place the back line of the house at the bottom of your sketch; let the top of the sketch be the rear property line.

To develop a straight-line pattern, draw a number of closely spaced lines (freehand again) from the back property line to the house. Repeat with closely spaced lines running at a 90-degree angle to the first lines — these lines must be at right angles to the side property lines. The effectiveness of this technique lies in having many lines close together rather than a few widely spaced lines.

The next step is to extract possible patterns that are suggested by tracing over selected lines of the grid. You may want to start with the patio, or possibly the planting beds and activity areas. Your goose-egg study will tell you where open spaces are needed for activity and use areas, and your site analysis will tell you where you need screening, privacy, etc. Keep your goose-egg study and site analysis in mind as you evolve your pattern. You should not be so tied to the goose-egg study that a good design is lost simply because the pattern areas do not fall exactly where one or two of your assigned activity areas are located in the goose-egg study. At this point, you should think of the goose-egg study as a suggested guide that can be modified to accommodate a good pattern design.

Draw a minimum of three to five thumbnail sketches. Do not spend a great deal of time on each sketch — be loose and free. If one sketch doesn't work or is obviously not appropriate, discard it and try another. Don't attempt to erase or draw over — just begin again. With a little practice, you should be able to develop several studies in 10 minutes.

After you have made your straight-line-pattern studies, do a similar number of diagonal-pattern studies. The procedure is the same except that the closely spaced lines should be drawn diagonally across the backyard area at a 45-degree angle to the house. Be sure that the cross lines that form the diagonal grid are at a 45-degree angle to the house but in the opposite direction. Draw out the various patterns suggested by the grid lines. Compare these patterns with the goose-egg study and site analysis to see whether the ideas developed in the patterns are compatible with the earlier studies.

Finally, you should explore some possible curved patterns. Draw your thumbnail sketches of the area. The lines you will use to develop the patterns will be scribbling marks over the entire area. Scribbling is not as easy as it may seem because adults are too self-conscious to scribble without practice. The results should resemble those of a child who is just learning to mark with a pencil. Your scribbles should be loose and flowing, crossing the paper in all directions — up and down, crisscross, diagonally, and everything in between. Be sure that you have many lines and that they are close together.

Study the scribbles to see what curved patterns can be developed. If you have developed a strong, bold curve but there is no transition line where you know that you need one, you must interpolate — in other words, add a line even though the scribble pattern doesn't suggest one at that point. This is also true for the straight-line and diagonal-line patterns.

All curved patterns need to be strong and bold to be readable in the landscape. A "soft" curve (a slightly curving line) cannot be distinguished from a straight line when viewed at a distance. Soft curves often leave the viewer wondering what the designer intended — a curve or a straight line. Another type of curved line to be avoided is a "snaky" one — a series of small curves that constantly change direction. It is distracting to look at and difficult to maintain. Do not attempt to duplicate nature as seen in meadows and wooded areas. Curves can be used to suggest this naturalness, but you are obviously working in a controlled and designed space, and this fact should be reflected in your curved patterns.

Designs consisting of bold outcurves blending into equally bold incurves are quite satisfactory. The curve must have a pleasing transition from the outcurve to the incurve, and the transition is best accomplished with a straight line. This pattern requires a great deal of ground space. Since the use of curves on small properties necessitates skillful design, straight-line and diagonal patterns are preferred. These patterns reflect and repeat the basic lines and masses seen in the architecture and property outlines.

A compromise between bold curves and one of the straight-line patterns is the **arc-and-tangent**. This pattern is also compatible with the lines of the property and the house, and is as visually satisfactory as the outcurve-incurve pattern. It consists of straight lines connected by small curves or arcs, and has the advantage of reflecting lines and patterns of the property and building, while being softened by the arc or curve that serves as a transition from one direction to another.

Make three to five thumbnail sketches for both the diagonal and curved patterns. Again use your goose-egg study and site analysis as the basis for checking these sketches. After you have selected your pattern, tape a clean sheet of tracing paper over the base plan of your house and yard. Lightly pencil in your selected pattern to scale on this sheet. Since your thumbnail sketches were not to scale, you will probably have to make adjustments in the pattern as you draw it to scale. If you have maintained good proportional relations between the sketch and the scale size of the base plan, you will not destroy the character of your pattern when you draw it to scale.

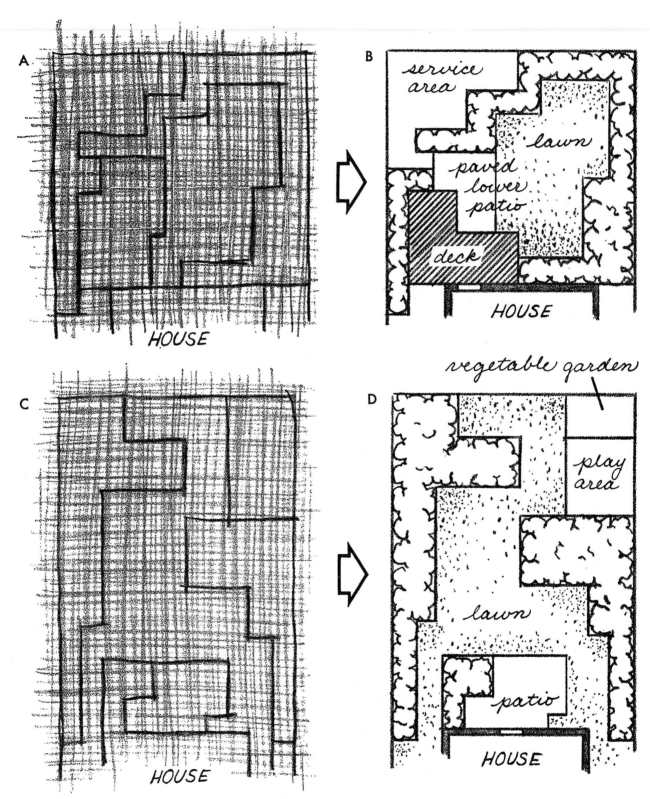

The thumbnail sketches (A) and (C) show two possible straight-line patterns. (A) is a basic pattern that closely parallels the goose-egg plan in which various use areas were assigned on the ground plane. Although the pattern is not drawn to scale, it establishes an elementary layout that can be further refined as it is transferred to the scale plan. For example, the area designated in (A) for the patio or outdoor living space has been modified in the final scale drawing (B) to include an enlarged deck that "wraps around" the lower patio. Notice the interesting units of space developed out of the overall site defined by the property lines: a service area screened by baffle plantings, and a private outdoor living area (deck and patio) looking out upon an enclosed lawn space. There are only minor changes between the thumbnail sketch (C) and the scale plan (D).

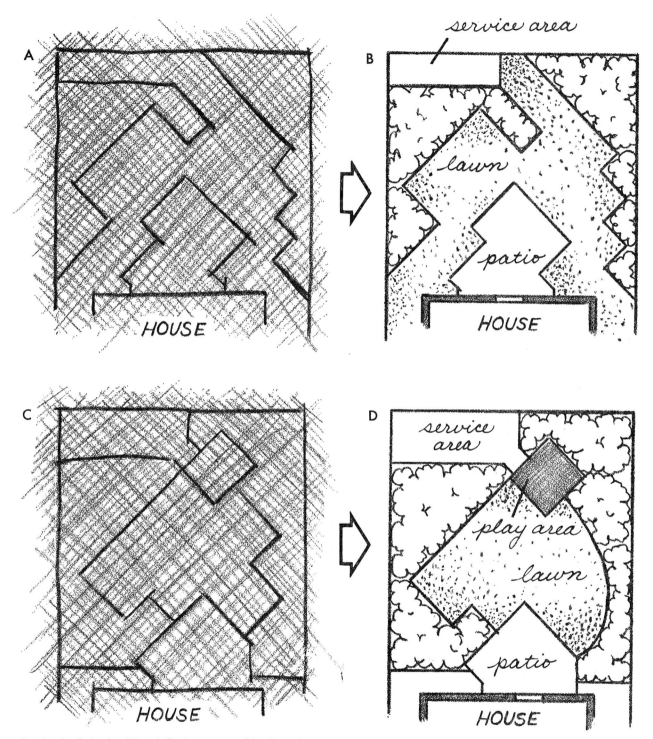

The thumbnail sketches (A) and (C) show two possible diagonal patterns. (A) was transferred to the final scale drawing (B) with only minor modifications. (C) underwent significant design changes during the transfer to the scale drawing (D). Notice that the area at the right side of (D) has been changed from a "stepped" planting bed to a curved bed. The outline of this curved bed offers a pleasing contrast in line and form that was not present in the thumbnail sketch (C).

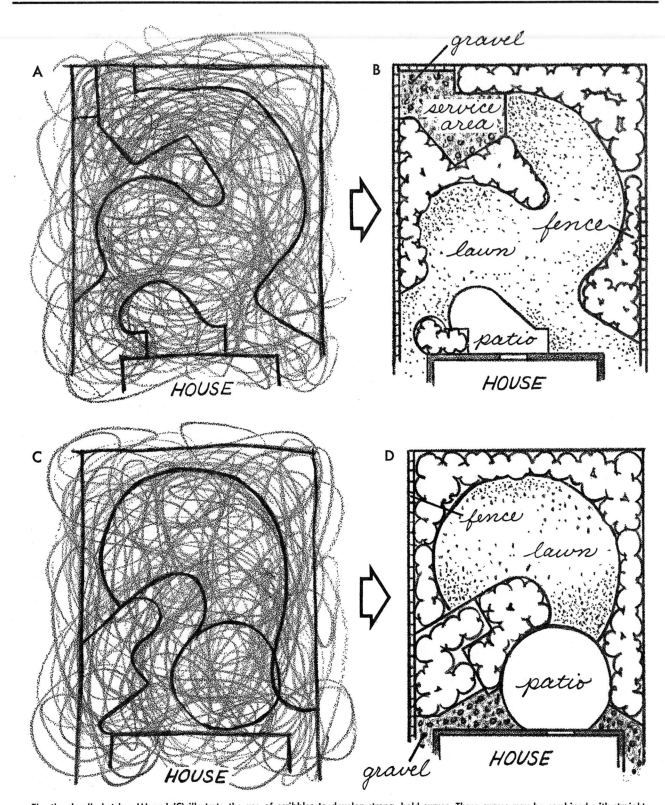

The thumbnail sketches (A) and (C) illustrate the use of scribbles to develop strong, bold curves. These curves may be combined with straight lines to form either an arc-and-tangent pattern (A) or an interlocking circular pattern (C). Notice the alterations that are introduced in the refined scale drawings (B) and (D). Remember — a curved pattern is the most difficult pattern to develop successfully in a limited space that is bounded and dominated by straight lines.

A mini-deck establishes a pleasing transition from interior to exterior spaces, and allows people to become oriented to the new environment before descending steps to another level.

Check over the pattern to be sure that it provides for the various areas needed, such as terrace, utility space, vegetable garden, shrub borders, paved and loose aggregate surfaces, etc. Consider needed grade changes and how you will develop them — whether by retaining walls, steps, or improved slopes. Next, locate trees. Since trees give a sense of overhead protection, definition, and enclosure along the sides of the space, their location and selection are important to the success of the outdoor living area. You may be fortunate enough to have trees already on your property, but most people have to start with young trees. In a few years, young trees will begin to spread out and arch over the garden to give a sense of overhead enclosure.

The location of background trees is important. They should provide shade for the sitting area, patio, or terrace, serve as a backdrop for the house as seen from the street, act as a canopy over the living area, and perhaps screen an object or frame a view. Plant trees that are deep-rooted and rapid-growing. It is difficult to find trees with both of these qualities, but they are available.

When you have worked out a simple, well-proportioned pattern, lay another sheet of paper over your base plan to refine the paved areas. The size and shape of a paved area will depend upon the use of that area. The desirable minimum size for a patio is about 15 feet by 20 feet (300 square feet), and the preferred size is 400 square feet. The shape of your patio area should be both functional and designed as an integral part of the total living-area pattern. Be sure that the pattern of the patio relates to the planting beds, lawn, etc. in the outdoor living area. Don't

be reluctant to experiment in working out relationships. Draw over, erase, or change anything that looks wrong. Tracing paper is inexpensive, and it is certainly worth a few sheets to insure a good investment.

Check to see if your pattern design allows for enclosures such as fencing or plants for shade, windbreak, and privacy. Determine whether you have a balance between open spaces and plantings. Too much planting to the amount of open space remaining can be overpowering. You can judge the proportion of open space to the planting mass by crosshatching the planting areas on tracing paper placed over the pattern design. Make any adjustments that you believe would be helpful to achieve a good balance. Be sure that your pattern design allows enough space for planting areas. These areas can vary in depth from 1 foot to 15 feet. Plant a narrow space with flowers, a vine, or low shrubs, if their spread can be contained within the area. Since most shrubs will grow about the same width as their height, allow 8 feet of depth for an 8-foot screen.

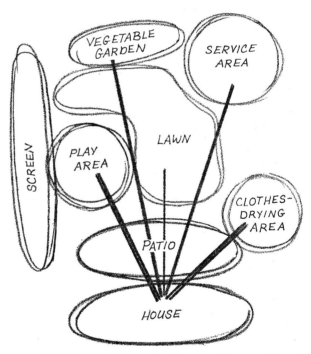

Before beginning your pattern development, indicate anticipated traffic routes on the goose-egg plan. These routes or "trip lines" establish movement from the house to the various use and activity areas. In the above drawing, the routes over which regular, heavy traffic can be expected are considerably darker than those that will be used only occasionally. Turf would probably support the traffic for these occasional routes. Where heavier traffic is expected, a more durable and permanent surfacing should be used. Try to integrate the heavy traffic routes into areas that require permanent and durable paving such as the patio and terrace.

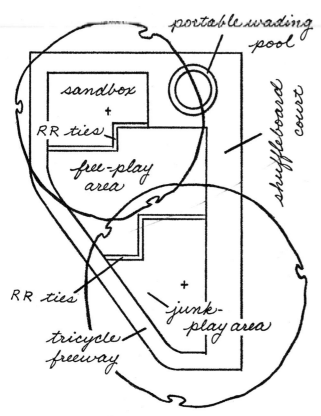

portable wading pool

sandbox

RR ties

free-play area

shuffleboard court

RR ties

junk-play area

tricycle freeway

An imaginative children's play area on your property will help to overcome the shortcomings of the standard playground experience of swings, slides, and teeter-totters. The plan illustrated above accommodates both children and adults. The sandbox satisfies the child's urge to dig and mold a world of his own; the portable wading pool, which is placed on concrete, provides an opportunity for water play without killing the lawn or creating "mud flats"; and the concrete "tricycle freeway" serves to contain the soft or loose surfacing (wood chips) in the free-play and junk-play areas. This "freeway" is widened on the right to allow for the adult game of shuffleboard. The center section of the play area is devoted to free play and the lower section to "junk play." In this lower section, the child can put together scrap lumber, boxes, or other discarded materials to create forts, houses, cubby holes, etc.

Flower beds should be from 2 to 5 feet deep. Beds that are too narrow look sparse and out of scale if you are trying to develop a shrub border. Narrow bed areas are better used for linear screen plantings. Wide planting areas should be used as shrub borders. The wider the flower bed, the more difficult it is to work in. Ideally, a flower bed should be about 2 to 5 feet deep, and backed by 6-foot shrubs to make the flowers stand out. You can also back up flowers with a fence and avoid the problem of competition between shrub and flower roots when they are planted too close together.

As you develop your planting design, remember that you are using woody plant materials that will provide a basic three-dimensional framework in the landscape. When screening is the only function of planting, you should use only one kind of plant. This does not mean that the same plant must be repeated for screening effects in other locations. It is perfectly acceptable to have different materials used in different locations.

When larger planting areas are available, a greater combination of different plants can be used. Review the "backward process" described in Chapter 8. Since you have already established the design of your planting bed, your next step is the selection and arrangement of plants that will strengthen your pattern design and refine the spaces being created. For best results, develop your abstract studies on the basis of the direction and angle from which they will most commonly be viewed.

You should also consider what part of the garden will be used in good weather and what part you will simply look at from within the house. Try to make each view as pleasant as possible. Move from room to room at the back of the house to determine if what you see outside is attractive and should be featured, or whether it is unattractive and should be screened.

After making this inside survey, look over the property from the outdoor sitting area. Notice where you have to protect your privacy or screen out an unsightly view. Locate all fencing on your garden plan; then sketch in all trees and shrub screens needed for privacy. Put in any shrub borders and flower beds. Study and locate seat walls and retaining walls to be sure that their lines and forms blend with the area.

Locate the terrace or patio on your plan early in the designing process, and design the remainder of the garden to take advantage of the patio location. A patio gives an excellent vantage point from which to enjoy the remainder of the yard.

A raised bed provides interest in a flat yard. Even as little as 4 inches of change can emphasize a particular planting mass, a tree planter, or specialized planting areas close to the terrace, patio, or sitting area. Raised planting beds can be created by building low walls of masonry or wood. You can put a cap on top of the wall so that it will serve both as a seat and as a retainer for the raised bed. The walls or retainers used to create these raised beds emphasize specific lines, and are important design features where strong patterns are to be developed. They can be used to divide the garden into areas, or as a special feature in conjunction with the patio. They are also useful in breaking the monotony of the level ground. Plant flowers, shrubs, or specimen plants in these raised beds.

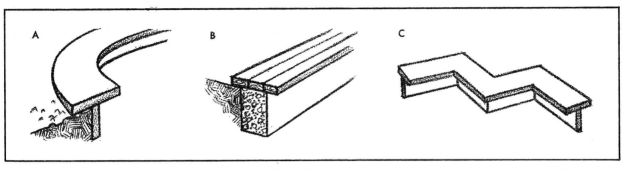

Low seat walls. (A) curved; (B) straight; (C) stepped. Seat walls can be wood, brick, brick support with wood top, concrete with wood top, or concrete block with wood top. Garden seating may be a freestanding element or part of a retaining wall designed to hold soil. Low walls used for soil retention or raised beds may also be used as seat walls.

You may wish to consider other landscape embellishments at this time so that you can properly integrate them with the rest of your design. You may use any of the embellishments mentioned earlier, but don't use so many that the design becomes cluttered. Be sure to create the proper setting for featuring a particular element; provide an appropriate background against which to view it; and arrange other landscape elements (structures and plants) to direct attention to the element and possibly frame it.

Elements can be natural or man-made. For example, you may wish to enhance the beauty of your garden with large boulders or a piece of sculpture used as a freestanding, three-dimensional unit. If you include sculpture, be sure that its design complements the theme, mood, and style of your landscape. Small accessories — those below 3 feet in height — should be large enough in diameter or mass to be in scale with the surrounding landscape. For example, plant containers that are an appropriate size for use within the house may be insignificant out-of-doors. To "read" well, these smaller accessories must be larger than their counterparts within the house.

Garden furniture should be selected with as much care as other embellishments. It will take a little searching to find chairs and tables that are both durable and well designed. Most of the furniture that is readily available is much too large. It often has ugly proportions and gaudy colors, and is constructed of materials that lack warmth, charm, and elegance.

Consider the type of garden furniture you will need to make your patio function according to its planned use. You will probably want chairs with backs for sitting comfort. Select chairs with the appropriate back angles for eating and for reading or conversation. Some chairs have adjustable backs to serve several of these functions. Footstools add lounging comfort in

chairs, and provide additional seating for large groups. Lounges for relaxation and sunning may also be appropriate. Several types of tables should be considered. A table for dining will probably be necessary, but you might also wish to include end tables and coffee tables.

Storage of furniture pads and cushions should be convenient to the patio. If you need to protect the furniture itself during the winter, you must provide adequate storage space. This space does not need to be located close to the patio, since it is used only once or twice a year.

Recheck your studies on paving and surfacing to decide whether you need more of these materials. You may want to add more ground cover or soft-surfaced material to the lawn and hard-surfaced areas.

Now it is time to polish and refine your plan. You can emphasize the important lines in your garden in many ways. Retaining walls or seat walls, fencing, and shrubs provide this emphasis. You may also wish to use brick or concrete edging to outline bed areas. A short line of low plants, either clipped or allowed to grow naturally, can emphasize shapes and divisions. Plants or a low seat wall do not necessarily have to extend the full length of the line. The viewer's imagination will carry the line beyond a small section.

Study the shapes and line directions in your plan. The eye tends to follow long lines to their terminus. Long lines are useful to draw attention to some special object or section of the garden, but they can be disturbing if they do not lead to a particular point. One line should meet another at a right angle or as close to a right angle as possible. Avoid a junction of two lines that is sharp or pinched. This applies both to the meeting points of curves and those of straight lines.

Place any pools or water effects in your garden so that they can be seen easily from the terrace or patio.

Water in a garden always gives a pleasant, cooling effect, and you can add interest to a pool by using one of a variety of shapes. In home-landscape areas where space is limited, it is not practicable to try to duplicate the shapes of bodies of water found in nature. It is much better to use water in basins that are more architectural in character and design. This is a straightforward use of water that indicates human design and control over the area. You can add motion to the water with bubblers or short jets of spray, or by recirculating water that spills from one basin to another. Or you may prefer to leave the water quiet as a clear, reflecting pool. To obtain the most effective reflections, paint the pool basin black.

You may want to rework your design on the basis of some of these suggestions. Don't worry about an occasional doubt that your design might not be a good one. Your garden will unquestionably be far better than if you had not planned it at all. There is no one "best way." It is not a matter of what is right or wrong, but what is attractive, satisfying, and functional for you and your family.

Thus far this discussion has centered upon trying to make a pattern plan that looks pleasing on a flat sheet of paper. Since a garden has three dimensions, however, you must also consider height and space. The basic rule is that different objects should be of different heights, while similar objects should be of similar heights. For example, matching planter boxes and groups of similar plants in different parts of the garden should be the same height.

But real interest in the garden is a result of height contrasts. Different groups of shrubs should definitely be of different heights — use medium shrubs with tall ones, low shrubs with ground cover, etc. Shrubs near a fence should be taller or shorter than the height of the fence.

Proportion must be considered along with height. Everything in a garden should be definitely wider than it is tall. That is why shrubs are recommended in groups of two or three or more of a kind. If you have two plantings, both of which are higher than the fence, the exposed portion of the fence should be wider than it is high.

Look at your rough plan. Are the tall shrubs and trees in balance, or is there more tall material on one side than on the other? Do your plantings interrupt the tops of fences and walls to help soften these structures and blend them into the design? Try to visualize how the plants will look when they are mature so that you allow enough space for them to grow.

To apply the final polish to the rough sketch, you might ask yourself several additional questions. For example, would raised beds or low retaining walls around part of the planting be worth the effort? Will you want to put any ornamental objects in the garden? Recheck designated flower-bed areas, tree locations, lines, forms, and patterns to be sure that they are free-flowing and not cramped or twisted. Is the garden easy to move through? Garden openings must be larger than those in the house (6 to 10 feet wide).

After you have checked over your detailed plan and asked yourself these or other questions, you should have a plan that will show the proposed layout and arrangements of your garden. Now, with your completed plan, you are at last ready to choose construction materials and the best plants for your design. Don't hesitate to make changes as you select plants and materials. It is almost impossible to plan ahead for everything.

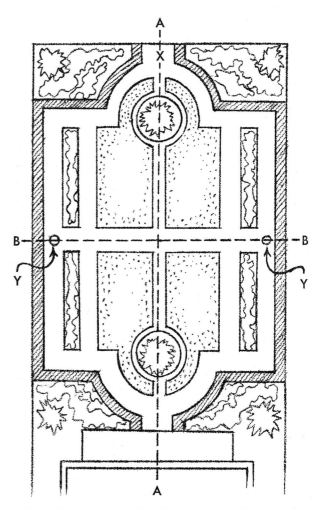

A formal design has symmetrical balance on each side of a major axis (A). In other words, whatever appears on one side of this axis is duplicated exactly on the other side. Every formal design also has a secondary axis (B). This secondary axis is used primarily for developing minor focal points (Y). Major focal points are always at (X). Formal gardens require a rectangle of 7 to 3 or 7 to 4 proportions. All shapes in the design are geometric figures or segments of them.

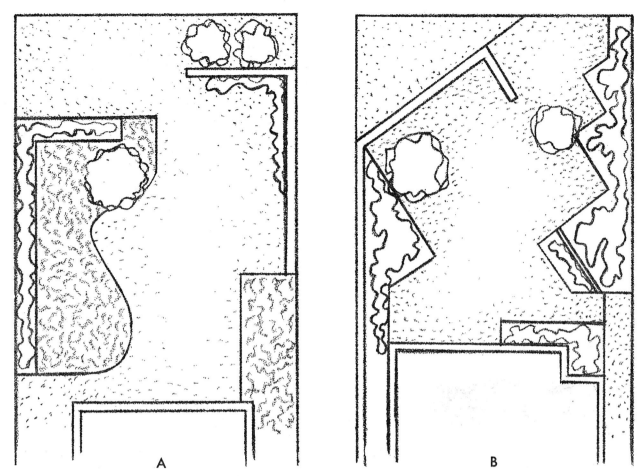

An informal design has asymmetrical balance and more natural lines (A), and is not confined by rectangular forms or straight lines. The architectural or stylized informal design has definite lines, patterns, and shapes. These can be either straight or curved, but tend to be geometrical. The stylized design shown in (B) is characterized by asymmetrical balance.

One landscape element for which some planning ahead is necessary is *landscape lighting.* There are two primary types of lighting in the outdoor living area: (1) lighting that creates dramatic garden effects; and (2) functional lighting that illuminates an area adequately for entertaining (playing cards, eating, lounging), play (croquet, horseshoes, badminton), or safety (walks, steps, paths).

Dramatic garden lighting extends your enjoyment of the landscape into the evening hours when the patio is most often used. By featuring trees, specimen shrubs, flower borders, sculpture, water, boulders, or fences and walls, you can create charming nighttime scenes. *Do not try to light everything.* The overall effect should be a complete composition or picture, not linear or scattered areas of lights surrounded by large areas of darkness.

Functional lighting is intended to guide people through darkness. For this reason, it is important that the lights be located either below or well above eye level. Lights at eye level (about 5 feet high) may temporarily "blind" a person moving into an illuminated area from a dark area. Low lighting is most effective because it lights the path of movement without causing eyestrain. If you light above eye level, be sure that the light beam is not directed toward your neighbors or passersby on the street.

Begin your lighting layout on the landscape plan that includes your final design for structures and plantings. First, determine the locations (both indoors and outdoors) from which you will be viewing the landscape. Next, identify all features (either plants or objects) in your plan that are potential subjects for lighting and those that may serve as your center of interest. Indicate the electrical power source from which wiring will be run so that you can establish a preliminary wiring layout pattern.

Place your lighting so that you create depth of space and establish perspective by manipulating the interplay of light and shadow.

It is often desirable to incorporate off-property views into the land-scape. To be effective, these views should be framed with plant materials. The general garden layout should have dominant flowing lines from the house or terrace leading the eye to the view. If the character of the view is predominantly vertical (above), use trees as the framing elements to repeat this vertical quality. A view that is predominantly horizontal (below) can be emphasized by tapering the ends of planting arms to the ground to repeat this horizontal character.

You can create depth of space by setting a visual boundary with lighting that is not too strong or uniform, or by forming a continuous line of illumination. A combination of light areas and shadow areas will effectively delimit the boundaries.

You can establish perspective by varying the light levels between the foreground, middle ground, and background. If the patio will have a rather high level of light, use the lowest light level in the middle ground and a medium intensity of light in the background. If the patio area will have a low level of illumination, then the middle ground should be left in shadow, with the strongest intensity of light in the background. Another way to establish perspective is to arrange lighting of appropriate intensity for all three areas (foreground, middle ground, and background) so that they establish a visual line or path for the eye to follow. This line should terminate at your center of interest.

As you select the light intensity for each area, consider the reflective qualities of the object you are lighting. Evaluate surface quality (smooth or textured), leaves, bark, and the lightness or darkness of an object. Light objects require less light, while dark objects need more light. Locate your lighting so that the eye will move over the night-lighted landscape in much the same way as it does in the daytime.

A basic rule of night lighting is to avoid placing the light fixtures so that the beam of light is directed head-on to the object. This results in "flattening" the object and eliminating its shadows, texture, and contours. To bring these qualities out, you should use two lights on either side of the object, with more light intensity on one side than on the other. Successful lighting of trees, shrubs, sculpture, flower borders, and flat surfaces requires experimenting with light placement to achieve the most pleasing effects. Some of the more common lighting techniques used in the landscape are described below.

Downlighting is used to illuminate plants, foliage, or other parts of the landscape from a light source well above the ground. It is important that the light source be hidden and that the light be directed straight down, not at an angle. Downlighting creates pools of light that resemble the natural light source of the sun.

Uplighting is achieved by placing a source of light at or below ground level with the light directed upward. This technique results in shadow patterns that emphasize and dramatize the object being illuminated. Uplighting is also effective in casting shadows on a flat surface. It is usually desirable to combine downlighting and uplighting in the various areas of your landscape.

Silhouetting results from backlighting an object (for example, the foliage of a tree) so that the object is viewed against darkness, or by lighting the background (wall, fence, or shrub border) so that the object is viewed against the illuminated surface.

Grazing is the "brushing" of light over the surface of the object to emphasize the textural qualities of bark, foliage, fences, or masonry walls.

Highlighting is employed when you want a particular focal point in your landscape (fountain, sculpture, etc.) to be the center of attention. The level of illumination is increased, with the light source located either above or some distance away from the object. Where you locate the light source depends upon the direction of light that will best feature and give focal emphasis to the object.

Contouring brings out the depth and three-dimensional character of the object through the use of two or three lamps aimed at different angles and with a stronger intensity of light from one side than the other. Locating the lights too close will "wash out" the contour effect. Try various distances between the light source and the object until you get the desired results.

Washing is the illumination of a vertical surface either through uplighting or downlighting. This technique can also be used to make the light bounce off the vertical surface onto objects in front of it.

Crosslighting is achieved by using a light from two different light sources placed so as to oppose each other — one light in front of the object to be lighted and one in the rear, or one light on one side and another on the opposite side. The fixtures for this kind of lighting are usually at ground level, and the light intensity of both fixtures is not the same.

The primary goal of lighting is to bring out the texture, shadows, and contours of the element being lighted. Walls and fences can be used as reflecting surfaces, and as a source of interesting shadow patterns. The light should be placed to the front but slightly off to the side to cast the shadow. To silhouette the plant, illuminate it from the back. This effect is further enhanced by using a weaker intensity of light on the front of the object from slightly off the side. Texture is featured when the light is placed close to the object. If the branching habit of the plant is loose and the foliage is open, use uplighting. If the plant has somewhat dense foliage, the light should come from the side at a sharp angle. Light greens or glossy foliage will reflect greater quantities of light than darker, dull surfaces. You may have to decrease the intensity of light on highly reflective surfaces and increase the intensity on darker colored and duller surfaced areas.

Each plant should be analyzed individually. Some plants look better lighted from above, others from below, and still others need to be silhouetted. Trees with an open structure and finer texture are better subjects for lighting than those that are coarse and dense. Canopy trees are most effective when uplighted either from the ground or lower part of the crown. Columnar trees should be lighted from the ground, with the lamps placed in a circular pattern.

Trees with dramatic form, irregular shapes, or handsome trunk and branching structure can be accentuated by uplighting so that the light grazes the trunks and branches. You may silhouette a tree to emphasize its form, or you may want to locate lights high in the crown and possibly out toward the drip line to cast the shadow patterns of its branches on the lawn. Because of their dense foliage, evergreen trees are most effectively lighted when only the tips (10 to 12 inches) of the branches are illuminated.

Shrubs can be lighted in much the same way as trees. Shrubs with interesting forms or habits of growth should be angle-lighted to accent their structure; those that are more open and airy can be backlighted, with the lamps throwing light upward. In some cases, low downlighting fixtures can be used to advantage.

The effective lighting of flowers requires flowering plants with large, showy blossoms that are carried well above the foliage. Low fixtures with shades that direct the light downward provide the best lighting. You will want to experiment with the height of the light above the flowers. It is seldom desirable for the light to be lower than 12 inches or higher than 24 inches.

It is difficult to determine the number and types of fixtures you may need without first experimenting with different lighting techniques on each object. You may wish to have a landscape architect review your plans and recommend lighting techniques to be used at the various locations. The return for this small investment will be many years of nighttime pleasure.

You can choose from two types of lighting systems — the low-voltage system and the standard voltage system. The low-voltage system is a major step forward in exterior landscape lighting. This system uses a cable that can be buried or placed on top of the ground. The standard 110 voltage is reduced to 12 volts through the use of a grounded transformer. This transformer should be selected on the basis of the total wattage load of all the fixtures to be used. Be sure that the minimum wattage is at least one-half of the transformer rating.

Mount the transformer 1 foot above the ground and within 5 to 6 feet of 110/120 volt receptacles. The wattage requirements must *not exceed* the rating of the transformer; if they do, two transformers are needed.

The low-voltage system does not require wire splicing, since the fixtures have pin-type connectors that clamp to the cable. The 12-volt current used in this system is the same as that used in a toy electric train, and it is equally safe. Since the fixtures are small, they can be moved to new locations with little difficulty as the landscape changes and matures, and they do not become a prominent part of the landscape.

The standard voltage systems (110/120 volts) can be installed more cheaply than in the past through the use of Type UF wire with a neoprene jacket that allows for direct burial in the ground, eliminating the need for a metal conduit or lead sheathing. Check your local codes to determine the underground wiring requirements in your community. Some communities still require wire to be placed in a conduit or sheathing.

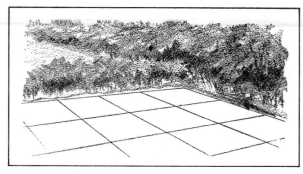

Low plants, seat walls, or low retaining walls give line and pattern to the design and create space by serving as divisions. They do not have to extend the full width of the yard. A short distance is sufficient, since the viewer's imagination will carry the effect of a division.

Install Type UF wire in an 18-inch trench. Cover the bottom of the trench with 2 inches of sand for drainage. Lay the wire in the trench and cover with 2 inches of soil. Place a 3-inch-wide board over the soil to prevent accidental cutting of the wire with a shovel or other garden equipment, and complete backfilling. At those locations where the wire emerges from the ground to a fixture, the wire must be enclosed in a rigid electrical conduit. Ordinary pipe is not suitable.

Once you have determined where you want outdoor lighting, consult your local electrical supply firm or electrical contractor about wiring and fixture installation. Both the standard and the low-voltage systems have lamps (bulbs) that provide a small, concentrated beam (spot) or a spreading beam of light that is not as intense. A number of colored lenses can be used for different effects. A green lens brightens greens but washes out pink and red. A blue lens emphasizes blue and green but dilutes the strength of warm colors. A red lens is best used in areas where red and orange tones predominate. An amber lens accentuates yellows, oranges, and browns, and does not attract insects. A clear lens brings out all colors and intensifies textures.

The most commonly used bulb is the PAR 38. This bulb is weatherproof, and it is available in floodlight or spotlight bulbs of 75, 100, and 150 watts. Clear lenses are standard on the 75- and 150-watt bulbs. There are also PAR 38 mercury vapor lights available in a 100-watt size. This light, which requires a ballast, gives a bluish cast to objects. Use only permanent wiring with waterproof sockets. The sockets should always be installed by an electrical contractor. Check your local building codes and ordinances governing outdoor lighting.

Finally, consideration should be given to developing the outdoor living areas for *row houses* or *town houses*. With the increased emphasis on high-density living, these housing units (often referred to as **condominiums** if they are privately owned) are becoming popular. They present special landscape problems because of the limited space available for development. The types of housing units discussed here are those that give the family direct access to the ground. The landscape principles are essentially the same as those for conventional housing, although the scale of the area to be developed is considerably reduced, and the problems of privacy versus open space and communal areas (interspaces formed by the layout patterns of the buildings) are somewhat more critical.

The planning approach for a row house is the same as that for a detached house. First, inventory your needs and resources; then analyze your site and become familiar with its potentials and limitations. Since the area over which you have control is extremely limited, it is very important to have a scale plan.

Before designing or modifying the public area, find out what you are permitted to do. Even if you own the unit, the owners' association usually does not allow any individual involvement in public or communal spaces. Because of the close proximity of one entry to another or a common building entry for two units, the design of the public area requires a cooperative landscape development. The developer or owners' association is usually responsible for the entire area between the street and buildings, as well as the interior common spaces. This responsibility should entail more than merely scattering a few plants and trees across the front of the building.

As a means of protecting their investment and enhancing the desirability of living in the project, the developer or owners' association should retain a landscape architect to design all public and communal spaces. The public-area planting design should help to articulate space and introduce the element of human scale in an area where there is an extensive building mass complicated by architectural features and detailing far in excess of those in single-family housing. The design problem at this scale is too complex to offer guidelines and specific suggestions for a "do-it-yourself" approach.

Your private space, which is usually an extension of your living unit, gives you an opportunity to undertake your own landscape design. Although these private spaces are usually small (typically 18′ x 24′), you can do a great deal to make them functional units that will allow you to extend your living activities into the outdoors. At the same time, the design should be strong, attractive visual space when viewed from within the unit.

The proper development of this private area within the boundary screen requires restraint and a discriminating choice of materials. You cannot include everything that you would like. Select only those elements that will add to the functional and aesthetic role of the area. You must use fewer elements and arrange them with extreme care. Since this space is small, choose only those materials that will exploit its full potential.

As in all landscape developments, you need to consider the floor, walls, and ceiling. You can later add enriching elements within this basic framework. Your plans should include surfacing patterns, a few selected shrubs, perhaps vines for screening, ground covers for flowers, and possibly a tree for shade. These are elements that add human scale by providing a bridge between the human body and large-scale buildings. They are also an essential part of space organization and enrichment.

The boundaries of your private space should be defined with a privacy fence or screen planting if these are not already in existence. The height of the fence between adjacent units should be higher (usually 6 feet) than the portion of fence that forms the rear of your space. This rear portion should be only 4 feet high to permit viewing into the central common areas. If it is too high, you will feel "boxed in," and the size of the space will be visually diminished. Check with the developer or the owners' association about restrictions for enclosure heights. A fence is usually preferable to a planting screen because it requires less ground space.

Determine areas where you are particularly vulnerable to viewing from other units in the complex or from neighboring properties. Before attempting to solve this problem, evaluate the plantings in the common area. This is the area usually located behind the buildings, and it is formed by the layout patterns of the buildings in the complex. If these plantings are relatively new, you need to anticipate their mature height and spread so that you can determine their ultimate effect on your area and your privacy. Then you can decide whether you need to try to block the view by plantings in your private area.

Surfacing should be either a deck or hard paving to accommodate intensive use and to provide easy maintenance. The same procedures for pattern development described for detached houses also apply to row houses. Since this space is pictorial as well as usable, however, more strength can be given to the ground pattern than in a detached home. For example, a strong diagonal pattern or a carefully conceived straight-line arrangement can help create an illusion of greater space.

The surfacing material can be modular units such as brick, exposed aggregate concrete, or a deck. A deck has the advantage of allowing you to extend the floor level within the house into the patio court. This deck pattern should be integrated with plantings and ground-cover patterns to assure that the combined planting and surface areas are unified. Usually, more space should be allotted to surfacing than to planting, but the planting area should be large enough to provide visual contrast between surface and enclosure elements.

Once you have a satisfying scheme of surfacing and enclosure, you are ready to consider adding enriching elements (boulders, water features, shrubs, flowers, specimen plants, etc.) to the picture. At this point, it is particularly important to exercise restraint. You must avoid turning the space into a confused jumble of individual elements fighting for attention. Use a few elements carefully arranged. Each element is meaningful and effective only in its relation to every other element in the design.

You should now check your design to be sure that you have a well-conceived layout for your private area. Form, color, and texture in all three basic units (floor plan, enclosure, and overhead) should be strongly contrasted. The design should have bold patterns that strengthen space organization, provide pictorial quality, and reflect sophisticated use of embellishments for maximum richness.

Shrubs used with a fence (or wall) should be shorter or taller than the fence. The exposed portion of fence, like all other elements in the landscape, should be wider than it is tall.

GROUND PATTERNS

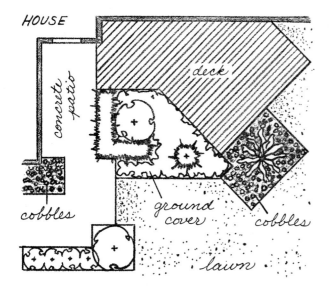

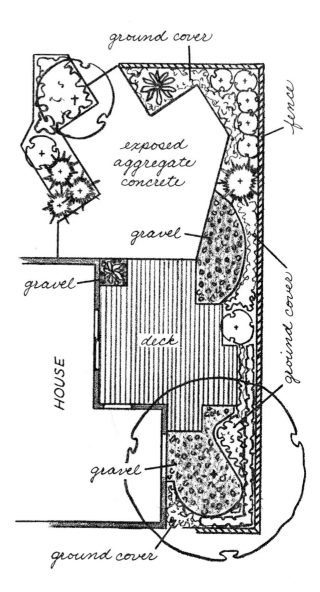

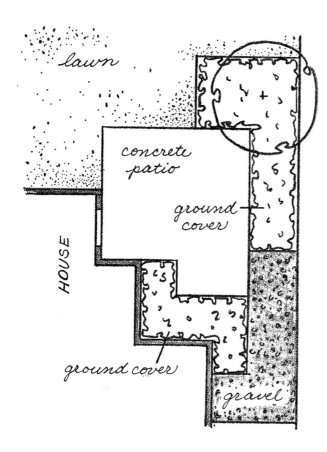

Select surfacing materials on the basis of their suitability for each area. By using several different materials, you can create a strong, interrelated pattern. Be sure that the ground pattern does not overwhelm the other units — enclosures, overheads, and embellishments. A good design balances the ground pattern with all of the other units that create three-dimensional space.

The following sketch plans and perspectives will help you in evaluating and developing your own landscape design. The first six sketches (pages 172-177) illustrate the use of general landscape principles in straight-line, diagonal, and curved patterns. They show space organization through the use of various materials, as well as refinement of the primary use areas. After reviewing these six sketches, return to your plan and analyze it in the same way that the sketches are analyzed in the book. Use page 178 to jot down ideas or note changes that you may wish to make in your plan.

The remaining 10 sketches (pages 179-188) are "case studies" dealing with typical site problems faced by homeowners (long, narrow lots, odd-shaped lots, shallow but wide lots, etc.). They should be studied not only for their patterns but for the functional and aesthetic use of plants and structures.

The 16 sketches are intended to give you a better understanding of how space can be organized to achieve a harmonious and usable landscape. You should not impose any of these designs directly on your own property. The degree of slope, climate, and orientation of your property, as well as your family's interests and needs, present unique problems that must be solved by your own landscape design.

Many patterns can be created by combining various surfacing materials, shrubs, trees, and vertical structures into the overall design. In the above drawing, dominant patterns have been evolved from the use of curved and straight lines. The wood fence used to screen the service area to the left of the house also serves as an enclosure along that side of the property. The raised planting bed created by a seat wall adds interest by giving a change in grade on a level lot. The patio has a hard surface, and the balance of the area is in lawn and plantings.

The above design illustrates the effective use of *repetition*. Notice the repetition of the curved bed line in the form of the patio. The small planting bed to the right of the patio is devoted to a specimen plant (stag horn sumac) and ground cover (Japanese spurge). At the rear of this planting is a fence panel that provides a backdrop for the planting and screens the neighbors' view at the same time. An additional section of fence is located on the property line to extend privacy on the right side of the yard. The same fencing is used to screen the service area at the upper left and to give protection on the left property line. The strong patterns formed by the planting beds, lawn, and patio add interest, and the repetition of line and material gives unity and harmony to the overall design.

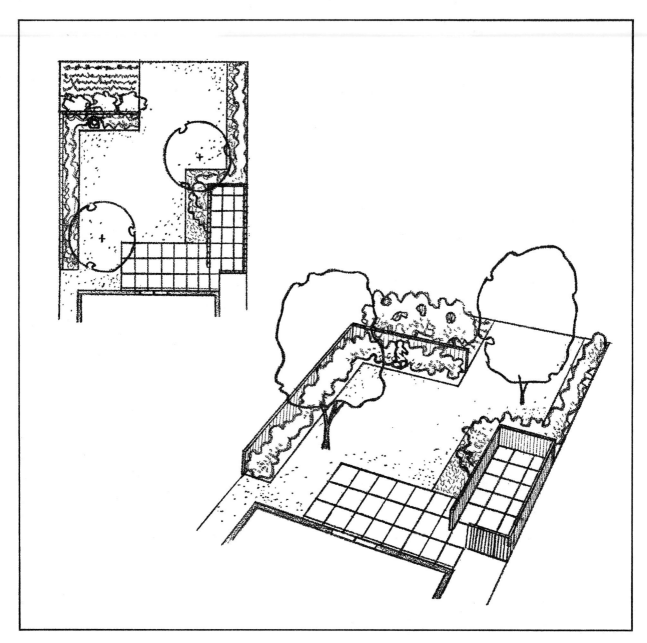

This asymmetrical design has been worked out entirely with straight lines. It shows good space organization for the service, leisure, sports, and vegetable-garden areas. The service area, located just off the patio, is close to the utility room, and there is easy access to the outdoor living area from the kitchen. An interesting scene has been created for viewing from within the house, as well as from the patio. The fence screening the vegetable garden at the upper left may be continued along the property line, depending upon the need for screening or privacy. The fence screening the service area should be more refined than the fence along the property line and vegetable garden because of its nearness to the patio. Notice the use of gravel and ground-cover surfacing in addition to lawn and patio surfacing. Remember — straight lines should lead to *something*. For example, the fence panel by the vegetable garden could have a piece of garden sculpture (as shown) or a specimen plant as a terminus for the straight line.

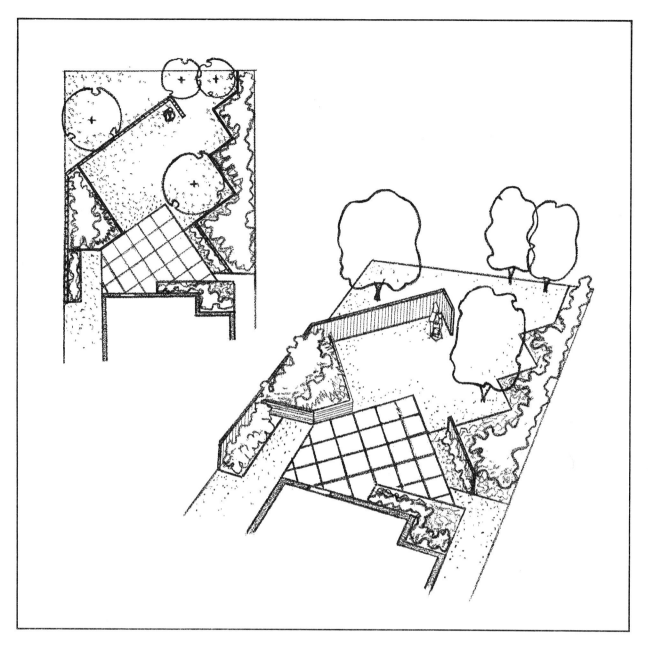

The design shown above was created through the use of straight lines in a diagonal pattern. The irregular shapes of lawn, paving, and planting beds all fit together. It is the pattern formed by the relations between these shapes, rather than the individual shapes themselves, that is of primary importance. The line that separates shapes can be straight, curved, or a series of steps, but it must defiine an interesting shape on both sides — not just on one side. Be sure that this dividing line is pleasing, not complicated with unnecessary bumps or jogs. Carefully consider the proportions of the two areas it defines. There should be enough difference between the length and width of each area to create interest. Notice the diagonal fence screening the service area at the upper left. The panel of fence set at right angles creates a focal point for a specimen plant, sculpture (as shown), or other garden ornamentation. The dark lines in the drawing could be raised beds or well-defined dividers between lawn and planting beds to emphasize shapes and patterns. The diagonal fence panel to the right of the patio provides protection from the wind and helps tie the design together.

This informal design combining curves and straight lines shows one way to treat a long, narrow lot. The only highly refined and intensely developed area is the patio. The patio, which extends directly from the house, is set off from the remainder of the private area by fencing units that also give privacy. The wide opening at the upper righthand corner of the patio allows a view of the balance of the yard, preserving a sense of spaciousness even with three sides enclosed. Notice the contrast of shapes in the patio. The hard surfacing is curved in sharp contrast to the strong rectangular shape of the area. Loose surfacing material is used adjacent to the circular patio area. Trees behind the service-yard fence at the upper right soften the harshness and relieve the monotony of a length of fence. The added height of the trees also screens the property from a large two-story house on a high foundation. A single row of screen plantings extends along the property line at the rear and left side. A screen planting of greater interest and variation has been developed along the right side of the property.

The informal design shown above uses both curves and straight lines. The strong curved line dividing the lawn and plantings blends into the patio, with a transition to straight lines achieved by a stepped seat wall, fence panels, and a planting area in the righthand corner of the patio. This effect is repeated in the lower left-hand corner, serving to screen the patio from the adjacent property at left. Access to the patio is from the living room, and access to the service area at the lower lefthand corner is from the kitchen. This design lends itself well to incorporating flowers at the upper left and at the strong incurve at the upper right of the planting bed. Notice the small clump of flowering trees at the left used to balance the seat walls and planting bed at the upper righthand corner of the patio. Fencing for screening or privacy is not required because the plantings give sufficient protection to the areas at the rear of the property.

Notes

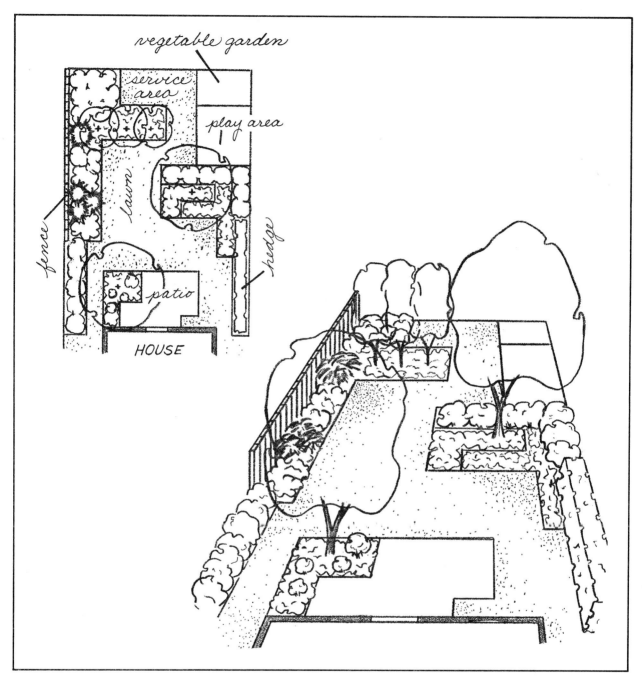

vegetable garden

service area

play area

lawn

fence

hedge

patio

HOUSE

A property that is considerably longer than it is wide requires a design that will stop the eye from viewing directly along its full length to the rear property line. A linear pattern following the outline of the property would only accentuate the depth of the lot. A pattern that extends the planting units inward (at right angles) from the side property lines, however, prevents the eye from "reading" the total length of the property in one scan. The illusion of greater width is created by organizing the area into subspaces of more pleasing proportions through the use of right-angle plantings in front of the play and service areas.

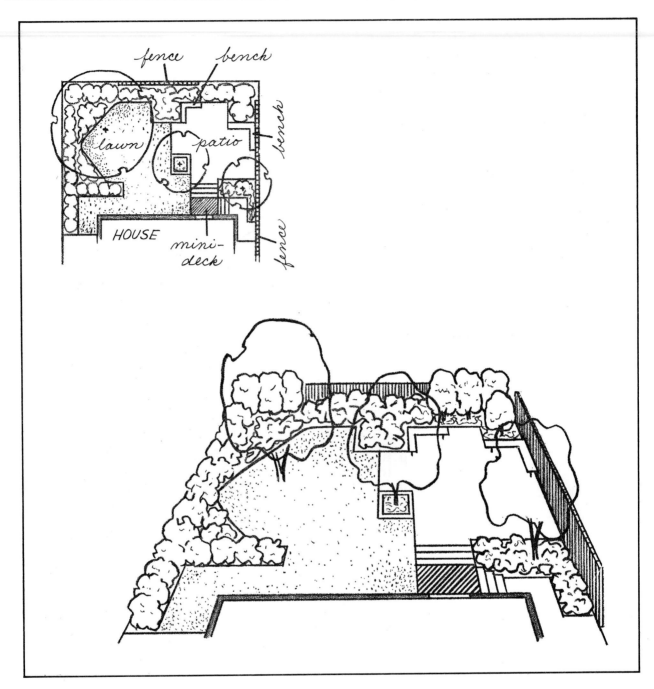

A striking pattern that "reads" well in both plan and perspective can be developed for a rear property that is wider than it is deep. The property is divided into two unequal areas. The smaller is the patio area. A mini-deck provides a transition between the house and the outdoor living area. The dominance of the rectilinear space is repeated in the basic straight-line design. The diagonal pattern gains added interest from the introduction of the diagonal lines in the lawn area. These diagonal lines are compatible with the basic straight-line style established, but their change in direction provides contrast and variety. Notice the projecting arms at the lower left corner of the lawn and at the upper center between the patio and lawn. The mini-deck also projects into the yard area. Each of these units succeeds in *reproportioning* the total space to suggest greater depth to the property than actually exists.

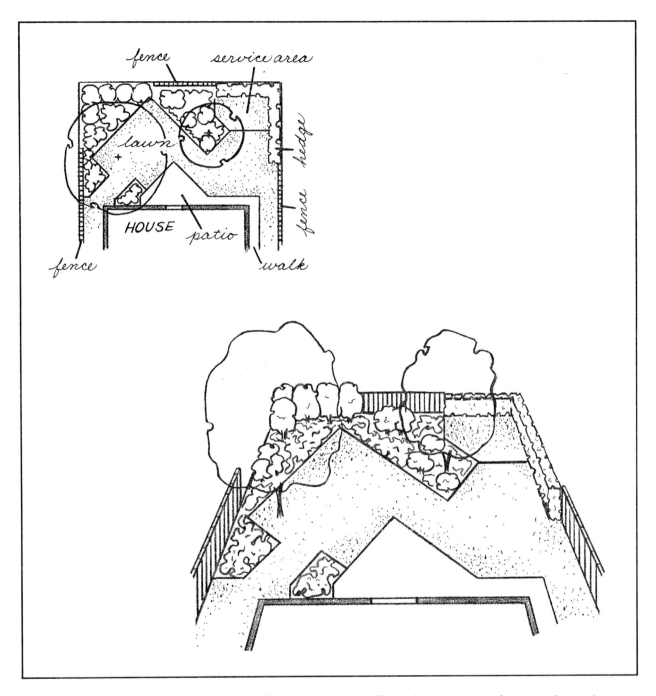

The diagonal lines in the ground pattern divert the viewer's attention from a rear property whose depth from the back of the house to the rear property line is less than its width from the side property lines. The diagonal unit projecting into the yard from the rear not only defines and encloses the outdoor living space but effectively separates and screens the service area from the living areas. Notice the two sections of fence connected by a hedge of equal height. This combination avoids the monotony and "imprisoning" effect of using only one continuous vertical element.

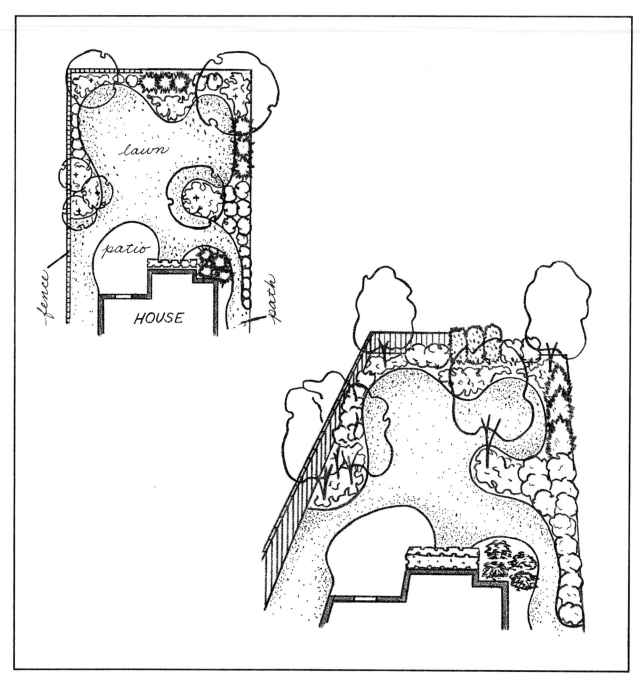

A rear area that has greater depth than width can more easily accommodate a curved plan because of the greater horizontal distance for achieving a transition reverse curve from an outcurve to an incurve. Notice the smooth flow of the curved pattern. This pattern presents a strong, bold contrast that overcomes the dominance of the straight lines of the house and property boundaries. The patio is designed into the setback of the rear line of the house, but it pro- jects into the yard to integrate the patio with the rest of the landscape. Since the bay in the upper right corner is not wholly visible from the house or patio, people are encouraged to move out and into the area. If you partially mask an area to pique curiosity, be sure to incorporate a special-interest landscape element (sculpture, seating, flower beds, etc.) into the design to justify the effort of walking into this hidden space.

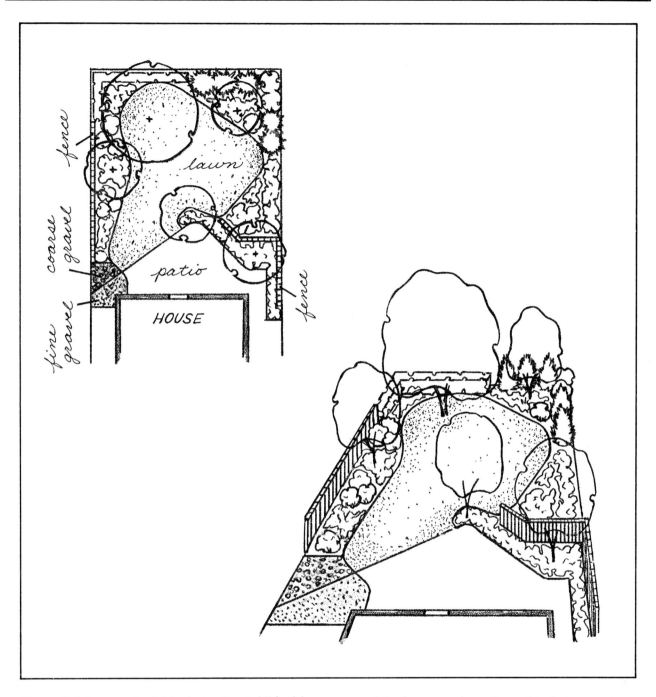

The spatial framework of this design is established by a curvilinear pattern that features arc-and-tangent lines. The lines and angles that separate the lawn area, planting beds, and patio provide a strong visual interest and establish flowing, freeform spaces. With the proper selection and combination of surfacing materials, fences, and plantings, this design produces a framework that invites the viewer to inspect the details of each area. It succeeds in providing a maximum of living space, as well as a sense of enclosure and privacy.

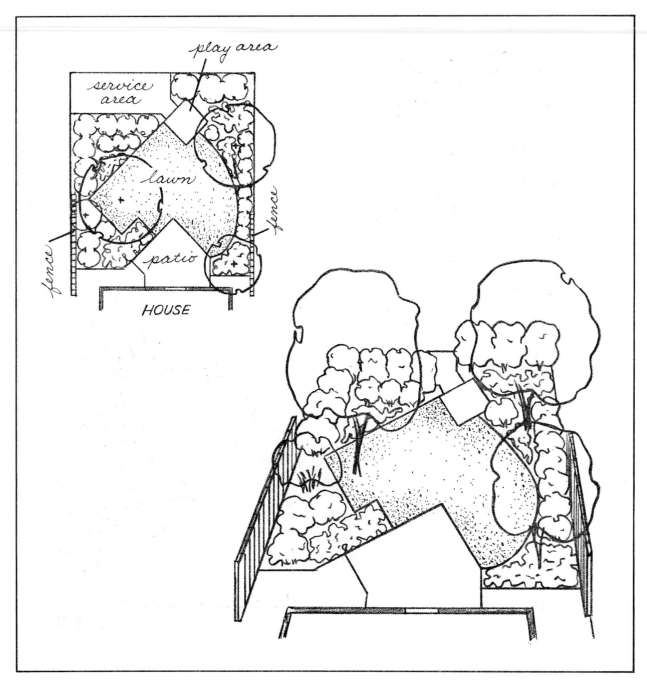

The design shown above has predominately diagonal lines that are given added emphasis by the introduction of the bold curved line on the right side of the property. This curved line adds variety and contrast to the total design, preventing monotony through excessive repetition of straight lines. The overall layout provides an orderly and sequential movement of the viewer's eye and attention. Notice that the straight lines of the house are extended into the landscape before the diagonal pattern is introduced. This transition between the house and the landscape is important with curved or diagonal patterns. The design allows for future adjustments. The children's play area is located so that it can easily be redesigned for integration into the basic design framework when it is no longer needed.

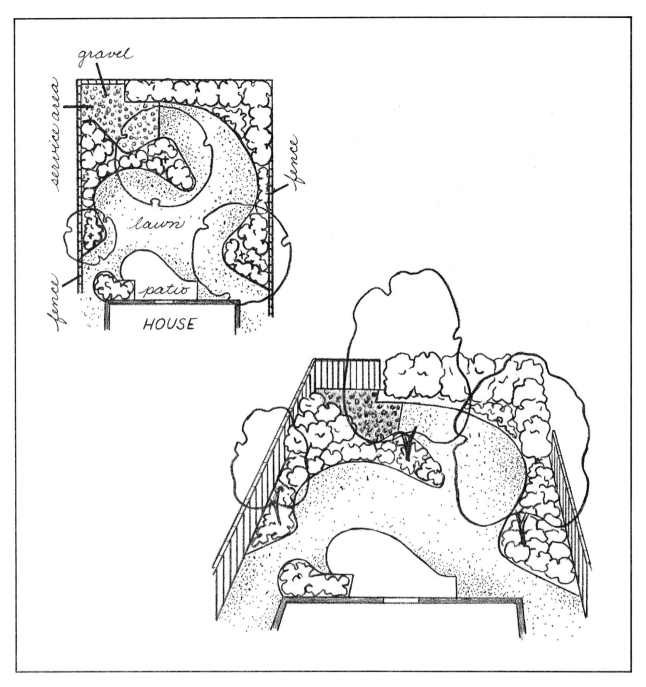

In the drawing above, the flowing yet bold curved line introduces a "naturalistic" quality to the design. This layout works well for a small property because the curved lines form an easily recognizable pattern that gives order to the composition. Notice the use of the arc-and-tangent design to achieve pleasing transitions from large, dominant incurves into the straight lines of the property boundary, or where changes in direction are required. The three trees serve to articulate the primary space and tie the pattern together. The form of the patio has the same form as that produced by the lines dividing the lawn and planting beds. The result suggests an interlocking of the two patterns. Blending loose, irregular groups and masses of plants within the controlled curved pattern strengthens the "naturalistic" quality of the design.

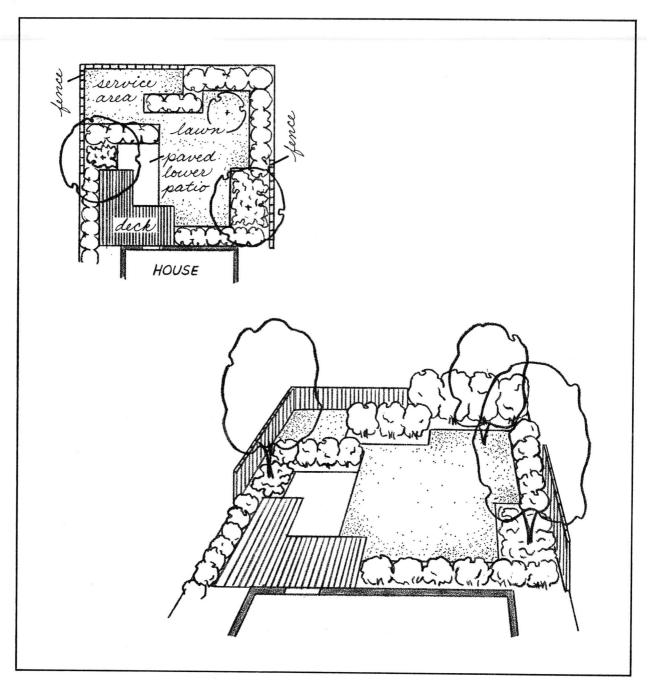

Visual interest and intriguing spatial relations are produced by this straight-line design that utilizes a series of interlocked patterns for various use areas. The deck establishes a comfortable transition between indoor and outdoor spaces, and it is large enough to be usable for outdoor living activities. The paved lower patio gives added flexibility for these activities. The plantings along the left side and at the rear of the deck-patio area define this roomlike space and direct attention to the balance of the landscape. The overall shape and proportion of the site has been consciously subordinated by the strong internal pattern and sub-spaces. Notice the baffle effect used to mask both the entry to the service area and the service area itself.

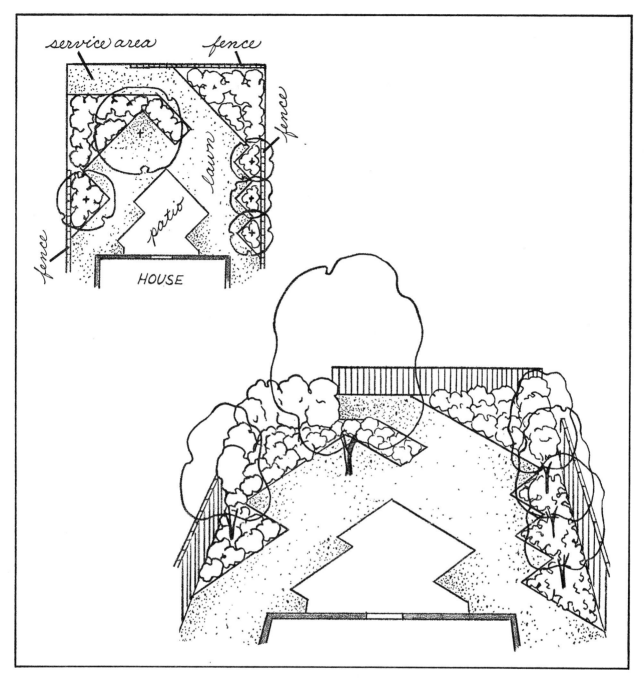

This diagonal-line pattern produces an orderly yet irregular arrangement that creates a strong sense of direction. The design qualities of the plant materials must be carefully considered because plants are used to reinforce the diagonal pattern. The design of the plantings and the patio give this composition an enclosed, intimate feeling. Notice how the small trees along the right side establish "visual stops" that avoid confusion in the stepped-pattern arrangement.

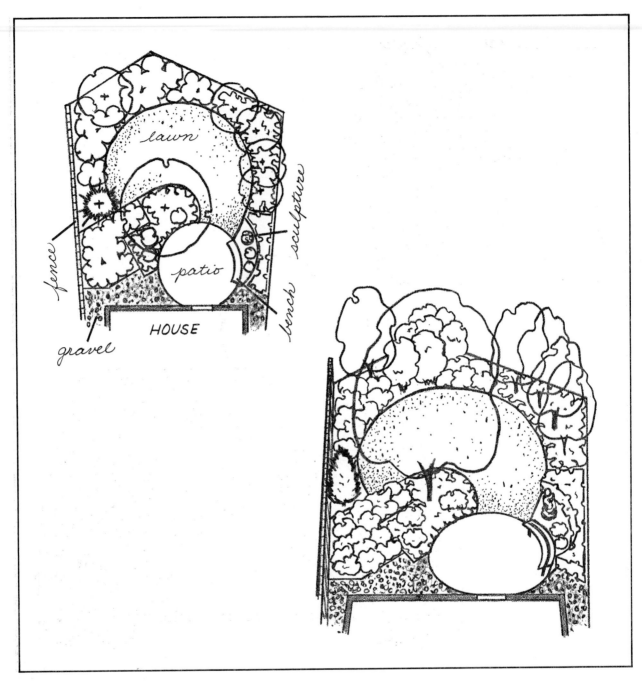

A basic rule to follow in developing a property that has an irregular or odd-shaped boundary is to establish a strong internal pattern that prevents the viewer from "reading" the unusual shape of the area. This can be accomplished with straight-line, diagonal, or circular patterns. In the above drawing, the repetition of the circular outline for the patio and lawn and planting areas successfully diverts the viewer's attention from the irregular shape of the property. The permanent bench reinforces the circular pattern and directs the view from the patio into the remainder of the landscape.

12: Buying And Planting Plants

You may be confused by the many places where you can buy plants and about what to look for to be assured of vigorous and healthy stock. If possible, buy locally grown material. Local plants are adapted to your climate, and are most likely to be in good condition. Shipping plants long distances may dry them out too much and lower their vigor and chances for survival.

A possible source of plants, particularly trees, is from a native grove. You may have to mark the plants you want when they are in bloom or in foliage, and then move them out later when they are dormant.

It is more difficult to reestablish trees from a woods than nursery-grown trees because their root systems are not as compact. Another disadvantage of transplanting native trees is that they grow so close together in the woods that it may be difficult to find well-shaped specimens. Try to choose trees that are growing in a large, open area because these trees are more likely to have well-formed crowns. They will also be easier to dig out with more root system.

Small trees do not need to be root-pruned, but large trees from a woods should be root-pruned for two years before moving them. A root-pruned tree has a much better chance to survive transplanting. Root pruning will encourage the development of fine hair roots on the remaining roots. To root-prune, draw a circle on the ground a few feet from the trunk and divide it into 6 pie-shaped sections. In the spring or fall, trench and backfill around the outside of *every other section,* cutting all roots. The following year, trench and backfill the other three sections.

The American Nurserymen's Association and the American Standards Association have set up standards to describe the quality and grades of nursery stock. Some of these standards are discussed below.

The height of deciduous shrubs (those that lose their leaves in winter) is usually given in inches up to 24 inches. For plants taller than 24 inches, the height is stated in feet. When measurements are stated in series (for example, 12 to 15 inches, or 2½ to 3 feet), the height of the material will not be less than the smaller figure nor greater than the larger figure.

In buying a deciduous shrub, actual height is not as important as the number of stems. It is important to select a plant with a dense, well-shaped crown and a root system that is as undamaged as possible. You should also consider the plant's general condition and appearance.

Evergreen shrubs keep their foliage all year, and their measurements depend upon the type selected. Evergreens include spreading types such as Waukegan or Pfitzer junipers, and upright types such as pines and spruce. Measurements for the spreading types give the spread, not the height. Spread measurement is usually an average rather than the largest diameter of the plant. Height measurement for the upright type is given in inches up to 24 inches, and in feet for plants taller than 24 inches. The term "specimen" indicates exceptionally heavy, well-shaped plants that are denser and thicker than the average.

Tree standards are given either as height or caliber measurements. Height is expressed in feet as a minimum to maximum height for the species or variety listed. Caliber refers to the diameter of the trunk. This measurement is usually taken 6 inches above the ground for trees whose caliber does not exceed 4 inches, and 12 inches above the ground for those with a caliber larger than 4 inches. Height is not as important as caliber in tree selection.

Tree quality is determined by a bushy crown and a well-developed root system. Because of extreme differ-

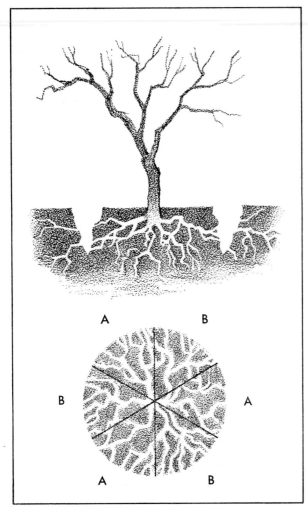

To root-prune a large tree, draw a circle around the trunk. The distance from the trunk should be about 5 inches for each 1 inch of trunk diameter. Divide this circle into 6 pie-like sections. The first year, dig a trench deep enough to cut all roots in the areas marked (A). Mix excavated soil with well-rotted manure or commercial fertilizer before replacing it in the trench. The second year, follow the same procedure for sections marked (B). The tree can be moved in the third year.

ences in growth rates and habits of trees, it is difficult to set standards for crown height and breadth with relation to total height or caliber.

An understanding of the way a nursery retail yard or garden center handles plant materials will help you to choose vigorous plants that will quickly adapt to their new location. Plant materials will be handled in the salesyard either as packaged bare-root, mechanically balled bare-root, balled-and-burlapped, or container stock.

Many people prefer to transplant locally grown plants selected in the field. Since these plants are freshly dug, they will be subject to the least amount of moisture loss and shock between digging and

replanting. A recent innovation in the nursery industry makes it possible to have top-quality plants that were dug in the fall. These plants are stored in translucent structures over winter so that they are not weakened by extreme temperature changes or by excessive moisture loss because of high winds. If properly stored, this plant material is equal to or even better than freshly dug material.

Balled-and-burlapped plants, often referred to as "B & B," are dug with a ball of soil around the root system. This ball is then wrapped with burlap or placed in a papier-mâché wrapper.

Evergreen plants must be balled to be moved, and deciduous plants must be balled when moved in leaf. The ball of earth containing undisturbed roots must be wrapped to keep it from breaking apart during the moving. Always carry a balled-and-burlapped plant under the ball, and handle it carefully.

Keep the ball as small as possible so that it will not crack open under its own weight. You will have to take enough soil for the plant to reestablish itself in its new location. Standard ball diameter is about one-third or one-fourth of the plant height. Exceptions are extremely small or extremely large plants, when the relative size of the ball may be larger for a small plant and somewhat smaller for a large plant.

To take out a balled plant, dig a trench around the plant a little farther out than you want the ball. Widen the trench as you dig deeper, and shape the ball as you go down. Slip a piece of burlap under the ball as you cut underneath, and roll the ball onto the burlap. When the ball rolls free, carefully wrap burlap around it. Hold the burlap in place with nails and tie securely with twine or rope. When planting, be sure to cut the twine to prevent girdling, especially around the trunk.

If you are digging and moving deciduous plants on your property, you will probably move them bareroot. It is best to move these in early spring or late fall when they are out of leaf. The entire plant is then dormant and the roots need little water. Dormant, bare-rooted deciduous plants are less likely to suffer from the shock of being moved.

For bare-root transplanting, you need only to dig up the plants, saving as many roots as possible. Don't let the roots dry out after digging — cover them immediately with burlap, soil, or sawdust while moving the plant to its new location. Even a few minutes in the air will dry roots out enough to kill the plant. You can store plants for several weeks or more by heeling them in and keeping the roots damp.

Packaged bare-root stock has roots in packing material such as sawdust or bark, and it is usually wrapped with plastic to reduce moisture loss from the roots. An artificial ball has peat or a peat-soil mixture compressed around the roots. The procedures for planting packaged or mechanically balled bare-root stock are the same as those for planting container or balled-and-burlapped material. Be sure to remove the plastic wrapping.

Many evergreens and deciduous materials come from a nursery in containers. The soil starts to dry out as soon as the container is cut open, and it is difficult to keep the roots moist. Set these plants out immediately in the ground, or store them with moist soil or sawdust covering the roots. Keep all the soil in contact with the roots, and plant the entire contents.

Plant container plants in the same way that you plant balled-and-burlapped, packaged, or mechanically balled bare-root stock. After removing the container, slice vertically with a knife through the soil and roots at three or four places to prevent the roots from growing in a circular pattern that could girdle the plant.

Prices of plants vary with their source. A mail-order house may offer a more attractive price than your local nurseryman, but you must usually add the cost of postage and express or freight charges to the mail-order price. The final cost may be close to that of freshly dug material from your local nurseryman. Shipped-in plants are often badly dried out when you get them, unless the shipper has protected the roots and crowns.

To be sure that you obtain a handsome evergreen or deciduous shrub or tree, purchase your materials from a reliable source. The desire to get your money's worth is understandable, and cut-rate prices may appeal to your sense of economy. But the nursery industry as a whole tries to maintain a price level that will result in a fair price for the buyer and a reasonable return to the grower. The important point is to buy only from a reputable local dealer or a mail-order firm that will back up its material with a guarantee.

Neighbors, relatives, and friends who offer their surplus stock are a good source of plants. But don't accept everything that is offered to you. Discipline yourself to follow through with your landscape plan. After all your work in planning your design, you can appreciate the importance of using the correct material in a particular location.

Before you plant anything, you must prepare the soil properly — perhaps even condition it. Conditioning means more than just fertilizing — it means altering the physical makeup of the soil. For example, you must correct the physical balance of soil that has too much clay in it, or sand that contains too little organic matter. Topsoil is usually better for plant growth than subsoil because it has larger amounts of decayed organic matter in it. For best growth, topsoil should be at least 8 to 12 inches deep. If your soil is poor and you cannot afford to add 6 inches of topsoil, you should have at least enough good soil on hand to fill planting holes properly.

If sandy soil does not have sufficient organic matter, it will lose water and plant nutrients through leaching. Sandy soils can be improved by mixing in organic matter (peat moss, sewage sludge, compost, etc.) and topsoils. If soil has too much clay, it may not drain well. Clay soils can be improved by adding coarser materials such as sand, calcined clay, and humus.

A soil test will tell you the fertility level of your soil. You can get a soil test by sending a soil sample to your county cooperative extension office.

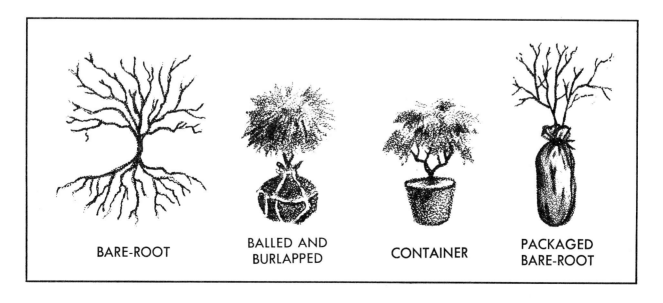

BARE-ROOT   BALLED AND BURLAPPED   CONTAINER   PACKAGED BARE-ROOT

To take a proper soil sample for a test, dig in random areas over the entire property. Dig out a shovelful of soil, and then slice a thin section from the hole and put it on a sheet of paper. When you have slices from various locations in your yard, mix them thoroughly in a jar and send them in for your soil test. If you are interested in the soil from one area, take soil only from that area.

Your soil test will tell you how much of each kind of fertilizer to add. Fertilizers may be organic (bonemeal, fishmeal, sewage sludges, etc.), synthetic, or inorganic. Inorganic fertilizers are readily available to plants, while organic fertilizers break down slowly and become available over a longer time.

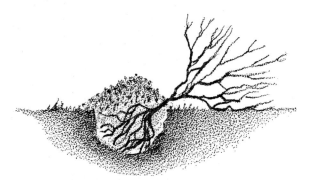

If you cannot place a new plant in the ground immediately, protect its roots from drying out. This plant has been heeled into a trench with soil covering its roots.

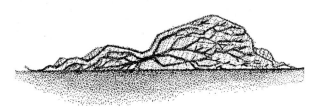

If the plant is going to be planted soon, it is usually sufficient to cover the entire plant with burlap canvas, or opaque plastic. Dampen before covering.

The roots of a balled-and-burlapped plant must be kept moist. Dampen the soil and cover the ball with soil or sawdust to reduce drying.

All plants need nitrogen, phosphorus, and potash for satisfactory growth. These elements are listed in that order by numbers on fertilizer bags. For example, a 16-8-6 combination indicates 16 percent nitrogen, 8 percent phosphoric acid, and 6 percent potassium oxide. A fertilizer containing all three of these nutrient elements is referred to as a "complete" fertilizer. Use a high-nitrogen fertilizer on foliage plants. Nitrogen is important for growth of new leaves and stems.

However, too much nitrogen supplied to flowering plants will cause them to produce leaves and stems rather than flowers. For this reason, use a high-nitrogen fertilizer primarily on trees, shrubs, and lawn. Use a high-phosphorus fertilizer (0-20-0) on plants to encourage flowering.

Soil pH indicates the relative acidity or alkalinity of the soil. The neutral point is 7.0 in a scale that runs from 0 through 14. Soil that tests below a pH of 7.0 is acid, and soil above 7.0 is alkaline. These pH values are based on logarithms, and a pH of 5.0 is 10 times more acid than a pH of 6.0. Most plants will thrive in a pH of 5.5 to 7.0. Some plants are indifferent to soil pH, while others are definitely sensitive and prefer either a strongly acid or alkaline soil.

Soil pH can be changed by adding certain materials. For example, if a soil test shows that your soil is too acid to grow most plants successfully, you can raise the pH by adding lime to the soil.

Some plants grow best in acid soils. If your soil is not acid enough for the plants you want, you can add small amounts of ferrous sulfate or elemental sulfur. Acid-loving plants often need partial shade, a rich organic soil, plenty of water, and good drainage.

Although plants need water, few plants do well if water collects around them in the soil without draining away. Water can shut off the air supply in the soil and "drown" the plants. If you have this problem, you can put in "pockets" of topsoil for growing plants in tight soil. Before planting and backfilling with new soil, be sure that the subsoil allows for proper drainage.

If the subsoil does not have good drainage, install a vertical drain in the planting hole. A vertical drain can be constructed by digging a 6-inch hole through the impervious layer of soil with a post-hole digger. This hole should be placed at an angle to carry the water away from the root zone. Fill the hole with river stone. Do not use crushed limestone or place gravel in the bottom of the planting hole. Gravel creates an interface that interferes with the capillary movement of water in the soil.

When you get ready to plant, have some good topsoil on hand that is rich in organic matter and nitrogen, phosphorus, and potash. Good topsoil helps the plant adapt itself quickly to its new location and facilitates its early growth.

For best results, dig the holes before the plants are delivered, and get the plants in the ground as soon as they arrive. If the root system dries out, you can do nothing to repair the damage, and the plant will die. If you can't get the holes dug first, cover the roots with moist material while waiting to plant. Heel the plants into a trench to keep the roots covered with moist soil until you can plant them.

Dig the hole for bare-root stock wide enough so that you can spread out the root system naturally without cramping or twisting it. Hold the plant in the air —the pattern that the roots take should be the planted pattern. Dig the hole about 4 inches deeper and 4 inches wider than the spread of the root system. Don't shortchange yourself by putting an expensive plant in a poorly prepared planting hole.

To enrich the soil that has been taken from the hole, mix it with well-rotted manure or other organic matter. Put a 4-inch layer of this mixture in the bottom of the hole, and use it for backfill.

Never let fertilizers come in contact with newly planted roots. Cover the fertilizer mixture with 2 inches of plain soil. Evergreens should not be buried any deeper than the depth at which they originally grew, although they may be planted slightly higher. Deciduous materials should be planted at their original depth or slightly lower. Use the prepared soil mixture in the bottom of the hole to set the plant at the correct height.

Plant so that you can see the best side of the tree or shrub from the terrace or patio. Fill in soil around the roots to prevent air pockets. Tamp the fill with a shovel handle or your foot. When the roots are about half-covered, soak well with water, finish filling the hole, tamp, and then soak again to settle the soil around the roots for good soil and root contact. Finally, make a ridge of dirt around the edge of the fill to hold water over the roots.

Follow this same procedure with container, packaged bare-root, or balled plants. Make the hole twice as wide and twice as deep as the ball, if possible. Put the prepared soil mixture in the bottom of the hole, and then fill with plain soil until the top of the ball is slightly higher than the surrounding ground. Plant balled-and-burlapped plants with the burlap still around the plants. Loosen it around the top, if you wish. Burlap rots away quickly and causes no problem. Cut all twine around the trunk and ball. Remove the plastic wrapping on packaged or mechanically balled bare-root stock. Remove container stock from the

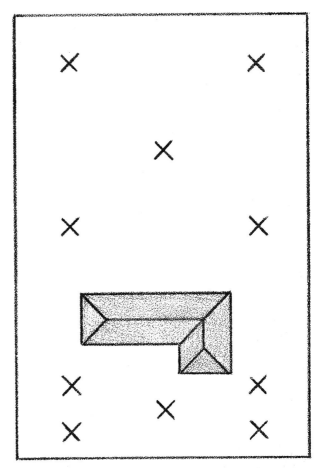

Take samples for a soil test of your yard in a random pattern similar to that indicated by the X's in the above drawing.

container, and slice down the sides of the soil, cutting the roots.

There is a balanced relationship between the roots and the top of a plant. The roots below the surface spread laterally, as well as descend into the soil. When roots are cut, the reduced root system will slow top growth. When you move a large tree, it may stay about the same size for several years while restoring its root system. If too few roots remain, the plant may not get enough water and die.

When root loss has been severe, prune back the top of the plant for compensation. An overbalance of leaves over roots will draw more water than the roots can supply, and the plant will wilt and die. Branches taken off at transplanting time will grow back as fast as the root system develops to handle them. In pruning after transplanting, try to keep the natural shape of the plant, but take off about one-fourth to one-third of the top to balance root loss.

You can prune back a branch to a bud, or all the way back to the main stem. In either case, always

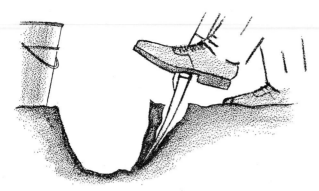

To dig a soil sample, remove one shovelful of soil; then slice a thin section from the hole and place it in a bucket or on a sheet of paper.

make a prune cut on a slant and as close to the bud as possible. Prune back to buds on the outside of the branch. If stubs of branches are left above the bud, they will eventually rot and offer easy access to insects or disease.

It may be best to prune the tree before planting so that you can reach the top easily. When you prune during the dormant season, you need not worry about painting the wound to halt bleeding. But such profuse "bleeders" as birch and beech cannot be pruned in spring.

Water newly planted trees and shrubs well. Soak the soil around them thoroughly twice a week for the first month or two after planting. One way is to let the hose run gently into the basin around the plant. But be sure that the running water doesn't erode the soil around the roots or the ridge.

During the remainder of the growing season, water new plants once a week. In the second growing season, water every second or third week. Watering deep is the secret to success. Make sure that the water gets into the soil where the roots are located. Watering by sprinkler only wets the surface. Fill the basin around new plants several times at each watering. It is difficult to overdo watering if drainage is good, but it is easy not to water enough.

It is normal for most plants to wilt slightly soon after transplanting. Shade severely wilted plants by covering them with heavy paper, cloth, or burlap. Keep this shade material wet and the ground soaked. A critical period for wilting may last for two or three weeks or even longer in hot weather. If the plant does not recover in a week or two, prune severely to lessen the amount of water lost by the plant.

Some plants will drop their leaves when transplanted in foliage and will develop a new set later. If you suspect that your plant is dead after it has dropped

all its leaves, scrape the bark with your fingernail. A green underlying surface indicates that the plant is still living and should not be pulled up. Don't damage the plant or kill it with too much scraping.

If you plant evergreens in the fall, provide some kind of protective shade from winter winds and sun to cut down moisture loss from the foliage. This is particularly important if the plants are planted on the south or west sides of the house. Winter winds can have a great drying effect on evergreens.

Wrap deciduous trees with sisal kraft paper whether you plant them in spring or fall. Spiral the paper from the ground level to the first branches. Secure the paper with twine wound around the full length of the trunk. The paper helps to protect the trunk from sunscald, which injures so many newly planted trees. An unprotected trunk may split when the sun warms up the bark on the south and west sides during the winter months. This alternating freezing and thawing action may crack the trunk lengthwise. Leave the tree wrapped for at least two growing seasons. After one growing season, check to be sure that the twine is not girdling the tree.

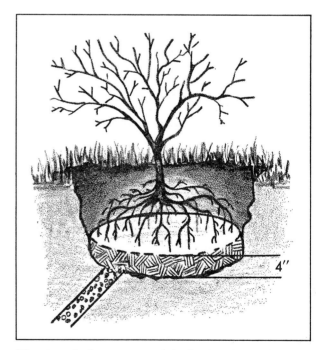

When transplanting, prepare a hole that is 4 inches wider and 4 inches deeper than required by the plant. Place 4 inches of prepared soil in the bottom of the hole. Add more soil to bring the plant to the same depth as that at which it was planted previously. In poorly drained soils, it may be necessary to install a vertical drain to remove excess moisture from the root area. A 4- to 6-inch soil borer can be used to make the channel for the vertical drain. Gravel placed in this channel will facilitate the removal of water. One vertical drain is adequate for shrubs, but several may be needed for large trees (3-inch caliber or over).

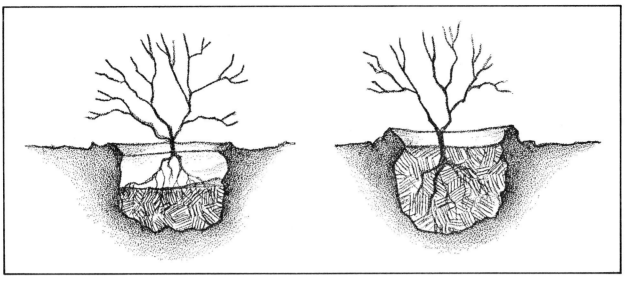

After the plant is located at the proper depth in the hole (left), backfill with topsoil to one-half the depth of the hole. Tamp thoroughly to remove air pockets. Allow water to filter through the filled area. Complete the backfilling of the hole to ground level (right), tamp, and water again. Then use the remaining soil to form a basin around the plant. This basin will facilitate watering.

Stake newly planted trees with 2 × 2″ or 2 × 4″ stakes to prevent the trees from being whipped by wind or loosened by freezing and thawing. High winds can interfere with soil-root contact in a bare-root planting and cause shifting and possible root damage in a balled-and-burlapped planting. Stake in two directions. The stakes should be directly opposite each other but located outside the ball. Drive the stakes below the excavated area and well into undisturbed soil so that they are secure and do not move.

Fasten the tree to the stakes with wire. Loop the wire around the tree in three places — where the first branches start, midway down the trunk, and about 6 inches above the groundline. Use plastic tubing or rubber hose to prevent these loops from cutting into the bark. Unprotected wire loops can girdle and kill the tree. Keep the wires tight. The tree should be tied to the stakes for at least two years.

You can transplant successfully in both spring and fall. Spring planting may be better because the plant has a full growing season to reestablish its root system before going through the rigors of winter. With new horticultural innovations, however, a plant can be transplanted at anytime except when there is a "flush" of new growth. Most thin-barked trees and fleshy rooted plants such as magnolias transplant best in spring and summer.

You can move balled-and-burlapped plants or plants in cans at any time, but you must also shade and water them to be sure that they survive.

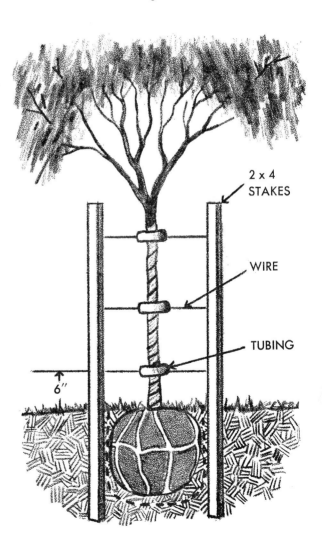

2 x 4 STAKES

WIRE

TUBING

6″

A number of roots are lost when a tree is transplanted. To restore a balance between the roots and the top, remove one-third to one-fourth of the top, as indicated by the cross marks in the drawing at left. This pruning should preserve the basic form of the plant, as shown at right.

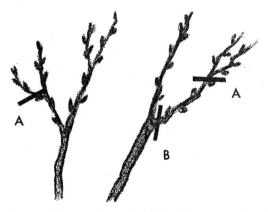

Branches should be pruned to a bud (A) or flush to parent branches (B). Be sure that the bud is facing in the direction in which you want the new growth. Make the cut at an angle, and as close to the bud as possible.

If your new plants become severely wilted because of loss of moisture from sun and wind, they may need artificial protection. You can protect plants with burlap screens attached to a wood frame, or by wrapping the plant with burlap to reduce moisture loss. Do not wrap the plant so tight that air movement is restricted beneath the burlap.

13: Taking Care Of Your Plants

Every landscape needs a certain amount of maintenance to remain attractive. You will be working with living, growing material that is constantly changing and demanding water, fertilizer, spraying, pruning, and cultivation.

An understanding of plant function is basic in plant care. Plants need light, water, air, and mineral elements to carry out their life processes. In selecting plants for your landscape, first consider their environmental requirements — light, tolerance to low temperatures, effects of wind and climate, and need for water. Each yard has its own environment. You can reduce maintenance considerably by choosing plants whose normal requirements are closest to the environmental conditions in your garden.

To care for outdoor plants properly, you should know some general facts about soil. Soil is the growing medium for plants. A knowledge of soil structure, pH reactions, amendments (materials added to the soil to improve the soil), and fertilizers will help you give your plants better care.

Soil Conditioning

Putting lime on your soil can correct acidity, change soil structure, hasten bacterial action and the decomposition of organic materials, and speed the liberation of plant foods. You can apply lime as ground limestone. Put the lime on the surface and then work it into the soil. Successive applications may be harmful. Ask your county extension office for recommendations as to the amount you need.

To increase soil acidity, apply either elemental sulfur or ferrous sulfate. You should not add phosphorus at the same time that you apply ferrous sulfate; if you do, the ferrous sulfate may not be available to plants. Elemental sulfur is slower to act than ferrous sulfate, but it is longer lasting. Common powdered sulfur is not recommended, since it takes three to six months to produce results.

Sand, calcined clay, sawdust, and ashes may be used as amendments to improve such fine-textured soil as clay. Decayed sawdust and peat have a beneficial effect on soil structure, but the bacteria responsible for this decay require large amounts of nitrogen. For this reason, add 6 pounds of ammonium nitrate per cubic yard as you put sawdust or bark on the soil, or they will tie up available nitrogen and slow plant growth. Ashes from nonlignite coal can be used after screening out the clinkers. Although wood ashes improve soil structure, they have little fertilizing value.

Humus is also important for good soils. Compost, peat, manure, sawdust, and shavings are all sources of humus.

Fertilizing

The use of commercial fertilizers is the most economical means for adding plant nutrients to the soil. Nitrogen, phosphorus, and potassium are the three nutrients most important to plant growth. (See the discussion of fertilizers in Chapter 12.)

Nitrogen is essential for plant growth, but too much nitrogen stimulates an overgrowth of foliage at the expense of flowers and fruits and keeps new growth from maturing before freezing weather sets in. Since nitrogen tends to disappear from the soil, it must be replaced with commercial fertilizer.

One source of nitrogen alone is ammonium sulfate, which can be applied at the rate of 1 to 2 pounds per 100 square feet of garden area. Another source is urea, a synthetic form of nitrogen that should be applied at the rate of 1 pound per 100 square feet.

Phosphorus is also essential for plant growth. It aids redevelopment and encourages flower and fruit production. Phosphorus becomes "fixed" in the soil (does not leach out or move) when it is applied. For

To fertilize a mature tree, you must get the fertilizer in the area of the hair roots so that they can take advantage of it. These roots are usually located at the drip line of the crown. Drill holes 18 to 24 inches deep and 2 to 2½ feet apart in this area. Be sure that you have one circle of holes beyond the drip line and several circles within the drip line. Fill these holes with fertilizer and water.

this reason, it is important to apply phosphorus where you want it to be available to the plants.

The chief source of phosphorus is superphosphate (0-20-0), which is applied at the rate of 2 or 3 pounds per 100 square feet. Bonemeal contains up to 25 percent phosphorus, but releases it so slowly that its value is questionable.

Potassium is important to the general vigor of plants. It increases disease resistance and has a general balancing effect on other plant nutrients. One source of potassium is potassium chloride. The recommended application rate is 1 pound per 100 square feet.

Some trace elements are needed for plant growth, although only minute amounts are required. Complete fertilizers often contain several of these trace elements, such as iron, boron, manganese, and sulfur.

A complete fertilizer in the ratio of 10-10-10 or 16-8-6 will usually produce desirable results on lawns, shrubs, and trees. A high-phosphorus fertilizer encourages flowers and fruit production. A 0-20-0 fertilizer works well on flowers and other plants where flower and fruit production are important.

You can fertilize shrubs and trees anytime from early spring to midsummer, and from September 15 to the last of November. Application between July 15 and September 15 may stimulate a late succulent growth. This growth will not have a chance to harden off properly before the killing frosts of fall cause dieback of the twigs.

Since the feeding roots of large trees extend as far as or even beyond the spread of the branches, apply fertilizer around this "drip line" area. Drive holes 24 to 30 inches apart and 18 to 24 inches deep in concentric circles around the trunk under the spread of the branches. Do not punch holes closer than 3 to 5 feet from the trunk. Put a complete fertilizer in each hole; then fill the holes with water to dissolve the fertilizer. Use a funnel to put the fertilizer in the holes, particularly on lawn areas where spilled fertilizer might harm the grass.

Shrubs and flowers also benefit from fertilization. Use a balanced fertilizer, and vary the amount with the size of the shrub and the frequency with which you apply it. The first number on a fertilizer bag represents the number of pounds of *actual nitrogen* in 100 pounds. For example, if you want to apply 2 pounds of actual nitrogen per 1,000 square feet, you will need 5 pounds of 16-8-6 fertilizer. A high-nitrogen fertilizer is a good one to use for shrubs. Apply it from near the base of the plant to the outer spread of the branches. Most of the feeding roots are in this area. Use 2 cups of 10-10-10 or 1 cup of 16-8-6 fertilizer, and work it into the upper soil surface.

Certain fertilizers can burn the foliage of growing plants. *Do not apply* any fertilizer except when the foliage is dry. Water thoroughly immediately after fertilizing. Put on enough water to carry the fertilizer down into the soil.

For flowers, work a handful of fertilizer into the soil around the base of both perennials and annuals. Use a fertilizer that is high in phosphorus content, such as 0-20-0.

Watering

Shrubs and trees may lack expected vigor because they are not getting enough water. On a warm summer day, a mature tree may lose as much as 10 to 20 barrels of water by evaporation through its foliage. During dry weather, a tree should be watered thoroughly about every 10 days to make up for this loss. Frequent light waterings do little good because the water does not sink deeply enough into the soil for the tree to use it.

There are no exact rules for watering plants. Use the condition of the soil and plant as a general guide. Consider the environmental needs of the plants you have used in your landscape. Those that resist drouth may not need much water between rains. Other plants that grow in shade and like moist conditions should have frequent waterings to survive in very hot summer weather. A watering lance is useful for getting water into the root zone.

Apply water slowly so that it will soak into the soil. To find out how slowly water penetrates, water an area for 15 minutes, and then dig down to see how far the water has gone. The rate of penetration depends upon the soil type. If runoff occurs, you have probably watered too much or too rapidly.

Soak the soil deeply to encourage root development. Spraying only the surface of the soil encourages shallow root development that may result in plant damage if you don't water for a day or two and there is a sudden hot spell.

Watering in late afternoon encourages disease on many plants. Do not water too much. Water passing through the soil may dissolve nutrients and carry them away, causing nutrient deficiencies. Excess water standing in the root zone can "drown" a plant by shutting off its soil air supply.

One deep watering every 5 to 7 days is usually enough for most plants. Don't forget the plants close

to a wall or under the eaves. These plants don't get much natural rainfall, and will need to be watered.

Shrubs, trees, and evergreens give off moisture into the air. This process is called *transpiration*. To replenish the water in the stem and leaf area, the plant absorbs moisture from the soil. Unless the plant is watered artificially, transpiration continues during extended dry periods or drouths until the plant dies. Evergreens give off moisture even during the winter months. If the ground is frozen so that the plant cannot restore its moisture, part of the plant will turn brown. If this condition, known as "winter burn," persists over a long period, the entire plant will brown and die.

Water lawn, trees, or shrubs slowly. Soak the soil to a depth of 8 to 10 inches to encourage deep root penetration. If the planting is new, apply the water slowly in the basin formed when transplanting. Water an area for 15 minutes, and then dig to find the depth of moisture penetration. This method will help you to determine the length of time required for deep watering.

Pruning

Pruning is a very important part of caring for and maintaining plants that is often either overdone or completely ignored. Pruning is the art of cutting out unwanted growth to make a plant respond as desired. Most plants need some pruning to serve as intended in the landscape. But if you have selected plants with the correct form and mature size, you won't have to prune severely at any time.

Pruning helps to produce more or better blooms, develops and keeps the desired shape, rejuvenates plants by removing older stems and encouraging vigorous young growth, repairs injuries, and removes diseased or injured parts, as well as winterkilled and dead wood. It differs from shearing or barbering.

You can find evidence in almost any neighborhood of the "frustrated barber" approach to pruning shrubs. The tops are sheared round or cut straight across. Pruning involves selection and judgment; shearing merely involves clipping.

If you cut back a branch only part way, many new shoots will grow out below the cut at awkward angles. These shoots then grow upward to create an unattractive broomlike appearance. To prevent this result, cut off a branch only where it joins a larger branch, and cut it off flush so that no stub is left.

Cut off a main stem at the ground level. Do not leave any stub. A stub not only produces new branches below the cut that disfigure the plant but it is also subject to decay and a point of entry for disease and insect damage. If a branch extends beyond the rest of the crown, do not cut it back only to the length of the other branches. Cut it back to where it joins a larger branch or back to the ground level. A pruned shrub may appear a little thin when you finish, but it will fill out nicely.

Don't prune too much at one time. Too severe pruning encourages the growth of suckers — long branches with larger than normal foliage. A rule of thumb for pruning flowering shrubs is to remove one-fourth to one-third of all older wood at ground level. This pruning stimulates growth of new wood from that area. Old wood is larger and has darker colored bark than new wood. Pruning also emphasizes a plant's natural shape by making each branch stand out separately. This is especially desirable for specimen plants.

Prune summer-flowering shrubs and small trees when they are dormant (between December and

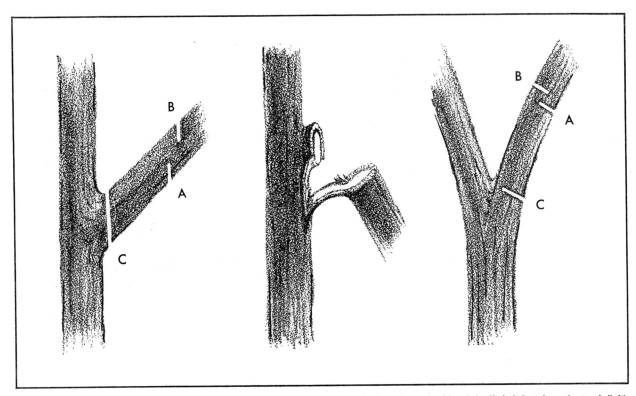

Remove a large limb from a tree in three steps. The first cut (A) should be made from the underside of the limb 1 foot from the trunk (left). The second cut (B) is made from the top about 2 inches from the undercut. Continue this cut until the limb falls. By using this method, you avoid peeling away the trunk bark (middle). The third cut (C) is made flush with the trunk to remove the stub. Notice the procedure for a split crotch (right). Cut (C) has to be made from underneath to avoid damaging the remaining limb.

Pruning cuts that are larger than 1½ inches in diameter should be dressed with a commercial tree paint or shellac to prevent excessive bleeding. If large cuts are unattended, they may cause disease and insect problems.

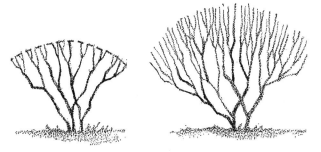

Plants should be allowed to grow into their natural shape. *Do not* shear plants (left) into balls, squares, or other rigid and unnatural shapes. These artificial shapes fit only into formal designs. Shearing is *not* pruning. Excessive sucker growth (right) develops as a result of shearing.

March). Prune spring-flowering shrubs as soon as they have finished flowering. Most shrubs and trees bloom before the end of June. Blooms result from flower buds formed the previous year in spring-flowering plants. If you prune these plants before they bloom, you will cut off most of the flower buds. Forsythia, spirea, deutzia, and mockorange are examples of spring-flowering plants.

Shrubs that bloom after June usually do so on growth made the same year. As a result, they have plenty of time to grow their flowering stems. Prune this group of shrubs in the winter when they are dormant. Examples of this group include buddlea,

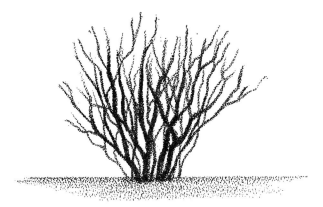

Prune the oldest wood from an established shrub at ground level. This wood is easily recognized because it is the largest and has the darkest color. Remove one-fourth to one-third of this wood annually to preserve the shrub's natural form and to stimulate flowering.

crepe myrtle, althea, white hydrangea, and vitex. They produce their flowers on the new wood that grows each spring.

Shade trees need relatively little pruning. Remove dead or diseased wood and cut out crowding or interfering branches. Pruning small, dead branches will often keep large branches or the trunk from rotting. To remove a dead branch, cut into live wood where it joins a larger branch. To remove large branches, cut from below part way through the branch, and then finish the cut from the top a short distance from the undercut. The lower cut will keep the weight of the branch from ripping off a section of bark just before the saw cuts through. After the branch has fallen, cut the stump that remains to a flat surface flush with the parent branch or trunk, and cover it with a wound dressing. You can make small cuts without danger of the tree bleeding, but large cuts should be protected with pruning paint or dressing wax.

Mulching

Mulching is recommended for plants to prevent erosion, control weeds, conserve moisture, and protect the plants. Nature mulches plants with fallen leaves and other organic materials. As practiced by gardeners, mulching is simply an adaptation of this natural process. Since most mulch is organic material, it helps to improve soil structure by adding humus as the mulch decays.

The greatest advantage of mulching over clean cultivation is the moisture-saving ability of mulch. Mulch greatly reduces evaporation losses by protecting the soil from sun and wind. It absorbs rainfall, keeps the soil from packing, and controls erosion.

Another advantage of mulching is weed control. Mulching is especially important in controlling weeds around shallow-rooted plants that cannot be cultivated, such as azalea, rhododendron, and camellia. Using a chemical weed killer with mulch increases the benefits even more.

Mulch also helps to control soil temperature. A lower soil temperature in summer favors plant growth, and in winter there is less frost penetration under mulch. This is important for evergreens, since they need moisture in winter as well as in summer. A winter mulch for evergreens helps to keep a supply of moisture available for a longer period and minimizes the effects of alternate freezing and thawing.

Although the advantages of mulching far outweigh its disadvantages, there are a few drawbacks. Mulching materials are sometimes costly or difficult to obtain. Some mulches, such as straw and dried leaves, are a fire hazard at certain times. Rodent problems may increase around mulched plants. And you may get a nitrogen deficiency when you use corncobs or bark chips as a mulch, since the bacteria that decompose these materials use nitrogen. When you apply corncobs or bark chips, add nitrogen fertilizer to prevent nitrogen deficiency.

Bark is easy to obtain in many parts of the United States. Apply it 3 to 4 inches deep. It is low in nutrients and decomposes slowly. If you mulch with sawdust, wood chips, bark, or shavings, add ammonium nitrate at the rate of 1 pound per 100 square feet (⅓ pound or 5 ounces per bushel of bark or sawdust or 6 pounds per cubic yard).

Peat moss is an attractive mulching material, but it is usually too expensive for large areas. Apply it to a depth of 1 to 2 inches. Before spreading, dampen the bale thoroughly for easier handling. Do not allow the peat moss to dry out — it is difficult to rewet. Ground or cracked corncobs and bark are also excellent for mulching and for improving soil structure. They should be applied to a depth of 3 to 4 inches.

Controlling Weeds

In addition to mulch, several chemicals are available to help in the fight against weeds. Weeding may be a definite problem for the first year or two after planting and fertilization. It is important to keep weeds controlled before they can go to seed.

Weed seed will continue to germinate in the soil until controlled by good cultural practices. You can kill most weed seedlings by hoeing about 1 inch deep and letting the soil dry out. Dry surface soil acts much like a mulch, helping to reduce the number of weed seeds that sprout and decreasing moisture loss from the soil. Hoe only deep-rooted plants. Shallow-rooted plants such as rhododendrons and azaleas may be injured by hoeing.

Controlling Diseases and Insects

Plant diseases are difficult to diagnose. If part of the plant dies, or if the leaves turn brown and fall off early, the cause may be either a disease or an environmental condition. For example, too much water in the soil will cause these symptoms.

A good preventive program provides the best disease control. Clear all weeds and debris out of your garden each spring and fall. In the spring, cut out all dead wood and turn under or remove winter mulch. In the fall, remove and dispose of all dead flower stalks, leaves, and annual plant stalks so that diseases and insects will not be carried through the winter.

Insect problems will vary from season to season. Apply preventive sprays to plants that are attacked each year by aphids, bagworms, red spiders, and other insects. Be on the alert for signs of insect damage to foliage, bark, or flowers. Apply control measures promptly to check the damage and keep the insects from spreading.

Protecting Plants

Be sure to provide adequate winter protection for your plants. The amount of protection needed depends upon the natural hardiness of the plant and the severity of the climate.

Extreme cold will cause twigs, stems, and branches to freeze. Too much moisture loss or severe cold often causes winterkilling, particularly in evergreens. Most

A corncob, sawdust, or straw mulch prevents the soil from freezing as quickly as exposed soil and reduces the depth of frost penetration. As a result, mulching helps keep the plant supplied with moisture during the winter. To prevent "winter burn" from excessive moisture loss during the winter, water evergreens thoroughly before the ground freezes in mid-November. Water again during midwinter thaws.

winter moisture loss results from strong drying winds on sunny days. The plant may die if the roots can't supply enough moisture.

For this reason, one of the most important ways to prepare all woody plants, especially evergreens, for winter is to make sure that the soil has a large reserve supply of moisture. If autumn rainfall has been light, thoroughly soak the ground around the plants before the first hard freeze. Then put on a heavy 4- to 6-inch mulch of ground corncobs, bark, wood chips, etc. to keep the ground from freezing too deep. The plant will then continue to receive moisture from the ground to replace the moisture lost by winter evaporation. Since the plants under the eaves do not receive adequate moisture, it is especially important to water these plants thoroughly before the ground freezes.

You can shield less hardy evergreens from winter sun and wind damage with burlap, straw, or boxes. Attach burlap to a frame around the plant as a

Place a lath frame over plants close to buildings to prevent damage from snow sliding off the roofs.

screen, or wrap the burlap on the plant itself. Leave the wrapping loose enough to allow some air movement through the burlap. An evergreen located under the roofline may need a lath shield to prevent damage from snow sliding off the roof.

You will have a chance to replenish moisture loss from the plants and soil during the usual winter thaws. Whenever the ground is not completely frozen, you can water the plants well to get moisture back into the soil. Check the mulch during the winter to be sure that it is still in place and not washing away.

Do not remove such winter-protective devices as screens, wrappings, and snow supports too early in the spring. In areas subject to many late heavy snowstorms and temperature extremes, early mulch removal might be a serious mistake. Leave mulch on until well into the spring to be sure that your plants get maximum protection.

You set the stage for winter plant protection by the kinds and numbers of plants that you choose for your garden. If you like to work outdoors with plants, you may want to use a few semihardy plants to get the variety you want. But you will have to take extra precautions to keep these plants flourishing. If you do not have the time or the inclination to test semiexotic plants in your yard, choose hardy plants that need only minimum care.

Wrap upright evergreens with burlap or straw mats to protect them from drying effects of winter sun and wind. Do not wrap the plants so tight that air movement inside is restricted.

List Of Plant Materials

The list of plant materials is divided into two sections: trees and shrubs classified according to their use in the home landscape, and descriptive outlines of trees, shrubs, vines, and ground covers. This list is, of course, a selected one, and many materials suitable for ornamental plantings are not included.

Trees are classified as accent trees, lawn trees, specimen trees, and street trees, or on the basis of their use in group plantings, planter boxes, screens, shrub borders, and in forming hedges. Shrubs are classified as accent plants, facer plants, and specimen plants, or on the basis of their use in foundation plantings, group plantings, hedges, planter boxes, screens, and shrub borders.

The fact that a tree or shrub appears in a particular group does not mean that it is restricted in its use to that group. For example, a shrub listed as a "foundation planting" may be used with equal effectiveness in a shrub border or a group planting. There is, however, an exception to this general rule. Only trees listed as street trees are satisfactory for that use. Although any of the street trees can be used as lawn trees, the reverse is not true.

The detailed descriptive outlines of trees, shrubs, ground covers, and vines have been organized so that you can find whatever information you need for a particular plant quickly and easily. Height and spread, exposure and soil requirements, texture, etc. are set in bold type for easy reference.

Each plant is listed alphabetically by its *common name*. The *botanical name* is given after the common name. Be sure to include the botanical name when ordering your plants. There may be several common names for a plant, but the botanical name identifies the plant without question.

Before choosing a tree, shrub, ground cover, or vine for your home landscape, make sure it will grow in your area. The term *hardiness* is used to express a plant's tolerance to temperatures and climates. The *zone number* that appears after each plant name in the descriptive outlines refers to the hardiness of that particular plant. A question mark following the zone number indicates that the plant may not thrive in certain areas within that zone.

The zones shown on the map on page 208 are those used by the U.S. Department of Agriculture. Each of these ten zones represents an area of winter hardiness based upon average minimum winter temperatures ranging from −50° F. or below in Zone 1 to +30° to 40° F. in Zone 10. Although these minimum temperatures are of primary importance for plant survival, there are other conditions that determine whether a plant will survive in a particular zone — frost occurrence, seasonal rainfall distribution, humidity, soil characteristics, and duration and intensity of sunlight.

A plant species that lives in one part of a zone can be expected to live in other parts of the same zone or in a warmer zone if growth conditions (rainfall, soil, summer heat, etc.) are comparable or capable of being made comparable through irrigation, soil correction, wind protection, partial shade, or humidity control. Despite your best efforts, however, a plant considered adapted to your zone may not survive the winter because of cultural conditions affecting the plant's hardiness, or a more severe winter than usual.

Following the zone number is a brief description of the plant's *habits of growth* and any qualities or problems worthy of special notice. The average mature *height and spread* is given for each tree and shrub, the *height* only for vines, and the *height and spacing* for ground covers. Spacing is measured from the center of one plant to the center of the next.

The *climbing method* of each vine is given to help you determine the kind of support that will be required, and the *rooting habit* of each tree is listed so that you can select the tree that best fits your situation. Deep-rooted trees do not compete with lawn and nearby plantings for nutrients and water and seldom interfere with underground water or sewer lines, but trees with shallow or spreading roots should not be located close to underground utilities.

Some plants will grow only in shade and others demand sun. The preferred *exposure* of each shrub and ground cover is included so that you can easily select a plant for any of the exposures on your property. *Soil preferences* and *special soil requirements* are also noted. The texture of each plant is given to help you develop pleasing contrasts among plants and other landscape elements.

Flower and fruit effects are described unless they are not outstanding or do not contribute significantly to the design. In that case, they are either omitted or indicated as "not showy." Consider color carefully to insure a harmonious color scheme. Remember that the flowers are usually of interest only for a short time. Don't base your selection entirely on flower effects.

Fall color is a quality that contributes to the late-season appearance of the landscape. When a plant has outstanding foliage color in the fall, the color is indicated; otherwise it is omitted.

At the end of the descriptive outline, following landscape uses, a list of *other varieties* of the plant may be recommended. A brief statement following each variety identifies those characteristics that distinguish that variety from the parent plant.

In some cases, the name of the plant is enclosed in single quotation marks, indicating that the plant is a *cultivar*. Strictly speaking, a cultivar is not a *botanical variety,** but in the interests of simplicity, cultivars are listed as varieties in this publication.

To show how these lists can help you select a plant appropriate to your needs, it may be helpful to go through the steps for selecting a shrub for the corner of your home. For the purposes of this illustration, let us assume that you live in Zone 4 and that your house is red brick. The eave line is 8½ feet from the ground, and the distance between the house and the entry walk is 8 feet. The exposure is sunny, except for some morning shade.

Your first step would be to check under *Foundation Plants — Corner* in the listing of shrubs classified according to use. Make a list of those plants that you think you might like; then check the descriptive outline of each plant on your list to determine which plant would probably be the most satisfactory.

For example, Lemoine Deutzia is recommended for use in a corner planting. The descriptive outline for this plant (page 230) is as follows:

DEUTZIA, LEMOINE
(*Deutzia* × *lemoinei*).　　　　**Zone 4**
Fast growing. Dense, upright. Handsome and reliable. Showy flowers.
Height: 6–7 feet.　　**Spread:** 4–6 feet.
Exposure: sun or partial shade.
Texture: medium fine.
Flower effects: white in June.
Fruit effects: not showy.
Use: corner, group, shrub border.
Varieties: 'Compacta' (see detailed description above); 'Erecta' (low, upright growing).

The process you should follow to evaluate the plant's suitability to your situation is outlined below:

Step 1. Check the *hardiness zone number* to be sure that the plant will survive in your geographic area. Since Lemoine Deutzia is hardy in Zone 4, it should be suitable for your area or in zones with higher numbers, such as Zone 5.

Step 2. Note the *mature height and spread* to be sure that the plant will not exceed your height and horizontal space requirements. Since your house has an eave line of 8½ feet, the mature height of your corner planting should not exceed 6 feet; and, since the distance between the house and entry walk is 8 feet, the plant should not exceed 6 to 7 feet in width (see Chapter 10). The mature height of Lemoine Deutzia is listed as 6 to 7 feet and the spread as 4 to 6 feet. Although this plant will probably meet your requirements, you should remember that these are average growth dimensions, and it is possible that the plant might grow considerably under or over the average size.

Step 3. Be sure that the preferred *exposure* for the plant is compatible with your situation. Lemoine Deutzia tolerates either sun or partial shade. Since the exposure at the corner of your house is sunny with some morning shade, the plant should thrive in this location.

Step 4. Determine whether the *texture* of the plant will complement the texture of nearby plant and architectural materials. You want to select a plant that either repeats or contrasts with the medium texture of your brick siding. Lemoine Deutzia has a medium texture that repeats the texture of the brick. Assuming that its texture is also compatible with the other plant materials in your foundation planting, this shrub would be satisfactory.

Step 5. Evaluate the *foliage and flower color* to be sure that the plant will harmonize with surrounding architectural and landscape units. If the foliage color is unusual (purple, variegated, etc.), this fact is noted in the descriptive outline; otherwise, you can assume

---

* Horticulturists disagree as to the precise definition of cultivars. According to Michael A. Dirr of the Department of Horticulture, University of Illinois at Urbana-Champaign, *cultivars* are "an assemblage of plants that possess distinguishing morphological, physiological, or cytological characteristics. These characteristics are retained when the cultivar is reproduced asexually (vegetatively) and, in certain cases, when reproduced sexually (from seed). Most woody plants must propagate vegetatively to retain characteristics consistent with the parent. If propagated from seed, the chances of the offspring being similar to the parent are almost nil. A *botanical variety* is a plant type subordinate to a species. The identifying characteristics are marked, but usually are not as clear or pronounced as those in the species. A botanical variety generally produces offspring similar to the parent when grown from seed."

that the foliage is green. Since Lemoine Deutzia does not have unusual foliage color, its foliage would be compatible with red brick. Plants with red or purplish foliage should be avoided because the color of the foliage would probably clash with or provide poor contrast with the color of the brick. The white flowers of the Lemoine Deutzia would blend well with the house and surrounding materials.

From this step-by-step evaluation, it appears that Lemoine Deutzia would meet your requirements for hardiness, height, spread, exposure, texture, and color. You will notice that there are two entries listed under other varieties in the descriptive outline. These, too, should be considered in your evaluation.

'Compacta' and 'Erecta' are the two recommended variations of Lemoine Deutzia. The notation following 'Compacta' refers you to the descriptive outline above. A complete descriptive outline of 'Compacta' is given because it differs significantly from the parent plant, and it is popular enough to warrant a detailed description. 'Erecta' is not commonly available, however, and this cultivar differs from Lemoine Deutzia only in its more erect habit of growth. For this reason, only a brief description of 'Erecta' is provided. From these descriptions you can quickly determine that neither of these plants meets your basic requirements either for height or habit of growth.

After following these steps for each plant on your list, you may want to examine the plants at a nursery before making your final decision.

The author wishes to acknowledge use of the following books as references in compiling the list of plant materials: *Shrubs and Vines for American Gardens* by Donald Wyman, Macmillan Company, New York, 1969; *Trees for American Gardens* by Donald Wyman, Macmillan Company, New York, 1965; and *Useful Trees and Shrubs* by Florence Bell Robinson, The Garrard Press, Champaign, Illinois, 1960. You may want to refer to these books for further information about plants suitable for your area.

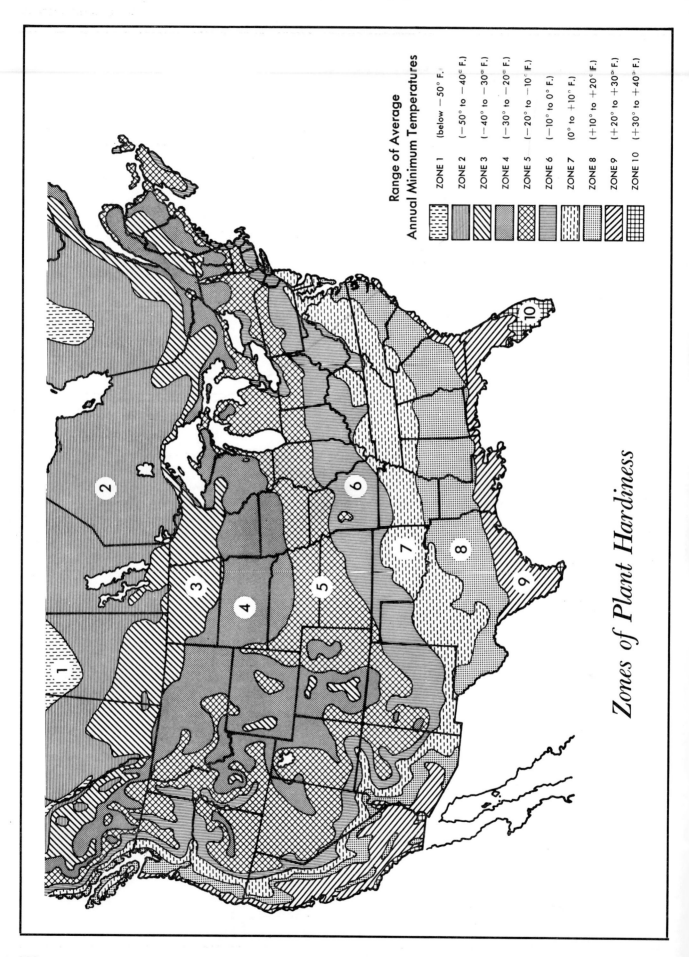

Range of Average
Annual Minimum Temperatures

ZONE 1 (below —50° F.)
ZONE 2 (—50° to —40° F.)
ZONE 3 (—40° to —30° F.)
ZONE 4 (—30° to —20° F.)
ZONE 5 (—20° to —10° F.)
ZONE 6 (—10° to 0° F.)
ZONE 7 (0° to +10° F.)
ZONE 8 (+10° to +20° F.)
ZONE 9 (+20° to +30° F.)
ZONE 10 (+30° to +40° F.)

Zones of Plant Hardiness

Trees Classified According to Use

ACCENT TREES

Birch, River
Crabapple, Flowering
(various species)
Maple, Japanese
Umbrellapine, Japanese

GROUP PLANTINGS

Alder, Speckled
Birch, Canoe or Paper
Birch, Sweet
Crabapple, Carmine
Crabapple, Flowering
(various species)
Crabapple, Selkirk
Crabapple, Snowdrift
Dogwood, Corneliancherry
Douglas-fir
Enkianthus, Redvein
Euonymus, Eastern Wahoo
Fringetree, White
Hawthorn, Washington
Laburnum, Waterer
Lilac, Japanese Tree
Maple, Japanese
Mulberry, White
Sassafras, Common
Serviceberry, Allegany
Serviceberry, Shadblow
Smokebush
Spruce, Blue Colorado
Tupelo (Black Gum)

HEDGES

Clipped

Dogwood, Corneliancherry
Hawthorn, Washington
Hornbeam, American
Hemlock, Canada
Hemlock, Carolina

Unclipped

Hornbeam, American

LAWN TREES

Small
(35 feet or under)

Alder, Speckled
Ash, Moraine
Birch, Gray
Buckeye, Red
Cherry, Autumn Higan
Cherry, Fugenzo Oriental
Cherry, Hally Jolivette
Cherry, Kwanzan Oriental
Cherry, Weeping Higan
Crabapple, Carmine
Crabapple, Flowering
Crabapple, Japanese Flowering
Crabapple, Radiant
Crabapple, Redbud Zumi
Crabapple, Red Jade
Crabapple, Selkirk
Crabapple, Siberian
Crabapple, Snowdrift
Crabapple, Tea
Dogwood, Corneliancherry
Dogwood, Flowering
Dogwood, Japanese (Kousa)
Enkianthus, Redvein
Euonymus, Aldenham Spindle Tree
Euonymus, Eastern Wahoo
Euonymus, Midwinter
Fringetree, White
Goldraintree, Panicled
Hawthorn, Cockspur
Hawthorn, Lavalle
Hawthorn, Paul Scarlet English
Hawthorn, Washington
Hawthorn, Winter King Green
Hornbeam, American
Katsura Tree*
Laburnum, Waterer
Lilac, Japanese Tree
Magnolia, Saucer*
Magnolia, Star
Magnolia, Sweetbay
Maple, Amur
Maple, Japanese

Maple, Paperbark
Maple, Tatarian
Mountainash, European
Mulberry, White
Redbud
Russianolive
Sassafras, Common*
Sea-Buckthorn, Common
Serviceberry, Allegany
Serviceberry, Shadblow
Silverbell, Carolina
Smokebush
Viburnum, Nannyberry
Viburnum, Siebold

Medium
(60 feet or under)

Ash, Green
Birch, Canoe or Paper
Birch, European White
Birch, River*
Corktree, Amur
Cherry, European Bird
Crabapple, Flowering (varieties)
Elm, Chinese
Hemlock, Carolina
Hophornbeam, American
Hornbeam, European
Horsechestnut, Common
Horsechestnut, Ruby Red*
Linden, Crimean
Linden, Greenspire Little-leaf
Linden, Little-leaf
Maple, Autumn Flame Red
Maple, Fassen's Black Norway
Maple, Norway
Maple, Red
Maple, Schwedler Norway
Mountainash, Korean
Oak, Pin*
Pagodatree, Japanese*
Pear, Bradford Callery
Sorrel Tree (Sourwood)
Sweetgum
Yellowwood, American
Zelkova, Japanese*

Trees Classified According to Use

Large Lawn Trees (over 60 feet)

Ash, Blue
Ash, Marshall Seedless
Baldcypress
Beech, American
Beech, European
Birch, Sweet
Cherry, Sargent
Coffeetree, Kentucky
Douglas-fir
Fir, White
Ginkgo
Hackberry, Common
Hackberry, Southern (Sugar)
Hemlock, Canada
Honeylocust, Thornless Common
Linden, American
Linden, Silver
Magnolia, Cucumber Tree
Maple, Sugar
Oak, English
Oak, Northern Red
Oak, White
Planetree, London
Pine, Austrian
Pine, Eastern White
Pine, Scotch
Spruce, Blue Colorado
Tuliptree
Tupelo (Black Gum)
Umbrellapine, Japanese

PLANTER BOXES OR CONTAINERS

Cherry, European Bird
Cherry, Hally Jolivette
Euonymus, Aldenham Spindle Tree
Euonymus, Midwinter
Hawthorn, Winter King Green
Hornbeam, European
Sea-Buckthorn, Common
Viburnum, Nannyberry
Viburnum, Siebold

SCREENS

Arborvitae, Mission Eastern
Douglas-fir
Hemlock, Canada
Hemlock, Carolina
Maple, Amur
Pine, Eastern White

SHRUB BORDERS

Buckeye, Red
Crabapple, Carmine
Crabapple, Flowering
    (various species)
Dogwood, Corneliancherry
Dogwood, Flowering
Euonymus, Aldenham Spindle Tree
Fringetree, White
Hawthorn, Washington
Magnolia, Star
Redbud
Sassafras, Common
Serviceberry, Allegany
Silverbell, Carolina
Smokebush
Tupelo (Black Gum)
Viburnum, Nannyberry
Yellowwood, American

SPECIMEN TREES

Beech, American
Beech, European
Birch, Canoe or Paper
Birch, European White
Birch, Sweet
Buckeye, Red
Cherry, Autumn Higan
Cherry, European Bird
Cherry, Fugenzo Oriental
Cherry, Hally Jolivette
Cherry, Kwanzan Oriental
Cherry, Sargent
Cherry, Weeping Higan
Crabapple, Carmine
Crabapple, Flowering
    (various species)
Crabapple, Japanese Flowering
Crabapple, Radiant
Crabapple, Redbud Zumi
Crabapple, Red Jade
Crabapple, Selkirk
Crabapple, Snowdrift
Crabapple, Tea
Dogwood, Corneliancherry
Dogwood, Flowering
Dogwood, Japanese (Kousa)
Douglas-fir
Enkianthus, Redvein
Euonymus, Aldenham Spindle Tree
Fir, White
Fringetree, White
Ginkgo
Goldraintree, Panicled
Hawthorn, Cockspur
Hawthorn, Lavalle
Hawthorn, Paul Scarlet English
Hemlock, Canada
Hemlock, Carolina
Laburnum, Waterer
Lilac, Japanese Tree
Magnolia, Saucer
Magnolia, Star
Maple, Amur
Maple, Japanese
Maple, Paperbark
Maple, Tatarian
Mountainash, Korean
Oak, Pin
Pine, Eastern White
Pine, Scotch
Redbud
Russianolive
Serviceberry, Allegany
Serviceberry, Shadblow
Smokebush
Sorrel Tree (Sourwood)
Spruce, Blue Colorado
Sweetgum
Tupelo (Black Gum)
Umbrellapine, Japanese
Viburnum, Nannyberry
Viburnum, Siebold
Yellowwood, American

Trees Classified According to Use

STREET TREES

Ash, Green
Ash, Marshall Seedless
Ash, Moraine
Cherry, Autumn Higan
Cherry, Fugenzo Oriental
Cherry, Kwanzan Oriental
Cherry, Sargent
Corktree, Amur
Dogwood, Flowering
Dogwood, Japanese (Kousa)
Ginkgo
Goldraintree, Panicled
Hackberry, Common
Hackberry, Southern (Sugar)
Hawthorn, Lavalle

Hawthorn, Paul Scarlet English
Hawthorn, Washington
Hawthorn, Winter King Green
Honeylocust, Thornless Common
Hornbeam, American
Hornbeam, European (var. *globosa*)
Lilac, Japanese Tree
Linden, Crimean
Linden, Greenspire Little-leaf
Linden, Little-leaf
Linden, Silver
Magnolia, Cucumber Tree
Maple, Amur
Maple, Autumn Flame Red
Maple, Norway
Maple, Paperbark

Maple, **Red**
Maple, Schwedler Norway
Maple, **Sugar**
Maple, Tatarian
Mountainash, European
Oak, Northern **Red**
Oak, **Pin**
Pagodatree, Japanese
Pear, Bradford Callery
Planetree, **London**
Redbud
Silverbell, Carolina
Sorrell Tree (Sourwood)
Sweetgum
Tuliptree
Viburnum, Siebold
Zelkova, **Japanese**

Shrubs Classified According to Use

ACCENT PLANTS

Holly, Burford Chinese
Hydrangea, Oak-Leaved
Redcedar, Canaert Eastern
Weigela (various species)
Yew, Hatfield or Hicks
Yew, Upright Japanese

FACER PLANTS

Abelia, Glossy
Almond, Flowering Dwarf
Andromeda, Mountain
Azalea, Karens
Barberry, Japanese
Barberry, Mentor
Bayberry, Northern
Bluebeard
Bushcherry, Nakai Chinese
Cherry, Western Sand
Cinquefoil, Bush
Coralberry, Chenault
Coralberry, Indiancurrant

Cotoneaster, Cranberry
Cotoneaster, Rock or Rockspray
Currant, Alpine
Deutzia, Compact Lemoine
Deutzia, Slender
Euonymus, Dwarf Winged
Forsythia, Bronx
Holly, Convexleaf Japanese
Holly, Heller Japanese
Hollygrape, Oregon
Honeysuckle, Clavey Dwarf
Juniper, Bar Harbor Creeping
Juniper, Blue Rug Creeping
Juniper, Compact Pfitzer
Juniper, Dwarf Common
Juniper, Sargent Chinese
Juniper, Waukegan Creeping
Kerria, Japanese
Mockorange, Frosty Morn
Ninebark, Dwarf
Quince, Flowering Japanese
Rhododendron, P.J.M. Hybrid
Rhododendron, Wilson

Rose (Floribunda Type)
  (various species)
St. Johnswort, Sungold
Spirea, Anthony Waterer
Spirea, Garland
Stephanandra, Cutleaf
Sumac, Fragrant
Virburnum, Dwarf European
  Cranberrybush
Yew, Dwarf Spreading Japanese
Yew, Taunton Anglojap
Yew, Ward Anglojap

Shrubs Classified According to Use

FOUNDATION PLANTINGS

Corner

Abelia, Glossy
Almond, Flowering
Barberry, Wintergreen
Bayberry, Northern
Buckthorn, Common
Cherry, Manchu
Cotoneaster, Spreading
Deutzia, Lemoine
Dogwood, Yellowtwig Redosier
Euonymus, Dwarf Winged
Euonymus, Spreading
Euonymus, Winged
Firethorn, Laland Scarlet
Fringetree, White
Honeysuckle, Winter
Hydrangea, Hills-of-Snow
Jetbead, Black
Juniper, Blue Rug Creeping
Juniper, Compact Pfitzer
Juniper, Dwarf Common
Juniper, Pfitzer Chinese
Juniper, Sargent Chinese
Juniper, Waukegan Creeping
Lilac, Persian
Nandina
Ninebark, Dwarf
Pine, Dwarf Mugo
Plum, Flowering
Privet, Regel Border
Quince, Flowering Japanese
Viburnum, American Cranberrybush
Viburnum, Arrowwood
Viburnum, Burkwood
Viburnum, Compact American
    Cranberrybush
Viburnum, Compact European
    Cranberrybush
Viburnum, Fragrant Snowball
    (Carlcephalum)
Viburnum, Koreanspice
Viburnum, Leatherleaf
Viburnum, Mapleleaf
Weigela (various species)
Yew, Anglojap

Yew, Dwarf Spreading Japanese
Yew, Hatfield or Hicks
Yew, Spreading Japanese
Yew, Taunton Anglojap
Yew, Upright Japanese
Yew, Ward Anglojap

Doorway

Azalea, Karens
Azalea, Mollis Hybrid
Barberry, Mentor
Barberry, Truehedge Columnberry
Bayberry, Northern
Cotoneaster, Cranberry
Cotoneaster, Rock or Rockspray
Currant, Alpine
Deutzia, Compact Lemoine
Deutzia, Slender
Dogwood, Kelsey Redosier
Euonymus, Bigleaf Wintercreeper
Euonymus, Dwarf Winged
Euonymus, Sarcoxie
Holly, Convexleaf Japanese
Holly, Heller Japanese
Hollygrape, Oregon
Honeysuckle, Clavey Dwarf
Juniper, Blue Rug Creeping
Juniper, Compact Pfitzer
Juniper, Dwarf Common
Juniper, Sargent Chinese
Juniper, Waukegan Creeping
Lavender, True
Pine, Dwarf Mugo
Quince, Flowering Japanese
Spirea, Alpine Japanese
Spirea, Anthony Waterer
Viburnum, Compact European
    Cranberrybush
Viburnum, Dwarf European
    Cranberrybush
Yew, Dense
Yew, Dwarf Spreading Japanese
Yew, Taunton Anglojap
Yew, Ward Anglojap

General Use

Box, Common
Box, Littleleaf
Bushcherry, Nakai Chinese
Leucothoe, Drooping
Mockorange, Frosty Morn
Mockorange, Mont Blanc Lemoine
Rhododendron, P.J.M. Hybrid
Rhododendron, Wilson
St. Johnswort, Sungold
Viburnum, Witherod

GROUP PLANTINGS

Abelialeaf, Korean
Alder, Speckled
Almond, Flowering Dwarf
Andromeda, Japanese
Azalea, Exbury Hybrids
Azalea, Karens
Azalea, Mollis Hybrid
Barberry, Wintergreen
Bluebeard
Blueberry, Highbush
Box, Common
Box, Littleleaf
Cherry, Manchu
Cherry, Purple Sand
Coralberry, Chenault
Cotoneaster, Cranberry
Crabapple, Sargent Flowering
Currant, Alpine
Deutzia, Compact Lemoine
Deutzia, Lemoine
Dogwood, Yellowtwig Redosier
Enkianthus, Redvein
Euonymus, Eastern Wahoo
Euonymus, Spindle Tree
Euonymus, Spreading
Euonymus, Winged
Euonymus, Yeddo
Falsecypress, Hinoki
Forsythia (various species)
Forsythia, Border
Forsythia, Bronx
Fothergilla, Dwarf
Fothergilla, Large
Fringetree, White

Shrubs Classified According to Use

Holly, American
Holly, Blue Girl
Holly, Foster's
Holly, Inkberry
Holly, Winterberry
Hollygrape, Oregon
Honeysuckle, Arnold Gotha
Honeysuckle, Clavey Dwarf
Honeysuckle, Winter
Honeysuckle, Zabel Blueleaf
Hydrangea, Hills-of-Snow
Juniper, Blue Rug Creeping
Juniper, Dwarf Common
Juniper, Japgarden
Juniper, Pfitzer Chinese
Juniper, Sargent Chinese
Kerria, Japanese
Leucothoe, Drooping
Lilac (various species)
Lilac, Japanese Tree
Lilac, Persian
Mockorange (various species)
Mockorange, Frosty Morn
Mockorange, Minnesota Snowflake
Mockorange, Mont Blanc Lemoine
Nandina
Pearlbush
Photinia, Oriental
Plum, Flowering
Plum, Thundercloud
Privet, Lodense
Privet, Regel Border
Quince, Flowering
Redcedar, Canaert Eastern
Rose (Floribunda Type)
   (various species)
Rose of Sharon (Shrubalthea)
St. Johnswort, Shrubby
St. Johnswort, Sungold
Sand Cherry, Purpleleaf
Serviceberry, Shadblow
Spicebush
Spirea, Alpine Japanese
Spirea, Bridalwreath
Spirea, Garland
Stephanandra, Cutleaf

Viburnum, American Cranberrybush
Viburnum, Burkwood
Viburnum, Compact American
   Cranberrybush
Virburnum, Compact European
   Cranberrybush
Viburnum, European Cranberrybush
Viburnum, Fragrant Snowball
   (Carlcephalum)
Viburnum, Japanese Snowball
Viburnum, Koreanspice
Viburnum, Leatherleaf
Viburnum, Linden
Viburnum, Nannyberry
Viburnum, Siebold
Viburnum, Witherod
Weigela (various species)
Witchhazel, Vernal
Witchhazel, Common
Yew, Dwarf Spreading Japanese
Yew, Taunton Anglojap
Yew, Ward Anglojap

HEDGES

Clipped

Barberry, Japanese
Barberry, Mentor
Barberry, Truehedge Columnberry
Barberry, Wintergreen
Box, Common
Box, Littleleaf
Cinquefoil, Bush
Cotoneaster, Peking
Currant, Alpine
Euonymus, Bigleaf Wintercreeper
Euonymus, Sarcoxie
Ninebark, Dwarf
Privet, Amur
Privet, Ibolium
Privet, Lodense
Privet, Regel Border
Quince, Flowering
Quince, Flowering Japanese
Yew, Dense
Yew, Hatfield or Hicks

Unclipped

Abelia, Glossy
Aralia, Fiveleaf
Arborvitae, Mission Eastern
Barberry, Japanese
Barberry, Mentor
Barberry, Wintergreen
Box, Common
Box, Littleleaf
Buckthorn, Columnar (Tallhedge)
Buckthorn, Common
Cinquefoil, Bush
Currant, Alpine
Deutzia, Slender
Euonymus, Dwarf Winged
Germander, Chamaedrys
Holly, Convexleaf Japanese
Holly, Heller Japanese
Honeysuckle, Winter
Honeysuckle, Zabel Blueleaf
Jetbead, Black
Ninebark, Common
Ninebark, Dwarf
Pachistima, Canby
Privet, Amur
Privet, Ibolium
Privet, Lodense
Privet, Regel Border
Rose (Floribunda Type)
   (various species)
Rose of Sharon (Shrubalthea)
Spirea, Anthony Waterer
Yew, Dense
Yew, Hatfield or Hicks

Shrubs Classified According to Use

PLANTER BOXES OR CONTAINERS

Azalea, Mollis Hybrid
Barberry, Japanese
Bayberry, Northern
Cotoneaster, Bearberry
Cotoneaster, Peking
Dogwood, Kelsey Redosier
Euonymus, Bigleaf Wintercreeper
Euonymus, Sarcoxie
Firethorn, Laland Scarlet
Germander, Chamaedrys
Holly, Convexleaf Japanese
Holly, Heller Japanese
Lavender, True
Pachistima, Canby
Pine, Dwarf Mugo
Viburnum, Dwarf European
  Cranberrybush
Yew, Dense
Yew, Dwarf Spreading Japanese
Yew, Hatfield or Hicks

SCREENS

Aralia, Fiveleaf
Arborvitae, Mission Eastern
Blueberry, Highbush
Buckthorn, Columnar
Currant, Clove
Euonymus, Eastern Wahoo
Euonymus, Midwinter
Forsythia (various species)
Holly, Foster's
Holly, Inkberry
Holly, Winterberry
Honeysuckle, Amur
Honeysuckle, Morrow
Honeysuckle, Tatarian
Honeysuckle, Zabel Blueleaf
Lilac (various species)
Lilac, Japanese Tree
Lilac, Persian
Mockorange (various species)
Peashrub, Siberian
Photinia, Oriental
Privet, Amur
Privet, Ibolium

Redcedar, Canaert Eastern
Rose of Sharon (Shrubalthea)
Spirea, Van Houtte
Sweetshrub, Common (Carolina
  Allspice)
Viburnum, American Cranberrybush
Viburnum, Arrowwood
Viburnum, European Cranberrybush

SHRUB BORDERS

Abelialeaf, Korean (Abeliophyllum)
Almond, Flowering Dwarf
Andromeda, Japanese
Azalea, Exbury Hybrids
Azalea, Karens
Barberry, Japanese
Beautybush
Bluebeard
Blueberry, Highbush
Box, Common
Box, Littleleaf
Buckeye, Bottlebrush
Buckeye, Red
Buckthorn, Common
Bushcherry, Nakai Chinese
Cherry, Manchu
Cherry, Peking
Cherry, Purple Sand
Cherry, Western Sand
Chokeberry, Red
Clethra, Summersweet
Cotoneaster, Peking
Cotoneaster, Spreading
Currant, Clove
Deutzia, Lemoine
Dogwood, Gray
Dogwood, Redosier
Dogwood, Yellowtwig Redosier
Elaeagnus, Cherry
Enkianthus, Redvein
Euonymus, Eastern Wahoo
Euonymus, Midwinter
Euonymus, Spindle Tree
Euonymus, Spreading
Euonymus, Winged
Forsythia (various species)

Forsythia, Border
Fothergilla, Dwarf
Fothergilla, Large
Hazel, American or Filbert
Holly, American
Holly, Blue Girl
Holly, Burford Chinese
Holly, Foster's
Holly, Inkberry
Holly, Winterberry
Honeysuckle, Amur
Honeysuckle, Clavey Dwarf
Honeysuckle, Morrow
Honeysuckle, Tatarian
Honeysuckle, Winter
Honeysuckle, Zabel Blueleaf
Hydrangea, Hills-of-Snow
Jetbead, Black
Juniper, Pfitzer Chinese
Kerria, Japanese
Leucothoe, Drooping
Lilac (various species)
Lilac, Japanese Tree
Lilac, Persian
Magnolia, Sweetbay
Mockorange (various species)
Mockorange, Minnesota Snowflake
Mockorange, Mont Blanc Lemoine
Nandina
Ninebark, Common
Pearlbush
Peashrub, Siberian
Photinia, Oriental
Plum, **Flowering**
Privet, Amur
Privet, Ibolium
Privet, Lodense
Privet, Regel Border
Quince, Flowering
Rhododendron, Catawaba
Rhododendron, P.J.M. Hybrid
Rhododendron, Wilson
Rose, Father Hugo
Rose of Sharon (Shrubalthea)
St. Johnswort, Shrubby
Serviceberry, Shadblow
Snowberry, Common
Spicebush

Shrubs Classified According to Use

Spirea, Bridalwreath

Spirea, Van Houtte

Sweetshrub, Common (Carolina Allspice)

Viburnum, Arrowwood

Viburnum, Burkwood

Viburnum, Compact American Cranberrybush

Viburnum, Compact European Cranberrybush

Viburnum, European Cranberrybush

Viburnum, Fragrant Snowball (Carlcephalum)

Viburnum, Japanese Snowball

Viburnum, Koreanspice

Viburnum, Leatherleaf

Viburnum, Linden

Viburnum, Mapleleaf

Viburnum, Nannyberry

Viburnum, Siebold

Viburnum, Witherod

Weigela (various species)

Witchhazel, Vernal

Witchhazel, Common

Yew, Anglojap

Yew, Spreading Japanese

SPECIMEN PLANTS

Andromeda, Japanese

Azalea, Karens

Buckeye, Bottlebrush

Buckeye, Red

Cherry, Manchu

Cotoneaster, Cranberry

Cotoneaster, Rock or Rockspray

Cotoneaster, Spreading

Crabapple, Sargent Flowering

Enkianthus, Redvein

Euonymus, Spindle Tree

Euonymus, Winged

Euonymus, Yeddo

Falsecypress, Hinoki

Firethorn, Laland Scarlet

Fringetree, White

Hazel, Contorted European

Holly, American

Holly, Blue Girl

Holly, Burford Chinese

Holly, Convexleaf Japanese

Holly, Foster's

Holly, Heller Japanese

Honeysuckle, Arnold Gotha

Honeysuckle, Tatarian

Hydrangea, Oak-Leaved

Lavender, True

Leucothoe, Drooping

Lilac (various species)

Lilac, Japanese Tree

Magnolia, Saucer

Magnolia, Star

Mockorange, Minnesota Snowflake

Nandina

Photinia, Oriental

Plum, Thundercloud

Rhododendron, P.J.M. Hybrid

Rose, Father Hugo

Rose of Sharon (Shrubalthea)

Sand Cherry, Purpleleaf

Serviceberry, Shadblow

Snowbell, Japanese

Spirea, Alpine Japanese

Spirea, Garland

Stephanandra, Cutleaf

Sumac, Staghorn

Viburnum, Burkwood

Viburnum, Fragrant Snowball (Carlcephalum)

Viburnum, Japanese Snowball

Viburnum, Koreanspice

Viburnum, Leatherleaf

Viburnum, Linden

Viburnum, Siebold

Witchhazel, Vernal

Witchhazel, Common

Yew, Spreading Japanese

Yucca (Adamsneedle)

Descriptive Outlines of Trees

ALDER, SPECKLED
(Alnus rugosa).   **Zone 3**

Medium to fast rate of growth. Large, spreading, ascending. Valued for its form, interesting bark, and suitability to wet situations.

Height: 8–25 feet.   **Spread:** 10–15 feet.
Rooting habit: spreading.
Soil: moist to wet.
Texture: medium to fine.
Flower effects: reddish.
Fruit effects: not showy.
Fall color: yellow.
Use: group. See also under Shrubs.

ASH, BLUE
(Fraxinus quadrangulata).   **Zone 2**

Fast growing. Broad, rounded form. Handsome foliage. Heavy, corky bark.

Height: 70–80 feet.   **Spread:** 60 feet.
Rooting habit: fibrous, spreading.
Soil: any good soil. Tolerates limestone.
Texture: medium.
Fall color: yellow to purple.
Use: lawn.

ASH, GREEN (Fraxinus pennsylvanica lanceolata).   **Zone 2**

Fast growing. Dense, oblong to round form. Subject to breakage and oystershell scale.

Height: 60 feet.   **Spread:** 40–50 feet.
Rooting habit: spreading, shallow.
Soil: moderately moist.
Texture: medium.
Flower effects: not showy.
Fruit effects: not showy.
Fall color: yellow.
Use: lawn, street.
Varieties: 'Honeyshade' (fast growing, glossy green leaves); 'Marshall Seedless' (see detailed description below); 'Summit' (female, upright, pyramidal, glossy foliage).

ASH, MARSHALL SEEDLESS (Fraxinus pennsylvanica lanceolata 'Marshall Seedless').   **Zone 4**

Fast growing. Seedless tree with a definite, uniform pyramidal shape. Rich, dark, glossy green foliage. Dense crown.

Height: 60 feet.   **Spread:** 50 feet.
Rooting habit: spreading, somewhat shallow.
Soil: moderately moist.
Texture: medium.
Fall color: yellow.
Use: lawn, street.

ASH, MORAINE (Fraxinus holotricha 'Moraine').   **Zone 5**

Fast growing. Small, low-growing tree with upright, narrow form. Glossy green foliage. Bears very little seed.

Height: 35 feet.   **Spread:** 20–25 feet.
Rooting habit: fibrous.
Texture: medium.
Fall color: yellow to purple.
Use: lawn, street.

BALDCYPRESS
(Taxodium distichum).   **Zone 4**

Medium rate of growth. Narrow, pyramidal form while young; broadly rounded at maturity. Foliage appears late, light feathery appearance. Limited use on small properties because of huge size.

Height: 100 feet or more.   **Spread:** 12–20 feet.
Rooting habit: long, horizontal.
Soil: rich, moist.
Texture: very fine, soft.
Flower effects: not showy.
Fruit effects: not showy.
Fall color: yellowish-orange to brown.
Use: lawn.

BEECH, AMERICAN
(Fagus grandifolia).   **Zone 3**

Slow growing. Oval to pyramidal. Stately, horizontal branching extends to the ground. Interesting form, excellent foliage, attractive winter bark.

Height: 70–80 feet.   **Spread:** 50 feet.
Rooting habit: spreading, shallow.
Texture: medium.
Flower effects: not showy.
Fruit effects: not showy.
Fall color: yellow-orange.
Use: lawn, specimen. Also effective planted in masses.

BEECH, EUROPEAN
(Fagus sylvatica).   **Zone 4**

Slow growing. Oval to pyramidal. Dense, stately, horizontal branching extends to the ground. Available in cut-leaf, columnar, and purple-leaf varieties.

Height: 70–80 feet.   **Spread:** 50–70 feet.
Rooting habit: spreading, shallow.
Soil: light.
Texture: medium.
Flower effects: not showy.
Fruit effects: not showy.
Fall color: red to yellow or brown.
Use: lawn, specimen.

Varieties: 'Dawyck' (narrow, columnar form); 'Laciniata' (cut-leaf); 'Pendula' (weeping form); 'Rivers' (young foliage red, then turns purple; holds color through summer; best of purple forms).

BIRCH, CANOE OR PAPER
(Betula papyrifera).   **Zone 2**

Medium rate of growth. Graceful, upright, slender. Interesting bark.

Height: 60 feet.   **Spread:** 30 feet.
Rooting habit: spreading, descending.
Soil: moist.
Texture: medium in summer, fine in winter.
Flower effects: yellow catkins in early spring.
Fruit effects: brown, conelike in summer.
Fall color: yellow.
Use: group, lawn, specimen.

BIRCH, EUROPEAN WHITE
(Betula pendula).   **Zone 2**

Fast growing. Oval, pendulous form. Graceful and airy. Interesting bark color. Subject to attack by the bronze birch borer.

Height: 40 feet.   **Spread:** 25 feet.
Rooting habit: spreading, descending.
Soil: light, moist.
Texture: fine.
Flower effects: pale yellow catkins, before leaves.
Fruit effects: brown, conelike clusters in late summer and fall.
Fall color: yellow.
Use: lawn, specimen.
Varieties: 'Fastigiata' (upright, narrow spire); 'Laciniata' (cut-leaf form); 'Young' (pendulous habit).

BIRCH, GRAY
(Betula populifolia).   **Zones 3–4**

Fast growing. Grows in clumps with slender, resilient trunks. Bark is white with triangular black markings.

Height: 30 feet.   **Spread:** 20–25 feet.
Rooting habit: spreading, descending.
Soil: rocky to wet.
Texture: fine.
Flower effects: yellow catkins.
Fruit effects: brown, conelike clusters in late summer.
Fall color: yellow.
Use: lawn.

Descriptive Outlines of Trees

BIRCH, RIVER
(Betula nigra).   **Zone 4**
Fast growing. Open, pyramidal form. Paper-thin, red-brown, exfoliating bark. Valued for ability to grow in wet places. Resistant to bronze birch borer.
Height: 50–90 feet.   **Spread:** 30–60 feet.
Rooting habit: spreading.
Soil: moist to wet.
Texture: medium-fine.
Flower effects: greenish-yellow catkins.
Fruit effects: brown, conelike.
Fall color: yellow.
Use: accent, lawn (best in wet areas).

BIRCH, SWEET
(Betula lenta).   **Zone 3**
Medium rate of growth. Pyramidal in youth and rounded at maturity. Bark cinnamon-brown to black. Beautiful fall color and shape.
Height: 60–70 feet.   **Spread:** 30–35 feet.
Rooting habit: fibrous, spreading, descending.
Soil: generally good, well-drained soil.
Texture: fine.
Fall color: brilliant yellow.
Use: group, lawn, specimen.

BUCKEYE, RED
(Aesculus pavia).   **Zone 4**
Moderately fast rate of growth. Loose, open, rounded form with ascending branches. Interesting flowers.
Height: 18–20 feet.   **Spread:** 10–20 feet.
Rooting habit: fibrous, descending. Tends to sucker.
Soil: rich loam.
Texture: medium to coarse.
Flower effects: bright red.
Use: lawn, shrub border, specimen. See also under Shrubs.

CHERRY, AUTUMN HIGAN
(Prunus subhirtella autumnalis).   **Zone 5**
Medium rate of growth. Dense, rounded form. Semidouble flowers that last a long time. Unique because of fall flowering if weather remains warm.
Height: 25–30 feet.   **Spread:** 15–25 feet.
Rooting habit: fibrous, spreading.
Soil: any good soil with normal moisture.
Texture: fine.
Flower effects: pink.
Fall color: bronze.
Use: lawn, specimen, street.

CHERRY, EUROPEAN BIRD
(Prunus padus).   **Zone 3**
Fast growing. Upright, somewhat open in form. Leaves appear in early spring. Flower clusters pendulous, fragrant. Dependable.
Height: 45 feet.   **Spread:** 35–45 feet.
Rooting habit: spreading.
Soil: any good soil with normal moisture.
Texture: medium.
Flower effects: white clusters in May.
Fruit effects: black cherries in July.
Use: containers, lawn, specimen.
Varieties: 'Commutata' (large, single flowers in very early spring); 'Plena' (long-lasting, large, double flowers); 'Spaeth' (pendulous flower clusters; dependable); 'Waterer' (best single-flowered variety, flowers 8 inches long).

CHERRY, FUGENZO ORIENTAL
(Prunus serrulata 'Fugenzo').   **Zone 5**
Medium rate of growth. Wide, spreading form with graceful structure. Large, rosy pink, double flowers. Popular variety.
Height: 20–25 feet.   **Spread:** 20–25 feet.
Rooting habit: spreading.
Exposure: full sun.
Soil: any good soil with normal moisture.
Texture: medium.
Flower effects: rosy pink fading to light pink.
Use: lawn, specimen, street.

CHERRY, HALLY JOLIVETTE
(Prunus 'Hally Jolivette').   **Zone 5**
Medium to slow rate of growth. Dense, rounded form that tends to be shrubby. Double flowers. Flowering extends over period of 10–20 days.
Height: 15–18 feet.   **Spread:** 18–20 feet.
Rooting habit: spreading.
Soil: any good soil with normal moisture.
Texture: fine.
Flower effects: pink buds, white flowers in mid-spring.
Fruit effects: insignificant.
Use: lawn, planter boxes, specimen.

CHERRY, KWANZAN ORIENTAL
(Prunus serrulata 'Kwanzan').   **Zone 5**
Medium rate of growth. Upright with graceful structure. Outstanding, double pink flowers (2½ inches in diameter) contrast with early spring foliage of reddish copper. Glossy, colorful bark.

Height: 18–25 feet.   **Spread:** 8–10 feet.
Texture: medium-coarse.
Flower effects: double, pink.
Use: lawn, specimen, street.

CHERRY, SARGENT
(Prunus sargentii).   **Zone 4**
Fast growing. Upright with rounded top. Excellent tree in flower and foliage. Leaves emerge a colorful bronze, then turn green. Interesting bark. Hardiest of oriental cherries.
Height: 50–75 feet.   **Spread:** 40 feet.
Rooting habit: spreading.
Exposure: full sun.
Soil: any good soil with normal moisture.
Texture: medium.
Flower effects: rich pink.
Fall color: orange to red.
Use: lawn, specimen, street.
Variety: 'Columnar' (columnar form).

CHERRY, WEEPING HIGAN
(Prunus subhirtella pendula).   **Zone 5**
Fast growing. Erect, graceful weeping form. Spring foliage bronze; summer foliage green to red-green. Flowers appear before leaves.
Height: 20–30 feet.   **Spread:** 15–25 feet.
Rooting habit: fibrous, spreading.
Soil: any good soil with normal moisture.
Texture: fine.
Flower effects: pale pink in mid-spring.
Fall color: bronze.
Use: lawn, specimen.

COFFEETREE, KENTUCKY
(Gymnocladus dioicus).   **Zone 4**
Medium rate of growth. Oval form. Tree structure interesting in winter. Fruit can become a nuisance. Plant male form only. Best used in large areas.
Height: 60–80 feet.   **Spread:** 40–50 feet.
Rooting habit: descending.
Texture: medium when in foliage, coarse during winter.
Flower effects: not showy.
Fruit effects: brown pod in fall.
Fall color: yellow.
Use: lawn.

Descriptive Outlines of Trees

CORKTREE, AMUR
(Phellodendron amurense).   **Zone 3**
Fast growing. Handsome round form. Striking bark. Tolerates heat and drouth. Heavy feeder. Sexes separate.
Height: 40–60 feet.   **Spread:** 30 feet.
Rooting habit: spreading, shallow.
Texture: medium in summer, coarse in winter.
Flower effects: white, not showy.
Fruit effects: black in fall.
Fall color: bronze.
Use: lawn, street.

CRABAPPLE, CARMINE
(Malus × atrosanguinea).   **Zone 4**
Medium rate of growth. Dense, mounded form. Glossy dark-green foliage. Flowers heavily each year. Disease resistant.
Height: 20 feet.   **Spread:** 25 feet.
Rooting habit: spreading, descending.
Soil: tolerant.
Texture: medium.
Flower effects: carmine in mid-May.
Fruit effects: red.
Use: group, lawn, shrub border, specimen.

CRABAPPLE, FLOWERING
(various species).   **Zones 2–5**
Medium rate of growth. Oval, round, spreading, depending on variety. Striking plant in flower and fruit. Wide selection of flower color, form, and size.
Height: 8–45 feet.   **Spread:** 12–35 feet.
Rooting habit: spreading, descending.
Texture: medium.
Flower effects: many colors ranging from white to red, in spring.
Fruit effects: red, yellow, or green in summer and fall.
Fall color: yellow, orange, or red, according to variety.
Use: accent, group, shrub border, specimen.

CRABAPPLE, JAPANESE FLOWERING
(Malus floribunda).   **Zone 4**
Medium rate of growth. Rounded form with dense foliage. Extremely reliable where hardy. Flowers as a young tree.
Height: 20–30 feet.   **Spread:** 30 feet.
Rooting habit: fibrous, spreading.
Soil: any good soil.
Texture: fine.
Flower effects: pink to red. Flowers annually.
Fruit effects: red.
Use: lawn, specimen.

CRABAPPLE, RADIANT
(Malus 'Radiant').   **Zone 4**
Medium rate of growth. Compact, upright form. Good ornamental flowers and fruit. Disease resistant.
Height: 30 feet.   **Spread:** 25 feet.
Rooting habit: spreading.
Soil: any good soil.
Texture: medium.
Flower effects: deep red buds, annual pink flowers.
Fruit effects: bright red through winter.
Fall color: sometimes reddish.
Use: lawn, specimen.

CRABAPPLE, REDBUD ZUMI
(Malus zumi calocarpa).   **Zone 5**
Medium rate of growth. Dense, pyramidal form. Flowers in alternate years. Fruit is showy and remains long into winter.
Height: 25 feet.   **Spread:** 18 feet.
Rooting habit: fibrous, spreading.
Soil: any good soil.
Texture: medium to coarse.
Flower effects: pink buds, white flowers.
Fruit effects: bright red.
Use: lawn, specimen.

CRABAPPLE, RED JADE
(Malus 'Red Jade').   **Zone 4**
Medium rate of growth. Upright with pendulous branches. Fruit lasts well into winter. Bears heavily, but in alternate years.
Height: 20 feet.   **Spread:** 25–30 feet.
Rooting habit: spreading.
Soil: any good soil.
Texture: medium to fine.
Flower effects: white, not so showy as some crabapples.
Fruit effects: bright red.
Use: lawn, specimen.

CRABAPPLE, SELKIRK
(Malus 'Selkirk').   **Zone 4**
Medium rate of growth. Dense, somewhat rounded form. Excellent foliage and fruit display that persists well into fall and winter.
Height: 25 feet.   **Spread:** 20 feet.
Rooting habit: spreading.
Soil: tolerant.
Texture: medium.
Flower effects: rose-red.
Fruit effects: purple-red, ½ inch in size.
Use: group, lawn, specimen.

CRABAPPLE, SIBERIAN
(Malus baccata).   **Zone 2**
Slow growing. Narrow, upright form. One of the largest and hardiest crabapples. Many varieties available; one of the best is 'Jackii'. Resistant to apple scab.
Height: 30–40 feet.   **Spread:** 15–20 feet.
Rooting habit: spreading, descending.
Soil: any good soil.
Texture: medium.
Flower effects: white, annual.
Fruit effects: red in fall.
Use: lawn.
Varieties: gracilis (slightly pendulous branches, white flowers); 'Jackii' (outstanding in its glossy red fruit).

CRABAPPLE, SNOWDRIFT
(Malus 'Snowdrift').   **Zone 4**
Medium rate of growth. Rounded form. Excellent growth habit and size recommend it for small properties. Disease resistant.
Height: 20 feet.   **Spread:** 20 feet.
Rooting habit: spreading.
Soil: tolerant.
Texture: medium.
Flower effects: yellow.
Use: group, lawn, specimen.

CRABAPPLE, TEA
(Malus hupehensis).   **Zone 4**
Medium rate of growth. Picturesque vase-shaped form. Flowers full length of stem. Blooms in alternate years only.
Height: 24 feet.   **Spread:** 15–18 feet.
Rooting habit: fibrous, spreading.
Soil: any good soil.
Texture: fine.
Flower effects: deep pink turning to white.
Fruit effects: yellow to red in fall.
Use: lawn, specimen.

DOGWOOD, CORNELIANCHERRY
(Cornus mas).   **Zone 4**
Medium rate of growth. Oval form. Valued for early flowers, which appear before leaves.
Height: 25 feet.   **Spread:** 20 feet.
Rooting habit: spreading, descending.
Soil: rich, well-drained.
Texture: medium.
Flower effects: yellow in early spring.
Fruit effects: scarlet in summer.
Fall color: red to green.
Use: group, clipped hedge, lawn, shrub border, specimen.

Descriptive Outlines of Trees

DOGWOOD, FLOWERING
(Cornus florida).   **Zone 4**

Slow growing. Flat crown, horizontal branches. Picturesque. Attractive foliage, flower, and brilliant red berries.

Height: 25 feet.   **Spread:** 15 feet.

Rooting habit: descending.

Soil: rich, well-drained.

Texture: medium.

Flower effects: white in early spring.

Fruit effects: red in early fall.

Fall color: red to violet.

Use: lawn, shrub border, specimen, street. Effective underplanting in woodland plantings.

Varieties: 'Cherokee Chief' (flowers reddish to pink); 'White Cloud' (creamy white flowers, unusually heavy flowering).

DOGWOOD, JAPANESE (KOUSA)
(Cornus kousa).   **Zone 4**

Medium to slow rate of growth. Outstanding horizontal branching, fruit, and foliage. Showy flowers appear later than *C. florida.* Good fall color.

Height: 21 feet.   **Spread:** 15 feet.

Rooting habit: descending.

Soil: rich, well-drained.

Texture: medium.

Flower effects: white to buff in mid-June.

Fruit effects: red in late summer.

Fall color: scarlet.

Use: lawn, specimen, street.

Varieties: 'Milky Way' (flowers heavily).

DOUGLAS-FIR (Psuedostuga
mensiesii [taxifolia]).   **Zone 4**

Fast growing. Open, pyramidal form. Dense, dark evergreen foliage. Excellent overall qualities recommend it for ornamental use.

Height: 150–200 feet.   **Spread:** 12–18 feet.

Rooting habit: taproot.

Soil: any good soil if moist.

Texture: medium.

Fruit effects: pendulous cones.

Use: group, large-scale screen, specimen.

Varieties: 'Compacta' (conical form); 'Pendula' (weeping branches).

ELM, CHINESE
(Ulmus parvifolia).   **Zone 5**

Fast growing. Rounded form. Bark matted and exfoliating. Should not be confused with Siberian Elm (*U. pumila),* which is mistakenly referred to and sold as Chinese Elm. True Chinese Elm is a good, fast-growing, ornamental tree.

Height: 50 feet.   **Spread:** 30 feet.

Rooting habit: spreading.

Soil: tolerant.

Texture: fine.

Use: lawn.

ENKIANTHUS, REDVEIN
(Enkianthus companulatus).   **Zone 4**

Medium rate of growth. Large, upright, rounded. Valued for flowers and autumn color. Must have acid soil.

Height: 10–20 feet.   **Spread:** 10–15 feet.

Rooting habit: spreading.

Soil: acid.

Texture: medium.

Flower effects: yellow to orange.

Fruit effects: not showy.

Fall color: scarlet.

Use: group, specimen. See also under Shrubs.

Varieties: 'Albiflorus' (white flowers); pabilinii (red flowers).

EUONYMUS, ALDENHAM SPINDLE TREE
(Euonymus europaeus 'Aldenhamensis').
    Zone 3

Medium-fast growing. Rounded form. Excellent foliage and more colorful fruit than *E. europaeus.* (See Shrubs.) Subject to scale infestations.

Height: 20–30 feet.   **Spread:** 10–20 feet.

Rooting habit: compact, fibrous.

Exposure: sun or partial shade.

Soil: very tolerant.

Texture: fine.

Flower effects: not showy.

Fruit effects: pink capsules in fall.

Fall color: red.

Use: containers, lawn, shrub border, specimen.

Other varieties: 'Alba' (white fruit); intermedia (bright red fruit).

EUONYMUS, EASTERN WAHOO
(Euonymus atropurpureus).   **Zone 3**

Slow growing. Spreading. Outstanding foliage and fruit color. Subject to scale infestations.

Height: 15–20 feet.   **Spread:** 8–15 feet.

Rooting habit: spreading.

Texture: medium.

Flower effects: not showy.

Fruit effects: red in fall.

Fall color: purple to red.

Use: group, lawn. See also under Shrubs.

EUONYMUS, MIDWINTER
(Euonymus bungeana).   **Zone 4**

Fast growing. Round, irregular form. Light-green foliage. Subject to scale infestations.

Height: 18 feet.   **Spread:** 25 feet.

Rooting habit: spreading.

Soil: tolerant.

Texture: medium to fine.

Flower effects: not showy.

Fruit effects: yellow.

Use: containers, lawn. See also under Shrubs.

Varieties: 'Pendulous' (gracefully drooping to weeping branches).

FIR, WHITE
(Abies concolor).   **Zone 4**

Fast growing. Narrow, pyramidal. Long, upcurving needles of blue-gray green. Handsome tree with softer appearance than the Blue Spruce. Withstands some drouth. Superior to Blue Spruce.

Height: 100–120 feet.   **Spread:** 25–35 feet.

Rooting habit: taproot.

Soil: moist, well-drained. Dislikes heavy clay.

Texture: medium-coarse.

Fruit effects: cones.

Use: lawn, specimen.

Varieties: conica (dwarf, pyramidal, slow growing); violacea (bluish-white foliage).

FRINGETREE, WHITE
(Chionanthus virginicus).   **Zone 4**

Slow growing. Round, spreading, upright. Showy, fragrant flowers. Leaves appear in late spring. Sexes usually separate. Withstands city conditions. Subject to scale infestations.

Height: 10–20 feet.   **Spread:** 8–20 feet.

Rooting habit: spreading.

Soil: moist.

Texture: coarse.

Flower effects: white in late spring.

Fruit effects: blue in late summer.

Fall color: yellow.

Use: group, lawn, shrub border, specimen. See also under Shrubs.

Descriptive Outlines of Trees

GINKGO
(Ginkgo biloba). **Zone 4**
Slow growing. Male tree has pyramidal form. Handsome foliage. Excellent for city conditions. Free of pests and diseases. Plant male tree only; female fruit has objectionable odor.
Height: 70 feet. **Spread:** 40 feet.
Rooting habit: spreading.
Texture: medium.
Flower effects: not showy.
Fruit effects: drupe (ill smelling).
Fall color: yellow.
Use: lawn, specimen, street.
Variety: 'Sentry' (columnar habit).

GOLDRAINTREE, PANICLED
(Koelreuteria paniculata). **Zone 5**
Fast growing. Handsome round tree. Showy in blossom, followed by attractive fruit. Tends to have weak wood. Tolerates drouth and wind. Prefers sun.
Height: 30 feet. **Spread:** 20 feet.
Rooting habit: descending.
Soil: tolerates alkaline soil.
Texture: medium.
Flower effects: yellow in midsummer.
Fruit effects: yellow to brown in late summer.
Fall color: brown.
Use: lawn, specimen, street.
Varieties: 'Fastigiata' (very narrow, columnar; 'September' (usually flowers in late August or September).

HACKBERRY, COMMON
(Celtis occidentalis). **Zone 4**
Fast growing. Oblong to vase-shaped plant resembling American elm. Reliable. Subject to witches' brooms, which do not harm the tree but make it somewhat unsightly in winter.
Height: 90 feet. **Spread:** 50 feet.
Rooting habit: spreading, shallow.
Texture: fine to medium.
Flower effects: not showy.
Fruit effects: purple in early fall.
Fall color: yellow.
Use: lawn, street.

HACKBERRY, SOUTHERN (SUGAR)
(Celtis laevigata). **Zone 5**
Fast growing. Rounded form. Spreading, sometimes pendulous branches. Foliage open and fine.
Height: 70 feet. **Spread:** 50–60 feet.
Rooting habit: spreading, descending.
Texture: fine.
Flower effects: not showy.

Fruit effects: hard, black berry.
Fall color: yellow.
Use: lawn, street.

HAWTHORN, COCKSPUR
(Crataegus crus-galli). **Zone 4**
Fast growing. Form usually rounded, but sometimes flat. Dense, horizontal branches with long thorns. Foliage glossy, lustrous, and dense. Withstands shearing; good for hedges. Thornless variety available.
Height: 35 feet. **Spread:** 25–30 feet.
Rooting habit: descending to taproot.
Texture: medium-fine.
Flower effects: white.
Fruit effects: bright red, persist into winter.
Fall color: orange to scarlet.
Use: lawn, specimen.

HAWTHORN, LAVALLE
(Crataegus × lavallei). **Zone 4**
Fast growing. Dense branching gives irregular, rounded form. Valued for flowers, fall color, and fruit that persists through winter. Subject to aphids and fire blight.
Height: 20–25 feet. **Spread:** 20–25 feet.
Soil: tolerant.
Texture: medium.
Flower effects: white in late spring.
Fall color: red to bronze.
Use: lawn, specimen, street.

HAWTHORN, PAUL SCARLET ENGLISH
(Crataegus oxyacantha 'Paulii'). **Zone 4**
Fast growing. Dense, rounded form. The only hawthorn available with pink to red flowers. In some areas foliage tends to scorch along edges.
Height: 15–18 feet. **Spread:** 12–15 feet.
Rooting habit: taproot.
Soil: heavy, dry loam.
Texture: medium-fine.
Flower effects: bright scarlet, double flowers in May.
Fruit effects: small, scarlet.
Fall color: not showy.
Use: lawn, specimen, street.
Other variety: plena (double white flowers, few fruits).

HAWTHORN, WASHINGTON
(Crataegus phaenopyrum). **Zone 4**
Fast growing. Oval to upright. Good color and texture. Excellent in flower, foliage, and fruit. Tolerates pruning.
Height: 30 feet. **Spread:** 20–25 feet.
Rooting habit: taproot.

Texture: medium to fine.
Flower effects: white in midspring.
Fruit effects: red in late summer through winter.
Fall color: red to bronze.
Use: group, clipped hedge, lawn, shrub border, street.
Varieties: 'Fastigiata' (columnar form); pyramidal (pyramidal form).

HAWTHORN, WINTER KING GREEN
(Crataegus viridis 'Winter King'). **Zone 4**
Medium rate of growth. Dense, spreading but rounded form. Glossy foliage, silver bark. Fruits heavily as young plant.
Height: 36 feet. **Spread:** 30–36 feet.
Rooting habit: taproot.
Soil: tolerant.
Texture: medium to fine.
Flower effects: white in late May.
Fruit effects: red. Fruit remains through winter.
Fall color: yellow to brown.
Use: lawn, planter boxes, street.

HEMLOCK, CANADA
(Tsuga canadensis). **Zone 3**
Medium to fast growing. Gracefully pyramidal with slightly drooping branches. Rich dark-green foliage. Tolerant of pruning and shearing; makes good hedge or screen. Can be held to 3 or 4 feet with proper pruning. One of the best evergreen ornamentals.
Height: 60–90 feet. **Spread:** 20–25 feet.
Rooting habit: shallow, spreading.
Exposure: sun or shade.
Soil: moist, but well-drained.
Texture: fine.
Fruit effects: cones.
Use: clipped hedge, screen, specimen.
Varieties: 'Bradshaw' (dense, pyramidal growth); 'Pomfret' (fast growing, dense, pyramidal).

HEMLOCK, CAROLINA
(Tsuga caroliniana). **Zone 4**
Fast growing. Deeper in color, more compact, and more tolerant of city conditions than the Canada Hemlock. Tolerant of shearing and pruning. Excellent evergreen tree.
Height: 40–50 feet. **Spread:** 20–25 feet.
Rooting habit: shallow, spreading.
Exposure: shade.
Soil: rich, moist.
Texture: fine.
Fruit effects: cone.
Use: clipped hedge, screen, specimen.

Descriptive Outlines of Trees

HONEYLOCUST, THORNLESS COMMON
(Gleditsia triacanthos inermis).   **Zone 4**
Fast growing. Round and spreading, somewhat horizontally branched. Provides light shade. Withstands city conditions. Blends well with contemporary architecture. Patented varieties below are both thornless and sterile. All types subject to mimosa webworm.
Height: 75 feet.   **Spread:** 40–50 feet.
Rooting habit: descending.
Texture: fine.
Flower effects: not showy.
Fruit effects: brown pods in late summer.
Fall color: yellow.
Use: lawn, street.
Varieties: 'Imperial' (graceful, spreading, 30–35 feet wide); 'Moraine' (wide-spreading form); 'Shademaster' (upright form); 'Skyline' (pyramidal form); 'Sunburst' (yellow-tipped leaves).

HOPHORNBEAM, AMERICAN
(Ostrya virginiana).   **Zone 4**
Slow growing. Pyramidal form with dense foliage. Somewhat difficult to transplant. Free from serious insects and diseases.
Height: 40–60 feet.   **Spread:** 20–25 feet.
Soil: tolerates dry situations.
Texture: medium-coarse.
Flower effects: not showy.
Fruit effects: clusters of bladderlike pods.
Fall color: clear yellow.
Use: lawn.

HORNBEAM, AMERICAN
(Carpinus caroliniana).   **Zone 2**
Slow growing. Dense, compact. Tolerates pruning. Excellent color.
Height: 30 feet.   **Spread:** 15 feet.
Rooting habit: shallow.
Texture: medium.
Flower effects: not showy.
Fruit effects: not showy.
Fall color: yellow, orange, red.
Use: hedge (clipped or unclipped), street (small areas).
Variety: 'Pyramidalis' (V-shaped growth with rounded top, about 40 feet high).

HORNBEAM, EUROPEAN
(Carpinus betulus).   **Zone 5**
Very slow growing. Upright habit. Tends to become vase-shaped in old age.
Height: 60 feet.   **Spread:** 30–40 feet.

Rooting habit: fibrous, shallow.
Soil: tolerant if not too acid.
Texture: medium-fine.
Flower effects: not showy.
Fruit effects: not showy.
Fall color: yellow.
Use: containers, lawn.
Varieties: 'Columnaris' (narrow, columnar, somewhat wider at base); 'Fastigiata' (upright to somewhat vase shaped); 'Globosa' (globe form; good street tree).

HORSECHESTNUT, COMMON
(Aesculus hippocastanum).   **Zone 3**
Medium rate of growth. Handsome, oval. Showy in flower. Casts dense shade.
Height: 40 feet.   **Spread:** 30 feet.
Rooting habit: spreading, descending.
Texture: coarse.
Flower effects: white in spring.
Fruit effects: nut in fall.
Fall color: yellow-brown.
Use: lawn.
Variety: 'Baumann' (double white flowers).

HORSECHESTNUT, RUBY RED
(Aesculus carnea 'Brioti').   **Zone 3**
Medium rate of growth. Large, round. Ornamental tree with striking spring color.
Height: 50–75 feet.   **Spread:** 30–40 feet.
Rooting habit: spreading, descending.
Texture: coarse.
Flower effects: scarlet in spring.
Fruit effects: nut in fall.
Use: lawn.

KATSURA TREE
(Cercidiphyllum japonicum).   **Zone 4**
Fast growing. Rounded, broad spreading (particularly when grown with several trunks). Low branching. Excellent form, foliage, and fall color. Insect resistant. Sexes separate.
Height: 30–40 feet (occasionally to 80 feet). **Spread:** 30 feet (almost as broad as high).
Rooting habit: broad, spreading, shallow.
Soil: rich, moist.
Texture: fine.
Flower effects: not showy.
Fruit effects: not showy.
Fall color: yellow to scarlet.
Use: lawn.

LABURNUM, WATERER
(Laburnum × watereri)   **Zone 4**
Commonly sold as *Laburnum × vossi*. Slow growing. Upright to vase-shaped. Outstanding, pendulous yellow flowers. Hardiest of genus.
Height: 30 feet.   **Spread:** 18–20 feet.
Rooting habit: descending.
Soil: any good, well-drained soil.
Texture: fine.
Flower effects: yellow in late May.
Use: group, lawn, specimen.

LILAC, JAPANESE TREE
(Syringa amurensis japonica).   **Zone 4**
New nomenclature lists as *Syringa reticulata reticulata*.
Medium rate of growth. Pyramidal but somewhat open form. Showy, late flowers and interesting cherrylike bark on older plants. This variety is more treelike than *S. amurensis*. Subject to scale infestations and bores.
Height: 15–30 feet.   **Spread:** 12–15 feet.
Rooting habit: fibrous.
Soil: any good soil.
Texture: medium-coarse.
Flower effects: creamy white in mid-June.
Fruit effects: not showy.
Use: group, lawn, specimen, street, windbreak. See also under Shrubs.

LINDEN, AMERICAN
(Tilia americana).   **Zone 2**
Medium rate of growth. Oval to round form. Excellent shade. Requires little attention. Some European species are superior.
Height: 70–80 feet.   **Spread:** 50–60 feet.
Rooting habit: spreading, descending.
Soil: well-drained.
Texture: coarse.
Flower effects: white to yellow in summer, fragrant.
Fruit effects: not showy.
Fall color: yellow-brown.
Use: lawn.

LINDEN, CRIMEAN
(Tilia euchlora).   **Zone 4**
Medium rate of growth. Round, somewhat pendulous. Excellent bright, glossy foliage.
Height: 50 feet.   **Spread:** 40–50 feet.
Rooting habit: spreading, descending.
Texture: medium to coarse.
Flower effects: yellow to white, fragrant.
Fruit effects: not showy.
Use: lawn, street.
Variety: 'Redmond' (pyramidal form).

Descriptive Outlines of Trees

LINDEN, GREENSPIRE LITTLE-LEAF
(Tilia cordata 'Greenspire'). Zone 3
Medium rate of growth. Narrow, oval form. Dense foliage. Tolerates city conditions. Patented variety.
Height: 50 feet. **Spread:** 20–25 feet.
Rooting habit: spreading, descending.
Texture: medium.
Flower effects: yellow to white in early summer.
Fruit effects: nutlet in fall.
Fall color: yellow.
Use: lawn, street.

LINDEN, LITTLE-LEAF
(Tilia cordata). Zone 3
Medium rate of growth. Dense, tight, pyramidal. Tolerates city conditions.
Height: 50 feet. **Spread:** 40 feet.
Rooting habit: spreading, descending.
Texture: medium.
Flower effects: yellow to white in early summer.
Fruit effects: nutlet in fall.
Fall color: yellow.
Use: lawn, street.
Varieties: 'Greenspire' (see detailed description above); 'Pyramidalis' (wide, pyramidal habit); 'Swedish Upright' (narrow, upright).

LINDEN, SILVER
(Tilia tomentosa). Zone 4
Medium rate of growth. Dense, compact, broadly oval form with ascending branches. Underside of leaves are white. Tolerates heat and drouth.
Height: 90 feet. **Spread:** 40 feet.
Rooting habit: spreading and ascending.
Soil: very tolerant.
Texture: medium.
Flower effects: creamy white, fragrant, but not showy.
Fruit effects: not showy.
Use: lawn, street.

MAGNOLIA, CUCUMBER TREE
(Magnolia acuminata). Zone 4
Medium rate of growth. Fastest growing of magnolias. Pyramidal form. Valued for foliage and habit of growth.
Height: 60–90 feet. **Spread:** 40–45 feet.
Rooting habit: fleshy and brittle.
Soil: rich, moist.
Flower effects: greenish-yellow, not too showy.
Fruit effects: pink to red, cucumber-shaped.
Fall color: reddish-bronze.
Use: lawn, street.

MAGNOLIA, SAUCER
(Magnolia soulangiana). Zone 5
Medium rate of growth. Rounded form. Showy flowers effective in front of evergreens. Because of fleshy roots, plants should always be moved with a ball of earth.
Height: 25 feet. **Spread:** 30 feet.
Rooting habit: descending.
Soil: rich, moist.
Texture: coarse.
Flower effects: white to purple before leaves appear.
Fruit effects: rose-pink cone in fall.
Fall color: green to bronze.
Use: lawn, specimen. See also under Shrubs.
Varieties: 'Alba' (compact form, white flowers); 'Lilliputin' (smaller flowers and smaller habit than species, late flowering); 'Lombardy Rose' (flowers dark rose on undersurface, white above); 'San Jose' (flowers rosy purple, fragrant; vigorous growing); 'Verbanica' (petals rose-pink outside, white inside; late flowering; slow growing).

MAGNOLIA, STAR
(Magnolia stellata). Zone 5
Slow growing. Broad to round. Showy flowers appearing before leaves. Will not tolerate dryness, lime, fresh manure, or root competition from other plants. Because of fleshy roots, plants should always be moved with a ball of earth. Prefers sun.
Height: 8–15 feet. **Spread:** 10–15 feet.
Rooting habit: spreading, shallow.
Soil: rich, moist, slightly acid.
Texture: coarse.
Flower effects: white.
Fruit effects: rosy red in fall.
Fall color: green to bronze.
Use: lawn, shrub border, specimen. See also under Shrubs.
Varieties: rosea ('Pink Star') (buds pink, flowers fading to white in full bloom); 'Rubra' (flowers purplish rose); 'Waterlily' (more bushy, twiggy, and upright than species; pink buds, large white flowers).

MAGNOLIA, SWEETBAY
(Magnolia virginiana). Zone 5
Slow to medium rate of growth. Loose, open habit. Valued for flowers.
Height: 10–30 feet. **Spread:** 10–15 feet.
Rooting habit: spreading.
Soil: moist to wet.
Texture: medium.
Flower effects: creamy white, fragrant.
Fruit effects: red, conelike.
Use: lawn. See also under Shrubs.

MAPLE, AMUR
(Acer ginnala). Zone 2
Medium rate of growth. Very hardy, semi-round, dense. Excellent foliage.
Height: 20 feet. **Spread:** 10–20 feet.
Rooting habit: spreading.
Texture: fine to medium.
Flower effects: not showy.
Fruit effects: red in late summer.
Fall color: scarlet.
Use: lawn, screen, specimen, street.
Variety: 'Durand Dwarf' (dwarf, shrubby).

MAPLE, AUTUMN FLAME RED
(Acer rubrum 'Autumn Flame'). Zone 3
Medium rate of growth. Very hardy, oval, dense. Excellent foliage, brilliant crimson-red in fall. Leaves persist for longer time than on the Red Maple.
Height: 50–60 feet. **Spread:** 30–40 feet.
Rooting habit: spreading.
Texture: medium.
Flower effects: red, before leaves.
Fruit effects: red.
Fall color: crimson-red.
Use: lawn, street.

MAPLE, FASSEN'S BLACK NORWAY
(Acer platanoides 'Fassen'). Zone 3
Medium rate of growth. Broad oval shape. Extremely dense. Holds red leaf color throughout summer months. Difficult to grow grass underneath. Withstands city conditions.
Height: 50–60 feet. **Spread:** 30–50 feet.
Rooting habit: spreading, feeding roots close to surface.
Soil: moist but well-drained.
Texture: coarse.
Flower effects: yellow.
Fruit effects: not showy.
Fall color: red.
Use: lawn.

MAPLE, JAPANESE
(Acer palmatum). Zone 5
Very slow growing. Handsome crown irregular but rounded. Excellent small tree.
Height: 20 feet. **Spread:** 15–20 feet.
Rooting habit: fibrous.
Exposure: partial shade.
Soil: rich, well-drained.
Texture: fine.
Fall color: scarlet.
Use: accent, group, lawn, specimen.
Varieties: 'Atropurpureum' (leaves dark red throughout season); dissectum (cut-leaf form giving delicate, lacy effect); 'Rubrum' (leaves deep red in spring, green in summer).

Descriptive Outlines of Trees

MAPLE, NORWAY
(Acer platanoides).   **Zone 3**
Medium to fast growing. Broad oval shape, extremely dense. Difficult to grow grass underneath. Withstands city conditions. Showy in blossom.
Height: 50–60 feet.   **Spread:** 30-50 feet.
Rooting habit: spreading, feeding roots close to surface.
Soil: moist but well-drained.
Texture: coarse.
Flower effects: yellow in spring.
Fruit effects: not showy.
Fall color: yellow.
Use: lawn, street.
Varieties: 'Almira' (globe shape, 20 feet); 'Cleveland' (upright, oval); Columnare' (upright, narrow, 60 feet); 'Crimson King' (red-maroon foliage throughout season); 'Emerald Queen' (rapid growing, dark-green leaves, ascending branches); 'Fassen's Black' (see detailed description above); 'Globosum' (globe form, dense habit, 15–18 feet); 'Greenlace' (upright form; deeply cut, lacelike leaf; fast growing to 50 feet); 'Schwedler' (see detailed description below); 'Summershade' (fast growing, heat resistant, upright form, leathery foliage); 'Superform' (fast growing, heavy dark-green foliage, 50 feet).

MAPLE, PAPERBARK
(Acer griseum).   **Zone 5**
Medium to slow growing. Rounded, somewhat open form. Outstanding reddish-brown bark that exfoliates in paper-thin sheets.
Height: 20–25 feet.   **Spread:** 20 feet.
Rooting habit: spreading, descending.
Soil: any good, well-drained soil.
Texture: medium to fine.
Flower effects: not showy.
Fruit effects: not showy.
Fall color: yellow to orange.
Use: lawn, specimen, street.

MAPLE, RED
(Acer rubrum).   **Zone 3**
Fast growing. Excellent, oval, dense, spreading habit. Good color in all seasons. Showy flowers, brilliant fall color.
Height: 60 feet.   **Spread:** 30–40 feet.
Rooting habit: spreading (seeks water).
Texture: medium.
Flower effects: red, before leaves.
Fruit effects: red.
Fall color: crimson.
Use: lawn, street.

Varieties: 'Autumn Flame' (see detailed description above); 'Armstrong' (narrow, columnar, 35 feet); 'Bowhall' (slower growing than species, narrow, pyramidal); 'October Glory' (brilliant orange fall color, 50 feet); 'Red Sunset' (brilliant red fall color); 'Schlesinger' (outstanding fall color, 45 feet); 'Tilford' (globelike to broad, pyramidal form).

MAPLE, SCHWEDLER NORWAY
(Acer platanoides 'Schwedler').   **Zone 3**
Medium rate of growth. Oblong to oval, dense. Interesting foliage; color changes from red in spring to a muted purple-green in summer. Withstands city conditions.
Height: 60 feet.   **Spread:** 30 feet.
Rooting habit: deep, wide-spreading.
Texture: coarse.
Flower effects: not showy.
Fruit effects: not showy.
Fall color: red.
Use: lawn, street.

MAPLE, SUGAR
(Acer saccharum).   **Zone 3**
Slow growing. Oval, dense. Excellent foliage and fall color. Reliable. One of our finest native trees.
Height: 80–120 feet.   **Spread:** 50–80 feet.
Rooting habit: spreading, descending.
Texture: medium.
Flower effects: not showy.
Fruit effects: not showy.
Fall color: yellow, orange, red.
Use: lawn, street.
Varieties: 'Globosum' (dense, rounded form to 10 feet); 'Green Mountain' (upright, oval crown, dark-green foliage, scarlet fall color); 'Newton Sentry' ('Columnare') (compact, narrow, upright to 40 feet, 12 feet wide); 'Temple's Upright' ('Monumentale') (slender ascending form, no central leader, 50 feet).

MAPLE, TATARIAN
(Acer tataricum).   **Zone 4**
Medium rate of growth. Well-shaped, upright, elliptical form. Good fall color and interesting fruit color.
Height: 20–30 feet.   **Spread:** 20–30 feet.
Rooting habit: fibrous, spreading.
Soil: very tolerant.
Texture: fine.
Flower effects: not showy.

Fruit effects: red in summer.
Fall color: red to yellow.
Use: lawn, specimen, street.

MOUNTAINASH, EUROPEAN
(Sorbus aucuparia).   **Zone 3**
Fast growing. Oval tree. Dramatic when in fruit. Attracts birds. Prefers sunny location. Problem with bores and fire blight.
Height: 35 feet.   **Spread:** 25 feet.
Rooting habit: spreading, shallow.
Texture: medium to fine.
Flower effects: white in spring.
Fruit effects: orange in midsummer.
Fall color: yellow-orange.
Use: lawn, street.
Varieties: 'Asplenifolia' (cut-leaf, graceful form); 'Brilliant Pink' (pink fruit); 'Carpet of Gold' (yellow to orange fruit); 'Fastigiata' (upright form); 'Scarlet King' (scarlet fruit); 'Wilson' (columnar form).

MOUNTAINASH, KOREAN
(Sorbus alnifolia).   **Zone 4**
Medium rate of growth. Pyramidal in youth and rounded at maturity. Lustrous, dense, bright green foliage. Smooth gray bark. Beautiful fall color in foliage and fruit. An outstanding specimen.
Height: 60 feet.   **Spread:** 30–40 feet.
Rooting habit: spreading.
Soil: does not like acid soils.
Texture: medium.
Flower effects: white, flat clusters.
Fruit effects: scarlet to orange fruit.
Use: lawn, specimen.

MULBERRY, WHITE
(Morus alba).   **Zone 4**
Fast growing. Broad, rounded. Excellent color, texture, and form. Fruit attracts insects. Use sterile variety if available.
Height: 30 feet.   **Spread:** 25–35 feet.
Rooting habit: spreading, shallow.
Texture: medium.
Flower effects: not showy.
Fruit effects: pale red in late summer.
Fall color: yellow.
Use: group, lawn.
Variety: 'Pendula' (pendulous branches forming umbrellalike head, often grafted).

Descriptive Outlines of Trees

OAK, ENGLISH
(Quercus robur). Zone 5
Medium rate of growth. Broad, rounded form. Strong and massive. Some insect problems.
Height: 75–125 feet. **Spread:** 80–120 feet.
Rooting habit: taproot.
Texture: medium to coarse.
Flower effects: not showy.
Fruit effects: acorn.
Fall color: bronze (not as intense as other oaks).
Use: lawn.
Varieties: 'Asplenifolia' (cut-leaf form, fine texture); 'Atropurpurea' (deep purple); 'Fastigiata' (narrow, columnar habit).

OAK, NORTHERN RED
(Quercus borealis). Zone 3
New nomenclature lists as *Quercus rubra*.
Medium rate of growth, but faster than most oaks. Broad and round. Excellent shade. Transplants easily.
Height: 70 feet. **Spread:** 60–75 feet.
Rooting habit: taproot.
Soil: well-drained.
Texture: medium to coarse.
Flower effects: not showy.
Fruit effects: brown acorn in fall.
Fall color: red-bronze.
Use: lawn, street.

OAK, PIN
(Quercus palustris). Zone 4
Fast growing. Pyramidal, becoming round in old age. Well-defined horizontal branching. Excellent foliage. Blends well with contemporary architecture. Not suitable for compacted soils or soils with a high pH. The latter can result in iron deficiencies.
Height: 40–70 feet. **Spread:** 40–50 feet.
Rooting habit: spreading.
Soil: rich, moist.
Texture: medium.
Flower effects: not showy.
Fruit effects: brown acorn in fall.
Fall color: bronze-scarlet.
Use: lawn, specimen, narrow street.
Variety: 'Sovereign' (branches angle upward).

OAK, WHITE
(Quercus alba). Zone 4
Slow growing. Sturdy, majestic; broad, rounded form. Difficult to transplant.
Height: 80–100 feet. **Spread:** 50–90 feet.

Rooting habit: taproot.
Soil: well-drained.
Texture: coarse to medium.
Flower effects: not showy.
Fruit effects: acorn in fall.
Fall color: red to wine.
Use: lawn.

PAGODATREE, JAPANESE
(Sophora japonica). Zone 4
Fast growing. Reliable, broad oval tree. Showy flowers late in season. Withstands city conditions.
Height: 45–70 feet. **Spread:** 30 feet.
Rooting habit: spreading, shallow.
Soil: tolerates poor, dry soil.
Texture: fine.
Flower effects: yellow in late summer.
Fruit effects: not showy.
Fall color: yellow.
Use: lawn, street.
Varieties: 'Fastigiata' (columnar habit); 'Pendula' (weeping form, seldom flowers); 'Regent' (oval form with glossy green foliage, white flowers).

PEAR, BRADFORD CALLERY
(Pyrus calleryana 'Bradford'). Zone 4
Medium rate of growth. Upright while young, broad oval in maturity. Outstanding in fall color. Pest-free.
Height: 40–50 feet. **Spread:** 30 feet.
Rooting habit: spreading, descending.
Texture: medium.
Flower effects: white.
Fruit effects: small, russet. Bears infrequently.
Fall color: yellow, bronze-red to dark-purple.
Use: lawn, street.

PINE, AUSTRIAN
(Pinus nigra). Zone 4
Fast growing. Compact, pyramidal in youth becoming broad and somewhat flat-topped. Foliage rigid, dark green. Withstands city conditions.
Height: 60–90 feet. **Spread:** 30–40 feet.
Rooting habit: taproot.
Soil: very tolerant.
Texture: coarse.
Fruit effects: cone.
Use: mass, windbreak.
Variety: 'Pyramidalis' (narrow, pyramidal).

PINE, EASTERN WHITE
(Pinus strobus). Zone 3
Fast to medium growing. Pyramidal in youth, picturesque and flat-topped at maturity. Delicate, soft-green foliage makes ideal background. Tolerates shearing. Subject to windburn.
Height: 100 feet or more. **Spread:** 50–60 feet.
Rooting habit: taproot.
Soil: moist but well-drained.
Texture: fine.
Fruit effects: cone.
Use: mass, screen, specimen (if sufficient space is available), windbreak.
Varieties: 'Fastigiata' (narrow, columnar); glauca (bluish-green foliage); 'Pendula' (pendulous branches giving weeping effect).

PINE, SCOTCH
(Pinus syvestris). Zone 2
Fast growing. Pyramidal when young, rounded to irregular when old. Bluish-green foliage and picturesque character. Not suitable for windbreaks. Subject to aphids and other insects.
Height: 60–100 feet. **Spread:** 40–50 feet.
Rooting habit: taproot.
Soil: well-drained.
Texture: medium.
Fruit effects: cone.
Use: mass, specimen (if sufficient room is available).
Varieties: 'Argentea' (silver-colored foliage); 'Fastigiata' (narrow, columnar habit); 'Waterer' (slow growing, dense, pyramidal, steel-blue color).

PLANETREE, LONDON
(Platanus acerifolia). Zone 5
New nomenclature lists as *Platanus hybrida*.
Fast growing. Rounded form. Interesting bark flakes off, exposing underbark of lighter color. Tolerates city conditions. Subject to anthracnose disease.
Height: 80 feet. **Spread:** 50–70 feet.
Rooting habit: spreading.
Soil: moist.
Texture: coarse.
Flower effects: not showy.
Fruit effects: not showy.
Fall color: brown to yellow.
Use: lawn, street.

Descriptive Outlines of Trees

REDBUD
(Cercis canadensis).   **Zone 4**
Medium rate of growth. Round. Excellent foliage. Attractive in bloom. Tolerates partial shade.
Height: 20 feet.   **Spread:** 12 feet.
Rooting habit: shallow.
Soil: rich, moist.
Texture: coarse to medium.
Flower effects: red in early spring.
Fruit effects: not showy.
Fall color: bronze to yellow.
Use: shrub border, specimen, street.
Varieties: 'Alba' (white flowers); 'Purple Leaf' (young leaves deep purple).

RUSSIANOLIVE
(Elaeagnus angustifolia).   **Zone 2**
Fast growing. Wide-spreading, irregular form. Attractive gray foliage and shredding brown bark. Often picturesque. Subject to verticillium wilt in wet areas.
Height: 20 feet.   **Spread:** 18–20 feet.
Rooting habit: shallow, spreading.
Soil: usually tolerant. Withstands sandy, dry, alkaline soils.
Texture: fine to medium.
Flower effects: small, yellow, fragrant.
Fruit effects: yellow to gray berries.
Use: lawn, specimen.

SASSAFRAS, COMMON
(Sassafras albidum).   **Zone 4**
Medium to slow growing. Oval form. Fragrant flowers. Excellent fall color. Sexes may be separate.
Height: 30–60 feet.   **Spread:** 25–40 feet.
Rooting habit: deep descending.
Soil: well-drained.
Texture: coarse.
Flower effects: yellow in early spring.
Fruit effects: blue in late summer.
Fall color: orange-red.
Use: group, lawn, naturalistic planting, shrub border.

SEA-BUCKTHORN, COMMON
(Hippophae rhamnoides).   **Zone 3**
Medium rate of growth. Rounded, open form. Valued for fruit and willowlike silver-gray foliage. Sexes separate. Use three pistillate (female) plants to one staminate (male) plant.
Height: 15–30 feet.   **Spread:** 10–20 feet.
Rooting habit: fibrous, may sucker.
Soil: very tolerant.
Texture: fine.
Flower effects: not showy.
Fruit effects: large orange clusters of berries in fall (on female plants.)
Use: containers, lawn.

SERVICEBERRY, ALLEGANY
(Amelanchier laevis).   **Zone 4**
Slow growing. Irregular but graceful and airy. Interesting bark. Tolerates shade.
Height: 35 feet.   **Spread:** 15 feet.
Rooting habit: spreading, shallow.
Texture: fine.
Flower effects: white in midspring.
Fruit effects: purple in late spring.
Fall color: red-bronze.
Use: group, lawn, shrub border, specimen.

SERVICEBERRY, SHADBLOW
(Amelanchier canadensis).   **Zone 4**
Often listed as *Amelanchier aborea*. Fast growing. Loosely round to oval. Good combined with broadleaf evergreens.
Height: 25 feet.   **Spread:** 12 feet.
Rooting habit: spreading.
Soil: well-drained.
Texture: fine.
Flower effects: white in early spring.
Fruit effects: purple berry in early summer.
Fall color: orange to red.
Use: group, lawn, specimen. See also under Shrubs.

SILVERBELL, CAROLINA
(Halesia carolina).   **Zone 5**
Medium rate of growth. Low, ascending narrow head. Showy in flower. Should be in sheltered location.
Height: 30 feet.   **Spread:** 20 feet.
Rooting habit: descending.
Soil: well-drained.
Texture: medium.
Flower effects: white in midspring.
Fruit effects: not showy.
Fall color: yellow.
Use: lawn, shrub border, street. Most effective when used in front of an evergreen background.

SMOKEBUSH
(Cotinus coggygria).   **Zone 5(?)**
Medium rate of growth. Dense, oval form. Picturesque. Especially valued for smoky effect from summer flowers.
Height: 15 feet.   **Spread:** 15–20 feet.
Rooting habit: spreading.
Soil: prefers well-drained, poor soil.
Texture: medium.
Flower effects: yellow to lavender (smoky) in midsummer.
Fall color: yellow-orange.
Use: group, lawn, shrub border, specimen.

SORREL TREE (SOURWOOD)
(Oxydendron arboreum).   **Zone 5**
Slow growing. Pyramidal form. Glossy foliage leathery in appearance. Late flowering, outstanding fall color. Good choice for all season interest.
Height: 50–60 feet.   **Spread:** 25–30 feet.
Rooting habit: spreading.
Soil: good, slightly acid soil.
Texture: slightly coarse.
Flower effects: white.
Fall color: scarlet red.
Use: lawn, specimen, street.

SPRUCE, BLUE COLORADO
(Picea pungens glauca).   **Zone 2**
Slow growing. Stiffly pyramidal evergreen. Popular because of blue color. Huge size limits its use on small properties. Attractive in youth, but tends to lose lower branches in old age. Subject to spruce gall aphid.
Height: 80–100 feet.   **Spread:** 20–30 feet.
Rooting habit: taproot.
Soil: rich, moist.
Texture: medium-harsh.
Use: specimen or several in a group. Hard to combine with other plants.

SWEETGUM
(Liquidambar styraciflua).   **Zone 5**
Medium rate of growth. Handsome, pyramidal form. Rich foliage color all seasons. Difficult to transplant.
Height: 60 feet.   **Spread:** 40 feet.
Rooting habit: taproot.
Soil: moist.
Texture: medium.
Flower effects: not showy.
Fruit effects: brown balls in late summer.
Fall color: red-orange to yellow.
Use: lawn, specimen, street.

TULIPTREE
(Liriodendron tulipifera).   **Zone 4**
Medium rate of growth. Oblong to spreading form. Showy flowers appear after ten to twelve years. Handsome foliage.
Height: 80 feet.   **Spread:** 30–40 feet.
Rooting habit: spreading, descending.
Soil: well-drained.
Texture: coarse.
Flower effects: green and orange in midspring.
Fruit effects: not showy.
Fall color: yellow.
Use: lawn, street.
Variety: 'Fastigiatum' (upright in habit).

Descriptive Outlines of Trees

TUPELO (BLACK GUM)
(Nyssa sylvatica).   Zone 4
Medium rate of growth. Pyramidal in form. Excellent in all seasons. Lustrous foliage, outstanding fall color. Sexes separate.
Height: 70–90 feet.   **Spread:** 30–50 feet.
Rooting habit: descending to tap.
Soil: moist or wet.
Texture: medium.
Flower effects: not showy.
Fruit effects: blue in midsummer.
Fall color: orange, red, scarlet.
Use: group, lawn, shrub border, specimen.

UMBRELLAPINE, JAPANESE
(Sciadopitys verticillata).   Zone 5
Very slow rate of growth. Densely pyramidal, often spirelike. Evergreen with long, dark-green needles. Valued for dense habit and interesting texture. No disease problems. Dislikes hot, dry situation.
Height: 70–80 feet.   **Spread:** 30–40 feet.
Rooting habit: taproot.
Soil: tolerant.
Texture: coarse.
Fruit effects: cone.
Use: accent, specimen.

VIBURNUM, NANNYBERRY
(Viburnum lentago).   Zone 2
Fast growing. Most often grown as a shrub but can be trained to grow as a tree. Excellent, dense green foliage. Good fall color. Attracts birds.
Height: 10–30 feet.   **Spread:** 6–10 feet.
Rooting habit: fibrous. Tends to sucker.
Soil: very tolerant.
Texture: coarse to medium.
Flower effects: white in late May.
Fruit effects: black. Effective fall and winter.
Fall color: red to purple.
Use: containers, lawn, shrub border, specimen. See also under Shrubs.

VIBURNUM, SIEBOLD
(Viburnum, sieboldii).   Zone 4
Medium to fast rate of growth. Rounded, somewhat open form. Valued for dark lustrous foliage, flowers, and fruit. Attracts birds.
Height: 15–20 feet.   **Spread:** 10–15 feet.
Rooting habit: fibrous.
Soil: tolerant, but prefers moist soil.
Texture: coarse.
Flower effects: creamy white in late spring.
Fruit effects: red turning to black.
Fall color: green to red.
Use: containers, lawn, specimen, street. See also under Shrubs.

YELLOWWOOD, AMERICAN
(Cladrastis lutea).   Zone 3
Medium rate of growth. Broad oval form. Graceful, excellent foliage. Subject to scale infestations.
Height: 35–40 feet.   **Spread:** 40 feet.
Rooting habit: spreading, shallow.
Soil: rich, moist. Does well in alkaline soil.
Texture: medium.
Flower effects: white in late spring, fragrant.
Fruit effects: green in late summer.
Fall color: yellow.
Use: lawn, shrub border, specimen.

ZELKOVA, JAPANESE
(Zelkova serrata).   Zone 5
Fast growing. Graceful, vase-shaped. Excellent shade, similar to American elm.
Height: 50–90 feet.   **Spread:** 40–80 feet.
Rooting habit: spreading, shallow.
Soil: moist.
Texture: fine to medium.
Flower effects: not showy.
Fruit effects: not showy.
Fall color: yellow to russet.
Use: lawn, street.
Variety: 'Village Green' (vigorous grower with strong wood, interesting bark).

Descriptive Outlines of Shrubs

ABELIA, GLOSSY
(Abelia × grandiflora).   Zone 5
Medium rate of growth. Dense plant. Excellent foliage and small flowers appearing throughout most of the summer.
Height: 5 feet.   **Spread:** 4–5 feet.
Exposure: sun.
Texture: medium.
Flower effects: pink throughout summer.
Fruit effects: not showy.
Fall color: bronze to purple.
Use: corner, facer, unclipped hedge, informal hedge.

ABELIALEAF, KOREAN
(Abeliophyllum distichum).   Zone 5
Fast growing. Rounded plant with arching branches. Valued for fragrant flowers, appearing before leaves. Combines well with forsythia.
Height: 3–5 feet.   **Spread:** 3–4 feet.

Exposure: full sun.
Soil: tolerant.
Texture: medium.
Flower effects: white.
Fruit effects: not showy.
Fall color: yellow.
Use: group, shrub border.

ALDER, SPECKLED
(Alnus rugosa).   Zone 3
Medium to fast growing. Large, spreading, ascending. Valued for its form, interesting bark, and suitability to wet situations.
Height: 8–25 feet.   **Spread:** 10–15 feet.
Exposure: sun or shade.
Soil: moist to wet.
Texture: medium to fine.
Flower effects: reddish.
Fruit effects: not showy.

Fall color: yellow.
Use: group, underplanting. See also under Trees.

ALMOND, FLOWERING DWARF
(Prunus glandulosa).   Zone 4
Slow to medium growing. Upright. Single- or double-flowering varieties available. Subject to verticillium wilt.
Height: 4 feet.   **Spread:** 4 feet.
Exposure: sun.
Soil: rich, moist.
Texture: medium.
Flower effects: pink or white in May, according to variety.
Fruit effects: red, not showy.
Fall color: yellow.
Use: facer, group, shrub border.
Varieties: 'Albiplena' (double white flowers); 'Rosea' (pink flowers); 'Sinensis' (double pink flowers).

Descriptive Outlines of Shrubs

ANDROMEDA, JAPANESE
(Pieris japonica). **Zone 5**
Slow growing. Rounded plant. Lustrous, dark evergreen foliage that is bronze in spring. Valued for foliage and pendulous flower clusters. Several varieties available.
Height: 9 feet. **Spread:** 6–8 feet.
Exposure: sun, but tolerates shade.
Soil: well-drained, moist, acid.
Texture: medium.
Flower effects: creamy white.
Use: group, shrub border, specimen.

ANDROMEDA, MOUNTAIN
(Pieris floribunda). **Zone 4**
Slow growing. Rounded, dense evergreen plant. Outstanding foliage and flowers. Combines well with other broadleaf evergreens.
Height: 4–6 feet. **Spread:** 8–10 feet.
Exposure: partial shade.
Soil: sandy to well-drained loam, not too heavy.
Texture: medium.
Flower effects: white clusters.
Use: facer. Good with rhododendrons.

ARALIA, FIVELEAF
(Acanthopanax sieboldianus). **Zone 4**
Medium rate of growth. Upright form with arching branches. Valued for tolerance of city dust and smoke. Grows well in shade.
Height: 6–9 feet. **Spread:** 4–6 feet.
Rooting habit: may sucker.
Exposure: sun or shade.
Soil: tolerant, drouth resistant.
Texture: medium-fine.
Flower effects: not showy.
Fruit effects: not showy.
Use: unclipped hedge, screen, slopes.

ARBORVITAE, MISSION EASTERN
(Thuja occidentalis 'Techny'). **Zone 2**
Fast growing. Columnar plant that tolerates shearing. Dark-green foliage. Valued for color and low mature height.
Height: 8–10 feet. **Spread:** 5–6 feet.
Exposure: sun or shade.
Soil: prefers moist soil but tolerates good humus soils.
Texture: fine.
Use: unclipped hedge, screen.

AZALEA, EXBURY HYBRIDS
(Rhododendron hybrid crosses). **Zone 5**
Moderate rate of growth. Well-shaped, rounded to spreading form depending upon hybrid selection. Large flowers and striking colors in early June. Nonevergreen. Buy named clones.
Height: 4–5 feet. **Spread:** 4–5 feet.
Exposure: partial sun for best flower effect.
Soil: rich, well-drained, acid.
Texture: medium.
Flower effects: large, showy flowers ranging from near-whites to pink, orange, rose, and red.
Use: group, shrub border.

AZALEA, KARENS *(Rhododendron obtusum kaemferi 'Karens').* **Zone 6**
Medium rate of growth. Dense, twiggy. Showy flowers. Excellent plant.
Height: 3–4 feet. **Spread:** 3–5 feet.
Exposure: sun or partial shade.
Soil: rich, well-drained, acid.
Texture: medium.
Flower effects: lavender.
Use: facer, doorway, group, shrub border, specimen.

AZALEA, MOLLIS HYBRID
(Rhododendronx kosterianum). **Zone 5**
Slow growing. Low, well-shaped, symmetrical plant. Attractive foliage, showy flowers. Many varieties available in numerous flower colors.
Height: 3–6 feet. **Spread:** 3–5 feet.
Exposure: prefers sun but tolerates shade.
Soil: best on slightly acid, light soils with much humus.
Texture: medium.
Flower effects: yellow in early spring, before leaves.
Fruit effects: not showy.
Fall color: red-bronze.
Use: containers, doorway, group, mass.

BARBERRY, JAPANESE
(Berberis thunbergi). **Zone 4**
Slow growing. Dense, round plant. Good in all seasons.
Height: 5–7 feet. **Spread:** 4–7 feet.
Exposure: sun or shade.
Texture: fine.
Flower effects: yellow in May, but not showy.
Fruit effects: red in summer.
Fall color: scarlet.
Use: containers, facer, hedge (clipped or unclipped), planter boxes, shrub border, slopes, underplanting.
Varieties: atropurpurea (reddish leaves); 'Crimson Pigmy' (dwarf, 2–3 feet; red foliage); erecta (see detailed description below).

BARBERRY, MENTOR
(Berberis × mentorensis). **Zone 5**
Slow growing. Upright semievergreen plant. Withstands dry summers and low winter temperature. Good substitute for wintergreen barberry.
Height: 5–6 feet. **Spread:** 4–5 feet.
Exposure: sun or shade.
Texture: fine.
Flower effects: yellow in May, but not showy.
Fruit effects: red in fall.
Fall color: red.
Use: doorway, facer, hedge (clipped or unclipped).

BARBERRY, TRUEHEDGE COLUMNBERRY
(Berberis thunbergi 'Erecta'). **Zone 4**
Medium-slow growing. Excellent upright plant. Requires little pruning when used as a hedge.
Height: 4 feet. **Spread:** 4–5 feet.
Exposure: sun or shade.
Texture: fine.
Flower effects: yellow in May, but not showy.
Fruit effects: red in late summer.
Fall color: red.
Use: doorway, clipped hedge.

BARBERRY, WINTERGREEN
(Berberis julianae). **Zone 5**
Slow but strong growing. Dense, upright evergreen plant. Prominent spines.
Height: 6 feet. **Spread:** 4–5 feet.
Exposure: sun.
Texture: medium to fine.
Flower effects: yellow in May, but not showy.
Fruit effects: blue to black in fall.
Use: corner, group, hedge (clipped or unclipped), specimen.

BAYBERRY, NORTHERN
(Myrica pensylvanica). **Zone 2**
Slow to medium growing. Compact, rounded. Excellent fruit and semievergreen foliage. Sexes separate. Combines well with junipers.
Height: 5 feet. **Spread:** 3–10 feet.
Exposure: sun.
Soil: tolerates both moist and dry sterile soils.
Texture: medium.
Flower effects: not showy.
Fruit effects: blue to white in late summer and fall.
Use: corner, doorway, facer, planter boxes.

Descriptive Outlines of Shrubs

BEAUTYBUSH
(Kolkwitzia amabilis). **Zone 4**
Slow growing. Broad, vase-shaped.
Height: 6–10 feet. **Spread:** 6–9 feet.
Exposure: sun.
Soil: well-drained.
Texture: medium.
Flower effects: pink in May and June.
Fruit effects: not showy.
Fall color: reddish.
Use: shrub border.

BLUEBEARD
(Caryopteris clandonensis). **Zone 5**
Fast growing. Round, spreading. Valued
for late flowers. In Zones 1–4, top of
plant will die back to ground, and plant
will require heavy pruning in early
spring.
Height: 3–4 feet. **Spread:** 4 feet.
Exposure: sun.
Texture: medium fine.
Flower effects: blue in late summer and
fall.
Fruit effects: not showy.
Use facer, group, shrub border.

BLUEBERRY, HIGHBUSH
(Vaccinium corymbosum). **Zone 3**
Medium to slow growing. Upright,
rounded. Excellent shrub with good
foliage and fall color. Red twigs during
winter. Many varieties available. Use
more than one for good pollination.
Height: 6–12 feet. **Spread:** varies ac-
cording to variety.
Exposure: sun or partial shade.
Soil: acid.
Texture: medium.
Flower effects: white to pink.
Fruit effects: blue-black.
Fall color: scarlet.
Use: group, screen, shrub border.
Variety: 'Coville' (very large fruit).

BOX, COMMON
(Buxus sempervirens). **Zone 5**
Slow growing. Dense, rounded form.
Evergreen foliage has billowy appear-
ance. Many varieties from which to
choose.
Height: 15–20 feet. **Spread:** 15–20 feet
or more.
Exposure: sun or shade if protected
from winter winds.
Soil: tolerant.
Texture: fine, but dense.
Use: foundation, group, hedge (clipped
or unclipped), shrub border.

BOX, LITTLELEAF
(Buxus microphylla). **Zone 5**
Slow growing. Dense, compact ever-
green plant. In some species leaves will
turn brown in winter. Hardier than
Common Box (B. sempervirens).
Height: 4 feet. **Spread:** 5–6 feet.
Exposure: needs winter protection.
Soil: tolerant.
Texture: medium-fine.
Use: foundation, group, hedge (clipped
or unclipped), shrub border.
Varieties: 'Compacta' (dwarf, 12 inches
tall); koreana (foliage turns brown in
winter; hardy in Zone 4).

BUCKEYE, BOTTLEBRUSH
(Aesculus parviflora). **Zone 4**
Medium to fast growing. Broad,
rounded, many-branched shrub. Can be
trained into a tree form. Showy flowers.
Height: 8–12 feet. **Spread:** 8–16 feet.
Exposure: sun.
Texture: coarse.
Flower effects: white pyramidal clusters
in July.
Use: shrub border, specimen.

BUCKEYE, RED
(Aesculus pavia). **Zone 4**
Moderately fast growing. Rounded form
with ascending branches. Interesting
flowers.
Height: 18–20 feet. **Spread:** 10–20 feet.
Exposure: sun or partial shade.
Soil: rich loam.
Texture: medium to coarse.
Flower effects: bright red.
Use: shrub border, specimen. See also
under Trees.

BUCKTHORN, COLUMNAR (TALLHEDGE)
(Rhamnus frangula 'Columnaris'). **Zone 2**
Fast growing. Narrow, columnar shrub.
Valued as a hedge because of narrow
spread. Does not require side pruning;
top pruning easily maintains desired
height.
Height: 15 feet. **Spread:** 4 feet.
Exposure: sun to partial shade.
Soil: tolerant.
Texture: medium.
Flower effects: not showy.
Fruit effects: black.
Use: unclipped hedge, screen.

BUCKTHORN, COMMON
(Rhamnus cathartica). **Zone 2**
Medium rate of growth. Round, dense.
Handsome foliage. Tolerates pruning.
Height: 12 feet. **Spread:** 10–12 feet.
Exposure: sun or shade.
Texture: medium to coarse.
Flower effects: not showy.
Fruit effects: black berries in fall.
Fall color: holds deep green foliage into
late fall.
Use: corner, unclipped hedge, shrub
border.

BUSHCHERRY, NAKAI CHINESE
(Prunus japonica). **Zone 2**
Medium rate of growth. Rounded, low,
dense. Extremely hardy flowering plant.
Colorful fruit.
Height: 3–4½ feet. **Spread:** 3 feet.
Exposure: sun.
Soil: tolerant.
Texture: medium.
Flower effects: pink or white.
Fruit effects: red.
Use: facer, foundation, shrub border.

BUTTONBUSH
(Cephalanthus occidentalis). **Zone 4**
Medium rate of growth. Broad, loose to
dense. Not a refined plant. Use limited
to wet areas.
Height: 4–15 feet. **Spread:** 5–12 feet.
Exposure: sun or partial shade.
Soil: moist to wet.
Texture: coarse.
Flower effects: creamy white balls.
Fruit effects: not showy.
Use: mass.

CANDYTUFT, EVERGREEN
(Iberis sempervirens). **Zone 4**
Medium rate of growth. Low, dense
semievergreen. Abundant, brilliant white
flowers.
Height: 12 inches. **Spread:** 12 inches.
Exposure: sun, but tolerates partial
shade.
Soil: good, well-drained, slightly acid.
Texture: medium-fine.
Flower effects: white.
Fruit effects: not showy.
Use: edging, rock gardens. See also
under Ground Covers.
Varieties: 'Christmas Snow' (blooms a
second time in fall); 'Little Gem' (lower
growing than species); 'Snowflake'
(vigorous, spreads to 3 feet).

Descriptive Outlines of Shrubs

CHERRY, MANCHU
(Prunus tomentosa).　　　　**Zone 2**
Fast growing. Broad, spreading, rounded. Showy flowers.
Height: 8–10 feet.　**Spread:** 10–15 feet.
Exposure: sun or shade.
Soil: rich, moist.
Texture: medium.
Flower effects: white to pink in April.
Fruit effects: red in June and July.
Fall color: reddish.
Use: corner, group, shrub border, specimen.

CHERRY, WESTERN SAND
(Prunus besseyi).　　　　**Zone 3**
Medium rate of growth. Low, bushy, somewhat prostrate. Attractive glossy leaves.
Height: 3–7 feet.　**Spread:** 3–5 feet.
Exposure: sun or partial shade.
Soil: tolerant.
Texture: medium-fine.
Flower effects: white.
Fruit effects: purplish black, edible.
Use: facer, shrub border.

CHOKEBERRY, BLACK
(Aronia melanocarpa).　　　　**Zone 4**
Medium rate of growth. Broad, loose, open shrub. Good woodland edging plant.
Height: 3–5 feet.　**Spread:** 3 feet or more.
Rooting habit: suckering.
Exposure: sun or partial shade.
Soil: any good, moist soil.
Texture: medium to fine.
Flower effects: white.
Fruit effects: black.
Fall color: crimson.
Use: naturalistic planting.

CHOKEBERRY, RED
(Aronia arbutifolia).　　　　**Zone 4**
Medium rate of growth. Although erect in form, plant has graceful, rounded top. Valued for color in summer and fall and reddish twigs in winter.
Height: 6–9 feet.　**Spread:** 3–5 feet.
Exposure: sun or partial shade.
Soil: any good soil.
Texture: medium to fine.
Flower effects: white to reddish.
Fruit effects: red.
Fall color: crimson red.
Use: shrub border.

CINQUEFOIL, BUSH
(Potentilla fruticosa).　　　　**Zone 2**
Slow growing. Bushy, dense. Chief value lies in its long period of flowering. Can be pruned heavily.
Height: 3 feet.　**Spread:** 3 feet.
Exposure: sun.
Texture: fine to medium.
Flower effects: yellow from early summer to fall.
Fruit effects: not showy.
Use: facer, hedge (clipped or unclipped). Combines well with perennials.
Varieties: 'Farrer' (2 feet high, deep yellow flowers); 'Klondike' (dwarf, compact, deep yellow flowers into fall); 'Tangerine' (flowers orange in shade, yellow in sun).

CLETHRA, SUMMERSWEET
(Clethra alnifolia).　　　　**Zone 3**
Medium rate of growth. Erect shrub with round top. Slow to establish. Subject to red spider in dry areas.
Height: 3–10 feet.　**Spread:** 3–8 feet.
Rooting habit: suckering.
Exposure: partial shade.
Soil: moist, slightly acid.
Texture: fine.
Flower effects: white, fragrant.
Fruit effects: not showy.
Use: shrub border.

CORALBERRY, CHENAULT
(Symphoricarpos × chenaulti).　　**Zone 4**
Fast growing. Low, loose growth. Larger fruit than Indiancurrant Coralberry.
Height: 3–4 feet.　**Spread:** 4 feet.
Exposure: sun or shade.
Soil: well-drained.
Texture: fine.
Flower effects: pink in July.
Fruit effects: red to white in fall.
Use: facer, group, underplanting in woodland plantings.

CORALBERRY, INDIANCURRANT
(Symphoricarpos orbiculatus).　　**Zone 2**
Fast growing. Round, dense. Good in shade but tolerates sun. Clustered fruit persists.
Height: 3–4 feet.　**Spread:** 3–4 feet.
Exposure: shade.
Texture: medium to fine.
Flower effects: not showy.
Fruit effects: pink to coral in fall.
Use: banks, facer.

COTONEASTER, BEARBERRY
(Cotoneaster dammeri).　　　　**Zone 5**
Slow growing. Prostrate, woody evergreen. Glossy dark-green leaves, attractive fruit. There are several good cultivars available.
Height: 12 inches.　**Spread:** 6–12 inches.
Exposure: sun or shade.
Texture: fine.
Flower effects: pink in June.
Fruit effects: red in late summer.
Use: containers, planter boxes, slopes. See also under Ground Covers.

COTONEASTER, CRANBERRY
(Cotoneaster apiculata).　　　　**Zone 4**
Medium to fast growing. Low, mounding plant. Large fruit.
Height: 2 feet.　**Spread:** 5–8 feet.
Exposure: sun or partial shade.
Soil: well-drained.
Texture: fine.
Flower effects: small, pink in June.
Fruit effects: red berries in fall.
Fall color: reddish.
Use: doorway, facer, group, specimen, at top of retaining wall. Handsome with rocks.

COTONEASTER, PEKING
(Cotoneaster acutifolia).　　　**Zone 4(?)**
Slow growing. Erect, spreading. Requires little care. Tolerates pruning. Withstands wind.
Height: 8–10 feet.　**Spread:** 8–10 feet.
Exposure: sun.
Soil: does well even on poor soils.
Texture: fine.
Flower effects: white to pink in June.
Fruit effects: black berries in fall.
Use: containers, clipped hedge, shrub border.

COTONEASTER, ROCK OR ROCKSPRAY
(Cotoneaster horizontalis).　　　**Zone 4**
Slow growing. Low, dense, horizontally spreading plant. Excellent foliage and persistent fruit. Difficult to transplant.
Height: 2–3 feet.　**Spread:** 4–6 feet.
Exposure: sun.
Soil: well-drained.
Texture: fine.
Flower effects: pink in May and June, but not showy.
Fruit effects: red in fall.
Fall color: red-orange.
Use: doorway, facer, specimen, and at top of retaining wall. Handsome with rocks. See also under Ground Covers.

Descriptive Outlines of Shrubs

COTONEASTER, SPREADING
(Cotoneaster divaricata). **Zone 5**
Medium rate of growth. Arching, spreading. Excellent fruiting habit. Withstands wind. Difficult to transplant.
Height: 6 feet. **Spread:** 5–6 feet.
Exposure: sun.
Texture: fine.
Flower effects: pink in May and June.
Fruit effects: red in late summer. Fruit persists into fall.
Fall color: red.
Use: corner, shrub border, specimen.

CRABAPPLE, SARGENT FLOWERING
(Malus sargentii). **Zone 5**
Medium rate of growth. Low, dense, shrubby tree which branches to the ground. Valued for low height and spreading form.
Height: 6–8 feet. **Spread:** 8–10 feet.
Exposure: sun.
Soil: tolerant.
Texture: medium.
Flower effects: white.
Fruit effects: wine-red.
Fall color: yellow to orange.
Use: group, lawn, specimen.

CURRANT, ALPINE
(Ribes alpinum). **Zone 2**
Medium rate of growth. Compact, dense. Attractive foliage. Does well in shade. Tolerates pruning.
Height: 4–6 feet. **Spread:** 4–5 feet.
Exposure: sun or shade.
Texture: medium.
Flower effects: not showy.
Fruit effects: red berries during summer.
Fall color: yellow.
Use: doorway, facer, group, hedge (clipped or unclipped).

CURRANT, CLOVE
(Ribes odoratum). **Zone 4**
Medium rate of growth. Irregular shrub with arching branches. Flowers heavily, good fall color. Do not use where white pine blister rust is a problem.
Height: 6 feet. **Spread:** 8 feet.
Rooting habit: suckering.
Exposure: sun or shade.
Soil: tolerant.
Texture: medium.
Flower effects: yellow, fragrant.
Fruit effects: black.
Fall color: scarlet-red.
Use: screen, shrub border.

DEUTZIA, COMPACT LEMOINE
(Deutzia × lemoinei 'Compacta'). **Zone 4**
Medium growth rate. Dense, compact. Abundant flowers.
Height: 4 feet. **Spread:** 3–4 feet.
Exposure: sun or partial shade.
Texture: medium fine.
Flower effects: white in June.
Fruit effects: not showy.
Use: doorway, facer, group.

DEUTZIA, LEMOINE
(Deutzia × lemoinei). **Zone 4**
Fast growing. Dense, upright. Handsome and reliable. Showy flowers.
Height: 6–7 feet. **Spread:** 4–6 feet.
Exposure: sun or partial shade.
Texture: medium fine.
Flower effects: white in June.
Fruit effects: not showy.
Use: corner, group, shrub border.
Varieties: 'Compacta' (see detailed description above); 'Erecta' (low, upright growing).

DEUTZIA, SLENDER
(Deutzia gracilis). **Zone 4**
Slow growing. Low, compact. Abundant flowers. Reliable. Easy to transplant.
Height: 3–4 feet. **Spread:** 3 feet.
Exposure: sun or partial shade.
Texture: fine.
Flower effects: white in May.
Fruit effects: not showy.
Use: doorway, facer, unclipped hedge.

DOGWOOD, GRAY
(Cornus racemosa). **Zone 4**
Medium rate of growth. Erect, spreading. Sprouts from base. Tolerates pruning.
Height: 8–15 feet. **Spread:** 8–12 feet.
Exposure: partial shade.
Soil: moist.
Texture: medium.
Flower effects: white in June.
Fruit effects: white in fall.
Fall color: dull red.
Use: shrub border, underplanting.

DOGWOOD, KELSEY REDOSIER *(Cornus stolonifera [sericea] 'Kelsey').* **Zone 2**
New nomenclature lists as *Cornus sericea.*
Slow growing. Valued for its dwarf, round, compact form. In some areas leaf blight can be a serious problem.
Height: 18–24 inches. **Spread:** 12–18 inches.
Exposure: sun or shade.
Texture: coarse.
Use: doorway, planter boxes, under low windows.

DOGWOOD, REDOSIER
(Cornus stolonifera [sericea]). **Zone 2**
New nomenclature lists as *Cornus sericea.*
Slow growing. Broad, spreading shrub. Valued for its winter color. Bloodtwig Dogwood *(C. sanguinea)* is similar to this variety.
Height: 8 feet. **Spread:** 8–10 feet.
Exposure: sun or shade.
Texture: coarse.
Flower effects: white in April and May.
Fruit effects: white to blue in late summer.
Fall color: red to bronze.
Use: shrub border, woodland planting.
Variety: 'Kelsey' (see detailed description above).

DOGWOOD, YELLOWTWIG REDOSIER
(Cornus stolonifera [sericea] 'Flaviramea'). **Zone 2**
New nomenclature lists as *Cornus sericea.*
Medium to slow growing. Spreading shrub. Valued for yellow twigs during winter.
Height: 8 feet. **Spread:** 6–8 feet.
Exposure: sun or shade.
Texture: coarse.
Flower effects: white in May and June.
Fruit effects: white to blue in late summer.
Use: corner, group, shrub border.

ELAEAGNUS, CHERRY
(Elaeagnus multiflorus). **Zone 4**
Medium rate of growth. Somewhat thin, open shrub with flat top. Foliage dark green above, silvery below. Fruit attracts birds.
Height: 6–9 feet. **Spread:** 6–10 feet.
Exposure: sun or partial shade.
Soil: tolerant, drouth resistant.
Texture: medium-fine.
Flower effects: not showy.
Fruit effects: red berries.
Use: shrub border.

Descriptive Outlines of Shrubs

ENKIANTHUS, REDVEIN
(Enkianthus companulatus). Zone 4
Medium rate of growth. Large, upright, rounded. Valued for flowers and autumn color. Must have acid soil.
Height: 10–20 feet. **Spread:** 10–15 feet.
Exposure: sun or partial shade.
Soil: acid.
Texture: medium.
Flower effects: yellow to orange.
Fruit effects: not showy.
Fall color: scarlet.
Use: group, shrub border, specimen. See also under Trees.
Varieties: 'Albiflorus' (white flowers); pabilinii (red flowers).

EUONYMUS, BIGLEAF WINTERCREEPER
(Euonymus fortunei 'Vegetus'). Zone 5
Slow growing. Grows upright with support but otherwise forms a mounded mass. Evergreen plant with thick, leathery, glossy leaves. Subject to scale infestations.
Height: 2–4 feet. **Spread:** 2–3 feet.
Exposure: sun or shade. Often needs shade in winter.
Texture: medium.
Flower effects: not showy.
Fruit effects: orange in fall.
Use: containers, doorway, clipped hedge, planter boxes.

EUONYMUS, DWARF WINGED
(Euonymus alatus 'Compactus'). Zone 3
Slow growing. Dense, compact. Outstanding fall color. Transplants easily.
Height: 6 feet. **Spread:** 4 feet.
Exposure: sun or shade.
Texture: medium in summer, coarse in winter.
Flower effects: not showy.
Fruit effects: pink in fall.
Fall color: rose-red.
Use: corner, doorway, facer, unclipped hedge.

EUONYMUS, EASTERN WAHOO
(Euonymus atropurpureus). Zone 3
Slow growing. Treelike, spreading. Outstanding foliage and fruit color. Subject to scale infestations.
Height: 15–20 feet. **Spread:** 8–15 feet.
Exposure: sun or partial shade.
Texture: medium.
Flower effects: not showy.
Fruit effects: red in fall.
Fall color: purple to red.
Use: group, screen, shrub border. See also under Trees.

EUONYMUS, MIDWINTER
(Euonymus bungeana). Zone 4
Fast growing. Rounded, irregular form. Light-green foliage. Subject to scale infestations.
Height: 18 feet. **Spread:** 25 feet.
Exposure: sun or partial shade.
Soil: tolerant.
Texture: medium to fine.
Flower effects: not showy.
Fruit effects: yellow.
Use: screen, shrub border. See also under Trees.
Variety: 'Pendulus' (gracefully drooping to weeping branches).

EUONYMUS, SARCOXIE
(Euonymus fortunei 'Sarcoxie'). Zone 5
Slow growing. Handsome, upright broadleaf evergreen. Tolerates pruning. Subject to scale infestations.
Height: 6 feet. **Spread:** 3–4 feet.
Exposure: sun.
Texture: medium.
Flower effects: not showy.
Fruit effects: not showy.
Use: containers, doorway, clipped hedge, planter boxes.

EUONYMUS, SPINDLE TREE
(Euonymus europaeus). Zone 3
Medium rate of growth. Medium-dense, oval shrub. Sometimes treelike. Valued for profuse and colorful fruiting. Excellent foliage. Subject to scale infestations.
Height: 15–30 feet. **Spread:** 10–25 feet.
Exposure: sun or partial shade.
Texture: fine.
Flower effects: not showy.
Fruit effects: brilliant rose-pink capsules, persistent.
Fall color: reddish.
Use: group, shrub border, specimen.

EUONYMUS, SPREADING
(Euonymus kiautschovicus). Zone 5
Slow growing. Bushy, round semievergreen. Flowers attract flies.
Height: 5–6 feet. **Spread:** 6 feet.
Exposure: partial shade.
Texture: medium.
Flower effects: not showy.
Fruit effects: pink to red in fall.
Use: corner, group, shrub border.
Variety: 'Manhattan' (handsome, dark glossy foliage).

EUONYMUS, WINGED
(Euonymus alatus). Zone 2
Slow growing. Dense, broad, horizontally branched. Outstanding fall color. Reliable. Transplants easily.

Height: 8–10 feet. **Spread:** 6–8 feet.
Exposure: sun or partial shade.
Texture: medium in summer, coarse in winter.
Flower effects: not showy.
Fruit effects: pink in fall.
Fall color: rose-red.
Use: corner, group, shrub border, specimen.
Variety: compactus (see detailed description above).

EUONYMUS, YEDDO
(Euonymus yedoensis). Zone 4
Slow growing. Treelike with somewhat flat top. Large leaves.
Height: 10–15 feet. **Spread:** 8–10 feet.
Exposure: sun or partial shade.
Soil: tolerant.
Texture: coarse.
Flower effects: not showy.
Fruit effects: pink capsules.
Use: group, specimen.

FALSECYPRESS, HINOKI (Chamaecyparis obtusa). Zone 3
Medium rate of growth. Form varies according to variety. Frondlike evergreen foliage of bright green. Handsome plant where it thrives.
Height: variable. **Spread:** variable.
Exposure: sunny, open. Shelter from wind.
Soil: prefers soil that tends to be dry.
Texture: fine.
Use: group, specimen.
Varieties: 'Compacta' (dense, pyramidal, 8 feet high and wide); 'Nana' (dwarf to 3 feet, slow growing, globe-shaped); 'Nana Gracilis' (dwarf to 4 feet and 3 feet wide, lustrous green foliage).

FIRETHORN, LALAND SCARLET
(Pyracantha coccinea 'Lalandi'). Zone 5
Medium rate of growth. Broad, spreading. Deciduous in north, evergreen in south. Fruit adds vivid color to winter scene. Prominent thorns. Tolerates pruning. Subject to fire blight.
Height: 6 feet. **Spread:** 6–10 feet.
Exposure: requires sun but needs protection against sun and wind in winter months.
Soil: well-drained.
Texture: medium.
Flower effects: white in June.
Fruit effects: orange to red in fall and winter.
Use: containers, corner, espalier, specimen.

Descriptive Outlines of Shrubs

FORSYTHIA
(various species).   **Zones 4–5**
Fast growing. Erect, arching, and trailing varieties available. Reliable shrub. Transplants easily. Showy flowers and good foliage.
Height: 8–10 feet.   **Spread:** 10–15 feet.
Exposure: sun.
Soil: well-drained.
Texture: medium.
Flower effects: yellow in early spring.
Fruit effects: not showy.
Use: group, screen, shrub border.
Avoid overcrowding from planting too close.

FORSYTHIA, ARNOLD DWARF
(Forsythia 'Arnold Dwarf').   **Zone 5**
Medium to slow growing. Dense, mounding, wide-spreading form. Branches root when touching soil. Flowers, if any, not outstanding.
Height: 4–5 feet.   **Spread:** 8–10 feet.
Exposure: sun.
Soil: well-drained.
Texture: medium.
Flower effects: not showy.
Use: slopes. See also under Ground Covers.

FORSYTHIA, BORDER
(Forsythia × intermedia).   **Zone 5**
Fast growing. Upright, ascending habit. Large, showy flowers.
Height: 8–10 feet.   **Spread:** 8–10 feet.
Exposure: sun.
Texture: medium.
Flower effects: pale to deep golden yellow.
Use: group, shrub border.
Varieties: 'Beatrix Farrand' (flowers about 2 inches in diameter, flower bud more hardy than species); 'Karl Sax' (large flowers, flower bud more hardy than species).

FORSYTHIA, BRONX
(Forsythia viridissima 'Bronxensis').
                     Zone 5
Medium rate of growth. Very dwarf in habit. Small but abundant flowers.
Height: 2 feet.   **Spread:** 2–4 feet.
Exposure: sun.
Texture: medium.
Flower effects: small, yellow.
Fall color: green to yellow.
Use: facer, group. See also under Ground Covers.

FOTHERGILLA, DWARF
(Fothergilla gardenii).   **Zone 5**
Slow growing. Low, mounding. Irregular branching. Valued for two-season interest — spring flowers and fall color.
Height: 3–4 feet.   **Spread:** 3–4 feet.
Rooting habit: suckering.
Exposure: partial shade.
Soil: moist, acid.
Texture: coarse.
Flower effects: white.
Fruit effects: not showy.
Fall color: yellow-red.
Use: group, shrub border.

FOTHERGILLA, LARGE
(Fothergilla major).   **Zone 5**
Slow growing. Upright, pyramidal form. Showy flowers and good fall color. Combines well with evergreens.
Height: 6–9 feet.   **Spread:** 6–8 feet.
Exposure: partial shade.
Soil: moist, acid.
Texture: coarse.
Flower effects: white.
Fruit effects: not showy.
Fall color: yellow, orange, red.
Use: group, shrub border.

FRINGETREE, WHITE
(Chionanthus virginicus).   **Zone 4**
Slow growing. Round, spreading, treelike. Leaves appear in late spring. Showy, fragrant flowers. Sexes usually separate. Withstands city conditions. Subject to scale infestations.
Height: 10–20 feet.   **Spread:** 8–20 feet.
Exposure: sun.
Soil: moist.
Texture: coarse.
Flower effects: white in late spring.
Fruit effects: blue in late summer.
Fall color: yellow.
Use: corner, group, specimen. See also under Trees.

GERMANDER, CHAMAEDRYS
(Teucrium chamaedrys).   **Zone 5**
Medium to slow growing. Low, dense, woody evergreen. May need winter protection.
Height: 10 inches.   **Spread:** 8–12 inches.
Exposure: sun or shade.
Soil: well-drained.
Texture: medium to fine.
Flower effects: rose to purple in summer.
Fruit effects: not showy.

Use: low edging, unclipped hedge, planter boxes. See also under Ground Covers.

HAZEL, AMERICAN OR FILBERT
(Corylus americana).   **Zone 3**
Fast growing. Rounded mass with erect branches from the ground. Tends to sucker.
Height: 3–8 feet.   **Spread:** 5–10 feet.
Exposure: sun.
Soil: tolerant.
Texture: coarse.
Flower effects: yellow catkins in early spring.
Use: shrub border in large areas, woodland planting.

HAZEL, CONTORTED EUROPEAN
(Corylus avellana 'Contorta').   **Zone 3**
Medium to slow growing. Irregular growth habit with twigs curled and twisted.
Height: 6 feet.   **Spread:** 4–5 feet.
Exposure: sun or shade.
Texture: medium-coarse.
Use: specimen.

HEATHER, SCOTCH
(Calluna vulgaris).   **Zone 4**
Slow growing. Low, sprawling evergreen. Forms mat or mound. Many varieties.
Height: 10–24 inches.   **Spread:** 2 feet.
Exposure: sun.
Soil: well-drained, acid sand or light loam.
Texture: fine.
Flower effects: white to red, according to variety.
Fruit effects: not showy.
Use: edging, rock gardens. See also under Ground Covers.

HOLLY, AMERICAN
(Ilex opaca).   **Zone 5(?)**
Slow rate of growth. Pyramidal form with dense branches to the ground. Dense evergreen foliage with spiny tips. Sexes separate. Male and female required for fruiting. Difficult to transplant. Popular Christmas decoration.
Height: 18–40 feet.   **Spread:** 12–20 feet.
Rooting habit: tap, with laterals spreading wider than top.
Exposure: shade or partial shade.
Soil: light, well-drained.
Texture: medium-coarse.
Flower effects: not showy.
Fruit effects: red berries.
Use: group, shrub border, specimen.

Descriptive Outlines of Shrubs

HOLLY, BLUE GIRL
(Ilex × meservae 'Blue Girl').   **Zone 4**
Fast growing. Globe form. Rich dark-green, hollylike leaves. Evergreen. Outstanding red fruit. Sexes separate. Needs winter wind protection.
Height: 15(?) feet.   **Spread:** 8–10 feet.
Exposure: shade.
Soil: tolerant.
Texture: medium to coarse.
Flower effects: not showy.
Fruit effects: red.
Use: group, shrub border, specimen.

HOLLY, BURFORD CHINESE
(Ilex cornuta 'Burfordi').   **Zones 5–6**
Slow growing. Dense, globose shrub. Short, spreading branches. Glossy, evergreen leaves with deep rich color. Tolerates shearing. Requires winter shade.
Height: 6–25 feet.   **Spread:** 6–8 feet.
Exposure: sun or shade.
Soil: moist, slightly acid.
Texture: medium.
Flower effects: not showy.
Fruit effects: clusters of red berries.
Use: accent, shrub border, specimen.

HOLLY, CONVEXLEAF JAPANESE
(Ilex crenata 'Convexa').   **Zones 5–6**
Slow growing. Broadleaf evergreen that is broader than it is high. Tolerates pruning; can be held to any size. Good substitute for boxwood.
Height: 4–20 feet.   **Spread:** 4–15 feet.
Exposure: tolerant, but prefers partial shade.
Soil: moist, slightly acid.
Texture: medium.
Flower effects: not showy.
Fruit effects: not showy.
Use: doorway, facer, hedge (clipped or unclipped), planter boxes, specimen.
Other varieties: 'Heller' (see detailed description below); 'Hetzi' (dwarf, hardy in Zone 5).

HOLLY, FOSTER'S
(Ilex × fosteri No. II).   **Zone 5**
Slow growing. Upright or conical. Open habit. Small, dark evergreen leaves and bright red fruit.
Height: 25 feet.   **Spread:** 10–15 feet.
Rooting habit: shallow.
Exposure: shade or partial shade.
Soil: acid.
Texture: medium.
Flower: white.
Use: group, screen, shrub border, specimen.

HOLLY, HELLER JAPANESE
(Ilex crenata 'Helleri').   **Zone 5**
Slow growing. Dwarf, compact evergreen. Tolerates pruning.
Height: 4 feet.   **Spread:** 5 feet.
Exposure: sun or partial shade.
Soil: moist, slightly acid.
Texture: medium.
Flower effects: not showy.
Fruit effects: not showy.
Use: doorway, facer, unclipped hedge, planter boxes, specimen.
Other variety: 'Stokes' (hardier than species).

HOLLY, INKBERRY
(Ilex glabra).   **Zone 3**
Slow growing. Upright form with ascending branches. Dense, glossy, deciduous foliage. Good in summer and winter effects. Sexes separate.
Height: 5–9 feet.   **Spread:** 6–10 feet.
Exposure: sun.
Soil: good, light.
Texture: medium.
Flower effects: not showy.
Fruit effects: black, persistent.
Use: group, screen, shrub border.
Variety: 'Compacta' (dwarf, female clone).

HOLLY, WINTERBERRY
(Ilex verticillata).   **Zone 3**
Slow growing. Spreading. Excellent foliage. Fruit persists to midwinter. Interesting the year around. Easily transplanted.
Height: 6–8 feet.   **Spread:** 3–5 feet.
Exposure: partial shade.
Soil: rich soil. Tolerates damp or wet locations.
Texture: medium.
Flower effects: not showy.
Fruit effects: red in fall and winter.
Fall color: yellow.
Use: group, screen, shrub border.
Variety: 'Nana' (dwarf to 3½ feet, fruits heavily).

HOLLYGRAPE, OREGON
(Mahonia aquifolium).   **Zone 5**
Medium rate of growth. Round, upright evergreen. Interesting holly-shaped, lustrous foliage and grapelike clusters of fruit.
Height: 3–5 feet.   **Spread:** 2–3 feet.
Exposure: partial shade, winter protection.
Texture: coarse.
Flower effects: yellow in spring.
Fruit effects: blue to purple in fall.

Fall color: bronze to purple.
Use: doorway, facer, group.
Varieties: 'Compacta' (compact form, glossy leaves, bronze in winter); 'Mayhan Strain' (dwarf to 2½ feet, glossy foliage).

HONEYSUCKLE, AMUR
(Lonicera maackii).   **Zone 2**
Fast growing. Tall-growing, rounded shrub. Yellow-green foliage. Fruits heavily in late fall.
Height: 12–15 feet.   **Spread:** 12–15 feet.
Exposure: sun or partial shade.
Soil: tolerant.
Texture: medium to coarse.
Flower effects: white, fragrant.
Fruit effects: red.
Use: screen, shrub border.
Variety: podocarpa (blooms in early June, holds leaves well into fall; hardy in Zone 4).

HONEYSUCKLE, ARNOLD GOTHA
(Lonicera × amoena 'Arnold').   **Zone 5**
Medium rate of growth. Foliage delicate. Flowers heavily. Valued for flowers and graceful arching habit.
Height: 9 feet.   **Spread:** 6–8 feet.
Exposure: sun.
Soil: tolerant.
Texture: fine.
Flower effects: pinkish white.
Fruit effects: red in summer.
Use: group, specimen.

HONEYSUCKLE, CLAVEY DWARF
(Lonicera xylosteum 'Claveyi').   **Zone 4**
Medium to slow growing. Compact, dense.
Height: 6 feet.   **Spread:** 4–6 feet.
Exposure: sun or shade.
Texture: medium.
Flower effects: white in spring.
Fruit effects: red in summer.
Use: group, shrub border.

HONEYSUCKLE, MORROW
(Lonicera morrowii).   **Zone 4**
Fast growing. Dense mound, often wider than it is high. Good all-purpose honeysuckle.
Height: 6 feet.   **Spread:** 8–10 feet.
Exposure: sun.
Soil: tolerant.
Texture: medium.
Flower effects: white turning to yellow.
Fruit effects: dark red.
Use: screen, shrub border.
Variety: 'Xanthocarpa' (yellow fruits, white flowers).

Descriptive Outlines of Shrubs

HONEYSUCKLE, TATARIAN
(Lonicera tatarica). **Zone 3**
Fast growing. Broad-spreading, round plant. Flowers and fruits heavily every year. Excellent in all seasons. Disease and insect resistant. Several excellent varieties.
Height: 9–12 feet. **Spread:** 10–12 feet.
Exposure: sun or partial shade.
Soil: tolerant.
Texture: medium.
Flower effects: pink or white.
Fruit effects: red in summer.
Use: screen, shrub border, specimen.
Varieties: 'Alba' (pure white flowers); 'Arnold Red' (darkest red flowers of species); 'Lutea' (pink flowers, yellow fruit); 'Parvifolia' (best white flowers of species); 'Virginalis' (rose-pink flowers, largest flowers of species).

HONEYSUCKLE, WINTER
(Lonicera fragrantissima). **Zone 5**
Medium rate of growth. Round, spreading. Handsome foliage. Flowers are fragrant and appear in very early spring. Tolerates pruning.
Height: 6 feet. **Spread:** 6 feet.
Exposure: sun or partial shade.
Texture: medium.
Flower effects: white, before leaves.
Fruit effects: red in early summer.
Use: corner, group, unclipped hedge, shrub border.

HONEYSUCKLE, ZABEL BLUELEAF
(Lonicera korolkowii 'Zabelii'). **Zone 3**
Fast growing. Upright to spreading structure. Vigorous grower. Free of disease and insect pests. Good appearance in all seasons.
Height: 7–10 feet. **Spread:** 7–10 feet.
Exposure: sun or partial shade.
Texture: medium.
Flower effects: deep pink to red.
Fruit effects: red berries.
Fall color: blue-green.
Use: group, hedge, screen, shrub border.

HYDRANGEA, HILLS-OF-SNOW
(Hydrangea arborescens 'Grandiflora'). **Zone 4**
Fast growing. Broad, upright plant. Good texture accent. Showy flowers. Requires severe pruning in spring.

Height: 4–8 feet. **Spread:** 5–8 feet.
Exposure: sun or shade.
Soil: moist.
Texture: coarse.
Flower effects: white in August.
Fruit effects: dry flower clusters in fall.
Use: corner, group, shrub border.

JETBEAD, BLACK
(Rhodotypos scandens). **Zone 5**
Medium rate of growth. Spreading and open habit. Excellent flowers and foliage.
Height: 5–6 feet. **Spread:** 4–5 feet.
Exposure: sun or shade.
Soil: tolerates poor soil.
Texture: medium.
Flower effects: white, late spring through summer.
Fruit effects: black, summer into winter.
Use: corner, unclipped hedge, shrub border.

JUNIPER, BAR HARBOR CREEPING
(Juniperus horizontalis 'Bar Harbor'). **Zone 2**
Fast growing. Low, spreading, somewhat open and trailing evergreen. Foliage is bluish green.
Height: 6–10 inches. **Spread:** 6–8 feet.
Exposure: sun or partial shade.
Soil: tolerates dry, sandy soil.
Texture: fine.
Use: facer. See also under Ground Covers.

JUNIPER, BLUE RUG CREEPING
(Juniperus horizontalis 'Wiltoni'). **Zone 2**
Fast growing. Extremely flat, spreading evergreen. Vivid blue foliage year-round. Blight resistant.
Height: 6–8 inches. **Spread:** 6–8 feet.
Exposure: sun or partial shade.
Soil: tolerates dry, sandy soil.
Texture: fine.
Use: corner, doorway, facer, slopes. See also under Ground Covers.

JUNIPER, COMPACT PFITZER
(Juniperus chinensis 'Pfitzeriana Compacta'). **Zone 4**
Fast to medium growing. Dwarf, spreading evergreen. Plumelike foliage.
Height: 5 feet. **Spread:** 5 feet.
Exposure: sun.
Soil: tolerates sandy soil.

Texture: fine.
Flower effects: not showy.
Fruit effects: gray-white berry in fall.
Use: corner, doorway, facer.

JUNIPER, DWARF COMMON **(Juniperus communis 'Depressa').** **Zone 2**
Medium to slow growing. Low, spreading habit with ascending branches. Blight resistant.
Height: 3–4 feet. **Spread:** 6–8 feet.
Exposure: sun or partial shade.
Soil: tolerates dry, sandy soils.
Texture: fine.
Use: corner, doorway, facer, group.

JUNIPER, JAPGARDEN
(Juniperus procumbens). **Zone 5**
Medium rate of growth. Low, creeping, dense evergreen mat. Blue-green foliage.
Height: 2 feet. **Spread:** 6–8 feet.
Exposure: sun.
Soil: tolerant.
Texture: fine.
Use: group. See also under Ground Covers.

JUNIPER, PFITZER CHINESE **(Juniperus chinensis 'Pfitzeriana').** **Zone 4**
Fast growing. Large, spreading evergreen. Plumelike blue-green foliage.
Height: 8–10 feet. **Spread:** 8–10 feet.
Exposure: sun.
Soil: tolerates sandy soil.
Texture: fine.
Flower effects: not showy.
Fruit effects: blue berry in fall.
Use: corner, group, shrub border.
Other variety: 'Compact Pfitzer' (see detailed description above).

JUNIPER, SARGENT CHINESE **(Juniperus chinensis sargenti).** **Zone 4**
Fast to medium growing. Flat, spreading evergreen. Steel-blue foliage. Excellent, serviceable plant. Blight resistant.
Height: 12–18 inches. **Spread:** 8–10 feet.
Exposure: sun or partial shade.
Soil: tolerates dry, sandy soil.
Texture: fine.
Use: corner, doorway, facer, group, slopes. See also under Ground Covers.

Descriptive Outlines of Shrubs

JUNIPER, WAUKEGAN CREEPING (Juniperus horizontalis 'Douglasii').   **Zone 2**

Medium rate of growth. Flat, spreading, somewhat trailing evergreen. Blue-green foliage.

Height: 6–12 inches.   **Spread:** 5 feet.
Exposure: sun or partial shade.
Soil: tolerates sandy soil.
Texture: fine.
Flower effects: not showy.
Fruit effects: blue berry in winter.
Use: corner, doorway, facer, slopes.

KERRIA, JAPANESE (Kerria japonica).   **Zone 4**

Medium growing. Broad, loose habit. Flowers, foliage, and twigs give year-round interest. Requires annual pruning.

Height: 4–6 feet.   **Spread:** 6–8 feet.
Exposure: sun or shade. Best in partial shade.
Texture: fine.
Flower effects: orange-yellow in May.
Fruit effects: not showy.
Fall color: yellow.
Use: facer, group, shrub border.
Variety: 'Pleniflora' (double, ball-shaped flowers last longer than single variety).

LAVENDER, TRUE (Lavendula officinalis).   **Zone 5**

Medium rate of growth. Dense, compact. Gray, semievergreen leaves.

Height: 3 feet.   **Spread:** 12–18 inches.
Exposure: sun.
Soil: light.
Texture: fine.
Flower effects: fragrant lavender spikes.
Fruit effects: brown, fragrant.
Use: containers, doorway, specimen.
Varieties: 'Hidcote' (hardier than species, 15 inches tall); 'Mumstead' (deep flower color, compact, dwarf to 12 inches).

LEUCOTHOE, DROOPING (Leucothoe fontanesiana [catesbaei]).   **Zone 4**

Slow growing. Semievergreen plant with graceful, arching branches. Lustrous green foliage with fall color.

Height: 4–6 feet.   **Spread:** 2–6 feet.
Exposure: shade or partial shade.
Soil: rich, moist, acid loam.
Texture: medium.
Flower effects: waxy, white.
Fall color: bronze, purplish in sun.
Use: foundation, group, shrub border, specimen.
Variety: 'Nana' (dwarf to 2 feet, 5–6 feet across).

LILAC (various species).   **Zones 2, 5**

Medium rate of growth. Upright, round shrub. Handsome, showy flowers in both single and double varieties. Reliable.

Height: 6–15 feet.   **Spread:** 6–12 feet.
Exposure: sun.
Texture: medium to coarse.
Flower effects: white to lavender in May.
Fruit effects: not showy.
Use: group, screen, shrub border, specimen.

LILAC, JAPANESE TREE (Syringa amurensis japonica).   **Zone 4**

New nomenclature lists as *Syringa reticulata reticulata*.
Medium rate of growth. Pyramidal but somewhat open form. Showy, late flowers and interesting cherrylike bark on older plants. This variety is more tree-like than *Syringa amurense*. Subject to scale infestations and bores.

Height: 15–30 feet.   **Spread:** 12–15 feet.
Exposure: sun.
Soil: any good soil.
Texture: medium-coarse.
Flower effects: creamy white in mid-June.
Fruit effects: not showy.
Use: group, screen, shrub border, specimen. See also under Trees.

LILAC, PERSIAN (Syringa persica).   **Zone 5**

Medium rate of growth. Dense and shapely. Valued for flowers.

Height: 4–8 feet.   **Spread:** 5–10 feet.
Exposure: sun, but tolerates light shade.
Texture: fine.
Flower effects: violet to white in May.
Fruit effects: not showy.
Use: corner, group, screen, shrub border.

MAGNOLIA, SAUCER (Magnolia soulangiana).   **Zone 5**

Medium rate of growth. Rounded form. Showy flowers effective in front of evergreens. Because of fleshy roots, plants should always be moved with a ball of earth.

Height: 25 feet.   **Spread:** 30 feet.
Exposure: sun.
Soil: rich, moist.
Texture: coarse.
Flower effects: white to purple, before leaves.
Fruit effects: rose-pink cone in fall.

Fall color: green to bronze.
Use: specimen. See also under Trees.
Varieties: 'Alba' (compact form, white flowers); 'Lilliputin' (smaller flowers and habit than species, late flowering); 'Lombardy Rose' (flowers dark-rose on undersurface, white above); 'San Jose' (flowers rosy purple, fragrant; vigorous growing); 'Verbanica' (petals rose-pink outside, white inside; late flowering; slow growing).

MAGNOLIA, STAR (Magnolia stellata).   **Zone 5**

Slow growing. Broad to round. Showy flowers appearing before leaves. Will not tolerate root competition from other plants, dryness, lime, or fresh manure. Because of fleshy roots, plants should always be moved with a ball of earth.

Height: 8–15 feet.   **Spread:** 10–15 feet.
Exposure: sun.
Soil: rich, moist, slightly acid.
Texture: coarse.
Flower effects: white.
Fruit effects: rosy red in fall.
Fall color: green to bronze.
Use: specimen. See also under Trees.
Varieties: rosea (buds pink, flowers fading to white in full bloom); 'Rubra' (flowers purplish rose); 'Waterlily' (more bushy, twiggy, and upright than species; pink buds, large white flowers).

MAGNOLIA, SWEETBAY (Magnolia virginiana).   **Zone 5**

Slow to medium growing. Loose, open habit. Valued for flowers.

Height: 10–30 feet.   **Spread:** 10–15 feet.
Exposure: partial shade, sheltered.
Soil: moist to wet.
Texture: medium.
Flower effects: creamy white, fragrant.
Fruit effects: red, conelike.
Use: shrub border. See also under Trees.

MOCKORANGE (various species).   **Zones 4–5**

Slow growing. Varieties compact, rounded, or erect. Most are leggy in appearance. Best held to back of planting with lower plants in front. Valued for flowers, which are usually fragrant.

Height: 4–12 feet.   **Spread:** 4–12 feet.
Exposure: sun or partial shade.
Texture: medium to coarse.
Flower effects: white in May and June.
Fruit effects: not showy.
Use: group, screen, shrub border.

Descriptive Outlines of Shrubs

MOCKORANGE, FROSTY MORN
(Philadelphus 'Frosty Morn'). **Zone 4**
Medium rate of growth. Rounded plant. Fragrant flowers. Withstands extremely cold temperatures.
Height: 3–4 feet. **Spread:** 3½ feet.
Exposure: sun.
Soil: any good soil.
Texture: medium.
Flower effects: white, double.
Fruit effects: not showy.
Use: facer, foundation, group.

MOCKORANGE, MINNESOTA SNOWFLAKE
(Philadelphus × virginalis 'Minnesota Snowflake'). **Zone 3**
Moderate rate of growth. Rounded, dense form. Fragrant, double flowers. Valued because it branches all the way to the ground. Extremely hardy.
Height: 8 feet. **Spread:** 4–6 feet.
Exposure: sun.
Soil: any good soil.
Texture: medium.
Flower effects: white, double.
Fruit effects: not showy.
Use: group, shrub border, specimen.

MOCKORANGE, MONT BLANC LEMOINE
(Philadelphus × lemoinei 'Mont Blanc'). **Zone 5**
Medium rate of growth. Dense, mounding. Shows little winter injury.
Height: 4 feet. **Spread:** 3–4 feet.
Exposure: sun or partial shade.
Soil: any good soil.
Texture: medium-fine.
Flower effects: white, single.
Fruit effects: not showy.
Use: foundation, group, shrub border.

NANDINA
(Nandina domestica). **Zones 6–7**
Medium rate of growth. Upright, loose. Valued more for fruit than flowers. Not hardy.
Height: 3–8 feet. **Spread:** 6 feet.
Exposure: sun or partial shade.
Texture: medium.
Flower effects: white in July.
Fruit effects: red to purple in fall and winter.
Fall color: bright red to scarlet.
Use: corner, group, shrub border, specimen.
Variety: 'Alba' (white fruits).

NINEBARK, COMMON
(Physocarpus opulifolius). **Zone 2**
Fast growing. Loose, spreading shrub resembling spirea. Because of coarseness not recommended in small, refined gardens.
Height: 10 feet. **Spread:** 10 feet.
Exposure: sun or shade.
Texture: coarse.
Flower effects: white in June.
Fruit effects: red to brown in fall.
Use: hedge, shrub border, woodland planting.
Varieties: intermedius (more refined than species, smaller leaves, 4 feet); nanus (dwarf, about 2 feet).

NINEBARK, DWARF
(Physocarpus monogynus). **Zone 2**
Fast growing. Dense shrub with bright green foliage.
Height: 4 feet. **Spread:** 3 feet.
Exposure: sun or shade.
Texture: medium.
Use: corner, facer, hedge (clipped or unclipped).

PACHISTIMA, CANBY
(Pachistima canbyi). **Zone 5**
Medium rate of growth. Low, dense, rounded. Excellent texture accent when used in a mass.
Height: 12 inches. **Spread:** 6–12 inches.
Exposure: shade or partial sun.
Soil: acid, moist.
Texture: medium fine.
Fall color: bronze.
Use: containers, dwarf hedge (unclipped), planter boxes. See also under Ground Covers.

PEARLBUSH
(Exochorda racemosa). **Zone 4**
Medium rate of growth. Slender-branched, upright shrub with loose, irregular growth. Sometimes treelike. Becomes leggy in old age, requiring facer shrubs. 'Wilson' is heavier flowering.
Height: 10–15 feet. **Spread:** 10–15 feet.
Exposure: sun or partial shade.
Soil: well-drained. Does not tolerate lime.
Texture: fine.
Flower effects: pearllike white flowers.
Fruit effects: not showy.
Use: group, shrub border.

PEASHRUB, SIBERIAN
(Caragana arborescens). **Zone 2**
Fast growing. Oval, erect and thin with age. Useful in sandy areas. Good foliage mass.
Height: 15–18 feet. **Spread:** 12 feet.
Exposure: sun, but tolerates partial shade.
Texture: fine in summer, coarse in winter.
Flower effects: yellow in spring, but not showy.
Fruit effects: not showy.
Fall color: yellow.
Use: shrub border, screen.

PHOTINIA, ORIENTAL
(Photinia villosa). **Zone 4**
Medium rate of growth. Large treelike shrub. Oval crown with twiggy, horizontal branching. Subject to fire blight.
Height: 15–20 feet. **Spread:** 12–18 feet.
Exposure: sun or partial shade.
Soil: moist.
Texture: medium.
Flower effects: white clusters.
Fruit effects: red berries.
Fall color: red-bronze.
Use: group, screen, shrub border, specimen.

PINE, DWARF MUGO
(Pinus mugo mugo). **Zone 2**
Slow growing. Round evergreen. Easily confined to small size by pruning.
Height: 4–8 feet. **Spread:** 12–20 feet.
Exposure: sun or partial shade.
Soil: moist.
Texture: medium.
Flower effects: yellow, not showy.
Fruit effects: yellow-brown cones.
Use: corner, doorway, planter boxes.
Varieties: 'Compacta' (dense, globe-shaped); pumilio (usually prostrate).

PLUM, FLOWERING
(Prunus triloba). **Zone 5**
Fast growing. Rounded, spreading.
Height: 8–10 feet. **Spread:** 8 feet.
Exposure: sun or partial shade.
Soil: rich, moist.
Texture: medium.
Flower effects: double flowers, pink in April and May.
Fruit effects: not showy.
Fall color: yellow.
Use: corner, group, shrub border.

Descriptive Outlines of Shrubs

PLUM, THUNDERCLOUD (Prunus cerasifera 'Thundercloud'). Zone 4
Fast growing. Round.

Height: 15–20 feet. **Spread:** 10 feet.
Exposure: sun or partial shade.
Texture: medium.
Flower effects: white to pink in April to May.
Fruit effects: yellow-red in late summer.
Fall color: yellow to red.
Use: group, specimen.

PRIVET, AMUR
(Ligustrum amurense). Zone 3
Fast growing. Dense, upright branches with round top. Tolerates pruning.
Height: 10–15 feet. **Spread:** 6–10 feet.
Exposure: sun or shade.
Texture: fine to medium.
Flower effects: not showy.
Fruit effects: blue-black in fall.
Use: hedge (clipped or unclipped), screen, shrub border.

PRIVET, IBOLIUM
(Ligustrum × ibolium). Zone 4
Medium growing. Broad, spreading. Tolerant to pruning.
Height: 10–12 feet. **Spread:** 12 feet.
Exposure: sun or shade.
Texture: fine.
Flower effects: white in early summer.
Fruit effects: blue-black in fall and winter.
Fall color: green to purple.
Use: hedge (clipped or unclipped), screen, shrub border.

PRIVET, LODENSE
(Ligustrum vulgare 'Lodense'). Zone 4
Medium rate of growth. Low, dense plant. Glossy foliage. Tolerates pruning.
Height: 4–5 feet. **Spread:** 3 feet.
Exposure: sun.
Texture: medium.
Flower effects: white.
Fruit effects: black.
Use: hedge (clipped or unclipped), group, shrub border.

PRIVET, REGEL BORDER (Ligustrum obtusifolium regelianum). Zone 3
Medium rate of growth. Horizontally branching. Dense foliage. Reliable, excellent form.
Height: 6 feet. **Spread:** 6 feet.
Exposure: sun or shade.
Texture: medium.
Flower effects: not showy.

Fruit effects: blue-black in fall and winter.
Fall color: russet to purple.
Use: corner, group, hedge (clipped or unclipped), shrub border.

QUINCE, FLOWERING (Chaenomeles lagenaria). Zone 4
New nomenclature lists as *Chaenomeles speciosa*.
Fast growing. Spreading plant. Good foliage, showy flowers, winter color. Many varieties and colors from which to choose.
Height: 6–8 feet. **Spread:** 6 feet.
Exposure: sun.
Texture: medium to fine.
Flower effects: white, pink, and red in April and May.
Fruit effects: yellow in late summer.
Fall color: bronze.
Use: group, clipped hedge, shrub border.

QUINCE, FLOWERING JAPANESE (Chaenomeles japonica). Zone 4
Fast growing. Spreading. Good foliage, showy flowers, winter color.
Height: 3–4 feet. **Spread:** 4 feet.
Exposure: sun.
Texture: medium to fine.
Flower effects: white through deep red in May.
Fruit effects: yellow in late summer.
Fall color: green to bronze.
Use: corner, doorway, facer, clipped hedge.
Variety: alpina (dwarf to 12 inches, orange flowers, dense).

REDCEDAR, CANAERT EASTERN (Juniperus virginiana 'Canaerti'). Zone 2
Medium rate of growth. Slender, pyramidal evergreen. Loose, open habit.
Height: 20 feet. **Spread:** 8–10 feet.
Exposure: sun.
Soil: tolerates sandy soil.
Texture: fine.
Flower effects: not showy.
Fruit effects: blue in fall.
Use: accent, group.

RHODODENDRON, CATAWBA (Rhododendron catawbiense). Zones 4–5
Medium rate of growth. Broad, rounded evergreen shrub that is wider than it is high. Profuse flowers in late spring or early summer. Extremely hardy. A number of hybrids are available.
Height: 6–10 feet. **Spread:** 8 feet or more.

Exposure: shade or partial sun. Must be protected.
Soil: rich, well-drained, acid.
Texture: coarse, heavy.
Flower effects: white to purple, depending upon hybrid.
Use: shrub border, woodland planting.

RHODODENDRON, P.J.M. HYBRID Zone 5
Medium rate of growth. Broad, rounded shrub. Flowers heavily every year in spring. Excellent broadleaf evergreen.
Height: 6–8 feet. **Spread:** 6 feet.
Exposure: sun or shade.
Soil: rich, well-drained.
Texture: coarse.
Flower effects: vivid lavender-pink.
Fall color: rich purple through winter.
Use: facer, foundation, shrub border, specimen, woodland planting.

RHODODENDRON, WILSON (Rhododendron × laetevirens). Zone 4
Moderate rate of growth. Low-growing evergreen shrub. Neat habit of growth. Flowers small compared to other rhododendrons.
Height: 4 feet. **Spread:** 4–5 feet.
Exposure: shade or partial sun.
Soil: rich, well-drained, acid.
Texture: medium.
Flower effects: pink to purple.
Use: facer, foundation, shrub border.

ROSE (FLORIBUNDA TYPE) (various species). Zones 2–5
Medium rate of growth. Rounded, upright, small-growing rose. Flowers all season. Many varieties and flower colors from which to choose.
Height: 3–5 feet. **Spread:** 3–4 feet.
Exposure: sun.
Soil: well-drained.
Texture: medium.
Flower effects: white to red all summer.
Fruit effects: red in fall.
Use: facer, group, unclipped hedge.

ROSE, FATHER HUGO
(Rosa hugonis). Zone 5
Fast growing. Dense, rounded. Excellent, showy flowers.
Height: 6–10 feet. **Spread:** 10 feet.
Exposure: sun.
Soil: well-drained.
Texture: fine.
Flower effects: yellow in June.
Fruit effects: black in midsummer.
Fall color: yellow.
Use: shrub border, specimen.

Descriptive Outlines of Shrubs

ROSE OF SHARON (SHRUBALTHEA)
(Hibiscus syriacus). Zone 5

Slow to medium growing. Upright, somewhat vase-shaped. Showy flowers in late summer. Young plants are less winter-hardy than older plants. Tolerates city conditions. Several varieties are available.

Height: 10–15 feet. **Spread:** 6–10 feet.
Exposure: sun or partial shade.
Texture: medium.
Flower effects: various colors, single or double varieties, in August and September.
Fruit effects: not showy.
Use: group, unclipped hedge, screen, shrub border, specimen.

ST. JOHNSWORT, SHRUBBY
(Hypericum prolificum). Zone 4

Medium to fast growing. Dense, erect stems with rounded form. Large, showy flowers continuing for several weeks.

Height: 3 feet. **Spread:** 3 feet.
Exposure: sun, but prefers partial shade.
Soil: tolerant.
Texture: medium-fine.
Flower effects: yellow.
Fruit effects: not showy.
Use: group, shrub border.

ST. JOHNSWORT, SUNGOLD **(Hypericum patulum 'Sungold').** Zones 5–6(?)

Medium rate of growth. Dense, rounded. Showy flowers in summer.

Height: 3–4 feet. **Spread:** 3 feet.
Exposure: sun or partial shade.
Soil: tolerates sandy, dry soil.
Texture: medium fine.
Flower effects: yellow in July and August.
Fruit effects: not showy.
Use: facer, foundation, group, woodland planting.
Other variety: 'Hidcote' (top may freeze back in severe weather).

SAND CHERRY, PURPLELEAF
(Prunus × cistena). Zone 2

Medium rate of growth. Oval form. Outstanding in fruit and foliage color.

Height: 7 feet. **Spread:** 6–7 feet.
Exposure: sun.
Texture: medium.
Flower effects: white in May.
Fruit effects: dark purple in late summer.
Fall color: purple.
Use: group, specimen.

SERVICEBERRY, SHADBLOW
(Amelanchier canadensis). Zone 4

Often listed as *Amelanchier aborea*. Fast growing. Loosely round to oval. Good combined with broadleaf evergreens.

Height: 25 feet. **Spread:** 12 feet.
Exposure: partial shade, but tolerates sun.
Soil: well-drained.
Texture: fine.
Flower effects: white in early spring.
Fruit effects: purple berry in early summer.
Fall color: orange to red.
Use: group, shrub border, specimen, woodland planting. See also under Trees.

SNOWBELL, JAPANESE
(Styrax japonicum). Zone 5

Medium rate of growth. Wide-spreading shrub or tree. Dense foliage. Interesting bark and curving horizontal branches with a twiggy appearance.

Height: 12–30 feet. **Spread:** 12–20 feet.
Exposure: partial shade.
Soil: well-drained but moist. Prefers acid soil.
Texture: medium-fine.
Flower effects: white, pendulous.
Fruit effects: not showy.
Use: specimen.

SNOWBERRY, COMMON
(Symphoricarpos albus). Zone 3

Fast growing. Loose, arching branches give irregular appearance. Valued for ability to grow in heavy shade and for fruit effects.

Height: 3–6 feet. **Spread:** 3–6 feet.
Rooting habit: suckering.
Exposure: sun or shade.
Soil: tolerant.
Texture: medium to fine.
Flower effects: white, inconspicuous.
Fruit effects: white clusters.
Use: shrub border.

SPICEBUSH
(Lindera benzoin). Zone 4

Slow growing. Oval form. Fragrant flowers appearing before leaves. Good fall color. Requires little care.

Height: 8–15 feet. **Spread:** 4–8 feet.
Exposure: sun.
Soil: moist.
Texture: medium in summer, coarse in winter.

Flower effects: yellow.
Fruit effects: red.
Fall color: yellow.
Use: group, shrub border.

SPIREA, ALPINE JAPANESE
(Spiraea japonica alpina). Zone 5

Medium rate of growth. Dwarf, mounding. Excellent overall character.

Height: 12 inches. **Spread:** 12 inches.
Exposure: sun.
Soil: any good garden soil.
Texture: fine.
Flower effects: pink.
Fruit effects: not showy.
Use: doorway, group, specimen. See also under Ground Covers.

SPIREA, ANTHONY WATERER **(Spiraea × bumalda 'Anthony Waterer').** Zone 5

Fast growing. Low, broad, flat on top. Attractive foliage, tinged pink when it first appears.

Height: 2–3 feet. **Spread:** 3 feet.
Exposure: sun.
Texture: fine.
Flower effects: pink to crimson, spring to fall.
Fruit effects: not showy.
Fall color: reddish.
Use: doorway, facer, unclipped hedge.
Other variety: 'Froebel' (3–4 feet high).

SPIREA, BILLARD
(Spiraea × billardi). Zone 4

Fast growing. Rounded form. Best used only on banks because of suckering.

Height: 6 feet. **Spread:** 5 feet.
Rooting habit: suckering.
Exposure: sun.
Soil: any good soil.
Flower effects: rose spikes.
Fruit effects: not showy.
Use: banks.

SPIREA, BRIDALWREATH
(Spiraea prunifolia). Zone 4

Fast growing. Graceful, upright. Reliable. Showy flowers, excellent fall color. Double variety available.

Height: 6 feet. **Spread:** 6 feet.
Exposure: sun.
Soil: moist.
Texture: medium to fine.
Flower effects: white in early spring.
Fruit effects: not showy.
Fall color: orange.
Use: group, shrub border.

Descriptive Outlines of Shrubs

SPIREA, GARLAND
(Spiraea × arguta).   **Zone 4**
Medium rate of growth. Graceful arching branches form dense, rounded mass. Valued for early, abundant flowering and fine texture.
Height: 5–6 feet.   **Spread:** 3 feet.
Exposure: sun or partial shade.
Soil: any good soil.
Texture: fine.
Flower effects: white.
Fruit effects: not showy.
Use: facer, group, specimen.
Variety: 'Compacta' (only 4 feet tall).

SPIREA, VAN HOUTTE
(Spiraea × vanhouttei).   **Zone 4**
Fast growing. Vase-shaped plant with rounded top. Showy when in bloom.
Height: 8–10 feet.   **Spread:** 8 feet.
Exposure: sun.
Texture: medium.
Flower effects: white in May.
Fruit effects: not showy.
Fall color: orange to yellow.
Use: shrub border, screen.

STEPHANANDRA, CUTLEAF
(Stephanandra incisa).   **Zone 5**
Medium rate of growth. Low, graceful, rounded plant. Dense and compact, often wider than it is tall. Valued for fine texture. Hardiness varies.
Height: 3–8 feet.   **Spread:** 4–8 feet.
Exposure: sun or partial shade.
Soil: tolerant.
Texture: fine (feathery).
Flower effects: white.
Fruit effects: not showy.
Use: facer, group, specimen.
Variety: 'Crispa' (dwarf to 18–36 inches, roots along branches, good for hillsides).

SUMAC, FRAGRANT
(Rhus aromatica).   **Zone 3**
Medium rate of growth. Round and spreading. Valued for handsome foliage, flowers, and fall color.
Height: 2–4 feet.   **Spread:** 5–8 feet.
Exposure: sun or shade.
Texture: medium.
Flower effects: yellow in early spring.
Fruit effects: red, berrylike in summer.
Fall color: yellow, scarlet, and crimson.
Use: facer, slopes. Should not be used in dusty areas because leaves hold dust.

SUMAC, STAGHORN
(Rhus typhina).   **Zone 3**
Fast growing. Irregular, picturesque. Interesting fuzzy twigs that hold dust.
Height: 20–25 feet.   **Spread:** 20 feet.
Exposure: sun or shade.
Soil: tolerates sterile soil.
Texture: medium in summer, coarse in winter.
Flower effects: not showy.
Fruit effects: red in fall.
Fall color: orange-red.
Use: clump, mass, specimen. Not suitable for small properties and dusty areas.
Varieties: 'Dissecta' (leaves deeply cut); 'Laciniata' (leaves deeply divided).

SWEETSHRUB, COMMON (CAROLINA ALLSPICE) (Calycanthus floridus).   **Zone 4**
Medium rate of growth. Stiff, upright shrub. Glossy foliage fragrant when crushed.
Height: 6–9 feet.   **Spread:** 5–8 feet.
Exposure: sun or shade.
Soil: tolerant, but prefers moist soil.
Texture: coarse.
Flower effects: maroon-red, fragrant.
Fruit effects: brown capsule, fragrant when crushed.
Fall color: yellow.
Use: screen, shrub border.

VIBURNUM, AMERICAN CRANBERRYBUSH
(Viburnum trilobum).   **Zone 2**
Fast growing. Dense, broad, round. Fruit showy in color and mass.
Height: 6–12 feet.   **Spread:** 8–12 feet.
Exposure: sun or shade.
Texture: medium.
Flower effects: white in May and June.
Fruit effects: red in August.
Fall color: reddish.
Use: corner, group, screen.
Variety: 'Compactum' (see detailed description below).

VIBURNUM, ARROWWOOD
(Viburnum dentatum).   **Zone 2**
Fast growing. Upright, dense. Handsome foliage.
Height: 15 feet.   **Spread:** 6–12 feet.
Exposure: sun or partial shade.
Texture: medium to coarse.
Flower effects: white in May.
Fruit effects: blue in late summer.
Fall color: bronze-red.
Use: corner, group, screen, shrub border.

VIBURNUM, BURKWOOD
(Viburnum × burkwoodi).   **Zone 5**
Medium rate of growth. Upright. Fragrant flowers and attractive foliage.
Height: 4–8 feet.   **Spread:** 6–8 feet.
Exposure: sun.
Soil: tolerates poor but well-drained soil.
Texture: coarse.
Flower effects: white in April and May.
Fruit effects: red to black in late summer.
Fall color: muted red.
Use: corner, group, shrub border, specimen.

VIBURNUM, COMPACT AMERICAN CRANBERRYBUSH (Viburnum trilobum 'Compactum').   **Zone 2**
Medium rate of growth. Rounded, compact. Hardiest of cranberrybush types. Heavy fruit, suitable for preserves.
Height: 5–6 feet.   **Spread:** 5 feet.
Exposure: sun or partial shade.
Texture: medium to coarse.
Flower effects: white in May.
Fruit effects: scarlet in fall.
Use: corner, group, shrub border.
Other varieties: 'Andrews' (hardier than species); 'Hahs' (thick foliage, excellent fall color); 'Wentworth' (hardier than species).

VIBURNUM, COMPACT EUROPEAN CRANBERRYBUSH (Viburnum opulus 'Compactum').   **Zone 3**
Medium rate of growth. Upright, rounded. Flowers and fruits well.
Height: 5 feet.   **Spread:** 4–5 feet.
Exposure: sun or shade.
Texture: medium to coarse.
Flower effects: white in May.
Fruit effects: red berries in fall and winter.
Fall color: red.
Use: corner, doorway, group, shrub border.

VIBURNUM, DWARF EUROPEAN CRANBERRYBUSH (Viburnum opulus 'Nanum').   **Zone 3**
Medium rate of growth. Dense, dwarf shrub. Irregular, picturesque. Tolerates pruning.
Height: 2 feet.   **Spread:** 2 feet.
Exposure: sun or shade.
Texture: medium.
Fall color: reddish.
Use: doorway, facer, planter boxes, under low windows.

Descriptive Outlines of Shrubs

**VIBURNUM, EUROPEAN CRANBERRYBUSH
(Viburnum opulus).**   **Zone 3**
Medium rate of growth. Vase-shaped. Outstanding color and massing of fruit.
Height: 10–12 feet.   **Spread:** 12–15 feet.
Exposure: sun or shade.
Texture: medium to coarse.
Flower effects: white in May.
Fruit effects: yellow to crimson in fall.
Fall color: yellow-red.
Use: group, screen, shrub border.
Varieties: 'Compactum' (see detailed description above); 'Nanum' (see detailed description above); 'Xanthocarpum' (golden yellow fruits).

**VIBURNUM, FRAGRANT SNOWBALL
(CARLCEPHALUM) (Viburnum ×
carlcephalum).**   **Zone 5**
Medium rate of growth. Upright, slightly spreading. Handsome glossy foliage and large fragrant flowers.
Height: 9 feet.   **Spread:** 6–8 feet.
Exposure: sun.
Soil: well-drained.
Texture: medium-coarse.
Flower effects: small, white, in large clusters.
Use: corner, group, shrub border, specimen.

VIBURNUM, JAPANESE SNOWBALL (Viburnum plicatum [tomentosum sterile]).   **Zone 4**
Medium rate of growth. Handsome shrub characterized by horizontal branching. Outstanding in flower and fruit. Several excellent varieties.
Height: 9 feet.   **Spread:** 6–8 feet.
Exposure: sun or partial shade.
Soil: moist, well-drained.
Texture: medium.
Flower effects: white.
Fruit effects: red to black.
Use: group, shrub border, specimen.
Varieties: 'Maries' (flowers, larger than species, extend along length of branches; excellent red fruit); tomentosum (Doublefile V.) (often as broad as tall; good flowers and fruit, but smaller than 'Maries').

**VIBURNUM, KOREANSPICE
(Viburnum carlesi).**   **Zone 4**
Medium rate of growth. Upright. Fragrant flowers and attractive foliage.
Height: 4–8 feet.   **Spread:** 6–8 feet.
Exposure: sun.
Soil: well-drained.
Texture: coarse.
Flower effects: pink to white in April and May.

Fruit effects: red to black in late summer.
Fall color: muted red.
Use: corner, group, shrub border, specimen.
Variety: 'Compacta' (more compact than species).

**VIBURNUM, LEATHERLEAF
(Viburnum rhytidophyllum).**   **Zone 5**
Medium rate of growth. Upright evergreen. Lustrous, dark-green, puckered foliage.
Height: 9 feet.   **Spread:** 8–9 feet.
Exposure: partial shade.
Soil: well-drained.
Texture: coarse.
Flower effects: pink in June.
Fruit effects: red to black in fall.
Use: corner, group, shrub border, specimen.

**VIBURNUM, LINDEN
(Viburnum dilatatum).**   **Zone 5**
Medium rate of growth. Neatly rounded, compact, dense. Outstanding fruit display that covers plant. Good for residential use.
Height: 9 feet.   **Spread:** 6–8 feet.
Exposure: sun or partial shade.
Soil: tolerant.
Texture: medium.
Flower effects: creamy white.
Fruit effects: bright red.
Fall color: russet-red.
Use: group, shrub border, specimen.
Variety: 'Xanthocarpum' (yellow fruit).

**VIBURNUM, MAPLELEAF
(Viburnum acerifolium).**   **Zone 3**
Slow growing. Outstanding in foliage and fruit color.
Height: 4–6 feet.   **Spread:** 3–4 feet.
Exposure: shade or partial shade.
Soil: tolerates dry soil but prefers moist situation.
Texture: medium.
Flower effects: white in May and June.
Fruit effects: red to black in early fall.
Fall color: yellow-red.
Use: corner, shrub border, woodland planting.

**VIBURNUM, NANNYBERRY
(Viburnum lentago).**   **Zone 2**
Fast growing. Usually grown as a shrub but can be trained to grow as a tree. Excellent, dense green foliage. Good fall color. Attracts birds.

Height: 10–30 feet.   **Spread:** 6–10 feet.
Exposure: sun.
Soil: very tolerant.
Texture: coarse to medium.
Flower effects: white in late May.
Fruit effects: black. Effective fall and winter.
Fall color: red to purple.
Use: shrub border. See also under Trees.

**VIBURNUM, SIEBOLD
(Viburnum sieboldii).**   **Zone 4**
Medium to fast growing. Rounded, somewhat open form. Often treelike. Valued for dark lustrous foliage, flowers, and fruit. Attracts birds.
Height: 15–20 feet.   **Spread:** 10–15 feet.
Exposure: sun or partial shade.
Soil: tolerant, but prefers moist soil.
Texture: coarse.
Flower effects: creamy white in late spring.
Fruit effects: red turning to black.
Fall color: green to red.
Use: group, shrub border, specimen. See also under Trees.

**VIBURNUM, WITHEROD
(Viburnum cassinoides).**   **Zone 2**
Medium rate of growth. Dense, compact, rounded form. Outstanding in fruit and foliage. Excellent fall color.
Height: 5–6 feet.   **Spread:** 5–6 feet.
Exposure: sun or partial shade.
Soil: any good soil.
Texture: medium.
Flower effects: creamy white.
Fruit effects: red to black.
Fall color: red.
Use: foundation, group, shrub border, woodland planting.

**WEIGELA
(various species)**   **Zone 5**
Fast growing. Round, spreading. Showy flowers. Requires annual pruning because of general die-back of branches. Often suffers winter injury in north. Many varieties available.
Height: 4–6 feet.   **Spread:** 5–6 feet.
Exposure: sun.
Texture: coarse.
Flower effects: crimson-red in June.
Fruit effects: not showy.
Use: texture accent, corner, group, shrub border.

Descriptive Outlines of Shrubs

WITCHHAZEL, VERNAL
(Hamamelis vernalis).   **Zone 4**
Slow growing. Upright to spreading plant. Valued for early flowering and dense foliage. Root-prune before transplanting.
Height: 6 feet.   **Spread:** 6–8 feet.
Exposure: sun or partial shade.
Soil: moist.
Texture: medium to coarse.
Flower effects: yellow in late winter.
Fruit effects: not showy.
Fall color: bright yellow to brown.
Use: group, shrub border, specimen.

WITCHHAZEL, COMMON
(Hamamelis virginiana).   **Zone 4**
Slow growing. Loose, irregular habit. Attractive flowers appear before foliage drops in fall. Root-prune before transplanting. Tolerates city conditions.
Height: 12–20 feet.   **Spread:** 12–20 feet.
Exposure: sun or partial shade.
Soil: moist.
Texture: coarse.
Flower effects: yellow in October and November.
Fruit effects: not showy.
Fall color: yellow.
Use: group, shrub border, specimen.

YEW, ANGLOJAP
(Taxus × media).   **Zone 4**
Slow growing. Dense, broadly pyramidal. Rich dark color. Sexes separate. Tolerates pruning. Do not plant too deep.
Height: 40 feet.   **Spread:** 12 feet.
Exposure: shade.
Soil: tolerant if well-drained.
Texture: medium.
Fruit effects: red in fall and winter.
Use: corner, shrub border.
Varieties: 'Amherst' (dense, compact, about 12 feet tall); 'Berryhill' (female clone, about 6 feet tall); 'Brown' (dense, rounded form, 6–9 feet tall); 'Hatfield' or 'Hicks' (see detailed description below); 'Taunton' (see detailed description below); 'Wards' (see detailed description below).

YEW, DENSE
(Taxus media 'Densiformis').   **Zone 4**
Slow growing. Dense, upright evergreen. Rich dark color. Sexes separate. Do not plant too deep.
Height: 4–5 feet.   **Spread:** 4 feet.

Exposure: shade.
Soil: tolerant, but prefers well-drained soil.
Texture: medium.
Flower effects: not showy.
Fruit effects: red in fall and winter.
Use: doorway, hedge (clipped or unclipped), planter boxes.

YEW, DWARF SPREADING JAPANESE
(Taxus cuspidata nana).   **Zone 4**
Slow growing. Compact, spreading evergreen. Rich dark color. Sexes separate. Do not plant too deep.
Height: 3–4 feet.   **Spread:** 4–5 feet.
Exposure: best in shade, but tolerates sunlight.
Soil: tolerant, but prefers well-drained soil.
Texture: medium.
Flower effects: not showy.
Fruit effects: red in fall and winter.
Use: corner, doorway, facer, group, planter boxes.

YEW, HATFIELD OR HICKS (Taxus ×
media 'Hatfieldii' or 'Hicksii').   **Zone 4**
Slow growing. Dense, slender, conical evergreen. Tolerates pruning. Rich dark color. Sexes separate. Do not plant too deep.
Height: 8 feet.   **Spread:** 4–5 feet.
Exposure: shade.
Soil: tolerant, but prefers well-drained soil.
Texture: medium.
Flower effects: not showy.
Fruit effects: red in fall and winter.
Use: accent, corner, hedge (clipped or unclipped), planter boxes.

YEW, SPREADING JAPANESE
(Taxus cuspidata).   **Zone 4**
Slow growing. Spreading evergreen. Rich dark color. Sexes separate. Do not plant too deep.
Height: 8–10 feet.   **Spread:** 8–12 feet.
Exposure: best in shade, but tolerates sunlight.
Soil: tolerant, but prefers well-drained soil.
Texture: medium.
Flower effects: not showy.
Fruit effects: red in fall and winter.
Use: corner, shrub border, specimen.
Varieties: capitata (see detailed description below); nana (see detailed description above).

YEW, TAUNTON ANGLOJAP
(Taxus × media 'Tauntoni').   **Zone 4**
Slow growing. Excellent spreading evergreen, neat grower. Displays great resistance to "winterburn." Do not plant too deep.
Height: 6–10 feet.   **Spread:** 8–10 feet.
Exposure: prefers shade, but tolerates sunlight.
Soil: tolerant, but prefers well-drained soils.
Texture: medium.
Fruit effects: red in fall and winter.
Use: corner, doorway, facer, group.

YEW, UPRIGHT JAPANESE
(Taxus cuspidata capitata).   **Zone 4**
Slow growing. Erect, broad, pyramidal evergreen. Rich dark color. Sexes separate. Do not plant too deep.
Height: 10–40 feet.   **Spread:** 15–20 feet.
Exposure: best in shade, but tolerates sunlight.
Soil: tolerant, but prefers well-drained soil.
Texture: medium.
Flower effects: not showy.
Fruit effects: red in fall and winter.
Use: accent, corner.

YEW, WARD ANGLOJAP
(Taxus media 'Wardii').   **Zone 4**
Slow growing. Semispreading, dense habit of growth. Dark-green evergreen foliage. Do not plant too deep.
Height: 3–6 feet.   **Spread:** 5–8 feet.
Exposure: prefers shade but tolerates sunlight.
Soil: tolerant, but prefers well-drained soils.
Texture: medium.
Fruit effects: red in fall and winter.
Use: corner, doorway, facer, group.

YUCCA (ADAMSNEEDLE)
(Yucca filamentosa).   **Zone 4**
Fast growing. Stiff, upright, dramatic evergreen.
Height: 3 feet.   **Spread:** 3–4 feet.
Exposure: sun.
Texture: coarse.
Flower effects: yellow to white in July.
Fruit effects: not showy.
Use: specimen. Blends well with large rocks.

Descriptive Outlines of Ground Covers

BARREN-STRAWBERRY
(Waldsteinia fragaroides).   **Zone 4**
Fast growing. Produces a thick mat. Spreads quickly by underground roots. Glossy evergreen foliage closely resembles that of the strawberry plant.
Height: 6–12 inches.   **Spread:** 12 inches.
Exposure: sun or shade.
Soil: tolerant.
Texture: medium-coarse.
Flower effects: yellow.
Use: general landscape areas, banks, under shrubs.

BEARBERRY (KINNIKINNICK)
(Arctostaphylos uva-ursi).   **Zone 2**
Slow growing. Spreading woody evergreen. Handsome foliage and fruit. Difficult to transplant.
Height: 6 inches.   **Spacing:** 18–24 inches.
Exposure: sun or shade.
Soil: tolerates dry sandy soils; requires well-drained soil.
Texture: fine.
Flower effects: pink.
Fruit effects: red.
Use: low cover under broadleaf evergreens, steep slopes.

BUGLE, CARPET
(Ajuga reptans).   **Zone 4**
Fast growing. Herbaceous semievergreen. Easy to grow.
Height: 6 inches.   **Spacing:** 8–12 inches.
Exposure: sun or shade.
Soil: moderately moist.
Texture: coarse.
Flower effects: blue.
Fruit effects: not showy.
Use: excellent low cover around trees and rocks, on low banks.
Varieties: 'Atropurpurea' (dark-bronze leaves); 'Variegata' (leaves with yellow variegation); 'Rubra' (leaves dark purple).

BUGLE, GENEVA
(Ajuga genevensis).   **Zone 4**
Medium rate of growth. Herbaceous semievergreen. Spreads less rapidly than other varieties. Height is a disadvantage.
Height: 14 inches.   **Spacing:** 8–12 inches.
Exposure: sun or shade.
Texture: coarse.
Flower effects: blue.
Fruit effects: not showy.
Use: general.

CANDYTUFT, EVERGREEN
(Iberis sempervirens).   **Zone 4**
Medium rate of growth. Low, dense semievergreen. Abundant, brilliant white flowers.
Height: 12 inches.   **Spread:** 12 inches.
Exposure: sun, but tolerates shade.
Soil: good, well-drained, slightly acid.
Texture: medium-fine.
Flower effects: white.
Fruit effects: not showy.
Use: in masses in small planting areas, in rock gardens. See also under Shrubs.
Varieties: 'Christmas Snow' (blooms a second time in fall); 'Little Gem' (lower growing than species); 'Snowflake' (vigorous, spreads to 3 feet).

COTONEASTER, BEARBERRY
(Cotoneaster dammeri).   **Zone 5**
Slow growing. Prostrate woody evergreen. Glossy dark-green leaves, attractive fruit.
Height: 6–12 inches.   **Spacing:** 18–24 inches.
Exposure: sun or partial shade.
Soil: well-drained but moist.
Texture: fine.
Flower effects: white.
Fruit effects: red.
Use: general planting areas, low banks, around large rocks. See also under Shrubs.

COTONEASTER, CREEPING
(Cotoneaster adpressa).   **Zone 4**
Slow growing. Mounding, woody, deciduous. Difficult to transplant. Potted plants are preferable.
Height: 12 inches.   **Spacing:** 18–24 inches.
Exposure: sun.
Soil: well-drained.
Texture: fine.
Flower effects: pink.
Fruit effects: red.
Fall color: deep red.
Use: does well on banks. Handsome texture contrasts with rock surfacings.

COTONEASTER, ROCK OR ROCKSPRAY
(Cotoneaster horizontalis).   **Zone 4**
Slow growing. Low, dense, horizontally spreading plant. Excellent foliage and persistent fruit. Difficult to transplant.
Height: 2–3 feet.   **Spread:** 4–6 feet.
Exposure: sun.
Soil: well-drained.
Texture: fine.
Flower effects: pink in May and June, but not showy.

Fruit effects: red in fall.
Fall color: red-orange.
Use: general, gentle slopes. See also under Shrubs.

DAYLILY
(various species)   **Zone 3**
Fast growing. Deciduous plant that flowers abundantly. Requires little attention once established. Readily naturalizes. Winter appearance somewhat unattractive.
Height: 2 feet.   **Spread:** 18–24 inches.
Exposure: sun or shade.
Soil: tolerant.
Texture: medium-fine.
Flower effects: variety of colors available.
Use: general, rough areas, slopes.

DRAGON'S BLOOD *(Sedum spurium 'Dragon's Blood').*   **Zone 3**
Medium rate of growth. Forms dense mat in full sun; becomes open in shade. Semievergreen. Tolerates dry conditions once established. Requires little care.
Height: 6–8 inches.   **Spread:** 12 inches.
Exposure: sun.
Soil: tolerant.
Texture: fine.
Flower effects: red.
Use: general.

EUONYMUS, BABY WINTERCREEPER
(Euonymus fortunei 'Minimus').   **Zone 5**
Slow growing. Woody evergreen. Not a vigorous spreader.
Height: 2–6 inches.   **Spacing:** 12 inches.
Exposure: partial shade.
Texture: fine.
Use: general use in small areas.

EUONYMUS, COMMON WINTERCREEPER
(Euonymus fortunei radicans).   **Zone 5**
Slow growing. Woody evergreen. Tends to mound into dense growth. Requires pruning to give prostrate effect. Bigleaf wintercreeper *(E. fortunei vegetus)* can also be used.
Height: 6–24 inches.   **Spacing:** 18–24 inches.
Exposure: sun or shade. May need protection against sun and wind in winter.
Texture: medium.
Flower effects: not showy.
Fruit effects: orange in fall.
Use: general.

Descriptive Outlines of Ground Covers

EUONYMUS, PURPLELEAF (Euonymus fortunei 'Coloratus'). **Zone 5**

Slow growing. Woody evergreen. Vigorous, dense, close growing. Requires pruning of upright shoots to keep groundcover effect. Larger leaves than other varieties.

Height: 6–18 inches. **Spacing:** 15–18 inches.
Exposure: sun or shade.
Texture: medium fine.
Flower effects: not showy.
Fruit effects: not showy.
Fall color: purplish-red through winter.
Use: general.

FESCUE, TALL
(Festuca arundinacea). **Zone 2**

Fast growing. Grasslike cover. Excellent for rough areas and erosion control. Discourages encroachment of other plants. Not recommended for refined areas.

Height: 10–14 inches.
Exposure: sun or partial shade.
Soil: tolerates heavy clay and dry sand.
Texture: coarse.
Use: rough areas, banks.

FORSYTHIA, ARNOLD DWARF
(Forsythia 'Arnold Dwarf'). **Zone 5**

Medium to slow growing. Dense, mounding form. Wide spreading. Branches root when touching soil. Flowers, if any, not outstanding.

Height: 4–5 feet. **Spread:** 8–10 feet.
Exposure: sun.
Soil: well-drained.
Texture: medium.
Flower effects: not showy.
Use: slopes. See also under Shrubs.

FORSYTHIA, BRONX (Forsythia viridissima 'Bronxensis'). **Zone 5**

Medium rate of growth. Very dwarf in habit. Small but abundant flowers.

Height: 2 feet. **Spread:** 2–4 feet.
Exposure: sun.
Texture: medium.
Flower effects: small, yellow.
Fall color: green to yellow.
Use: slopes. See also under Shrubs.

GERMANDER, CHAMAEDRYS
(Teucrium chamaedrys). **Zone 5**

Medium to slow growing. Low, dense, woody evergreen. May need winter protection.

Height: 10 inches. **Spacing:** 8 inches.
Exposure: sun.

Soil: well-drained.
Texture: medium to fine.
Flower effects: rose-purple.
Fruit effects: not showy.
Use: general, edging. See also under Shrubs.
Variety: 'Prostratum' (heavy flowering, 8 inches tall).

GINGER, WILD
(Asarum canadense). **Zone 4**

Slow growing. Handsome deciduous plant that blends well with other garden plants. Excellent for entryways and protected areas.

Height: 7–10 inches. **Spread:** 10–15 inches.
Exposure: shade.
Soil: rich, moist, acid.
Texture: coarse.
Flower effects: not showy.
Use: general.

GOUTWEED
(Aegopodium podograria). **Zone 3**

Fast growing. Herbaceous, deciduous. Can become a weed.

Height: 8 inches. **Spacing:** 18 inches.
Exposure: sun or shade.
Soil: tolerates poor soils.
Texture: medium.
Flower effects: not showy.
Fruit effects: not showy.
Use: general garden areas; good in areas where many plants will not grow.
Variety: 'Variegatum' (leaves with white variegation).

HEATHER, SCOTCH
(Calluna vulgaris). **Zone 4**

Slow growing. Low, sprawling evergreen. Forms mat or mound. Many varieties.

Height: 10–24 inches. **Spread:** 2 feet.
Exposure: sun.
Soil: well-drained, acid sand or light loam.
Texture: fine.
Flower effects: white to red, according to variety.
Fruit effects: not showy.
Use: general. See also under Shrubs.

HONEYSUCKLE, HALLS JAPANESE
(Lonicera japonica 'Halliana'). **Zone 4**

Fast growing. Extremely vigorous. Popular fragrant vine. Good for all purposes.

Height: 2 feet. **Spacing:** 3 feet.
Exposure: sun or shade.
Texture: medium to coarse.

Flower effects: white to yellow in spring through fall.
Fruit effects: not showy.
Fall color: bronze.
Use: not recommended for small areas; good for long steep banks because of fast growth and rooting along stems. See also under Vines.

IVY, BALTIC ENGLISH
(Hedera helix 'Baltica'). **Zone 5**

Fast growing. Woody evergreen. Hardier than English ivy.

Height: 6 inches. **Spacing:** 6–12 inches.
Exposure: shade or partial sun.
Soil: rich, moist.
Texture: medium.
Flower effects: not showy.
Fruit effects: black in fall.
Use: general garden areas, gentle slopes, areas where grass will not grow.

IVY, BULGARIAN ENGLISH
(Hedera helix 'Bulgaria'). **Zone 4**

Fast growing. Woody evergreen. Rich, shiny leaves.

Height: 6 inches. **Spacing:** 6–12 inches.
Exposure: sun or shade.
Soil: rich, moist.
Texture: medium.
Flower effects: not showy.
Fruit effects: black in fall.
Use: general garden areas, gentle slopes, areas where grass will not grow.

IVY, THORNDALE ENGLISH
(Hedera helix 'Thorndale'). **Zone 4**

Medium to fast growing. Handsome evergreen foliage. Will climb walls or tree trunks. Once established, plant tolerates broad range of conditions: sun or shade, cool or hot, dry or moist.

Height: 8–10 inches. **Spread:** 12 inches.
Exposure: sun or shade.
Soil: tolerant.
Texture: medium.
Use: general, refined areas.

JUNIPER, BAR HARBOR CREEPING
(Juniperus horizontalis 'Bar Harbor').
Zone 2

Fast growing. Low, spreading, somewhat open and trailing evergreen. Foliage is bluish green.

Height: 6–10 inches. **Spread:** 6–8 feet.
Exposure: sun or partial shade.
Soil: tolerates dry, sandy soil.
Texture: fine.
Use: slopes. See also under Shrubs.

Descriptive Outlines of Ground Covers

JUNIPER, BLUE RUG CREEPING
(*Juniperus horizontalis 'Wiltoni'*). Zone 2
Fast growing. Extremely flat, spreading evergreen. Vivid blue foliage the year round. Blight resistant.
Height: 6–8 inches.   **Spread:** 6–8 feet.
Exposure: sun or partial shade.
Soil: tolerates dry, sandy soil.
Texture: fine.
Use: general planting areas, slopes, terraces. See also under Shrubs.

JUNIPER, CREEPING
(*Juniperus horizontalis*).   Zone 2
Medium rate of growth. Woody evergreen. Low, creeping, not too dense.
Height: 6–12 inches.   **Spacing:** 5–8 feet.
Exposure: sun.
Soil: tolerates poor soil.
Texture: fine.
Flower effects: not showy.
Fruit effects: blue berry.
Use: general level areas and banks.

JUNIPER, JAPGARDEN
(*Juniperus procumbens*).   Zone 5
Medium rate of growth. Low, creeping, dense evergreen mat. Blue-green foliage.
Height: 2 feet.   **Spread:** 6–8 feet.
Exposure: sun.
Soil: tolerant.
Texture: fine.
Use: general level areas, slopes, terraces. See also under Shrubs.

JUNIPER, SARGENT CHINESE
(*Juniperus chinensis sargenti*).   Zone 4
Fast to medium growing. Flat, spreading evergreen with steel-blue foliage. Excellent, serviceable plant. Blight resistant.
Height: 12–18 inches.   **Spread:** 8–10 feet.
Exposure: sun or partial shade.
Soil: tolerates dry, sandy soil.
Texture: fine.
Use: general planting areas, slopes, terraces. See also under Shrubs.

JUNIPER, WAUKEGAN CREEPING **(*Juniperus horizontalis 'Douglasi'*).   Zone 2**
Medium rate of growth. Woody evergreen. Blue in summer, turning lavender in fall.
Height: 6–12 inches.   **Spacing:** 5 feet.
Exposure: sun.
Soil: tolerates poor soil.
Texture: fine.

Flower effects: not showy.
Fruit effects: blue berry.
Fall color: lavender.
Use: large areas and banks.

LILYTURF
(*Liriope spicata*).   Zone 4
Fast growing. Makes excellent dense mat. Grasslike evergreen foliage. Flower spikes somewhat showy. Easily contained. Resists encroachment from other plants.
Height: 8–12 inches.   **Spread:** 12 inches.
Exposure: sun or partial shade.
Soil: tolerant.
Texture: fine.
Flower effects: purple to almost white.
Use: general.

MAHONIA, CREEPING
(*Mahonia repens*).   Zone 5
Slow growing. Woody evergreen that spreads by underground roots. Fragrant flowers.
Height: 10 inches.   **Spacing:** 18–24 inches.
Exposure: shade or partial shade.
Texture: medium to coarse.
Flower effects: yellow in spring.
Fruit effects: purple-black, grapelike in midsummer.
Use: general, rock gardens.

PACHISTIMA, CANBY
(*Pachistima canbyi*).   Zone 5
Medium rate of growth. Low, dense, rounded. Excellent texture accent when used in a mass.
Height: 12 inches.   **Spread:** 6–12 inches.
Exposure: shade or partial sun.
Soil: acid, moist.
Texture: medium fine.
Fall color: bronze.
Use: general. See also under Shrubs.

PERIWINKLE, COMMON (MYRTLE)
(*Vinca minor*).   Zone 4
Medium-slow growing. Reliable woody evergreen. Glossy, dark-green foliage. Subject to stem canker.
Height: 3–6 inches.   **Spacing:** 12 inches.
Exposure: sun or shade.
Soil: tolerates poor soil, but prefers moist situation.
Texture: medium.
Flower effects: blue to lavender.
Fruit effects: not showy.

Use: general level areas, short slopes, underplanting for trees or shrubs.
Varieties: 'Alba' (white flowers); 'Atropurpurea' (purple flowers); 'Aureovariegata' (yellow-spotted leaves); 'Bowles' (light-blue flowers, tends to grow in clumps, not as spreading as species).

PLANTAIN-LILY (FUNKIA)
(*Hosta decorata*).   Zone 5
Medium rate of growth. Coarse foliage lends itself to striking texture contrasts. Flowers showy in late summer. Dies back each winter leaving area planted bare.
Height: 12–24 inches.   **Spread:** 18 inches.
Exposure: shade.
Soil: tolerant, but prefers moist soil.
Texture: coarse.
Flower effects: white or purple.
Use: general, small areas.

PLANTAIN-LILY, VARIEGATED-LEAVED
(*Hosta undulata*).   Zone 3
Medium rate of growth. Leaves with white or yellow variegation die to ground in late fall and are slow to reappear in spring.
Height: 2–3 feet.   **Spread:** 12–24 inches.
Exposure: shade.
Soil: tolerant.
Texture: coarse.
Flower effects: purple.
Use: small areas, edging.

ROSE, MEMORIAL
(*Rosa wichuraiana*).   Zone 5
Slow growing. Dense, woody, deciduous.
Height: 12 inches.   **Spacing:** 8 feet.
Exposure: sun or partial shade.
Texture: fine.
Flower effects: white in midsummer.
Fruit effects: red in late summer.
Use: well adapted to banks; good barrier planting.

SNOW-IN-SUMMER
(*Cerastium tomentosum*).   Zone 2
Fast growing. Spreads quickly. Can spread up to 3 feet, but recommended planting distance is 18–24 inches apart. Evergreen. Good for hot, dry situations.
Height: 12–14 inches.   **Spread:** 3 feet.
Exposure: sun.
Soil: tolerant if well-drained.
Texture: fine.
Flower effects: white.
Use: general.

Descriptive Outlines of Ground Covers

SPEEDWELL, DRUG (GYPSY-WEED)
(Veronica officinalis). **Zone 4**
Medium rate of growth. Excellent low-growing mat about 4 inches high with flower stocks that extend about 8 inches above the foliage. Dense, creeping branches. Mostly evergreen. Requires little maintenance.
Height: 4–12 inches. **Spread:** 8–12 inches.
Exposure: sun or partial shade.
Soil: tolerant.
Texture: medium.
Flower effects: pale blue.
Use: general.

SPIREA, ALPINE JAPANESE
(Spiraea japonica alpina). **Zone 5**
Medium rate of growth. Dwarf, mounding. Excellent overall character.
Height: 12 inches. **Spread:** 12 inches.
Exposure: sun.
Soil: any good garden soil.
Texture: fine.
Flower effects: pink.
Fruit effects: not showy.
Use: general level areas. See also under Shrubs.

SPURGE, JAPANESE (PACHYSANDRA)
(Pachysandra terminalis). **Zone 4**
Slow to medium growing. Woody evergreen that gives good texture accent. Subject to stem rot.

Height: 6–8 inches. **Spacing:** 12 inches.
Exposure: shade or partial shade.
Texture: coarse.
Flower effects: not showy.
Fruit effects: not showy.
Use: general level areas, under trees where grass will not grow. Blends with yellow or yellow-green but not with blue-green.
Variety: 'Variegata' (white variegation on leaves).

STONECROP, LARGE LEAF
(Sedum acre sexangulare). **Zone 4**
Fast growing. Forms an attractive, dense, evergreen mat. Best of all yellow-flowered sedums. Do not use in traffic areas.
Height: 6–8 inches. **Spread:** 12 inches.
Exposure: sun.
Soil: tolerant if well-drained.
Texture: medium.
Flower effects: yellow.
Use: small refined areas.

THYME, CREEPING (MOTHER-OF-THYME)
(Thymus serpyllum). **Zones 1–3**
Fast growing. Reliable woody evergreen. Lowest growing of the ground covers.
Height: 1 inch. **Spacing:** 6–8 inches.
Exposure: sun or light shade.
Soil: tolerates poor soils.
Texture: fine.
Flower effects: rose to lilac.

Fruit effects: not showy.
Use: a good matting between paving stones on terraces or walks.

VIRGINIA CREEPER
(Parthenocissus quinquefolia). **Zone 3**
Fast growing. Rank grower. Woody deciduous plant. Will climb any object.
Height: 18 inches. **Spacing:** 2 feet.
Exposure: sun or shade.
Texture: medium to coarse.
Flower effects: not showy.
Fruit effects: purple in summer and fall.
Fall color: rich, crimson-red.
Use: large areas, well adapted to banks. See also under Vines.

YARROW, WOOLLY
(Achillea tomentosa). **Zone 2**
Medium rate of growth. Herbaceous evergreen. Withstands light traffic, such as between stepping stones.
Height: 6 inches. **Spacing:** 12 inches.
Exposure: sun.
Texture: medium-fine.
Flower effects: yellow.
Fruit effects: not showy.
Use: general.

Descriptive Outlines of Vines

AKEBIA, FIVELEAF
(Akebia quinata). **Zone 4**
Moderate to slow growing. Fragrant flowers. Gives light shade. Often becomes bare of foliage. May become a weed if it escapes.
Height: 12–40 feet.
Method of climbing: twining stems.
Soil: well-drained.
Texture: medium to fine.
Flower effects: violet to red in spring.
Fruit effects: purple in early summer (not often formed).
Use: fence, trellis, walls.

BITTERSWEET, AMERICAN
(Celastrus scandens). **Zone 2**
Medium rate of growth. Handsome and showy foliage and fruit. Must have male and female plants for fruit development. Can kill shrubs or trees used for support.
Height: 30–40 feet.
Method of climbing: twining stems.
Texture: medium to coarse.
Flower effects: not showy.
Fruit effects: yellow-red in fall.
Fall color: yellow.
Use: bank, fence; good vertical screen.

BITTERSWEET, ORIENTAL
(Celastrus orbiculata). **Zone 4**
Medium rate of growth. Rank grower. Handsome foliage. Must have male and female plants for fruit development. Can kill shrubs or trees used for support.
Height: 30–40 feet.
Method of climbing: twining stems.
Texture: medium to coarse.
Flower effects: not showy.
Fruit effects: yellow and orange in fall.
Fall color: yellow.
Use: bank, fence; good vertical screen.

Descriptive Outlines of Vines

CLEMATIS, JACKMAN
(Clematis × jackmanii).   **Zone 5**
Medium rate of growth. Rank grower. Striking appearance, good color accent. Many varieties available. Likes shade around roots. Can be heavily pruned in spring.
Height: 5–12 feet.
Method of climbing: twining stems and petioles.
Soil: moist, alkaline.
Texture: medium.
Flower effects: blue, red, or purple in summer and fall.
Fruit effects: not showy.
Use: flower gardens as accent or specimen.

DUTCHMANSPIPE, COMMON (Aristolochia durior [macropylla]).   **Zone 4**
Fast growing. Rank grower. Requires considerable space. Coarse texture provides accent, but could be out of scale in small gardens.
Height: 15–30 feet.
Method of climbing: twining stems.
Soil: well-drained.
Texture: coarse.
Use: fence, trellis.

FLEECEFLOWER, SILVERVINE
(Polygonum auberti).   **Zone 4**
Fast growing. Perennial climber. Valued for quick cover and for late flowers giving fleecy effect.
Height: 25 feet.
Method of climbing: twining stems and tendrils.
Texture: medium (fine when flowering).
Flower effects: white in spring and late summer.
Fruit effects: not showy.
Fall color: red-green.
Use: fence, slopes, walls.

GLORYVINE (GRAPE)
(Vitis coignetiae).   **Zone 5**
Fast growing. Rank grower. Covers large areas quickly. Handsome large foliage, brilliant autumn color. Reliable.
Height: 25 feet.
Method of climbing: forked tendrils.
Soil: moist, rich.
Texture: coarse.
Flower effects: not showy.
Fruit effects: purple in fall.
Fall color: brilliant scarlet.
Use: fence, slopes, wood or wire supports.

HONEYSUCKLE, HALLS JAPANESE
(Lonicera japonica 'Halliana').   **Zone 4**
Fast growing. Vigorous. Popular fragrant vine. Good for all purposes.

Height: 15–30 feet.
Method of climbing: twining stems.
Texture: medium to coarse.
Flower effects: white to yellow in spring through fall.
Fruit effects: black in midsummer through fall.
Fall color: bronze.
Use: fence, slopes, walls. See also under Ground Covers.

HONEYSUCKLE, TRUMPET
(Lonicera sempervirens).   **Zone 3**
Slow growing. Semievergreen. Showy flowers. Attracts hummingbirds.
Height: 10–20 feet.
Method of climbing: twining stems.
Soil: light, moist.
Texture: medium to coarse.
Flower effects: scarlet and yellow in spring and summer.
Fruit effects: orange-red in summer and early fall.
Fall color: blue-green.
Use: fence, slopes, walls.

HYDRANGEA, CLIMBING
(Hydrangea petiolaris).   **Zone 4**
Slow to establish, then fast growing. Rank grower. Attractive flowers. Tolerates either sun or shade, but flowers more heavily in sun. Red bark interesting in winter.
Height: 60–80 feet.
Method of climbing: aerial roots.
Soil: rich, moist.
Texture: coarse.
Flower effects: white in summer.
Fruit effects: not showy.
Use: fence, slopes, walls.

IVY, BOSTON
(Parthenocissus tricuspidata).   **Zone 4**
Fast growing. Handsome, rank grower. Withstands city conditions.
Height: 60 feet.
Method of climbing: tendrils.
Texture: coarse.
Flower effects: not showy.
Fruit effects: blue in fall.
Fall color: rich red-purple.
Use: fence, slopes, walls.

MONKSHOOD VINE
(Ampelopsis aconitifolia).   **Zone 4**
Slow growing. Delicately shaped leaves give texture variation.
Height: 10–30 feet.
Method of climbing: tendrils.
Texture: fine.
Fruit effects: yellow to orange in fall.
Use: fence, trellis, low walls.

TRUMPET VINE (TRUMPETCREEPER, COMMON) (Campsis radicans).   **Zone 4**
Medium rate of growth. Often bare of foliage at base. Showy flowers. Clings to wood and stone, but often needs support because of weight. 'Madame Galen' is attractive for northern areas.
Height: 30–50 feet.
Method of climbing: aerial roots and twining.
Soil: rich, well-drained.
Texture: medium.
Flower effects: orange in summer.
Fruit effects: brown pods, autumn through winter.
Use: accent, specimen, trellis, walls.

VIRGINIA CREEPER
(Parthenocissus quinquefolia).   **Zone 3**
Fast growing. Rank grower. Woody deciduous plant. Will climb any object.
Height: 30–50 feet.
Method of climbing: tendrils and aerial roots.
Texture: medium to coarse.
Flower effects: not showy.
Fruit effects: purple in summer and fall.
Fall color: rich crimson-red.
Use: fence, slopes, walls. See also under Ground Covers.

VIRGINSBOWER
(Clematis virginiana).   **Zone 4**
Medium rate of growth. Handsome flowering vine. Interesting fruit. Often has a thin base. Prefers sun.
Height: 12–20 feet.
Method of climbing: twining stems and petioles.
Soil: moist, alkaline.
Texture: medium.
Flower effects: white in summer.
Fruit effects: gray plumes in fall.
Fall color: yellow.
Use: banks, fence, trellis.

WISTERIA, JAPANESE
(Wisteria floribunda).   **Zone 4**
Slow growing. Handsome flowers and foliage. Good as climber or trained as a standard. Difficult to transplant, slow to reestablish. Many varieties available.
Height: 30 feet.
Method of climbing: twining stems form woody trunk or standard.
Soil: prefers rich loam but tolerates sand.
Texture: medium.
Flower effects: violet-blue in late spring.
Fruit effects: not showy.
Fall color: yellow.
Use: trellis, walls.